Diasporic Africa

Diasporic Africa

A Reader

EDITED BY

Michael A. Gomez

New York University Press

NEW YORK AND LONDON

NEW YORK UNIVERSITY PRESS
New York and London
www.nyupress.org

Library of Congress Cataloging-in-Publication Data
Diasporic Africa : a reader / edited by Michael A. Gomez.
p. cm.
Includes bibliographical references and index.
ISBN–13: 978–0–8147–3165–9 (cloth : alk. paper)
ISBN–10: 0–8147–3165–1 (cloth : alk. paper)
ISBN–13: 978–0–8147–3166–6 (pbk. : alk. paper)
ISBN–10: 0–8147–3166–X (pbk. : alk. paper)
1. African diaspora—History.   2. Blacks—History.
I. Gomez, Michael Angelo, 1955–
DT16.5.D54   2006
909'.0496—dc22   2005019518

New York University Press books are printed on acid-free paper,
and their binding materials are chosen for strength and durability.

Manufactured in the United States of America

c 10 9 8 7 6 5 4 3 2 1
p 10 9 8 7 6 5 4 3 2 1

To the Association for the Study of the
Worldwide African Diaspora (ASWAD),
whose maiden 2000 conference in New York City
was the occasion for many wonderful presentations,
including those prepared for this volume.

Contents

Introduction

Diasporic Africa: A View from History

Michael A. Gomez

It is a commonplace for many that the dawn of modernity commenced with the transatlantic slave trade. With the exportation of millions of Africans and their labor, parts of Iberia, the Mediterranean, and the New World were transformed into endless fields of agricultural (and in some instances mineral) production that proved critical to the economic and political development of various European states. Nascent imperialism was funded by an array of labor arrangements that included the indentured and those working for wages, but they were overshadowed, at least into the nineteenth century, by a practice of slavery that became almost exclusively tied to Africans and their descendants. The African presence and contribution was certainly foundational, but it was also ongoing in what would become the Americas.

The African was not the sole representative of the "Old" World in the New. Europeans and Asians also made the voyage, albeit under very different circumstances. Collective conditions obtaining in Old World provenances, ranging from the conceptual framework of the "nation" to the "tribe," retained some meaning in the Americas, but as these concepts had been previously developed within Europe or Asia as a means of distinguishing among territorially and culturally contiguous groups, their applicability to the starkly novel realities of the New World, where "Europeans" and "Asians" and "Africans" were now juxtaposed alongside native "Americans," underwent significant attenuation. Indeed, Europeans and Africans emerged in the New World, where only English and French and Wolof and Hausa and the intimacies of the village had existed in the Old.

Cultural affinities, seemingly closely related to anatomical concurrences, were not only suggested but also undergirded by the imperial project itself. As a result, "race" was eventually recruited to explain apparent difference and consequent privilege (not to mention to legitimize unspeakable atrocity and inhumanity), borrowed from the language of Old World derogation regarding the Irishman and the Jew.

In this way, the African, as a composite locus of relations configured according to a calculus of geography, language, appearance, and social condition, was no more novel than the creation of the European and the Asian (or the Native American, for that matter). All parties were in the process of becoming, precisely because they were now in cultural confluence directly informed by political conflict, with labor extraction and arrogation of land as objectives. In addition to the fact that such multiple contestations were concomitant and mutually reinforcing, they were being waged on soil foreign to many. In the multigenerational effort to distill the meanings of existence in the New World, connections with antecedent lands and ways of life became sites of pride and loathing, longing and dread, revelry and nightmare, with the Atlantic (and Pacific) as bridge and barrier. This was true for everyone.

For a multiplicity of reasons, and notably in contrast to the experiences of Europeans in the New World, the cultural and social transformations of transported Africans tend to invite a quality of critique unique in its level of elevated scrutiny, emphasizing distance and lacunae in the substance and circumstances separating Africa and the Americas. Although whiteness studies reflect the progress made in recognizing that social and cultural malleability was not confined to Africans (a refreshing, healthy, and laudable development), there remains substantial resistance to assigning enslaved Africans in the Americas a collective identity beyond "African" or simply "slave."[1] Opposition to such an approach is articulated in doubts about the ability of Africans to transfer collective perspectives to the Americas, and in ruminations that arguably overdetermine the conditions of slavery and the slave trades.[2] Rejection of the idea resides in the suspicion that European conceptual frameworks have been projected onto African human landscapes, such that African collectivities, it is argued, were often the creation of commercial expediency and colonization. Discussion of "creole" communities in the early Atlantic world, in which Africans and their descendants became fused with European influences via cultural and sexual interactions, further disrupt notions of a pristine transfer of African culture and community from one side of the pond to the other. Indeed, for certain regions of Africa, the inquiry has resulted in the questioning of any useful category of collective identity in Africa itself prior to the rise of the transatlantic slave trade. An (in)famous characterization of enslaved Africans in transit as "crowds" rather than socially configured aggregates has been extrapolated farther back in time and space, making their disaggregation an "African" phenomenon.[3]

It is therefore the case that collective terms for Africans and their descendants in the Americas are either completely eschewed or employed with the greatest hesitation, with all the caveats applicable. To avoid discursive minefields associated with these considerations, we are reduced to speaking of general regions of origin; ethnolinguistic groupings, towns and other immediacies with which captives may have been associated can only be broached with sufficiently nuanced and qualifying language. The consequence, whether intended or not, is, on the one hand, a deepening mystification of Africa and the African, and the reification of the African as the quintessential Other; and, on the other hand, the Negrofication of the African-descended in the Americas, by which Africa is of little or no significance to the experience and history of black people in the New World. A new heaven and earth may not have materialized, but a veritable new creature, for all practical purposes irreversibly deracinated, has been produced. We are in many ways back to erasure.

To the investigations of the historian and the anthropologist, for whom preceding times carry some import, must be added the intervention of "cultural studies," for whom history either does not seem to exist or does not play a significant role. Some theorists, in the name of anti-essentialism, question the usefulness of Africa in understanding the experiences of the African-descended elsewhere. "Essentialism," rather than an uninterrogated assumption of linkage both spatially and temporally, has come to signify a disdain for Africa itself, relegating interest in the continent to the atavistic. Ironically, this qualifies relevant components of the cultural studies project as a collaboration with forces long invested in processes of silencing and erasure. Such a reading of postmodernity, for all of its flexibility and inclusiveness, willfully embraces vacuities of the temporal.[4]

That views of the histories and experiences of the African-descended are variable and divergent is readily understandable. Indeed, those histories and experiences are complex and multitudinous, such that interpretations are bound to be myriad, ranging from the idiosyncratic to the systematically theoretical. No one lens of analysis could possibly capture such a vast and sweeping drama or series of dramas. Neither is a given perspective necessarily more salutary, penetrating, or superior of caste. When twin conditions of cogence and coherence are met, there is no discernible hierarchy of interpretive privilege, only preferences.

With the foregoing in mind, it is the argument of this book that the envisioning of an African diaspora vitally and inextricably linked to the histories, cultures, and communities of Africa is at least as valid as the notion of a black Atlantic that effectively excludes the continent (save as source of a primordial and unrecoverable inception). In fact, the conjunction of Africa and its diaspora is historically undeniable, intellectually defensible, and empirically demonstrable. In this way, the idea of an Atlantic world is realized with the inclusion of an Africa that is fully participatory throughout each phase of its development, from the dawn of the transatlantic slave trade to the present.

A real problem here, one fundamental source of discomfort with the notion of an Atlantic that actually extends to both Africa and the Americas (and, of course, Europe), seems to be located in limitations of the discursive. The artificialities of these demarcations are becoming increasingly obvious as interaction between Americanists and Africanists increases. However, Americanists must take the study of Africa seriously, and not simply be content to glean from the scholarship while moving in the occasional conjoined circle.

A configuration of the Atlantic world that is coterminous and interchangeable with a vision of an African diaspora that is fully engaged with Africa is certainly tenable. But it must be borne in mind that the African diaspora is in fact far more global of a concept, reaching into the Mediterranean and Europe, the Indian Ocean and adjoining lands, and inclusive of significant portions of Asia.[5] The asymmetries of the present volume, in which the majority of the contributions focus on the Atlantic, arise from the materials available for this particular publication and should in no way be read as prescriptive or normative of the African diaspora.

The imperative to twin the study of Africa and the African diaspora emerges from several concurrent considerations that may be best organized along a historical continuum. Beginning with the period of the slave trade, Africa and its diaspora are brought together by cultural affinities, political activities, and social conventions that could be highly exclusionary. If anything, ongoing research into these areas has strengthened rather than enfeebled emphases on the relational. From the middle of the nineteenth century through the turn, missions and migrations and repatriations further entwined populations of African descent on various sides of the Atlantic, such that a temporal distancing was countered by approxima-tions of the soul, however poorly conceived. The ideologies of the late nineteenth century would soon issue into a full flourishing of diasporic concern and sentiment for Africa in the earlier twentieth century, responding initially to the Berlin Conference (1884–85) and the Battle of Adwa (1896), while reaching the most notable crescendo of rhetorical flourish and organizational fervency in the Universal Negro Improvement Association.[6] World wars, both hot and cold, coincided with anticolonial and anti-imperial struggles around the globe, only deepening the interest of the African-descended in the plight of the continent, culminating in the successful overthrow of the racialized project in South Africa. While few struggles have galvanized blacks (and the enlightened) around the world like the anti-apartheid movement, the engagement with Africa has contin-ued with foci on governance, conflicts, natural resources (especially petro-leum), plagues, and natural disasters. Most recently, the reformulated African Union has begun to reverse the direction of attention with attempts to formally incorporate the African diaspora into its various mechanisms. Far from disengagement, if anything the momentum of reat-tachment is quickening, hastening to rhythms of musical and artistic tra-ditions in ever-increasing dialogue and interdependence.

Research into the experiences of Africans and their descendants has effectively responded to doubts regarding the African provenance of cul-tural practices of and their ongoing relevance for the African-descended in the Americas. To be sure, such phenomena were almost everywhere impacted by the cultures and sensitivities of non-Africans, resulting in spectacular displays of innovation and creativity. Novel expressions and entreaties and demeanors and sartorial splendor certainly emerged, and that in arresting and strikingly beautiful ways, but an inability or refusal to come to terms with those aspects of newness that were of African deriva-tion or import can only obfuscate rather than elucidate New World explic-ability. There is no inconsistency in identifying the sustained within the novel.

Enslaved Africans, first and foremost, brought skills to the Americas. They cultivated rice and tobacco and indigo in the northern climes of the hemisphere and passed those skills on to progeny and planters alike. They dived for pearls and mined for specie in the Caribbean and Latin America, skills often acquired in Africa. Their familiarity with animal husbandry was also recognized by slaveholders throughout the Americas, who exploited that expertise as well. And though sugarcane cultivation cannot necessarily be ascribed to Africa, Africans were well aware of its regimen long before setting sail for the Americas, as they worked in the cane fields of São Tomé, Principe, and the Mediterranean. Beyond these examples, Africans brought with them metallurgical abilities, experience with water craft, building techniques, and so on. Such skills transformed the New World.[7]

Of course, far more than their vocational and agricultural contributions, Africans are known for their various approaches to religion. Though such a focus arguably skews the overall assessment, there is no gainsaying that religion is an important category of analysis, and within that category Africa towers in significance. From North America to Latin America and the Caribbean, African religions went far beyond rites with which they are most famously associated, such as formations of sacred space and experiential worship styles, and have been central to articulations of familial relations that involved patterns of marriage, child-rearing, death, more broadly configured arrangements of community, self-help strategies, agricultural endeavors, revolutions and revolts and other expressions of rebellion, as well as what would appear to be behaviors consistent with acquiescence. Most African religions were closely associated with specific ethnolinguistic groups in Africa, and this remained true in the Americas as well. The most celebrated have been Yoruba-based expressions, most famously represented in *lucumí* or *santería* in places like Cuba and *candomblé* in Brazil. But there are others, including such clandestine religious organizations as the *abukuá* of Cuba, a society originating in the Cross River area of southeastern Nigeria and Cameroon. The blend of Ewe-Fon-Yoruba beliefs first begun on African soil further progressed in Saint Domingue, later Haiti, where West Central African infusions combined with those from West Africa to form *vodun*. So-called Akan religion, emanating out of what is now Ghana and the Ivory Coast, could be found in various Caribbean sites and as far north as the United States, and probably played some role in the eventual emergence of *obeah*, the use of supernatural powers to inflict harm, and *myalism*, the employment of spiritual resources and herbs to counteract witchcraft and other evil.[8]

What is missing from the literature is a more careful discussion of how these religions developed historically in the New World from the fifteenth through the nineteenth centuries, and this can probably best be accomplished by a critical rereading of contemporary materials left by observers. In fact, embedded in this approach are suggestions not only for African religions in the Americas, but also for Africa itself. For what is known about religions in West Africa during the transatlantic slave trade, leaving Islam aside for the moment, is best derived from a careful analysis of contemporary literature in tandem with the orature of the region and the anthropological record. What I am suggesting here is that literature from the Americas discussing the African presence can be read together with materials written expressly in and on Africa for the purpose of illuminating *African* history, not simply New World histories. The best known example of this kind of source is Olaudah Equiano, whose discussion of precolonial Igbo culture remains one of the most important, but there were millions of Africans transported to the New World, and there are additional sources of information about their behavior, traditions, beliefs, languages, and so on.[9] Such information has largely been mined only for interpretations of New World phenomena, but the moment has arrived for Africanists to take note of these documents for their potentially revelatory value for Africa itself.

Perhaps one of the most valuable kinds of sources within this category are Arabic manuscripts. Thousands of Muslims were imported into the Americas, where they left their considerable imprints from North America to Brazil. Individuals such as Abu Bakr as-Siddiq and Muhammad Kaba of Jamaica, Salih Bilali of Georgia, Mahommah Baquaqua of Brazil, Umar b. Said of Carolina, and Ibrahima Abd ar-Rahman of Mississippi all left evidence, often in Arabic, regarding their homelands, in some instances providing very rich details. As more of these manuscripts come to light, it becomes clear that they are sources not just of diasporic history, but of *African* history, and should be examined in conjunction with those materials more conventionally seen as the preserve of Africanists.[10]

Conversely, an accurate understanding of the African political context is vital to understanding African diasporic history. It is not enough to establish some facile rendering of the "cultural" chart of Africans entering the Americas, and to thence erroneously proceed with the New World narrative as if culture, though very important, is all that matters when it comes to Africans. It should also be recognized that individuals emerged out of ever-changing political and social contexts, and that such circumstances help to explain behavior in the New World. We cannot understand the 1835 *malê* revolt of Bahia, a Muslim-led event, without sufficiently coming to grips with jihadic activity in northern and southwestern Nigeria that preceded it. We cannot understand the 1739 Stono rebellion in South Carolina without first taking into consideration religious and political developments in West Central Africa. And as for the Haitian Revolution of 1791 to 1804, we are suspended between the French Revolution and marronage as explanations for conceptual sources, without considering those places and circumstances in Africa out of which nearly three-fourths of the enslaved population in Saint Domingue hailed. These are just a few examples cited to make the point.[11]

Mention of the Stono rebellion segues to a consideration of a series of engagements Africans developed with Christianity. It is now clear that the latter's establishment in West Central Africa in the late fifteenth century meant that some Africans were at least acquainted with, if not practitioners of, Catholicism prior to ever leaving African shores.[12] This form of Catholicism was heavily infused with African interpretation and deeply invested with African meaning, such that the extent to which it remained Catholicism is not a closed question. But the implications are obvious and startling: on both sides of the Atlantic were communities of Christians, Muslims, and adherents of ancestral religions, each practicing observances that would have been mutually intelligible to the corresponding community across the ocean. The Middle Passage therefore does not only signify what was lost, although that is a principal component of its meaning, but also what was preserved. This observation becomes even more signal when we recall that in some instances individuals (and some communities) were in sustained transoceanic dialogue.

The political circumstances out of which all Africans came, and which in turn informed some of the most spectacular political acts of resistance known to the New World, were themselves reinforced by bonds of religion hailing back to Africa, thus strengthening such ties. Thus, the Haitian Revolution began with *vodun* rites and was in turn preceded by the career of Mackandal, a "voodoo priest" who used his skills to confront the slaveocracy. Islam was central to the 1835 *malê* revolt in Bahia, as it probably was in early sixteenth-century Hispaniola, where rebellious Senegambians very much threatened the viability of the nascent experiment with servile labor as they wreaked havoc on plantations while forming maroon communities. Religion played a vital role in the Denmark Vesey conspiracy of 1822 in Charleston, where Vesey, an apparent Christian, organized his followers along lines that respected both African ethnicity and religious variation. Revolts throughout the English-speaking Caribbean were often characterized as "Akan" or "Coromantee" affairs and were preceded by Akan religious rites. Deported as malcontents to such places as New York City, these same rebels proceeded to foment insurrection in 1712 and 1741.[13]

Of course, there were many other cultural insignia maintained by Africans and their descendants in the slaveholding Americas that harkened back to Africa. They could certainly be identified in the music and closely related dance forms, and both music and dance were intimately connected to religion. Those of African descent were also capable of taking the inferior clothes earmarked for them and transforming them into revelatory statements of self-expression; the presentation of the body did not end with clothes, but also included hairstyles and patterns of cicatrization. Even a cursory review of the foodways introduced into the Americas by Africans serves to reinforce the notion of sustained ties within the Atlantic world.[14]

The slaving data indicate that, while the English and American interdictions of the slave trade in 1807/8 may have had some effect, the trade in Africans went on, both clandestinely (in North America) and overtly (in Latin America and parts of the Caribbean).[15] Through the first half of the nineteenth century, Africans continued to arrive on American shores in significant numbers. Far from "dying out," African cultures were continually replenished in places like Cuba and Brazil. But even in areas like the British-held Caribbean, where the Apprenticeship (1834–38) had ended slavery, African workers continued to be recruited. Some 36,120 so-called postemancipation Africans, seized from slave ships and often taken to Sierra Leone and St. Helena in West Africa, were subsequently reexported to the British-held Caribbean between 1839 and 1867. Cultural ties to Africa were therefore reinvigorated wherever they settled, with data for such places as Trinidad both abundant and supportive.[16] But black folk were not only moving east to west; they were also circulating in a variety of patterns throughout the Atlantic world as seafarers, both slave and free, usually in the company of whites and others. As traders, raiders, and slavers, such individuals were positioned to carry news of interest to black populations regarding blacks elsewhere. Hence, certainly not all, but at least some blacks (especially in the port cities) were connected to one another (and Africa) by means of these couriers.[17]

The collective evidence is simply overwhelming that African persons and African cultures arrived simultaneously in the New World, and that the latter, though transformed through contact with other cultures and under difficult circumstances, nevertheless persisted. Perhaps this is most clearly demonstrated with language, with creole glossolalia obviously reflecting a history of interaction and exchange. But even when European languages were spoken, they were (and continue to be) uttered with inflections and syntaxes that reveal African influence.

Although the nineteenth century saw the progressive ending of legal slavery and the predominance of creole or native-born populations throughout the Americas, there yet remained a consistent and important conversation between Africa and those removed. The nineteenth century also saw the beginning of a significant "return" movement among Africans and their descendants back to Africa. In Brazil, for example, those alleged to be complicit in the 1835 *malê* revolt in Bahia were in some instances sent back to West Africa, notably disembarking in what is now southwestern Nigeria and Benin. There they joined others from Brazil and Cuba who collectively pooled their resources to pay for the return passage, members of *cabildos* (in Cuba) and *irmandades* (Brazil), fraternal organizations based upon purported membership in ethnolinguistic groups. Upon their return, persons originally taken from the Bight of Benin (many of whom were Yoruba, Fon, and Ewe) became known as *agudas* and *amaros*. Similarly, some rescued at sea by the British and brought to Sierra Leone later returned to southwestern Nigeria and Benin, where they were referred to as *saros*.

In places like Jamaica and Trinidad, African men and women similarly petitioned the English government to provide them with safe passage to West Africa, an effort largely organized among Muslims that acquired particular urgency with the advent of Apprenticeship in 1834. And although whole communities were not successful in their attempts to repatriate, individuals were in fact successful, and they joined with others such as Ibrahima Abd ar-Rahman, who left Mississippi for West Africa. There is also the example of Paul Cuffe in North America, who personally transported thirty-eight persons back to Africa in 1815, financing the entire enterprise himself.

Such return efforts developed alongside anti-slavery campaigns, efforts revealing how participants in the same enterprise came with entirely different assumptions and motivations. For Africans and their descendants, the opportunity to return to Africa represented the possibility to escape the oppressive, racist atmosphere of the Americas and start over as pioneers or to fulfill a missionary zeal to bring the Christian gospel to "benighted heathens." Their struggle to return was supported by some whites in Britain, for example, who were interested in relocating the "black poor" to Africa, where they could both improve their lives and facilitate British interests in "legitimate" (nonslave) trade. Many whites in the

United States, on the other hand, advocated repatriation to rid the land of free blacks and thereby strengthen slavery. Whatever their various impulses, repatriation to Africa from Britain and Canada, the latter the destination for Jamaican maroons and a refuge for blacks who fought for the British during the American War of Independence, began in 1787 and centered on the British settlement at Sierra Leone. These initial groups would be joined by the aforementioned captives taken from slavers bound for the Americas. Sierra Leone received thousands of such recaptives, reaching a peak in the 1840s. As for the United States, repatriation became an organized, state-sanctioned enterprise beginning in 1817 with the founding of the American Colonization Society, which in 1822 began a colony in what would become Monrovia, Liberia. By the 1850s, a little less than 15,000 blacks had participated in the return, to which can be added recaptives liberated from slavers by the American navy. Africa therefore continued to loom large in the consciousness of both Africans in the Americas and their native-born progeny. Africa itself would be profoundly impacted by these returnees, especially in Liberia, Sierra Leone, and Nigeria, so that while an understanding of the Americas is unattainable without an appreciation of the African background, Africa itself cannot be understood without recourse not only to the transatlantic slave trade, but also to the consequences of the reversal of that trade, consequences that continue to reverberate.

Black folk were not simply moving in significant numbers back to Africa absent some conceptual framework. Rather, such movement was at times informed by an articulation of the Africa-Diaspora nexus that would serve as the foundation for the pursuit of pan-Africanism in the twentieth century. As early as Denmark Vesey in 1822 and David Walker in 1831, black thinkers have consistently displayed an awareness that the plight of their particular community was somehow tied to similar communities elsewhere. Specifics varied, but it was rare for a visionary to not have a sense of a more broadly defined, African-derived community extending beyond geopolitical boundaries. The last quarter of the nineteenth century through the first half of the twentieth century saw the growth of this principle. The activities of the proponents of this idea, in conjunction with labor migrations, advances in technology, and the reality of empire itself, helped disseminate the concept of an African diaspora among working class blacks. Reconnecting to Africa and others in the diaspora, initially envisioned as an intellectual quest or an ideological campaign, often led to concrete action.[18]

Many of the early leaders of pan-Africanism were Christian ministers, including Henry Highland Garnet who, in his 1843 *Address to the Slaves of the United States*, called for armed revolt against the slaveocracy, citing Toussaint L'Ouverture as an example to be emulated. Garnet further revealed a diasporic perspective in predicting that the islands of the Caribbean would eventually be "ours" (a reference to blacks in the Caribbean, not North America), and by his organization of the Cuban Anti-Slavery Committee in 1873. He completed the circle with his voyage to West Africa in 1882, where he died and remains buried. His contemporaries, Alexander Crummell, Martin R. Delany, and Henry McNeil Turner, all favored black emigration to either Africa or Central and South America. And Anna Julia Cooper, born to an enslaved mother and a white slaveholder, established in her 1892 *A Voice from the South* connections between racial and gender inequalities in the United States and downtrodden populations beyond its borders.[19]

This early generation of pan-Africanists included Edward W. Blyden, born in St. Thomas, Virgin Islands, who repatriated to West Africa in the 1860s, where and when he became a leading force in establishing educational institutions in Liberia and Sierra Leone, articulating in the process a vision of pan-Africanism unequaled in eloquence. His vision suffered, however, from a disdain of indigenous African culture (save for Islam, for which he had the highest regard), a shortcoming many in his and subsequent generations shared.[20] The civilizing mission of the pan-Africanists would impact the ways in which the imperial project unfolded and would play an important role in the selection and elevation of a western-educated African elite.

Arguments invested in the decoupling of Africa from its diaspora very much depend upon the logic of cultural distance increasing over time. But one of the most arresting aspects of the turn of the twentieth century was the intensity with which the diaspora increasingly focused on Africa, the fervor with which it took up the cause of the latter, and the degree to which it envisioned a future in which the fates of Africa and the diaspora were intertwined. No doubt, this was due in large part to developments in Ethiopia, from the defeat of the Italians at Adwa in 1896, to the Italian invasion in 1935. Within this period, the diaspora's turn to Africa was nowhere more pronounced than in the Caribbean and the United States, where perhaps the quintessential expression of diasporic political consciousness was the creation of the Universal Negro Improvement Association and African Communities League (UNIA) under Marcus Garvey.

Born in Jamaica in 1887, Garvey founded the UNIA in 1914, in which his wives Amy Ashwood and later Amy Jacques Garvey would play prominent roles. Venturing to the United States in 1916, he incorporated the UNIA in New York State in 1918, establishing his headquarters in Harlem. Garvey's "back-to-Africa" movement was more than a simple call for repatriation. Facing colonialism in both the Caribbean and Africa, he advocated the dismantling of European and American empires and the reconstruction of black societies everywhere. His businesses, such as the Black Star Line, were launched to promote trade between black communities in the Americas. His official organ, the *Negro World*, was the most widely circulated black publication in the world, appearing in English, French, Spanish, and Portuguese. By 1921, Garvey had achieved international recognition, his parades through Harlem, along with his annual August conventions, attracting thousands from all over the world. Centered in Harlem, the UNIA was the literal embodiment of pan-Africanism, and in time established 996 branches in forty-three countries, including Cuba, South Africa, Europe, and even Australia. Its membership is difficult to calculate, but it conceivably numbered in the hundreds of thousands.[21]

The UNIA was mismanaged, however, by Garvey and his advisors. There were also elements within the American black community appalled by his back-to-Africa message, at his ability to raise substantial sums of money, and at his rapid ascent. Britain also was uneasy with Garvey, and together with the United States covertly opposed the UNIA's attempt to acquire land and establish a presence in Liberia. The "Garvey Must Go" campaign resulted in his indictment on mail-fraud charges in 1921 and conviction in 1923. In 1925, he began serving a five-year term that was commuted in 1927. Garvey would return to Jamaica, and from there to London, where he died in 1940.

Although W.E.B. Du Bois proved to be Garvey's major nemesis, the former was also engaged in a lifelong dialogue with Africa. The fact that one of America's premier intellectuals, and the exemplar of the scholar-activist, was a principal spokesperson of pan-Africanism should not be lost in the current assessment of Africa's relationship to the diaspora. Born in Great Barrington, Massachusetts, Du Bois made incredible contributions to the struggle of black folk and the downtrodden throughout his life (1868 to 1963). Having founded the American Negro Academy as early as 1897, and having published the influential *Souls of Black Folk* in 1903, Du Bois led a Niagara Movement in 1909 that became subsequently institutionalized as the National Association for the Advancement of Colored People (NAACP).[22]

In the context of a civil rights struggle, Du Bois concluded that Garvey did not understand North American race relations and saw him as a menace. But one of the greatest ironies of the period is that both were deeply committed to the struggles of black people on an international scale. As long-time editor of the *Crisis*, official organ of the NAACP, Du Bois published articles and information that covered the whole of the African diaspora, and in that way paralleled the range of Garvey's *Negro World*. A series of several Pan-African Congresses, begun in 1900, saw Du Bois's organizational involvement in 1919, 1921, 1927, and 1945. These congresses, convened to marshal opposition to colonialism and racism, were not unlike Garvey's annual conventions, and the two men's efforts were often confused in the media. Du Bois would go on to incorporate a Marxist analysis into a powerful critique of capitalism, while Garvey remained an unabashed capitalist enthusiast. Tensions between Du Bois and the Garvey camp lessened, however, when Amy Jacques Garvey and Du Bois collaborated in organizing the 1945 Manchester Pan-African Congress. Du Bois's investment in Africa is perhaps best demonstrated in his relocation to Ghana in 1960, where he would renounce his American citizenship before his death in 1963. Perhaps the tempestuous relationship between Du Bois and Garvey as pan-Africanist pioneers was ultimately reconciled on African soil through Kwame Nkrumah, independent Ghana's first president. Having studied in the United States at Lincoln University, Nkrumah's pan-Africanist vision for Africa was directly inspired by both men. The discourse in the diaspora therefore translated into policy in Africa.

With respect to the Caribbean contribution to pan-Africanism, and in addition to Garvey and Blyden, Trinidadian Henry Sylvestre Williams called the first Pan-African Congress in London in 1900, and collaborated with Dr. Robert Love of Jamaica to establish branches of the Pan-African Association in Jamaica in 1906. Deeply disturbed by the 1935 Italian invasion of Ethiopia, Jamaican Harold Moody transformed his League of Coloured Peoples from an educational organization to a decidedly political one, while Trinidadians George Padmore and C.L.R. James responded by founding the International African Service Bureau in London in 1937, along with the future president of Kenya, "Burning Spear" Jomo Kenyatta. Padmore would control the bureau until it became the Pan-African Federation in 1944, and was instrumental in recruiting many of the organizers for the Manchester Congress the following year. He would precede Du Bois in Ghana, where in the 1950s he served as an advisor to Nkrumah.[23] In 1938, C.L.R. James published both *The Black Jacobins*, the seminal work on the Haitian Revolution, and *History of Negro Revolt*, centering people of African descent in world history, reflective of his deep engagement with anti-colonial struggles in Africa as well as the Caribbean and elsewhere.[24]

Rather than weakening, the impulse to connect with Africa in substantive and vital ways only quickened with the life and career of Paul Robeson.[25] Traveling to London in 1927 to study at the London School of Oriental Languages, he encountered James, Padmore, Kenyatta, and Nnamdi Azikiwe, first president of Nigeria, and would later recall "I discovered Africa in London." His 1934 publication, *What I Want from Life*, is one of the most incisive inquiries into the collective psyche of the African-derived. As a result of his travels to the Soviet Union and Spain in the 1930s, he began stressing the need to coordinate anti-colonial and anti-racist struggles globally. Becoming increasingly radical as his singing and acting careers soared, in 1937, he helped establish what became the Council on African Affairs (CAA), serving as its chair for most of its existence after 1942. Considering his activities along with those of other such "giants" of the age, it is clear that, far from the periphery, Africa occupied the very center of the diaspora's intellectual and political agendas.

Developments in the realm of the decidedly political were of course paralleled by the aesthetics of the times. Whether ideological or artistic (or both), the engagement with Africa was profound, best exemplified in the Harlem Renaissance, also called the New Negro Movement, spanning the 1920s and early 1930s. Langston Hughes's "The Negro Speaks of Rivers" certainly supports this observation, as does Countee Cullen's 1925 *Color*, in which one of his most famous poems, "Heritage," addresses this point. Jamaican Claude McKay, who in 1924 published *Home to Harlem*, was joined by Eric Walrond of British Guyana, and with others explored the meaning of connections among African-descended populations and Africa's meaning for the diaspora.[26] In addition to creative writers, there were also artists like Aaron Douglas, whose body of work evinces a sustained interest in African art (as well as cubism), as did Nancy Elizabeth Prophet, working in stone and wood and producing *Head of a Negro* and *Congolaise*.

Of course, *négritude* also posited connections between people of African descent, reinforcing the sense that Africa was of tremendous significance to the diaspora, in this instance its francophone component.

The work of sisters Paulette, Jane, and Andrée Nadal of Martinique, together with Léopold Senghor of Senegal and Aimé Césaire of Martinique, constitute a reiteration of this theme.[27] In tandem with *négritude* and the New Negro Movement, Spanish-speaking artists developed *negrismo*. African Cuban poet, writer, and journalist Nicolás Guillén is a prominent example, whose 1929 collection of poems, *Cerebro y Corazón* ("Brain and Heart"), celebrates African beauty while depicting black struggle. Luis Palés Matos of Guayama, Puerto Rico also focused on race, as is evident in his 1937 *Tuntún de pasa y grifería* ("Drumbeats of Kink and Blackness"). But perhaps the quintessential artist of the period was the Cuban painter Wilfredo Lam. Born of a Chinese father and a mother of African, European, and indigenous ancestry, Lam's work developed an intense engagement with African themes.

Consciousness of a black world also developed in Brazil, notwithstanding its complexities of racial identity.[28] In São Paulo, black newspapers such as *A Liberdade*, published early in the twentieth century, gave way to *A Voz da Raça* ("The Voice of the Race") in the 1930s, and sought to unify the African-descended community by emphasizing African Brazilian history and making connections to a larger black world. Black Brazilian consciousness took a momentous step forward between 1931 and 1937, when the Frente Negra Brasileira, or Black Brazilian Front, operated. A similar movement developed in Cuba, where the Partido Independiente de Color operated from 1907 to 1910, when it was outlawed and thousands of party members were slaughtered, including women and children.

The period 1945 to 1968 was also a time of tremendous struggle against racism and colonialism. Europe, seat of colonial power in Africa, was superceded by the United States and the Soviet Union as the two world superpowers, neither with territorial claims in Africa. The new Cold War facilitated anti-imperial struggle while transforming parts of Africa into a very Hot War, a veritable East-West theater of conflict. Africa's independence movement took place concurrently with parallel developments elsewhere, especially in India and China, and was also unfolding at a time of tremendous unrest in the United States, the Caribbean, and Latin America. The imagination of the African diaspora was especially captured by five developments in Africa: Ghana's independence under Kwame Nkrumah in 1957; the bloody struggle of Jomo Kenyatta and the Kenyan Land and Freedom Army (the so-called Mau Mau) against the British, culminating in Kenyan independence in 1963; Congo's independence (1960) and the assassination of its first prime minister, Patrice Lumumba (1961);

the Algerian War (1954–62), a particularly grim, intense struggle against the French; and the ongoing anti-apartheid campaign in South Africa. Like Senegal's Léopold Senghor, many anti-colonial leaders had studied in Europe and the United States and had been influenced by Garvey, Du Bois, Padmore, and others. This was true not only of Nkrumah, who envisioned a United States of Africa as a part of his pan-Africanism, but also Nnamdi Azikiwe, who also studied at Lincoln University and the University of Pennsylvania, and had Nkrumah as a student while teaching in Ghana. Azikiwe or "Zik" became Nigeria's president in 1963 and the father of Nigerian nationalism, a pragmatic leader and unifier of disparate groups. As such, the dawn of African independence included illumination from the diaspora, and the effect of simultaneous conflict in Africa and the diaspora resulted in closer cultural and political links between the two.

The period was artistically captured in the music, especially jazz. Trumpeter Dizzy Gillespie (and his *A Night in Tunisia*, for example), drummer Max Roach (who together with Clifford Brown recorded *Study in Brown* in 1955), and drummer Art Blakey (*Hard Bop*, 1956) experimented with forms that included specific African influences. The 1960s in turn saw the rise of avant-garde or free jazz, when the music became exploratory, decoupled from fixed chord progressions and tonality, and in many ways was in concert with the turbulence of the times.

An important example of interconnections in the African diaspora was the rise of Afro-Cuban jazz in New York. Led by the great Machito, the African Cuban percussionist, Afro-Cuban jazz (also known as Cubop) enjoyed an intimacy with dance, as it was associated with mambo, cha-cha, and guaguancó (a subdivision of rumba). Cuban-born Celia Cruz would draw upon similar sources to fashion salsa, while two other African-based dances, the tango and samba, would disseminate from Uruguay-Argentina and Brazil, respectively, and would impact dance around the world.

In North America, the political tenor of jazz was perhaps met only by the activism in the music of such greats as Nina Simone, Sam Cooke, and Curtis Mayfield; and by Trinidadian calypso (or kaiso) in the Caribbean, led by such artists as Atilla the Hun, Roaring Lion, Lord Invader, and Lord Kitchener in an earlier period, followed by the Mighty Sparrow in subsequent years. But perhaps the quintessential diasporic music establishing indissoluble and explicit links between Africa and black people everywhere was reggae, with the genre becoming an international phenomenon through the medium of Bob Marley's Rastafarian spirituality.

Black music from the Caribbean, Latin America, and the United States traveled the world over. In places like Britain, Caribbean forms have mixed with African genres to create new profusions, while in the United States these influences would eventually give rise to hip hop. In the African continent, diasporic musical forms, with their basis in earlier African traditions, were reintegrated into the work of such artists as Fela Anikulapo Kuti of Nigeria. Joining a highlife band in 1954, he launched what he called Afro-beat in 1968, a convergence of West African music with jazz (and a little James Brown). South African Hugh Masekela, the "father of African jazz," was similarly influenced by diasporic influences (and the politics of his society).[29]

The consideration of tangible, sustained, and vital links between Africa and its diaspora as both an intellectual project and as a series of lived experiences far exceeds the limitations of space provided here. Despite some five hundred years of disruption and dislocation, such links have endured and are incontrovertible. But whatever the academic position on the relevance of an African-Diaspora juxtaposition, it must also be borne in mind that working class people have made their own judgments about the matter, and in fact have participated in traditions underscoring a sustained global engagement, from music to dance to cinema to travel to literature to carnival to the presentation of the body. Stated differently, the African presence and contribution is *performed* throughout the diaspora every day, in countless ways, and by millions of people, African and non.

This volume seeks to make a contribution to that engagement.

NOTES

1. For examples of whiteness studies, see David R. Roediger, *The Wages of Whiteness: Race and the Making of the American Working Class*, rev. ed. (London: Verso, 1999); David R. Roediger, ed. *Towards the Abolition of Whiteness: Essays on Race, Politics, and Working Class History* (London: Verso, 1994); Michael Omi and Howard Winant, *Racial Formation in the United States, from the 1960s to the 1990s*, 2nd ed. (New York: Routledge and Kegan Paul, 1986); Ruth Frankenberg, *White Women, Race Matters: The Social Construction of Whiteness* (Minneapolis: U. of Minnesota Press, 1993); Noel Ignatiev, *How the Irish Became White* (New York: Routledge, 1995).

2. Examples of literature that argue for African ethnolinguistic relevance in the Americas include Michael A. Gomez, *Exchanging Our Country Marks: the Transformation of African Identities in the Colonial and Antebellum South* (Chapel Hill

and London: U. of North Carolina Press, 1998); John Thornton, *Africa and Africans in the Making of the Atlantic World, 1400–1800*, 2nd ed. (Cambridge and New York: Cambridge U. Press, 1998); Maureen Warner Lewis, *Central Africa in the Caribbean: Transcending Time, Transforming Cultures* (Kingston: U. of West Indies Press, 2003); Paul E. Lovejoy and David V. Trotman, eds., *Trans-Atlantic Dimensions of Ethnicity in the African Diaspora* (London and New York: Continuum Press, 2003).

3. For examples of literature reflecting these perspectives, see Sidney W. Mintz and Richard Price, *The Birth of African-American Culture: An Anthropological Perspective* (Boston: Beacon Press, 1992); Ira Berlin, *Generations of Captivity: A History of African-American Slaves* (Cambridge, Mass.: Belknap Press of Harvard U. Press, 2003); Ira Berlin and Philip D. Morgan, eds., *Cultivation and Culture: Labor and the Shaping of Slave Life in the Americas* (Charlottesville: U. Press of Virginia, 1993).

4. Consider such works as James Clifford, "Diasporas," *Cultural Anthropology* 9 (1994): 302–38; Stuart Hall, "Negotiating Caribbean Identities," *New Left Review* 209 (1995): 3–14; Stuart Hall, "Cultural Identity and Diaspora," in Jonathan Rutherford, ed., *Identity: Community, Culture, Difference* (London: Lawrence and Wishart, 1990); Homi Bhabha, *The Location of Culture* (London: Routledge, 1994); Homi K. Bhabha, "Frontlines/Borderposts," in Angelika Bammer, ed., *Displacements: Cultural Identities in Question* (Bloomington: Indiana U. Press, 1994); William Safran, "Diasporas in Modern Societies: Myths of Homeland and Return," *Diaspora* 1 (1991): 83–99; Robert J. C. Young, *Colonial Desire: Hybridity in Theory, Culture and Race* (New York: Routledge, 1995); Paul Gilroy, Lawrence Grossberg, and Angela McRobbie, *Without Guarantees; in Honour of Stuart Hall* (London and New York: Verso, 2000); David Scott, "That Event, This Memory: Notes on the Anthropology of African Diasporas in the New World," *Diaspora* 1 (1991): 261–84; Avtar Brah, *Cartographies of Diaspora: Contesting Identities* (London: Routledge, 1996); Paul Gilroy, *The Black Atlantic: Modernity and Double Consciousness* (Cambridge, Mass.: Harvard U. Press, 1993).

5. See, for example, Edward Alpers and Amy Catlin-Jairazbhoy, eds., *Sidis and Scholars: Essays on African Indians* (Trenton, N.J., Red Sea Press, 2004); J. O. Hunwick, "African Slaves in the Mediterranean World: A Neglected Aspect of the African Diaspora," in Joseph Harris, ed., *Global Dimensions of the African Diaspora*, 2nd ed. (Washington, D.C., Howard U. Press, 1993); Fitzroy A. Baptiste, "The African Presence in India," in *Africa Quarterly* 38, no. 2 (1998): 92–126; Bernard Lewis, *Race and Color in Islam* (1971); Lewis, *Race and Slavery in the Middle East; an Historical Enquiry* (New York: Oxford U. Press, 1990); Shaun Marmon, *Slavery in the Islamic Middle East* (Princeton, N.J.: M. Wiener, 1999); Ehud R. Toledano, *Slavery and Abolition in the Ottoman Middle East* (Seattle: U. of Washington Press, 1998); Joseph Harris, *The African Presence in Asia* (Evanston: Northwestern U. Press, 1971); Alexandre Popovic, *The Revolt of African Slaves in Iraq in the 3rd/9th*

Century (Princeton, N.J.: M. Weiner, 1999); St. Clair Drake, *Black Folk Here and There: An Essay in History and Anthropology*, 2 vols. (Los Angeles: Center for Afro-American Studies, U. of California Press, 1987, 1990); Mohammed Ennaji, *Serving the Master: Slavery and Society in Nineteenth-Century Morocco*, trans. Seth Graebner (New York: St. Martin's Press, 1999); John O. Hunwick and Eve Trout Powell, eds., *The African Diaspora in the Mediterranean Lands of Islam* (Princeton, N.J.: M. Weiner, 2002).

6. The Berlin Conference of 1884–85 saw European states negotiate the distribution of African territories, marking the official beginning of Europe's colonization of Africa. The Battle of Adwa and the Universal Negro Improvement Association are discussed later in this essay.

7. For starters, see Judith Ann Carney, *Black Rice: The African Origins of Rice Cultivation in the Americas* (Cambridge, Mass.: Cambridge U. Press, 2001).

8. See William Bascom, *Shango in the New World* (Austin, Texas: African and Afro-American Research Institute, 1972); Roger Bastide, *The African Religions of Brazil* (Baltimore: Johns Hopkins University Press, 1978); Roger Bastide, *African Religions in the New World* (New York: Harper and Row, 1971); Kim Butler, *Freedoms Given, Freedoms Won: Afro-Brazilians in Post-Abolition São Paulo and Salvador* (New Brunswick, N.J.: Rutgers U. Press, 1998); Lydia Cabrera, *Anaforuana: Ritual y símbolos de la iniciación en la sociedad Abakuá* (Madrid: Ediciones R, 1975); Lydia Cabrera, *La Sociedad Secreta Abakuá* (Havana: Ediciones C.R., 1959); Maya Deren, *Divine Horseman: Voodoo Gods of Haiti* (New York: Chelsea House Publishers, 1970); Rachel E. Harding, *A Refuge in Thunder: Candomblé and Alternative Spaces of Blackness* (Bloomington: Indiana U. Press, 2000); Zora Neale Hurston, "Hoodoo in America," *Journal of American Folklore* 44 (1931); Alfred Métraux, *Le Vaudou Haitien* (Paris: Gallimard, 1958). Translated as *Voodoo in Haiti* (New York: Oxford U. Press, 1959); Fernando Ortiz, *Hampa afro-cubano: Los Negroes Brujos* (Madrid: Editorial America, 1906); Jean Price-Mars, "Lemba-Petro: Un Culte secret," *Revue de la société d'histoire et de geographie d'Haiti* 9, 28 (1938); Albert J. Raboteau, *Slave Religion: The "Invisible Institution" in the Antebellum South* (New York: Oxford U. Press, 1978); G. E. Simpson, *Black Religions in the New World* (New York: Columbia U. Press, 1978); George Eaton Simpson, *Religious Cults of the Caribbean: Trinidad, Jamaica and Haiti* (Rio Piedras: Institute of Caribbean Studies, University of Puerto Rico, Monograph Series no. 15, 3rd ed., 1980); Robert Farris Thompson, *Flash of the Spirit: African and African-America Art and Philosophy* (New York: Random House, 1983); Robert Farris Thompson and Joseph Cornet, *The Four Moments of the Sun: Kongo Art in Two Worlds* (Washington, D.C.: National Gallery of Art, 1981); John K. Thornton, "On the Trail of Voodoo: African Christianity in Africa and the Americas," *Americas* 44 (1988): 261–78; Pierre Verger, *Notes sur le culture des orisa et vodun* (Dakar: IFAN, 1957).

9. Olaudah Equiano, *The Interesting Narrative of the Life of Olaudah Equiano,*

Written by Himself, ed. Robert Allison (Boston and New York: St. Martin's Press, 1995; orig. 1789).

10. See, for example, Ivor Wilks, "Abu Bakr al-Siddiq of Timbuktu" and "Salih Bilali of Massina" in Philip D. Curtin, ed., *Africa Remembered: Narratives of West Africans from the Era of the Slave Trade* (Madison: U. of Wisconsin Press, 1967); "Ben-Ali Diary," University of Georgia Library; Joseph H. Greenberg, "The Decipherment of the 'Ben-Ali Diary,' a Preliminary Statement," *Journal of Negro History* 25 (1940): 372–75; B. G. Martin, "Sapelo Island's Arabic Document: the 'Bilali' Diary in Context," *Georgia Historical Quarterly* 78 (1994): 589–601; "Autobiography of Omar ibn Said, Slave in North Carolina, 1831," *American Historical Review* 30 (1925): 787–95; Yacine Daddi Addoun and Paul Lovejoy, "The Arabic Manuscript of Muhammad Kaba Saghanughu of Jamaica, c. 1823," http://yorku.ca/nhp/shadd/kaba/index.asp

11. João José Reis, *Slave Rebellion in Brazil: The Muslim Uprising in 1835 in Bahia*, trans. Arthur Brakel (Baltimore: Johns Hopkins U. Press, 1993); Carolyn E. Fick, *The Making of Haiti: The Saint Domingue Revolution from Below* (Knoxville: U. of Tennessee Press, 1990); C.L.R. James, *The Black Jacobins; Toussaint Louverture and the San Domingo Revolution* (New York: Dial Press, 1938); John K. Thornton, "'I Am the Subject of the King of Congo': African Political Ideology and the Haitian Revolution," *Journal of World History* 4 (1993), 181–214; John K. Thornton, "African Dimensions of the Stono Rebellion," *American Historical Review* 96 (1991): 1101–13.

12. The major proponent of this perspective is John Thornton. In addition to works of his previously cited, also see his *The Kongolese Saint Anthony: Dona Beatrice Kimpa Vita and the Antonian Movement, 1684–1706* (Cambridge, U.K. and New York: Cambridge U. Press, 1998).

13. In addition to works already cited, see David Barry Gaspar, *Bondsmen and Rebels: A Case Study of Master-Slave Relations in Antigua, with Implications for Colonial British America* (Baltimore: Johns Hopkins U. Press, 1985); Michael Craton, *Testing the Chains: Resistance to Slavery in the British West Indies* (Ithaca, N.Y.: Cornell U. Press, 1982); Sterling Stuckey, *Slave Culture: Nationalist Theory and the Foundations of Black America* (New York: Oxford U. Press, 1987).

14. See, for example, Jessica B. Harris, "Same Boat, Different Stops: An African Atlantic Culinary Journey," in Sheila S. Walker, ed., *African Roots—American Cultures: Africa in the Creation of the Americas* (Lanham, Md.: Rowman and Littlefield, 2001).

15. On the transatlantic slave trade, see David Eltis, Stephen D. Behrendt, David Richardson, and Herbert Klein entitled *The Trans-Atlantic Slave Trade: A Database on CD-ROM* (Cambridge: Cambridge U. Press, 1999).

16. See, for example, Monica Schuler, *"Alas, alas Kongo": A Social History of Indentured African Immigration into Jamaica, 1841–1865* (Baltimore: Johns Hopkins

U. Press, 1980), and Maureen Warner-Lewis, *Guinea's Other Suns: The African Dynamic in Trinidad Culture* (Dover, Mass.: Majority Press, 1991).

17. Peter Linebaugh and Marcus Rediker, *The Many-Headed Hydra: Sailors, Slaves, Commoners, and the Hidden History of the Revolutionary Atlantic* (Boston: Beacon Press, 2000). Black mariners and revolt are also taken up in Julius S. Scott, "The Common Wind: Currents of Afro-American Communication in the Era of the Haitian Revolution" (Ph.D. thesis, Duke University, 1986). Jeffrey W. Bolster, *Black Jacks: African American Seamen in the Age of Sail* (Cambridge: Harvard U. Press, 1997).

18. Read carefully David Walker, *Walker's Appeal, in Four Articles: together with a preamble to the colored citizens of the world, but in particular, and very expressly to those in the United States of America. Written in Boston, in the State of Massachusetts, Sept 28th, 1929* (Boston: David Walker, 1829).

19. For a rather critical discussion of the early pan-Africanists, see Tunde Adeleke, *Un-African Americans: Nineteenth-Century Black Nationalists and the Civilizing Mission* (Lexington: U. of Kentucky Press, 1998).

20. See, for example, Edward Blyden, "Mohammedanism and the Negro Race," *Fraser's Magazine*, November 1875.

21. Amy Jacques-Garvey, *Philosophy and Opinions of Marcus Garvey*, 2 vols. (New York: Arno Press, 1968–69); Tony Martin, *Race First: The Ideological and Organizational Struggles of Marcus Garvey and the Universal Negro Improvement Association* (Dover, Mass.: Majority Press, 1986); Rupert Lewis, *Marcus Garvey: Anti-Colonial Champion* (Trenton, N.J.: Africa World Press, 1988); Robert A. Hill, ed., *The Marcus Garvey and Universal Negro Improvement Association Papers*, 9 vols. (Berkeley: U. of California Press, 1983–); Horace Campbell, *Rasta and Resistance: From Marcus Garvey to Walter Rodney* (Trenton, N.J.: Africa World Press, 1987); Ula Yvette Taylor, *The Veiled Garvey: The Life and Times of Amy Jacques Garvey* (Chapel Hill: U. of North Carolina Press, 2002); Barbara Bair, "Pan-Africanism as Process: Adelaide Casely Hayford, Garveyism, and the Cultural Roots of Nationalism," in Sidney Lemelle and Robin Kelley, eds., *Imagining Home: Class, Culture and Nationalism in the African Diaspora* (London and New York: Verso, 1994); Adelaide M. Cromwell, *An African Victorian Feminist: The Life and Times of Adelaide Smith Casely Hayford, 1868–1960* (Washington, D.C.: University Press, 1986); and Gerald Horne, *Race Woman: the Lives of Shirley Graham Du Bois* (New York: New York U. Press, 2000).

22. On Du Bois, begin with Arnold Rampersad, *The Art and Imagination of W.E.B. Du Bois* (New York: Shocken Books, 1990); Manning Marable, *W.E.B. Du Bois: Black Radical Democrat* (Boston: Twayne, 1986); and David Levering Lewis, *W.E.B. Du Bois: Biography of a Race, 1868–1919* (New York: H. Holt, 1993).

23. On Padmore, see James R. Hooker, *Black Revolutionary: George Padmore's Path from Communism to Pan-Africanism* (New York: Praeger, 1967).

24. On C.L.R. James, see Anthony Bogues, *Caliban's Freedom: The Early Politi-*

cal Thought of C.L.R. James (London and Chicago: Pluto Press, 1997), and Paul Buhle, *C.L.R. James: The Artist as Revolutionary* (London and New York: Verso, 1988).

25. On Robeson, see Martin B. Duberman, *Paul Robeson* (New York: Knopf, 1989); Sheila Tully Boyle, *Paul Robeson: The Years of Promise and Achievement* (Amherst: U. of Massachusetts Press, 2001); Penny M. Von Eschen, *Race Against Empire: Black Americans and Anticolonialism, 1937–1957* (Ithaca, N.Y. and London: Cornell U. Press, 1997).

26. A great deal has been written on the Harlem Renaissance. One can begin with Arna Bontemps, ed., *The Harlem Renaissance Remembered* (New York: Dodd, Mead, 1972); Nathan Huggins, *Harlem Renaissance* (New York: Oxford U. Press, 1971); and David Levering Lewis, *When Harlem Was in Vogue* (New York: Knopf, 1981).

27. Regarding *négritude*, see Janet G. Vaillant, *Black, French, and African: A Life of Léopold Sédar Senghor* (Cambridge, Mass.: Cambridge U. Press, 1990); Femi Ojo-Ade, *Leon Gontran-Damas: The Spirit of Resistance* (London: Karnak, 1993); and Léopold Senghor, *Négritude, arabisme et francité: réflexions sur le problème de la culture* (Beyrouth: Éditions Dar al-Kitab Allubnani, 1967); Tyler Stovall, *Paris Noir: African Americans in the City of Light* (Boston and New York: Houghton Mifflin, 1996); Brent Edwards, *The Practice of Diaspora; Literature, Translation, and the Rise of Black Internationalism* (Cambridge, Mass.: Harvard U. Press, 2003).

28. See Butler, *Freedoms Given, Freedoms Won.*

29. Their work on black music is voluminous. One can begin with LeRoi Jones (Baraka, Imamu Amiri), *Blues People: The Negro Experience in White America and the Music That Developed from It* (New York: William Morrow, 1963); Eileen Southern and Josephine Wright, *Images: Iconography of Music in African-American Culture, 1770s–1920s* (New York: Garland, 2000); Samuel A. Floyd, Jr., *The Power of Black Music: Interpreting Its Music from Africa to the Americas* (New York: Oxford U. Press, 1995); Angela Davis, *Blues Legacies and Black Feminism: Gertrude "Ma" Rainey, Bessie Smith, and Billie Holiday* (New York: Pantheon Books, 1998); Kwame Dawes, *Natural Mysticism: Towards a New Reggae Aesthetic in Caribbean Writing* (Leeds, Eng.: Peepal Tree Press, 1999); Chuck Foster, *Roots, Rock, Reggae: An Oral History of Reggae Music from Ska to Dancehall* (New York: Billboard, 1999); Lloyd Bradley, *This Is Reggae Music: The Story of Jamaica's Music* (New York: Grove Press, 2000); J. D. Elder, *From Congo Drum to Steelband: a Socio-Historical Account of the Emergence and Evolution of the Trinidad Steel Orchestra* (St. Augustine, Trinidad: U. of the West Indies Press, 1969); Donald R. Hill, *Calypso Calaloo: Early Carnival Music in Trinidad* (Gainesville: U. of Florida Press, 1993); Rudolph Ottley, *Women in Calypso* (Arima, Trinidad: s.n., 1992); Louis Regis, *The Political Calypso: True Opposition in Trinidad and Tobago, 1962–1987* (Barbados: U. of West Indies Press and Gainesville: U. of Florida Press, 1999); and Keith Q. Warner, *Kaiso! The Trinidad Calypso: a Study of the Calypso as Oral Literature* (Washington, D.C.: Three Continents Press, 1992).

Part I

Transformations of the Cultural and Technological during Slavery

This section establishes the connection between Africa and its diaspora as demonstrable and vital. Entirely written by historians, these three chapters explore such correspondences during slavery in the Americas. They interrogate the movement of technology, culture, and social organization from Africa to the Americas through the nineteenth century, breaking new ground with regard to ongoing debates about the specifics of such transfers.

Fred Knight's discussion of textile-working as an African importation helps to organize the framework of the argument. He illustrates that the transfer and adaptation of African technology in the New World was one necessarily accompanied by an attendant social organization that would also undergo transition. He avers that indigo production in both South Carolina and the Caribbean in the eighteenth century was the result of a West African agricultural "knowledge system." This especially involved the labor of women and included and was related to the cultivation of rice. Far from presenting uncomplicated "continuities," Knight is careful to detail those multiple factors that also help to explain the rise of indigo in South Carolina. He underscores that straightforward, pristine transmissions of any kind probably exist only as an imaginary construct. We are indebted to Knight for his patient discussion of the processes by which dye was produced in West Africa, an explanation informed by substantial primary documentation. We also learn that indigo production in the Caribbean, particularly in Barbados and Jamaica, rose and fell in conjunction with global economic currents generated not only by the economies of sugarcane production, but also the costs of indigo cultivation in India. Africans enslaved in Jamaica would add to their own expertise in indigo production processing techniques borrowed from the Indian experience, a "synthesis" that finds its way to South Carolina, where it resulted in the rise of a unique planter culture. Knight's contribution spans a considerable portion of the Atlantic world and is in fact global in its reach. As such, it is an important augmentation of the research undertaken by such scholars as Judith Carney (*Black Rice: the African Origins of Rice Cultivation in the Americas* [Cambridge, Mass: Harvard U. Press, 2001]) and Peter Wood (*Black Majority: Negroes in Colonial South Carolina from 1670 through the Stono Rebellion* [New York: W. W. Norton, 1974]). There is strong inference here that evidence of additional examples of African technology transfer during the period of the slave trade is on the horizon.

From North America the focus shifts to more southerly terrain, where João Reis provides another example of how far the literature regarding the African connection to the diaspora has traveled beyond uncomplicated notions of retention and continuity. The technological considerations of Knight's anglophone world connect with the kinetically and musically infused politics of lusophonic (Portuguese-speaking) space, where Reis focuses on Bahia (in Brazil). He follows the development of drumming and dance (*batuque*) in the first half of the nineteenth century, as it evolved from a form of black revelry celebrated along ethnic lines earlier to a much more ethnically homogeneous expression closely associated with slave insurrection. Along the way, Reis follows the shifts and turns in collective identities and relations between African-based groups, both enslaved and free, and African and *crioulo* (Brazilian-born). He presents a fascinating window into a decades-spanning debate between political and military leaders over the appropriate response to black revelry. For Reis, the issue is far from identifying the African origins of this or that cultural expression, but rather monitoring its unfolding and permutations for clues into the ways in which power and privilege were negotiated both within African-derived groups and between them and the slaveholding/supporting authorities. While always arguably a form of cultural rebellion, the *batuque* was certainly seen as precursory to sedition by the 1830s, a development concomitant with a series of Muslim- and Yoruba-based revolts. Stated differently, this essentially consistent cultural form acquired ever-changing investments of meaning for both the African-derived and authority-wielding communities with the passing of time, consistent with both the shifting demographics of the former and the evolving preoccupations of the latter.

The section ends with a chapter that also centers on Brazil, but extends its analysis to other parts of the Atlantic in ways that reinforce the observations not only of Reis, but also Knight and Archer (discussed in the next section). In fundamental ways, both Reis and Sweet provide rich insight into the cultural heritage of Brazil, but in his work, Sweet is concerned not so much with emendations in culture as he is with its erasure. More specifically, Sweet is concerned with *calundu*, a Central African practice involving spirit possession for purposes of divination. His study is an example of how certain African cultural forms have been decoupled from contexts of initial significance and otherwise (and subsequently) appropriated. Sweet is concerned with creolization as process, beginning with the unstable and contingent nature of "ethnicity" in Central Africa. Contesting the "creole" status of the "charter generation" of Africans arriving in Brazil in chains, Sweet argues that the *calundu* of Central Africans, introduced in Brazil by the seventeenth century, underwent certain alterities with the subsequent advent of West Africans. That is, an important "syncretism" took place among Africans of differing ethnolinguistic and regional backgrounds, such that *calundu* eventually came to represent a generic rather than ethnically specific gloss for African rituals. In this sense, what happens with *calundu* is the opposite of what occurs with *batuque*. The latter saw the culturally hegemonic rise of certain ethnolinguistic groups and therefore witnessed the transition from the diffuse to the particular. Having split into three different branches by the end of the eighteenth century, the religious components of *calundu* eventually merged with other religious diffusions with the progression of the nineteenth century, so that preceding African cultural forms were subsumed, in this case, by consequent ones. But *calundu* was apparently a hemispheric phenomenon, as Sweet turns up evidence for it in both Saint Domingue and what becomes the United States. His is a fascinating discussion and underscores that African cultural forms did not only change in response to European and Native American stimuli, but also as a consequence of intra-African exchange. Read correctly, Sweet's contribution serves as yet another caution against not only a presumption of cultural and political stasis in Africa itself during the transatlantic slave trade, but a reading of the African presence in the Americas that equally fails to take into consideration a negotiation of interiority.

1

In an Ocean of Blue

*West African Indigo Workers
in the Atlantic World to 1800*

Frederick Knight

> The forests gave way before them, and extensive verdant
> fields, richly clothed with produce, rose up as by magic
> before these hardy sons [and daughters] of toil. . . . Being
> farmers, mechanics, laborers and traders in their own
> country, they required little or no instruction in these
> various pursuits.   —Martin Delany[1]

Between 1740 and 1770, colonial South Carolina emerged as one of Great
Britain's principal suppliers of indigo, used as a blue textile dye. South
Carolinian indigo gained a reputation as a middle-grade commodity, next
in quality to the highest grade produced in Guatemala and the French
Caribbean. In 1750, the colony exported approximately 87,000 pounds of
indigo. Between midcentury and the American Revolution, South Carolina's indigo exports expanded more than tenfold to over one million
pounds per year.[2] During the South Carolina indigo boom, the colony also
increased its imports of workers from West Africa, particularly from the
Gold Coast, Windward Coast, and Senegambia region.[3] An infusion of
African workers, who carried experience with indigo production, fostered
the crop's development.

In this chapter, we will focus on a case study of the Lucas estate in
South Carolina in order to establish the impact of African workers on
South Carolina indigo production. The chapter also places the develop-

ment of indigo in South Carolina within a larger context by looking at the impact of African indigo workers on the larger Anglo-American world. On both sides of the Atlantic, African workers lived in an ocean of blue. A number of sources have portrayed Eliza Lucas Pinckney as the principal agent of South Carolina's indigo production. For instance, agricultural historian Lewis Cecil Gray, who made a lasting impact on the field, wrote, "The credit for initiating the [indigo] industry is due Eliza Lucas, who had recently come from the West Indies to South Carolina, where she resided on an estate belonging to her father, then governor of Antigua."[4] In a similar fashion, one recent colonial historian has written, "Eliza Lucas (later Pinckney) especially labored to introduce West Indian indigo cultivation."[5] In addition, Pinckney has been the subject of biographies, children's books, and a novel that mythologizes her "innovations" in indigo.[6] However, the focus on Lucas Pinckney obscures the ways in which African workers played a significant role in the shaping of indigo plantation development in South Carolina, as well as in other British American colonies.

Like most planters in colonial South Carolina, the Lucas family made their fortunes from their rice plantations, which depended upon African workers not only for physical labor but also for their expertise with the crop. Indeed, some colonial officials were aware of the expertise of African workers. For example, one colonial official from neighboring Virginia remarked, "We perceive the ground and Climate is very proper for [rice] as our Negroes affirme, which in their own Country is most of their food, and very healthful for our bodies."[7] African workers begat rice, which in turn begat more African workers experienced with rice, and the crop became the colony's most important export.[8] With increased flows of labor from Central and West Africa, coastal South Carolina attracted planters and prospective planters to the colony, and the Lucas family entered the Carolinas in this spirit. By 1713, John Lucas of Antigua established and owned in absentia a number of Carolina rice plantations. In 1738, his son George left Antigua to live on the Carolina estates. His political aspirations soon called George Lucas back to Antigua, leaving his daughter Eliza with the authority to take charge of his property for him. She managed three plantation sites, one at Wappoo, where the family lived; one at Garden Hill on the Combahee River, a fifteen hundred acre property that produced pitch, salt pork, tar, and other commodities; and a three thousand acre rice plantation on the Waccamaw River.[9]

In the early 1740s, the Lucas estate began and eventually succeeded with indigo experiments. Previous generations in South Carolina had tried indigo production, yet the Lucas experiment is notable because it produced the crop on a larger scale than their predecessors and inspired many more planters to turn to the crop. How did this conversion to indigo production happen? A number of factors shaped indigo production in South Carolina, including changes in the supply structure of indigo to Great Britain from India, inputs of knowledge from India and the Caribbean, and the opportunities created by a wartime crisis. Furthermore, as this chapter discusses, the colony's African workforce contributed knowledge to indigo production, as many of them brought, along with rice production skills, experience with the dye across the Atlantic.[10]

During the years of the transatlantic slave trade, a substantial number of workers in West Africa cultivated and processed indigo as part of their daily work activity. They did so despite the disruptions caused by the traffic in human cargo and the influence of European imports on West African craft production. For instance, a group of West African weavers added a dimension to their craft by unraveling imported cloth and interweaving the foreign thread with locally spun thread to produce new textile designs.[11] Though imported fabrics shaped African cloth production, the imports were unable to dislodge local textile weavers from their craft. During this period, imported textiles constituted only 2 percent of West Africa's clothing needs, so the output of indigenous cotton workers, spinners, dyers, and weavers far outweighed the textiles imported from European merchants.[12] The viability of African textile workers was not lost on European merchants in West Africa, many of whom sought to tap into its textile and related industries. For example, as early as the mid-sixteenth century, Portuguese merchants initiated an indigo trade on the coast of Sierra Leone.[13]

West African textile workers used different kinds of dyes in their craft, yet the most prevalent was indigo. Several contemporaries of the Atlantic slave trade attested to indigo production up and down the West African coast. Concerning textile production in Benin, the representative of the Dutch West India Company, David van Nyendael, noted, "The Inhabitants are very well skill'd in making several sorts of Dyes, as Green, Blue, Black, Red and Yellow; the Blue they prepare from Indigo, which grows here." Another agent of the company, Ph. Eyten observed indigo for sale in the market in the Slave Coast port town of Whydah.[14] Pieter de Marees noted that in Senegal the male elders "wear a long cotton Shirt, closed all around, made like a woman's chemise and with blue stripes," a style also prominent among elites in Allada, as surviving textiles from the mid-seventeenth century show.[15] Based upon first-hand accounts given to him about Benin, the Dutch geographer Olfert Dapper remarked, "The women wear over the lower part of their body a blue cloth, coming to below their calves." And in the interior town of Jenne, it was reported, "the Priests and Doctors wear white Apparel, and for distinction all the rest wear black or blew Cotton."[16] From the Senegambia region to the Slave Coast, Africans lived in worlds of blue textiles and indigo production.

Workers in West Africa, not unlike colonial South Carolina, linked indigo production with rice cultivation as part of an agricultural "knowledge system." This system consisted of experience with an indigenous West Africa red rice (*oryza glaberrima*); water and saline level management skills that involved constructing banks and sluices; expertise with rice cultivation in tidal floodplains, inland swamps, and upland areas; and the manufacture of tools such as the long-handled hoe (*kayendo*), mortar and pestle, and woven fanner baskets for separate phases of production.[17] It was not unusual for West African communities that grew rice as a staple crop to also grow indigo. The landscape of West Africa's rice region, which varied from the damp floodplains and swamps to drier upland fields, accommodated indigo cultivation that is suited to drier soils. Several eighteenth- and nineteenth-century sources testify to the ways that Africans managed these two crops. Michel Adanson, a British naturalist who surveyed the geography of the Senegambian region, observed, "the higher grounds were covered with millet; and there also the indigo and cotton plants displayed a most lovely verdure." In contrast, rice was "almost the only grain sown at Gambia in the lands overflown by the rains of the high season. The negroes cut all these lands with small causeys, which withhold the waters in such a manner, that their rice is always moistened."[18]

West African agriculturalists practiced similar methods in the following century, tying rice together with indigo production. As the Frenchman Gaspar Mollien passed through the regions of Futa Toro and Kabu in the early nineteenth century, he noted that the cultivators planted "large and small millet, cotton, which is very fine, excellent rice, indigo, and tobacco."[19] Richard Lander noted that between Boosa and Yaoorie, "The soil improved greatly as we drew near Yaoorie; and immense patches of land, cultivated with a variety of corn, also with rice, indigo, cotton, etc., were attended by a drummer, that they might be excited by the sound of his instrument to work well and briskly."[20]

Agriculturalists tied rice, indigo, and other crops together in a knowledge system in other ways as well, particularly in terms of processing methods. Throughout the West African rice region, women used mortar and pestles to remove rice grains from their hulls, and they employed similar techniques at certain stages of indigo production. Adanson remarked that after workers cultivated and harvested the indigo in Senegambia, they pound the leaves "in a mortar to reduce them to paste."[21] William Littleton, a commercial agent who worked on the Senegambia coast over the course of eleven years during the eighteenth century, observed that workers would first cultivate indigo and then "cut it, pound it in a wooden mortar, and hang it up in the form of sugar loaves." Cultivating and then transforming the indigo leaves into indigo balls were the first steps in the dyeing process.[22]

Workers carried out the final stage of production with other techniques and tools, taking the indigo, after being pounded in the mortar and dried, through another phase before it was ready for use. In order to make use of it for dyeing, they fermented the leaves in an alkaline solution or "ash water." To make the ash water, they took burnt wood, ash used for cooking, and ash and ash water leftover from previous dyeing on a sieve in a clay kiln. Next, they placed wood, old indigo leaves as well as the ashes in the bottom of a pot with a hole in the bottom. Into this pot, which sat atop another pot with a whole in its side, they poured water that dissolved the salt from the ashes and passed through the bottom hole. Craft workers collected the ash water in a pot they placed through the side of the bottom pot, and transferred the water to a dyeing pot or vat. Combined with the crushed indigo, the solution was ready for dyeing. Requiring agricultural, woodcarving, pottery, and other kinds of work skills, West Africa's indigo and blue textile workers embodied several layers of knowledge.[23]

Whether involved directly in its development or indirectly through trading or other kinds of relationships, West Africans, particularly women, carried indigo production knowledge systems across the Atlantic. As with rice production, indigo was produced through gendered divisions of labor, and, though in some places men dominated the craft of dyeing, indigo production and the dyeing process was usually a woman's art.[24] Embodying knowledge systems that included expertise with rice and indigo production, West African workers brought valuable skills to the Anglo-American colonies.[25]

To carve out their new American possessions, the Anglo-American colonists depended heavily upon a West African workforce. For example, during the 1640s, Barbados planters received most of their slave labor from West Africa through British slavers.[26] During the same decade, the island's workers produced indigo, which planters predictably used to buy more slaves. Though beset by overproduction and in spite of the sugar revolution at midcentury that transformed the Barbados export economy and its labor system from a society of slaves into a slave society, Barbados continued to produce small amounts of indigo into the 1660s, while many planters in the British Caribbean continued to view indigo as a viable crop.[27]

West African workers deployed a number of skills they carried across the Atlantic through the Middle Passage to shape indigo production in Barbados. Like indigo workers in Senegambia and other parts of West Africa, African workers in Barbados cultivated and harvested the indigo crop, and, according to one contemporary, "the plant is put in hollowed-out trees or troughs and water is poured over it. They let it lie there until it is quite soft and smooth, and then pound it with pestles until all is crushed." Furthermore, "Then they strain it and fully press out the left overs. The juice is then poured up to a hand's width high, into clean vessels, and is dried in the sun." The development of indigo in Barbados, in part a result of the experience of its West African workers, helped buoy the confidence of British colonists in the crop's viability.[28]

Within the first decade of the British occupation of Jamaica in 1655, indigo was among its chief exports, a product cultivated by a mixed labor force of indentured servants and slaves. And while the early African population of other colonies such as Barbados consisted of both West and Central Africans, imports of slaves to early Jamaica came primarily from West Africa, particularly from the Slave Coast and the Bights of Benin and Biafra. Because it could not absorb the approximately 3,800 slaves imported into the island between 1656 and 1665, many were dispersed to other islands. Yet, by 1662, hundreds of slaves populated the island, toiling alongside indentured servants, clearing the heavy forests, and cultivating indigo and other crops for export or subsistence. With the allure of profits from the dye, Jamaican elites invested in slaves and indigo works, so that in the final two decades of the century and into the next, indigo exports steadily increased in volume.[29]

Even as sugar became more important to the island, Jamaican landowners without enough capital to develop sugar plantations often made smaller investments in indigo production. This became especially important for the metropole, given changes in the structure of indigo production in India, one of England's principal suppliers of the dye in the seventeenth century. Late in the century, the cost of indigo in India went up, largely because of increased demand for indigo in Indian and Middle Eastern textile industries and also as a result of changes in the road tolls and tribute collected from Indian peasants. However, in the process of trade, the English learned indigo production techniques in India, and by the second half of the century these skills were transferred to the Caribbean; from 1671 to 1684, the number of indigo plantations increased from approximately nineteen to forty, with many of them concentrated in Clarendon Parish, Jamaica, along the Mino River.[30]

Reorganizing the development of indigo works to produce the dye on a large scale, the planter class introduced plans that demanded that Africans adapt their previous experience with indigo and woodcarving to different kinds of work. As on sugar estates, Caribbean indigo plantations conjoined agriculture with large-scale refinement works. And while some plantations specialized in indigo, others combined indigo with sugar, corn, and ginger and depended on slaves not only to cultivate the fields but also, along with white artisans, to work as carpenters.[31] These craft workers were needed to build indigo vats modeled after Indian vats, a central feature of indigo production in the Caribbean by the 1660s.

Within this wider context of movement and trade, African workers shaped indigo production by integrating their skills from Africa with knowledge from other fields. For example, after the crop was cultivated and the indigo leaves were harvested, the indigo was

> steept in proportionable Fats 24 Hours, then it must be cleared from the first Water, and put into proper cisterns; when it has been carefully beaten, it is permitted to settle about 18 Hours. In these Cisterns are Several Taps, which let the clear Water run out, and the thick is put into Linnen Bags of about three Foot long and half a Foot wide, made commonly of Ozenbrigs, which being hung up all the liquid Part drips away. When it will drip no longer, it is put into Wooden Boxes three Foot long, 14 inches wide, and one and a half deep. These boxes must be placed in the Sun till it grows too hot, and then taken in till the extreme Heat is over.[32]

As in West Africa, workers also pounded the leaves with a mortar and pestle before placing them in the indigo vats.[33] Synthesizing several valences of knowledge, including Indian indigo processing skills and African agricultural and woodworking skills, African workers on Jamaican indigo plantations helped supply Great Britain's market.

Because of the thirst for profits and British demands for indigo, the slave labor force faced a number of hazards. One Jamaican planter reported on "the high mortality of the negroes from the vapour of the fermented liquor (an alarming circumstance, that, as I am informed both by the French and English planters, constantly attends the process)." They also had to battle their way through fields that were occasionally subject to infestation and, as with other crops, the indigo crop failed at times because of unexpected, inadequate, or excessive rainfall. The enslaved were, like the indigo leaves in the mortar and pestles, pounded in the process of large-scale production. So, perhaps as result of sabotage by slaves, a portion of the indigo spoiled in the dyeing vats because it was steeped for too long.[34]

The structures and practices of slavery in the British Caribbean were brought into the Carolinas, whose development depended on West Indian capital and labor. The Lucas family of Antigua entered South Carolina within this larger context of Atlantic commerce and British colonial expansion. Aware of indigo development in the Caribbean, Eliza Lucas asked her father to send indigo seeds from the Caribbean. In July 1740, she wrote her father about the "pains I had taken to bring Indigo . . . to perfection, and had great hopes from the Indigo (if I could have the seed earlier next year from the West India's) than any of the rest of the things I had try'd."[35]

Lucas not only depended upon indigo seeds from the Caribbean, but she also looked to the islands for skilled craft workers to make indigo vats. In 1741, her father sent a worker to construct indigo vats and oversee the process of indigo manufacture. The estate first employed Patrick Cromwell and then his brother Nicholas, both from the island of Montserrat, but Eliza dismissed them both, suspecting that they had sabotaged the operation fearing that she and possibly other Carolinians would provide undue competition with their home island. In response, Governor Lucas looked elsewhere in the Caribbean for skilled labor.[36] In particular, he turned toward the French Caribbean, where African workers produced indigo for European markets. On small plantations of ten to twelve workers in Saint Domingue, Guadeloupe, and Martinique, slaves cultivated indigo, built vats, and reduced the plant to dye.[37] Given Governor Lucas's experience in Antigua, he was certainly aware of the French Caribbean indigo plantations and saw them as models for his own plantations on the mainland. According to one source, Lucas "sent out a negro from one of the French islands" to supervise the process in South Carolina. Soon after, the Lucas estate added indigo to its exports of rice, pitch, salt pork, and tar.[38]

The Lucas estate also mobilized workers from the Gold Coast region of West Africa. A 1745 inventory of slaves on the Garden Hill property, a site of indigo production beginning in 1744, listed 35 men, 16 women, 17 boys, and 11 girls including workers named "Quamina," "Quashee," "Quau," "Quaicu" (appearing twice), and Cuffee.[39] Their names indicate origins from the Gold Coast, either its interior or its periphery, where indigo-dyed textiles were produced along with a range of other agricultural and craft goods. Within these areas, indigo was produced and refined to support their cotton textile industries, such as those in the states of Bono and Akwapem and the town of Begho and its hinterland.[40] Swept through in the first half of the eighteenth century by Asante armies, who in turn sold the captives to European slave traders, these areas supplied South Carolina with slave labor.[41] Based upon the labor of workers from the Caribbean and West Africa who brought expertise in indigo production to the colony, the Lucas estate became a template of indigo cultivation and processing that other South Carolina planters followed.

Building upon the Caribbean model, the Lucas estate provided an example to other South Carolina planters who sought to move into indigo production. This became particularly significant because the War of Jenkins' Ear (1739–41) between England and Spain blocked international trade routes and the export of rice from South Carolina. As a result, South Carolina planters searched for alternative exports and decided upon indigo. By midcentury, it was South Carolina's second largest export, with 87,415 pounds being shipped from Charleston between November 1749 and November 1750.[42] Each enslaved indigo worker cultivated approximately two acres of land per year, producing a total of sixty pounds of indigo. Since the crop yielded an estimated thirty pounds per acre, each worker produced approximately sixty pounds of indigo per year while also cultivating their food provisions. Hence, to produce the 87,000 pounds of indigo exported from South Carolina in 1750, the colony's indigo plantations required at least 1400 workers.[43]

Indigo production grew substantially in the second half of the century, remaining South Carolina's second most important export. And, like the tobacco that shaped the culture of colonial Virginia, indigo helped to define the character of South Carolina culture among the planter class, in the fields, and within the slave quarters. Among elite Carolinians, indigo culture in South Carolina spread through an established network that connected colonial plantations with each other and the wider Atlantic commercial system. Through the slave trade and migration of free labor, through imports and exports, via books and private correspondence, through colonial newspapers and commercial documents, Carolinian elites participated in a global flow of labor and knowledge that stimulated the development of indigo in South Carolina on the one hand and supplied consumer demand across the Atlantic on the other.[44]

While planters acquired written knowledge of indigo production, slaves knew it through practical application. Many of them came directly from West Africa, particularly Senegambia, where, as we have seen, indigo production was fairly commonplace.[45] Their expertise with the crop fostered colonial indigo production and expansion, and slaves engaged in every aspect of production, from cultivating the labor-intensive crop in light, dry soils, to constructing indigo steeping vats, extracting the dye, and making the barrels in which the indigo was shipped. Although Africans brought experience with indigo to South Carolina, that experience underwent transformation in the New World. For instance, African workers in South Carolina performed little or no dyeing, as indigo left colonial ports packed in barrels exported across the Atlantic for English dyers. In particular, women who mastered cultivation, processing and dyeing techniques in Africa were now deskilled, being excluded from indigo processing and generally working only in the fields. Yet their agricultural expertise was not lost on planters such as Henry Laurens, whose slave Hagar developed the reputation for her "great care of Indigo in the mud."[46] Enslaved indigo workers such as Hagar generated fortunes for South Carolina planters.

The enslaved also saw within indigo spiritual riches, seeing metaphysical and healing properties in the blue dye. In contrast to the planter class's profit motivations, the slave community developed alternative ideas about indigo, some of which were related to West or Central African cosmologies. Into the nineteenth century, Afro-Carolinians attributed spiritual significance to the color blue. In some cases they painted their doors blue with residue from the indigo vats, and, in others, Gullah conjurers gave their patients blue pills for protection from harm. These practices complemented the wider set of African healing beliefs and practices in the antebellum South, as outlined by Jermaine Archer in the next section.[47]

For a century and a half, the American indigo plantations helped supply British demand, but as they turned again to India for indigo in the late eighteenth century, its production declined in the Anglo-American world.[48] Though indigo exports generally died out, it remained alive in other ways; for instance, South Carolina drew upon the colony's history of indigo development as a source of local pride. Yet commercial development of indigo, in South Carolina in particular and the British Americas more generally, can be better understood within a global context of movement and political change that bound together the histories of the North American mainland, Europe, the Caribbean, and India. And to the indigo fields and workshops of the Anglo-American World, West African workers carried critical knowledge from the other side of the Atlantic, skills which primarily benefited the colonial elite. As the planter class reasoned, slaves "must work, and suffer so that we, who must, can live."[49]

Research on the African diaspora in the Americas has enriched our perspective on the history of the New World and the contributions of Africans to American culture. From the spiritual practices of *quilondo* and *batuque* in Brazil, to the sacred dance of slaves in the Pinkster ceremony in Upstate New York, to the use of herbal medicines by healers such as Harriet Tubman, Africans shaped the landscape of the Americas. However, given that Africans landed in the Americas primarily to work, it is critical for scholars of the African diaspora to account for the impact of Africans as *workers* in the Western Hemisphere. For the Americas reaped the fruits of African labor skills and knowledge.

NOTES

I would like to thank a number of scholars who commented on previous versions of this essay: Jeffrey Fleisher, Michael Gomez, Dennis Laumann, Wende Elizabeth Marshall, Jemima Pierre, Hanan Sabea, Jesse Shipley, Sterling Stuckey, and Bryan Wagner.

1. Martin Delany, *The Condition, Elevation, Emigration, and Destiny of the Colored People of the United States* (Baltimore, Md.: Black Classics Press, 1993; reprint, 1852), 66.

2. Virginia Gail Jelatis, "Tangled Up in Blue: Indigo Culture and Economy in South Carolina, 1747–1800" (Ph.D. diss., The University of Minnesota, 1999), 160; Jenny Balfour-Paul, *Indigo* (Chicago: Fitzroy Dearborn Publishers, 2000; reprint, London: British Museum Press, 1998), 66; "Letters of Morris and Brailsford to

Thomas Jefferson," Richard Walsh, ed., *South Carolina Historical Magazine* 58 (1957), 137; "An Account of Goods Exported from Charles Town of the Produce of South Carolina from the 1st November 1749 to the 1st November 1750," in *British Public Records Office South Carolina, B. T.* vol. 16, 366–67.

3. William Pollitzer, *The Gullah People and Their African Heritage* (Athens: University of Georgia Press, 1999), 44–45.

4. Lewis Cecil Gray, *History of Agriculture in the Southern United States to 1860,* vol. 1 (New York: Peter Smith, 1941), 290.

5. Joyce Chaplin, *An Anxious Pursuit: Agricultural Innovation and Modernity in the Lower South, 1730–1815* (Chapel Hill: University of North Carolina Press, 1993), 192; Ira Berlin added, "Unlike the Africans who had grown rice prior to their capture, the slaves assigned to indigo production brought no knowledge of the task with them to the New World and often had to be directed by white artisans; still their on the job training gave them a special expertise in the intricacies of making the blue dye." *Many Thousands Gone: The First Two Centuries of Slavery in North America* (Cambridge, Mass.: Belknap Press of Harvard University Press, 1998), 148.

6. Elise Pinckney, "Eliza Lucas Pinckney: Biographical Sketch," in *The Letterbook of Eliza Lucas Pinckney, 1739–1762* (Chapel Hill: University of North Carolina Press, 1972), xvi–xxi; Nell S. Graydon, *Eliza of Wappoo: A Tale of Indigo* (Columbia, S.C.: R. L. Bryan Company, 1967); Frances Leigh Williams, *Plantation Patriot: A Biography of Eliza Lucas Pinckney* (New York: Harcourt, Brace & World, 1967); Harriott Horry Ravenel, *Eliza Pinckney* (New York: Charles Scribner's Sons, 1896); Susan Lee, *Eliza Lucas* (Danbury, Conn.: Children's Press, 1977).

7. *A Perfect Description of Virginia; Being a Full and True Relation of the Present State of the Plantation, Their Health, Peace, and Plenty, the Number of People, with the Abundance of Cattell, Fowl, Fish, etc.* (London, 1649), 14.

8. Peter Wood, *Black Majority: Negroes in Colonial South Carolina from 1670 through the Stono Rebellion* (New York: W. W. Norton, 1975 [repr. 1974]), 27–62; Judith Carney, *Black Rice: The African Origins of Rice Cultivation in the Americas* (Cambridge, Mass.: Harvard University Press, 2001).

9. Elise Pinckney, "Eliza Lucas Pinckney: Biographical Sketch," xvi–xviii.

10. Jelatis, "Tangled Up in Blue," 150–59; Daniel C. Littlefield, *Rice and Slaves: Ethnicity and the Slave Trade in Colonial South Carolina* (Baton Rouge: Louisiana State University Press, 1981), 76–77; Michael Gomez, *Exchanging Our Country Marks: The Transformation of African Identities in the Colonial and Antebellum South* (Chapel Hill: University of North Carolina Press, 1998), 93.

11. Thomas Phillips, *A Journal of a Voyage Made in the Hannibal of London, Ann. 1693, 1694, from England to Cape Monseradoe, in Africa; And thence Along the Coast of Guiney to Whidaw, the Island of St. Thomas, and So Forward to Barbadoes* (1746), in Answham Churchill, *A Collection of Voyages and Travels, Some Now First Printed from Original Manuscripts, Others Now First Published in English*, 3rd ed., vol. 6 (London, 1746), 236.

12. John Thornton, *Africa and Africans and the Making of the Atlantic World*, 2nd ed. (New York: Cambridge University Press, 1998), 49–50.

13. Carney, *Black Rice*, 15.

14. Nyendael quoted in Talbot, *The Peoples of Southern Nigeria: A Sketch of Their History, Ethnology and Languages, with an Abstract of the 1921 Census*, vol 3: *Ethnology* (London: Oxford University Press, 1926), 941–42; Basil Davidson, *West Africa Before the Colonial Era: A History to 1850* (London: Longman, 1998), 121; *The Dutch and the Guinea Coast, 1674–1742: A Collection of Documents from the General Archives of the Hague*, compiled and translated by Albert Van Dantzig (Accra: Ghana Academy of Arts and Science, 1978), 208–09.

15. Pieter de Marees, *Description and Historical Account of the Gold Kingdom of Guinea (1602)*, translated from the Dutch and edited by Albert Van Dantzig and Adam Jones (New York: Oxford University Press, 1987), 11; Adam Jones, "A Collection of African Art in Seventeenth-Century Germany: Cristoph Weickmann's Kunst-Und Naturkammer," *African Arts* 27:2 (April 1994), 28–43.

16. Olfert Dapper, *Description of Benin* (1668), trans. and ed. Adam Jones (Madison: African Studies Program, University of Wisconsin-Madison, 1998), 14; Richard Blome, *A Geographical Description of the World, Taken from the Works of the Famous Monsieur Sanson, Late Geographer to the Present French King, 1680, in Cosmography and Geography in Two Parts* (London, 1682), 380.

17. Carney, *Black Rice*, 30–106.

18. Michel Adanson, *Voyage to Senegal, The Isle of Goree and the River Gambia* (London, 1759), 151 and 166.

19. Gaspar Mollien, *Travels in the Interior of Africa to the Sources of the Senegal and Gambia* (London: Frank Cass and Co., 1967; reprint. London: Henry Colburn, 1820), 155 and 321.

20. Richard Lander, *The Niger Journal of Richard and John Lander* (New York: Praeger, 1965), 125.

21. M. Adanson, *Voyage*, 295.

22. Testimony of William Littleton, *Minutes of the Evidence Taken Before a Committee of the House of Commons, Being a Committee of the Whole House, to Whom It Was Referred to Consider the Circumstances of the Slave Trade, Complained of in the Several Petitions Which Were Presented to the House in the Last Session of Parliament, Relative to the State of the African Slave Trade* (London, 1789), 212. Eytzn noted that in the village of Keta, "they first soak the leaves and then make balls of them about the size of a fist, which they then put away. In this way, they seem to keep them in a good condition for more than a month." *The Dutch and the Guinea Coast, 1674–1742*, 206. Likewise, indigo workers in the Cape Verde Islands made the dye "by pounding the Leaves of the Shrub, while green, in a wooden Mortar . . . and so reduce it to a kind of Pap, which they form into thick round Cakes, some into Balls, and drying it, keep it 'till they have Occasion to use

it for dying their Cloths." George Roberts, *The Four Years Voyages of Captain George Roberts* (London, 1726), 397.

23. Adanson, *Voyage*, 296; Balfour-Paul, *Indigo*, 119–21; Judith Byfield, "Women, Economy and the State: A Study of the Adire Industry in Abeokuta, 1890–1930" (Ph.D. diss., Columbia University, 1993), 127–30; *Minutes of the Evidence*, 212; Mungo Park, *Journal of a Mission to the Interior of Africa, in the Year 1805* (London, 1815), 10–11; Claire Polakoff, *Into Indigo: African Textiles and Dyeing Techniques* (Garden City: Anchor Books, 1980), 25–26.

24. Mungo Park, *Journal of a Mission*, 10–11; Balfour-Paul, *Indigo*, 142; Byfield, "Women, Economy and the State," 124–27.

25. The theory that West Africans embodied knowledge systems is inspired by Pierre Bourdieu's ideas about embodied cultural capital in "The Forms of Capital," in *Handbook of Theory and Research for the Sociology of Education*, ed. John G. Richardson (New York: Greenwood Press, 1986), 241–58.

26. Ernst Van den Boogart and Pieter C. Emmer, "The Dutch Participation in the Atlantic Slave trade, 1596–1650," *The Uncommon Market: Essays in the Economic History of the Atlantic Slave Trade* (New York: Academic Press, 1979), 371. Boogart and Emmer note that from 1645 to 1647, British ships supplied the British Caribbean's slaves. See also George Frederick Zook, *The Company of Royal Adventurers Trading into Africa* (New York: Negro University Press, 1969), 72; Elizabeth Donnan, *Documents Illustrative of the Slave Trade to America*, vol. 1 (New York: Octagon Books, 1965; reprint, Carnegie Institution of Washington, 1930), 74–78. A. Hampete Ba discusses textile workers in the West African savanna and sahel in "The Living Tradition," *General History of Africa*, vol. 1: *Methodology and Prehistory*, ed. J. Ki-Zerbo (Los Angeles: University of California Press, 1981), 180–87.

27. Balfour-Paul, *Indigo*, 45–48; Hilary McD. Beckles, *White Servitude and Black Slavery in Barbados, 1627–1715* (Knoxville: University of Tennessee Press, 1989), 26; Gary Puckrein, *Little England: Plantation Society and Anglo-Barbadian Politics, 1627–1700* (New York: New York University Press, 1984); Richard Ligon, *A True and Exact History of the Island of Barbadoes* (London: Frank Cass & Co., 1970), 24. I distinguish between societies with slaves and slave societies based upon the research of Ira Berlin. Berlin, *Many Thousands Gone*, 1–14; John Scott, Sloane Manuscripts 3662, British Museum; Robin Blackburn, *The Making of New World Slavery: From Baroque to the Modern, 1492–1800* (New York: Verso Press, 1997), 230; Richard Dunn, *Sugar and Slaves: The Rise of the Planter Class in the English West Indies, 1624–1713* (Chapel Hill: University of North Carolina Press, 1972), 122–44 and 167–78.

28. "A Swiss Medical Doctors' Description of Barbados in 1661: The Account of Felix Christian Spoeri," Alexander Gunkel and Jerome S. Handler, ed. and trans., *The Journal of the Barbados Museum and Historical Society* 33:1 (May 1969), 7–8. Indigo production failed in Virginia during the 1620s because colonists did not

know how to process the crop. Philip Bruce, *Economic History of Virginia in the Seventeenth Century*, vol. 1 (New York: MacMillan and Co., 1896), 246.

29. Dunn, *Sugar and Slaves*, 167–68; David Eltis, et al., *The Trans-Atlantic Slave Trade: A Database on CD-ROM* (New York: Cambridge University Press, 1999); Eric Williams, *From Columbus to Castro: The History of the Caribbean* (New York: Vintage Books, 1980 [repr. 1970]), 114–15; David Eltis, "New Estimates of Exports from Barbados and Jamaica, 1665–1701," *William and Mary Quarterly*, 3d series, vol. 52, no. 4 (October 1995), 639 and 643; Frank Pitman, *The Development of the British West Indies, 1700–1766* (Hamden, Ct.: Archon Books, 1967 [repr. Yale University Press, 1917]), 234.

30. K. N. Chaudhuri, *The Trading World of Asia and the English East India Company, 1660–1760* (New York: Cambridge University Press, 1978), 334; Balfour-Paul, *Indigo*, 109–10; Eltis, "New Estimates," 639 and 643; Dunn, *Sugar and Slaves*, 169; Richard Sheridan places the number of indigo works in 1670 at 49. See *Sugar and Slavery: the Economic History of the British West Indies, 1623–1775* (Baltimore, Md.: Johns Hopkins University Press, 1973), 212; A. Lea, "A New Mapp of the Island of Jamaica" (1685), Geography and Map Division, Library of Congress.

31. Colonel Charles Long to Peter Haywood, 16 October 1707 to 6 May 1708, West Indies Folder, Rare Books and Manuscripts Division, New York Public Library.

32. John Oldmixon, *The British Empire in America*, 2nd ed. (London: J. Brotherton), vol. 2, 400. Another lengthy description of the fermentation process in Jamaica is in Bryan Edwards, *The History, Civil and Commercial of the British Colonies of the West Indies*, vol. 2 (London, 1793), 284–86. Some slaves drew upon their knowledge of indigo for domestic consumption. As the natural scientist Hans Sloane remarked, "Those of *Madagascar* beat Leaves to a Lump and make use of it to dye with." *A Voyage to the Islands of Madera, Barbadoes, Nieves, St. Christopher, and Jamaica*, vol. 2 (London, 1725), 36.

33. Jean Baptiste du Tertre, *Histoire Générale des Antilles Habitées par les François*, vol. 2 (Paris, 1667–71); Walter Edgar, *South Carolina: A History* (Columbia: University of South Carolina Press, 1998), 144–49.

34. Edwards, *The History, Civil and Commercial*, vol. 2, 287; Hans Sloane, *A Voyage to the Islands*, vol. 2, 35–36.

35. *The Letterbook of Eliza Lucas Pinckney, 1739–1762*, 8 and 16. Though it is not clear what kind of indigo was grown on the Lucas plantations, by the 1750s, at least two kinds predominated, *Indigofera tinctoria*, or "French" indigo, and *Indigofera suffruticosa*. David H. Rembert, Jr., "The Indigo of Commerce in Colonial North America," *Economic Botany* 33:2 (1979), 128–33.

36. Elise Pinckney, "Eliza Lucas Pinckney," xvii–xviii.

37. Blackburn, *The Making of New World Slavery*, 295; Clarence J. Munford, *The Ordeal of Black Slavery and Slave Trading in the French West Indies, 1625–1715*, vol.

2: *The Middle Passage and the Plantation Economy* (Lewiston, N.Y.: Edwin Mellen Press, 1991), 544–45.

38. Ravenel, *Eliza Pinckney*, 105.

39. Elise Pinckney, "Eliza Lucas Pinckney: Biographical Sketch," xv–xvi; Ravenel, *Eliza Pinckney*, 104; "Col. Lucas's List of Negroes at Garden Hill from Murray, May 1745," in Pinckney Family Papers, South Carolina Historical Society, Charleston, South Carolina.

40. For a treatment of Akan names, see Florence Dolphyne, *A Comprehensive Course in Twi(Asante) for the Non-Twi Learner* (Accra: Ghana Universities Press, 1996), 14; for Akan day names in Cote D'Ivoire, see Richard R. Day and Albert B. Saraka, *An Introduction to Spoken Baoule* (Washington: Center for Applied Linguistics, 1968), cycles 16–18; Sjarief Hale, "Kente Cloth of Ghana," *African Arts* 3:3 (1970), 26–29; Dennis M. Warren, "Bono Royal Regalia," *African Arts* 8:2 (Winter 1975), 16–21; James Anquandah, *Rediscovering Ghana's Past*, 93–94.

41. Ivor Wilks, "The Mossi and Akan States, 1500–1800," *History of West Africa*, 3rd ed., vol. 1, ed. J. F. A. Ajayi and Michael Crowder (Essex, England: Longman, 1985), 369; A. A. Boahen, "The States and Cultures of the Upper Guinea Coast," *General History of Africa*, vol. 5: *Africa from the Sixteenth to the Eighteenth Century*, ed. B. A. Ogot (Los Angeles: University of California Press), 428.

42. Elise Pinckney, "Eliza Lucas Pinckney," xvii; the figure of indigo exports is from "An Account of Goods Exported from Charles Town of the Produce of South Carolina from the 1st November 1749 to the 1st November 1750," 366–67.

43. "A Description of South Carolina: Containing Many Curious and Interesting Particulars Relating to the Civil, Natural and Commercial History of that Colony" (London: R. and J. Dodsley, 1761) in *Historical Collections of South Carolina; Embracing Many Rare and Valuable Pamphlets, and Other Documents, Relating to the History of That State, From Its First Discovery to Its Independence, in the Year 1776*, ed. B. R. Carroll, vol. 2 (New York: Harper and Brothers, 1836), 204.

44. Timothy Breen, *Tobacco Culture: The Mentality of the Great Tidewater Planters on the Eve of Revolution* (Princeton, N.J.: Princeton University Press, 1985); Jelatis, "Tangled Up in Blue"; Chaplin, *An Anxious Pursuit*, 190–208.

45. Pollitzer, *The Gullah People and Their African Heritage*, 44–45.

46. The method of producing indigo in South Carolina was essentially the same as in the Caribbean. Guion Griffis Johnson, *A Social History of the Sea Islands, With Special Reference to St. Helena Island, South Carolina* (Chapel Hill: University of North Carolina Press, 1930), 20–21; Peter Manigault to Benjamin Stead, 6 February 1770, Peter Manigault Letterbook (typescript in possession of the author); Jelatis, "Tangled Up in Blue," 150–59; Philip Morgan, *Slave Counterpoint: Black Culture in the Eighteenth-Century Chesapeake and Lowcountry* (Chapel Hill: University of North Carolina Press, 1998), 159–64.

47. Margaret Washington Creel, "*A Peculiar People*": Slave Religion and Commu-

nity-Culture among the Gullahs (New York: New York University Press, 1988), 321; Julie Dash draws upon these archetypes in *Daughters of the Dust*, as in the prominence of indigo-dyed textiles worn by and the blue-stained hands of Nana Peazant. *Daughters of the Dust*, prod. and dir. Julie Dash, 113 min. Kino Video, 1992 videocassette; Jermaine O. Archer, "Bitter Herbs and a Lock of Hair: Recollections of Africa in the Slave Narratives of the Garrisonian Era," in this volume.

48. Balfour-Paul, *Indigo*, 70–76.

49. Sterling Brown, *Collected Poems of Sterling Brown*, ed. Michael S. Harper (New York: Harper and Row, 1980), 190.

2

Batuque

African Drumming and Dance between Repression and Concession: Bahia, 1808–1855

João José Reis

The four million Africans imported to Brazil as slaves brought with them not only the physical energy to produce wealth, but also the religious, aesthetic, and moral values to create culture. It is commonplace to talk about the African contribution to different aspects of Brazilian culture, but little has been produced to document the tense and often conflictive history of the formation of Afro-Brazilian culture.[1] In this chapter I consider a small piece of that history, African drumming and dance (or *batuque*). However, I do not identify African origins of instruments, rhythms, and musical forms, but rather take African revelry as a window to discuss power relations under slavery in Bahia.

Blacks were involved in all kinds of celebrations in Brazil at the time of slavery. In white men's private parties, they figured at least as servants and often as musicians. They also participated in public festivities, be they civic or religious, segregated or mixed, with other sectors of society. They also produced their own celebrations, which were not always the same. Some had more, others less African density. Those produced by black Catholic brotherhoods, for instance, included processions and masses as well as African drumming, dancing, and singing. But there were also those celebrations which tried to reproduce more closely the experience that slaves had left behind in their homelands. The so-called *batuque* represented this kind of cultural manifestation.[2]

One way to consider black celebrations is to look at the degree of "africanity" among the revelers. There were those exclusively staffed by

African-born blacks, although unfortunately the documents usually hide their specific origins in Africa. What difference was there between the Yoruba and the Benguela *batuque*, for instance? The cultural exchange among Africans, which certainly happened all the time, can be perceived but rarely detailed. There were other possible differences regarding who were involved: slaves or freed/free people? Recently arrived or seasoned Africans? And how about the mixture of Africans from different ethnic groups, new and seasoned Africans, slaves and freed? Mixing leads to change. The problem is to establish the direction of the change. When we add the *crioulo* or Brazilian-born black, the detail is still lost, but our imagination suggests we are facing a deeper process of cultural change, of transculturation. There is more. Even the most densely African celebrations, including those of a religious character—like *calundu* and *candomblé*—could involve free *mestiços* (or mixed-bloods) and whites, initially only as curious observers, later as partners, but in the case of the *batuque* never representing a threat to the established African hegemony.

Despite the incorporation of foreign elements and despite change, the *batuque* continued to be a basic reference of black and slave identity until the late nineteenth century, as long as we understand identity not as a fixed point in the experience of a group. Identity can change and be multifarious. What is constant is a sentiment of alterity, collective singularity, and often opposition. That is the reason why all black celebrations under slavery, though some more than others, represented a means of expressing slave and black resistance and therefore a motive of concern for those in command. On the other hand, celebrations also developed as a means of negotiation with other sectors of society, with locally born blacks and mulattos as well as white people.

The several meanings and the many forms taken by slave celebration often confused those responsible for its control. Masters, police, and religious and political authorities regularly disagreed on what to do about it. On the one hand, they could see it as immoral, barbarous, bad for labor productivity, and, worse, as a rehearsal for rebellion. On the other hand, they could see it as good to placate the tensions in the slave quarters, as a healthy distraction, and even as a right as long as it could be considered "honest and innocent," to use the words of a seventeenth-century Jesuit priest.[3] The slaves of course often used the "honest and innocent" celebration as a smoke screen to exhibit deeply meaningful manifestations of their culture.

In this chapter I suggest some of the meanings acquired by black rev-elry under slavery, particularly the *batuque*. Given the restrictions of the available sources, all written by whites and mulattos with power and pres-tige, I discuss above all the attitudes and the views of masters, policemen, journalists, and politicians toward the *batuque*. For this reason I have cho-sen those festive manifestations more densely African or seen as such by these individuals. I discuss particularly what changed during the first half of the nineteenth century in their attitudes toward the *batuque*, which here generally means black percussion music usually accompanied by dance.

For this discussion I focus on three basic sources or episodes: a police report describing an African celebration in the sugar plantation town of Santo Amaro in 1808; a series of newspaper reports published between 1838 and 1841; and finally a debate by representatives in Bahia's Provincial Assembly in 1855. By moving through time I hope to be able to show both continuity and change.

In December 1808, a large African celebration took place in the streets of Santo Amaro, one of the most important towns in the sugar plantation region of Bahia, known as the Recôncavo. Those were days of prosperity in the sugar business, due to the Haitian revolution, which had destroyed slavery and plantation society in that former, prosperous French colony. The sugar boom meant more slaves in Bahia, who arrived in numbers that reached eight thousand a year. In 1815, the slave population of the large sugar zone where Santo Amaro was located is estimated to have been around ninety thousand souls.[4]

During the week that follows the Christmas celebration—not Christ-mas Day exactly—plantation slaves met with urban slaves in the streets of Santo Amaro, where they organized themselves according to their *nações* or nations, the way African ethnic groups were known in Brazil. Angolans (Africans exported through the port of Luanda), Jejes (Gbe-speaking peo-ples), Nagôs (Yoruba-speaking peoples), and Hausas—the last two together—occupied different parts of the town. On the plantations, while cleaning the soil, planting, cutting, and crushing the cane, they all proba-bly worked side by side; maybe they were allowed to live ethnically apart in the slave quarters. When celebrating, however, once free to organize themselves, they chose to reconstruct their differences, to assert their alter-ity among themselves.

Their ethnic severance, however, was clear but not perfect, not complete. Hausas and Nagôs had combined to produce the "brightest" group of them all, according to Militia Captain José Gomes. And he explained: "their bodies are half dressed, they [play] a big tambour, and some of them are decorated with some golden pieces, . . . they continued with their dances not only during the day but still a good part of the night, they dined in a nearby house in the same street . . . which they found empty . . . and there they had a lot to drink, paid by the same blacks."[5] The town had become a free territory for a few hours. Captain Gomes was disturbed, and he was probably not alone. He detected danger in so much physical energy lost to labor, exhibited in those seminaked, dancing black bodies, adorned with golden trinkets—nakedness and dance which suggested excessive sensuality, always unsettling for the white man in an environment where African women were scarce.

The captain also registered the existence of a large African drum, a sign that he was familiar with smaller, less threatening drums. But he considered them all "accursed instruments" in another passage of his report. He appeared to confront a sabbath of witches, appropriately including a large amount of food and drink, all paid for by the blacks themselves, which meant that some slaves had access to subsistence gardens and local markets, and others may have been slaves-for-hire in Santo Amaro and neighboring villages. This was additional evidence of African autonomy in that context, more fuel for fear. And besides dancing and drumming during the day, Nagôs and Hausas invaded the shadows of night in celebration, hours forbidden for slaves because they were ideal for planning plots against masters. As far as the captain was concerned, these elements constituted too much of a threat.

However, not all whites seemed to be as disturbed as he was. Free local people converged on the streets to watch the African celebration: "there were many people of all quality and sex," wrote the captain himself, meaning that individuals belonging to different classes and races, women and men, converged to watch the *batuque*. The masters of the African revelers themselves had allowed them to leave their plantations, and some may have been among the spectators. There was also compliance from the local councilmen and magistrates, "who rule the republic by hiding this insolence entitled divertissements . . . which is even consented by masters in their *engenhos* [sugar plantations and their surrounding environs] and farms, except for a few of them," reproached the intolerant captain. What figured as slave entertainment for masters, councilmen, and magistrates, meant slave insolence for the captain. Political power and military power were in disagreement. Good for the slaves.

The captain's words indicate that Santo Amaro slaves were gaining breathing space, at least along the cultural front. This interpretation is confirmed by another passage of his report, in which he wrote that such scenes represented "disorder . . . not unheard of in this village." For a good number of whites, nevertheless, this apparent disorder actually meant the true expression of order, in the sense that they believed that the slave who danced and sang represented less danger. I disagree with this interpretation and will return to this point. For the moment, let me introduce another distressed white into the plot.

His name was Ignacio dos Santos, the village priest. During the African afternoon function, he tried in vain to stop Nagôs and Hausas from singing and dancing. We do not know precisely what he told the revelers, but according to Captain Gomes "he approached them with apostolic zeal." We can imagine him trying to preach Christianity to Africans in the middle of a seemingly pagan celebration. He spoke in vain, according to Captain Gomes, "for the said blacks did not listen and responded with indecent words, and . . . they said that their masters had all week to amuse themselves while they only had one day, and asked him to leave or he would get what they had for him, and thus the said priest left pleading to God." God, however, apparently did not grasp the gravity of the situation, for He did not come forward to help His missionary.

Indecency, lack of decorum, nakedness, sensual dance, noisy drumming, in sum, cultural subversion, but also well-defined antagonistic words, heated that episode of class struggle in the 1808 summer of Santo Amaro. The attitude toward the slaves is evidence of class conflict. We have seen that Captain Gomes had represented slaves and masters in mutual cooperation, the former dancing, the latter letting them dance. Now that we are able to listen, however vaguely, to the Africans' words, there emerges a cutting critique of their masters' exploitative and privileged position in the social and economic structure. In lieu of seignorial concession, the words of the slaves conveyed the idea that freedom of cultural expression was a right they had fought to achieve, and this right, mixed with some lewdness, was thrown in the face of the man who represented the official, seignorial religion—the priest—as religion was the most powerful instrument of ideological control in Brazilian slavery.

Father Ignacio may have had Muslim slaves before him. The Hausas had come from lands largely controlled by Allah. They had been victims of the Fulani-led jihad begun in Hausaland by Shaikh Usuman dan Fodio in 1804, a holy war that was still in progress when the episode here discussed took place. One of the main goals of the jihad was to fight pagan practices which for the shaikh had been corrupting the souls of Muslims. Those Bahian slaves were probably in the shaikh's opposition camp in Africa. After all, he had written words against drumming that echoed those written in Bahia by intolerant whites: "My view is that a drum should be beaten only for some lawful purpose, such as calling a meeting, announcing when an army departs, or pitches camp or returns home and the like." The Prophet himself, according to the shaikh, had once called "beating the drum diversion in spite of the fact that it was being beaten for a legitimate purpose because it was not essential. How [much worse] then, is what the ignorant people do—playing musical instruments for entertainment and singing!"[6] Shaikh Usuman dan Fodio had something of Father Ignacio dos Santos. Because the Hausas associated with the Nagôs to dance in 1808, and the latter were predominantly "pagans," Santo Amaro may have become the stage for further estrangement between Hausas and a form of orthodox religion.

On both sides of the Atlantic, African celebrations divided those who had the power to subdue them, but who nevertheless did not have the determination of a Father Ignacio or a Shaikh dan Fodio to do so. To illustrate this point I now introduce to the reader another character, Francisco Pires de Carvalho e Albuquerque, member of a powerful planter family and captain-major of Santo Amaro, the highest local militia officer. It was to him that Captain Gomes had written his report. After reading it, the captain-major wrote to the colonial governor and Captain-general of Bahia, the Count of Ponte, a man who considered that social order depended on the absolute submission of slaves to masters and deference of free blacks to whites, in general. Such a vision was in conflict with expressions of African cultural autonomy, of course. He owned property in Portugal and Bahia, including sugar plantations and more than five hundred slaves. Therefore, besides defending the interests of the Portuguese crown, the Count defended his own private interests in ways he found more suitable. Contrary to the local planters, he considered African drumming and dances to be rehearsals to revolt, a thought that disturbed his mind more than the sound of slave drums disturbed his sleep.

In his report to the Count, the captain-major sought to soothe him by saying that "the reunion of blacks who came down from the plantations" did not have another goal other than promoting "their entertainment."[7]

But because disorders had happened in the past on such occasions, he asked the governor for instructions on how to behave in the future. Aware of his superior's hardline anti-slave politics, he could have acted severely against slave revelers, but because Santo Amaro masters allowed them to revel, he needed to back up his actions with written orders from the governor. And the latter did instruct him to forbid slave meetings, to arrest those who disobeyed, and to warn masters of the new regulations regarding slave control.[8]

Those were the methods of the Count of Ponte. And he was not alone. In spite of his hesitation, Captain-major Albuquerque agreed with the idea of hardening slave control, as did his subordinate Captain Gomes. They all seemed to have listened to the warnings of Luís dos Santos Vilhena, a Portuguese and Greek language teacher in Bahia, who had written the following words about the capital city, Salvador, in 1802:

> it does not seem to me to be sound politics to tolerate that in the streets [of this city] and its environs crowds of blacks of both sexes make their barbarous *batuques* to the sound of many and horrendous tambours, dancing impudently, and singing gentile songs, speaking diverse languages, and with such noise and such horrendous and disharmonious shouts that they cause fear and alienation . . . due to the consequences which can emerge from it, given the . . . number of slaves that exist in Bahia, a fearful corporation which deserves much attention in spite of the rivalry that is there between the creoles and those who are not [creoles], as well as among the several nations of which are composed the slaves brought from the coast of Africa.[9]

This is all very similar to what happened in Santo Amaro, both the noisy celebration and indecent dance. Vilhena proceeded by saying that slaves should be kept in a total state of subordination, not only to their masters, but to whites in general. Unfortunately, he maintained, Bahian slaves, especially those who belonged to powerful whites, treated lesser whites—like Vilhena himself or Captain Gomes and Father Ignacio—as if they were inferior to them.

That was precisely the situation the Count of Ponte believed he had found when he arrived in Bahia to become governor in December 1805. He reacted by following Vilhena's prescription, as if they had one day discussed the matter. In April 1807, he could write to Lisbon about his success in the struggle against many centers of African cultural resistance in the outskirts of Salvador, where he arrested numerous blacks who, according

to him, "with absolute liberty, with dances, capricious dress, false remedies, blessings and fanatical prayers, lounged about, ate, and celebrated
with the most scandalous offense to all rights, laws, ordinances, and public
order."[10] This is also very similar to what Santo Amaro witnessed during
that Christmas season. To the slaves' relief, the governor would die two
years later at only thirty-five years of age, perhaps a victim of "false remedies, blessings and fanatical prayers" well administered by the Africans.
However, he had lived long enough to make masters get used to his style of
slave control.

That was at least what the Count of Ponte's successor concluded. In
contrast to the dead governor, the Count of Arcos believed that Bahian
slaves were poorly fed, excessively punished, and forced to work long
hours without rest—and this kind of treatment, he thought, explained the
attempts to rebel. In 1813, he wrote to a magistrate in the Recôncavo that
"the safest and most efficient way to avoid the disorders caused by black
slaves is to allow them without hesitation to entertain themselves with
their dances on Sundays and Holy Days."[11] That was precisely what the
Santo Amaro masters had been doing before harsher methods of control
were introduced by the former governor. Arcos indicated several reasons
why slavery should be more flexible, all featuring African celebrations as a
principal vehicle. According to him, revelry contributed to the relief of
slaves' souls from oppression, making them forget for a few hours their
miserable lives, and more important, it helped promote ethnic division
among them.

Because of their well-defined differences regarding methods, the counts
of Ponte and Arcos represented opposing paradigms of slave control, the
hard versus the flexible.[12] Slave revelry was at the center of the question, for
approving or repressing it became metaphors of opposing methods for the
management of peace in the slave quarters. As a consequence, African revelry also became a focal point of slave resistance. It could evolve into rebellion, just as the Count of Ponte believed, or it could cause rebellion if
forbidden, as the Count of Arcos maintained. That is, neither repression
nor permission could guarantee peace. The Hausa and Nagô slaves, who
festively shook Santo Amaro in 1808, would shake Bahia with revolts for the
next thirty years. These apparently began in 1807, when the Count of Ponte
discovered and suppressed a conspiracy led by Hausa slaves. From then on,
Nagôs and Hausas, together or separately, would produce more than twenty
conspiracies and revolts, some of them fought to the sound of war drums.

. . .

After Brazil's independence from Portugal in 1822–23, local authorities tried to improve control over the slave population through provincial laws and municipal ordinances which included the prohibition of *batuques* and other forms of black revelry "everywhere and at any time."[13] These measures reflected the fear of slave rebelliousness on the one hand, and the dissemination of African customs on the other. There were strong reasons for such fears. African slaves continued to arrive by the thousands every year, even after the prohibition of the slave trade in 1831. At least 170,200 had been imported to Bahia between 1820 and 1850, the majority illegally.[14] Slaves formed 40 percent of the 65,000 inhabitants of Salvador in 1835. Approximately 60 percent of them had been born in Africa and, when added to the African freed men and women, amounted to 34 percent of the city's population. In addition, the Yoruba or Nagô represented two-thirds of the African community in the 1850s, which meant that old ethnic divisions had slowly declined and were being replaced by a kind of Nagô cultural hegemony. Revelry was therefore no longer an important vehicle of division among Africans. Maybe for this reason it gradually became more vigorous, which happened precisely at a time when the white elite sought to eradicate African culture from the streets of Salvador in order to "civilize" the city. And all of this was taking place in an era shaken by slave revolts, of which the 1835, predominantly Muslim and Nagô, uprising emerges as the most serious.[15]

The Muslim uprising occurred on a festive weekend in January, when Bahia celebrated Our Lord of Good End (Nosso Senhor do Bonfim), the most popular Catholic devotion in town. In 1835, the date coincided with the Lailat al Qadr, the Muslim celebration that closes Ramadan. Revelry and revolt then exchanged hands. The rebellion was eventually defeated, but there followed a period of great tension in the province, where every public festival that facilitated the reunion of blacks became a reason for alarm. Collective fear contributed to the circulation of usually unfounded rumors. In the beginning of February, news spread that slaves from several *engenhos* in Itaparica Island and Cachoeira were planning a revolt for Carnival. The fishermen festival in Salvador, on February 2, was canceled by the chief of police.[16]

In 1835, any *batuque* was largely interpreted as a revolt against slavery. A justice of the peace in Cachoeira received a warning that there was slave unrest in Iguape, the center of sugar agriculture. A police investigation, however, revealed that all that happened was "the diversion of black drumming, an amusement which is said to take place every Saturday" in a particular plantation.[17] The owner of this plantation simply followed the principle of those Santo Amaro masters accused of leniency by Captain Gomes in 1808. Just as he allowed his slaves to beat the drum and dance according to local custom, many whites and mestizos hoped that life would return to normal because they saw the January Nagô uprising as one more rebellion similar to many previous ones. But other Bahians surrendered to fear.

A segment of Bahia's press reflected and strengthened that fear by promoting the idea that all black celebration meant revolutionary revelry. The newspaper *Correio Mercantil* played this role perfectly. In 1838, for instance, it published a long article about a "noisy *batuque*" on the outskirts of Salvador that had brought "fright and terror to numerous families in that neighborhood." The newspaper had certainly received complaints from residents whose sleep had been disturbed by the sound of drums that conjured up images of Africans preparing for war. The *Correio* proceeded to say that it had already exposed similar developments in the same district and now added that numerous runaway slaves could also be found there. Thus, *batuque* and revolt were associated in the mind of the reporter.[18] This last *batuque*, however, did not assemble Africans only. The newspaper itself discussed the presence of "people of diverse qualities." This social mixture, though not as threatening as an African rebellion, frightened those who preached the elimination of the *batuque* as part of the plan to civilize the province the European way. The newspaper gives us the impression that Africans were having the upper hand in civilizing Bahia their way.

The following month the *Correio* would again denounce a lavish "African revelry" in the same district as well as other suburbs of the city. Additionally, "smaller *batuques*" occurred during a celebration of the departure of a military battalion from Salvador which had been brought in to fight a liberal rebellion that had engulfed the city from early November 1837 to early March 1838. This liberal rebellion gained the support of several sectors of the black population, and its defeat was followed by a bloodbath promoted by government forces, including the departing battalion.[19] According to the newspaper, "to show how relieved the Muslims were, they all sang, or rather howled in groups."[20] By identifying the Africans as Muslims, and then comparing them to beasts, the reporter fed the fear of his readers.

The following week, the *Correio* returned to the subject of *batuques* and Muslims.[21] The subject, however, would only regain full strength during the celebrations of the young Emperor D. Pedro II's coronation in 1841. Once again, a relatively prosaic incident would bring "fright to the peaceful inhabitants of this city." It seems that the arrest of an African slave carrying papers written in Arabic provoked a wave of rumors that the Muslims were trying a new version of the 1835 rebellion. The newsmen guided the eyes, ears, and minds of their readers to their interpretation of *batuques*:

> Horrifying scenes are witnessed in this city on Sundays and Holy Days, especially those which took place during the 8 days of celebration for the coronation. Let us speak clear: in view of the tumultuous and numerous African *batuques* that are seen all around everyday by the peaceful resident, which make him hurry in terror to reach his house, who would not justify, to a certain degree, the sudden terror that takes over a whole population ... when it has in mind the audacity with which the barracks were taken by surprise in 1835, etc, etc, etc?[22]

The "etc, etc, etc" belongs to the original document and it invited its readers to fill their minds with memories of 1835. Of course, their memories were now interrupted because, as the newspaper maintained, they had already been occupied by more recent terrifying *batuques*. The *Correio* would also use the episode to call vehemently for the elimination of *batuques* in Bahia. Alleging to be the voice of public opinion, particularly of those who attended the celebration, the reporter claimed that blacks had stolen the scene. He wrote: "multiple *batuques* ... in every plaza and public places, day and sometimes until late in the evening, struck the eyes and poor ears of those who tried to enjoy beautiful celebrations." And he fantasized about what a foreign tourist, a European, of course, would have thought in the face of such music and dance: "a foreigner who arrived in this city on this occasion would judge that he had before him an African village, so numerous and noisy were those *batuques*!" Had the author of these words been reading contemporary European travelers' accounts he would have known that, with or without *batuques*, they actually considered Salvador a kind of African village due to the overwhelming presence of blacks in the streets.[23] To change this impression, the *Correio*'s publisher should have known that Salvador would have to hide, expel, or exterminate the vast majority of its inhabitants, and by doing so cease to function. With 34 percent of its population born in Africa, with another 40 percent entirely or partially descendants of Africans, the city was predominantly African. But the newspaper's battle was not a demographic or economic one, it was cultural.

It was a fact—a journalistic fact at least—that the Africans had hegemonized culturally the 1841 celebrations, and that constituted a big problem. On that occasion, Bahian whites who converged on a particular neighborhood to watch the fireworks were "taken by terror" with the noise made by almost five hundred blacks who occupied that part of town. There was the terror produced by the threat of a new slave revolt, and there was fear of the cultural Africanization of the province. The African appropriation of the festive space meant they had won a battle in a symbolic war. But the politics of symbols would not distract the *Correio* from considering a possible, more serious political outcome, and it concluded its coverage of the episode, warning against "the bad results which emerge from these noisy and turbulent meetings, where the brutal fanaticism of this sect [Islam], exalted by rum, conceive ideas of extermination and canibalism."[24]

Fanatics, exterminators, cannibals as well as dancers and drunkards— voilá the profile of Muslims as depicted by the *Correio*. They seemed to resemble those Santo Amaro slaves in the now distant 1808. But the 1835 Muslims, according to numerous contemporary witnesses, were tuned to a more austere Islam, even though they did not seem to have reached the perfection recommended by Shaikh dan Fodio. There were reports that they promoted banquets but not *batuques*. There were also reports that they beat the drums in 1835 to make war, not to revel in peace.[25]

Reports such as those printed in the *Correio* helped create an image of the *batuque* which, though plausible, to a great extent did not exist. Nevertheless, this journalistic discourse contributed symbolic and ideological images and was written in a context that facilitated its reception. Africans had truly proven, in 1835 and other occasions, that they could turn feast into revolt. The collective energy of their *batuques*, often enveloped in mystery, seemed to many people a warning that they were preparing to attack again.

But in their frequency the drums announced another kind of movement, different from a frontal attack on the slave society. They communicated that the Africans and their descendants had not accepted being mentally enslaved. To reach such a goal blacks did not always have to be concerned with an image of whites ready to conquer their souls, having already enslaved their bodies. Getting together to celebrate African values and to think about themselves was a form of liberation. But such an Africa collectively reinvented in Bahia, which did not surrender culturally, was just as threatening as the Africa that rebelled physically. For those who thought the way the *Correio's* editors did, African revelry represented a threat to an imagined European civilization in the tropics as well as to the slave system.

However, not everyone in power and among the common white and mestizo folks agreed with the newspaper. We have already seen that people with different social backgrounds joined or attended as spectators the *batuques* reported by the *Correio*. Besides, the lavish black celebrations for the Emperor did not bother the police or political authorities of Bahia, who allowed them to happen and may have even encouraged them. They believed it was absolutely safe to see the members of the lowest social echelon celebrate so enthusiastically in honor of its highest political figure and chief symbol of stability.

In the 1850s, self-appointed civilized Bahians would fight vigorously what they considered barbarous African customs, like beating the drums in the streets of Salvador. With the final closure of the Atlantic slave trade in 1850, they increased their hope that the end of the *batuques* was near, now that African culture in Bahia could no longer be renewed with the help of imported slaves.

Although *batuques* took place under many different circumstances and disguises, it was during Catholic religious festivals that they occurred with greater regularity. The festival of Our Lord of Bonfim, the same celebration which had covered the Muslim conspiracy in 1835, was one of the most popular in town. For this reason local authorities paid close attention to it. In 1855, for instance, twenty drums were confiscated in *batuques* near the Bonfim church.[26] One year later the Englishman James Wetherell wrote in his diary:

> The "festas" at this church were formerly scenes of the wildest debauchery. Upwards of 20,000 blacks would be assembled and scattered over the hill, upon which the church is situated: hundreds would be dancing their national dances whilst thousands looked on, and these orgies would be incessantly continued. The dancers in public have been prohibited for some years, but immense crowds, dressed in the height of negro fashion, go there

during the three Sundays in January when the feast takes place. Dances are held in the houses, and even out doors, in spite of the prohibition, and all kinds of amusement in booths, which are erected round and near the church.[27]

In midcentury the siege of African revelry seemed to intensify and so did black resistance to it. Although it is difficult to measure, the *batuques* may have been expanding, dispersed here to reappear there, often under different forms such as indoor dance and drumming. This apparent paradox is in part explained by the attitudes of those with power to repress the *batuques*. The whites continued to be divided between permission and prohibition. A debate on the theme reached Bahia's Provincial Assembly in 1855.

That debate is a surprise because it was about the right to beat and dance to the drum, something that seemed to be already decided against for a long time, at least on the legal level. The debate arose as a result of a Municipal Ordinance from the town of Maragogipe, which required the approval of the Assembly in order to be enforced. The ordinance prohibited "*batuques* and shouts" in "public houses." This is something different from street drumming, which was generally forbidden even though it could be tolerated, depending on the mood or the character of the local police authority. The law, after all, often represented an instrument of negotiation more than one of punishment.[28]

The 1855 debate included a discussion on the meaning of *batuque*. A member of the Conservative Party and a district police officer (delegado), Antonio Luiz Affonso de Carvalho, favored the ordinance. He defined *batuques* as the gathering of people to dance "the most barbarian and immoral dances, with non-rhythmic and loud voices . . . the most complete orgy"; it was also a stage for drunkenness, fights, and crimes. *Batuques* were no "innocent amusement," he argued. He praised the Bonfim delegado for having recently dispersed and arrested "a great number of black Africans . . . who were giving themselves up to immoral dances in the middle of the most disturbing clamor."[29] Note his emphasis on the sensual aspect of the *batuques*, a typical white man's fear of supposedly exaggerated African sexuality.

Another conservative representative, José Pires de Carvalho e Albuquerque—who belonged to the same family as that captain-major of Santo Amaro in 1808—added an important economic angle: "Those who gather in *batuques* are in their majority slaves who run away from their masters' houses leaving them without workers."[30] This perspective is missing from the *Correio* campaign against *batuques*, and only suggested in the reports regarding the 1808 episode in Santo Amaro. The newspaper, remember, fought the "barbarism" of *batuques*—just as these politicians did—and warned about their role in bolstering slave resistance—a theme the assemblymen would not touch now. It makes sense: the *Correio* published its theses between the late 1830s and the early 1840s, when Muslim ghosts still haunted the province. When the Assembly discussed *batuques* in 1855, twenty years had passed without any serious slave uprising. The problem now was to subdue African customs, considered barbarous and immoral, and to make sure they did not disturb the business of slavery. The concern here was a form of resistance represented by slave flights, roving, and a lack of decorum, not a resistance represented by violent insurrection.

The strategy chosen by the assemblymen who opposed the anti-*batuque* ordinance was to defend the freedom to party indoors. The most articulate in the debate was the medical doctor, journalist, and liberal politician João José Barbosa de Oliveira. He did not defend the disorderly *batuques* or the runaway slaves identified by his conservative colleagues. He simply played by the liberal book, maintaining that it was an intolerable despotism to legislate about things that took place in private and behind doors. He chose to ignore the argument made by his opponents that the ordinance dealt with *batuques* in "public houses." "The municipal government," he argued, "cannot enter other people's houses." As for the *batuque*, he equated it with any other kind of music and dance, the latter consisting on "the cadence of more or less harmonious steps," and the former on "the sound of instruments and voices which can be loud or not." "It's a noisy singing," intervened José Pires with astonishment. João Barbosa calmly raised the surprising thesis that *batuque* singing could always be "in a submissive voice" and its drums be "softly played," which resulted in a "*batuque* without shouting." In sum, *batuque* was one thing, noise something else.[31]

He went on to define dance. Who, he asked, could forbid someone to dance "behind doors" the way he or she wished? There was no way to repress that kind of dance because there was no way to enter the human heart and say: "I hereby extinguish this source of passion." The consequences of passion, yes, those should be controlled as long as they offend a third party. Barbosa explained that the law should reconcile "civil liberty with social right." He refused to accept that the state could be allowed to control so completely the actions of individuals. He even accused the conservatives of being communists, for their drive "to reduce all individuals to the level of pupils . . . to eliminate natural rights . . . to establish communism and deliver to the State the tutelage of all individual actions."[32]

To be sure, Barbosa did not call for an absolute freedom to engage in drumming and dance the African way, but he was not against the *batuque* itself. He believed that police edicts and the criminal code were enough to control the excesses the municipal ordinance sought to punish. And in the end he won the day, despite the opposition of Bahia's archbishop (and assemblyman) Don Romualdo Seixas.

Politicians like João Barbosa belonged to an ideological lineage, which had a long history in Bahia, although according to the circumstances it adapted different strategies and arguments. Those who followed this line in the period of the slave revolts maintained that *batuques* appeased potential rebels; when the slave quarters quieted down, they came to the extreme of defending *batuques* as a civil right. In the meantime, those who followed the hard line mixed a concern with social order with moral and religious repugnance to *batuques*, though changing emphasis between the beginning of the century and the years that followed the 1835 rebellion. In this latter period, the struggle against African drumming and dance was portrayed as a fight between the peaceful civilization of the white man and the warlike barbarism of the Muslims. In the 1850s, the attack against moral barbarism still figured in the discourse of intolerance, but the concern with black rebelliousness would disappear, to be replaced by a concern with day-to-day resistance, namely, temporary flights and vagrancy, both favored by the Africa revelry.

Under the shadow of the rulers' doubts, black revelry continued to evolve. In the second half of the century, it would expand to include extra-African participation in people and symbols. But for many—whites, blacks, and mulattos—the *batuque* and later the samba would not lose its African identity. And its africanity was certainly not represented by a "submissive voice" or by instruments "softly played," suggested by the liberal politician João Barbosa. The Africans civilized Bahia in their own way, with soul sound. Usually quiet, cultural slave resistance in this case was not so silent.

NOTES

This article was written with the help of a research grant from the Brazilian Research Council—CNPq. It also appears as "*Batuque*: African Drumming and Dance between Repression and Concession. Bahia, 1808–1855" in the *Bulletin of Latin American Research*, vol. 24, no. 2, 2005, pp. 201–214 (Blackwell Publishing).

1. See, for instance, José Ramos Tinhorão, *Os sons dos negros no Brasil. Cantos, danças, folguedos: origens*, São Paulo, Art Editora, 1988, and *História social da música popular brasileira*, São Paulo, Editora 34, 1998.

2. The difficulty in defining the meaning of *batuque* in different contexts is discussed by Martha Abreu, *O Império do Divino: festas religiosas e cultura popular no Rio de Janeiro, 1830–1900*, Rio de Janeiro, Nova Fronteira, 1999, pp. 287–294.

3. André João Antonil, *Cultura e opulência do Brasil*, Belo Horizonte, Itatiaia, 1982, p. 82.

4. The 90,000 slaves in the Recôncavo in 1815 is an estimate by B. J. Barrickman, "The Slave Economy of Nineteenth-Century Bahia: Export Agriculture and Local Markets in the Recôncavo, 1780–1860," Ph.D., University of Illinois, 1991, p. 352.

5. Capitão José Roiz de Gomes to Capitão-mor Francisco Pires de Carvalho e Albuquerque, 20 January 1809, Arquivo Público do Estado da Bahia (APEBa hereafter), Capitães-mores. Santo Amaro, 1807–1822, maço 417-1. I have previously analyzed this document in João José Reis, "Identidade e diversidade étnicas nas irmandades negras no tempo da escravidão," *Tempo*, vol. 2, no. 3 (1997), pp. 7–10.

6. ʿUthmán Ibn Fúdì (Usuman dan Fodio), *Bayán Al-Hijra ʿAla ʿL-ʾIbad (The Exposition of the Obligation of Emigration upon the Servants of God)*, edited and translated by F. H. El Masri, Khartoum, Khartoum University Press; New York, Oxford University Press, 1978, p. 90.

7. Capitão-mor Francisco Pires de Carvalho e Albuquerque to Governor Conde da Ponte, 21 January 1809, APEBa, Capitães-mores. Santo Amaro, 1807–1822, maço 417-1.

8. Ibid. Despacho do Conde da Ponte, 27 January 1809.

9. Luís dos Santos Vilhena, *A Bahia no século XVIII*, Salvador, Itapuã, 1969, vol. 1, p. 134.

10. Conde da Ponte to Visconde de Anadia, 7 April 1807, Anais da Biblioteca Nacional do Rio de Janeiro, 37 (1918), pp. 450–451.

11. Conde dos Arcos para o Juiz de Fora de Cachoeira, 22 May 1813, APEBa, *Cartas do Governo*, 168, fl. 246.

12. I have discussed Ponte's and dos Arcos's methods in the context of Bahian slave rebellions in João José Reis, *Slave Rebellion in Brazil: The Muslim Uprising in 1835 in Bahia*, trans. Arthur Brakel (Baltimore: Johns Hopkins University Press, 1993), and "Quilombos e revoltas escravas no Brasil," *Revista USP*, no. 28 (1989), p. 24. The role of Ponte in the repression of a runaway slave community in the south

of Bahia is discussed in detail in my "Escravos e coiteiros no quilombo do Oitizeiro: Bahia, 1806," in J. J. Reis e Flávio Gomes (eds.), *Liberdade por um fio: história dos quilombos no Brasil* (São Paulo, Companhia das Letras, 1996), pp. 332–362. See also Reis, "Os escravos e o conde: resistência Africana no tempo do Conde da Ponte" (Unpublished manuscript, 2002).

13. See several examples in *Repertório de fontes sobre a escravidão existentes no Arquivo Municipal de Salvador: as posturas (1631–1889)*, Salvador, Fundação Gregório de Mattos, 1988, passim; *Legislação da Bahia sobre o negro: 1835–1888*, Salvador, Fundação Cultural do Estado da Bahia/Diretoria de Bibliotecas Públicas, 1996, pp. 125ff.

14. David Eltis, "The Nineteenth-Century Transatlantic Slave Trade: An Annual Time Series of Imports into the Americas Broken Down by Region," *Hispanic American Historical Review*, vol. 67, no. 1 (1987), p. 136.

15. Reis, *Slave Rebellion in Brazil*, pp. 15–20, passim. In "'The Revolution of the Ganhadores': Urban Labour, Ethnicity and the African Strike of 1857 in Bahia, Brazil," *Journal of Latin American Studies*, 29 (1997), p. 391, I estimate that 77 percent of slaves-for-hire in Salvador in the mid-1850s were Yoruba/Nagô. Using different sources, Maria Inês C. de Oliveira estimated that 79 percent were slaves in and around Salvador during the second half of the nineteenth century. See her "Retrouver une identité: jeux sociaux des Africains de Bahia (vers 1750–vers 1890)," Ph.D., Université de Paris-Sorbonne, 1992, pp. 107, 109.

16. Reis, *Slave Rebellion in Brazil*, pp. 189–190.

17. Juiz de Paz do 1° Distrito de Cachoeira to the Presidente da Província, 9 February 1835, APEBa, *Juízes. Cachoeira, 1834–1837*, maço 2272. The fear that Muslim rebels could be emulated outside of Bahia led to severe slave control in other parts of Brazil, above all in Rio de Janeiro. See Reis, *Slave Rebellion*, pp. 29–30; Flavio dos Santos Gomes, *Histórias de quilombolas: mocambos e comunidades de senzalas no Rio de Janeiro—século XIX*, Rio de Janeiro, Arquivo Nacional, 1995, p. 259; Carlos Eugênio L. Soares, "A capoeira escrava no Rio de Janeiro—1808–1850," Ph.D., UNICAMP, 1998, pp. 89ff, 92, 102, 277, 295ff. The fear of popular rebellions has already been studied in other historical contexts: see Jean Delumeau, *História do medo no Ocidente*, São Paulo, Companhia das Letras, 1989, chaps. 4 e 5. For convergences between revelry and revolt in France, see Yves-Marie Bercé, *Fête et révolte: des mentalités populaires du XVe au XVIIIe siécles*, Paris, Hachette, 1976, and Emmanuel Le Roy Ladurie, *Le Carnaval de Romans: de la Chandeleur au mercredi des Cendres, 1579–1580*, Paris, Gallimard, 1979.

18. *Correio Mercantil*, 4 July 1838.

19. For the Sabinada movement, see Paulo César Souza, *A Sabinada: a revolta separatista da Bahia, 1837*, São Paulo, Brasiliense, 1987, and Hendrik Kraay, "'As Terrifying as Unexpected': The Bahian Sabinada, 1837–1838," *Hispanic American Historical Review*, no. 72 (1992), pp. 501–527. The English traveler George Gardner, *Travels in the Interior of Brazil . . . , 1836–1841*, Londres, Reeve Brothers, 1846, p. 78,

wrote that the Sabinada began just after he left Salvador and that it was led by some whites but "supported by the majority of the black population."

20. *Correio Mercantil*, 2 August 1838.

21. *Correio Mercantil*, 7 August 1838.

22. *Correio Mercantil*, 30 September 1841. In previous issues the *Correio* described and commented with enthusiasm on official ceremonies around the Emperor's coronation.

23. See Moema Parente Augel, *Visitantes estrangeiros na Bahia oitocentista*, São Paulo, Cultrix, 1980, pp. 201–207.

24. *Correio Mercantil*, 30 September 1841.

25. Reis, *Slave Rebellion*, especially Part II. All religions have a center and a periphery. I am talking about the center or the most orthodox Muslims in 1835.

26. *Jornal da Bahia*, 17 March 1855, p. 2 and 19 March 1855, p. 1.

27. James Wetherell, *Stray Notes from Bahia*, Liverpool, Webb & Hunt, 1960, p. 122.

28. The debate is published in *Jornal da Bahia*, 17 March 1855 and 19 March 1855.

29. *Jornal da Bahia*, 17 March 1855, p. 1.

30. *Jornal da Bahia*, 19 March 1855, p. 1.

31. *Jornal da Bahia*, 17 March 1855, pp. 1–2.

32. *Jornal da Bahia*, 17 March 1855, p. 1.

3

The Evolution of Ritual
in the African Diaspora

Central African Kilundu *in Brazil, St. Domingue, and
the United States, Seventeenth–Nineteenth Centuries*

James H. Sweet

In the 1690s in the Brazilian town of Rio Real, Bahia, a slave woman
named Caterina was denounced before the Portuguese Inquisition for curing with "*ulundus*," which she said were "her relatives who died in Angola,
her homeland." Caterina cured "other negras" who suffered from a variety
of *lundus* that plagued their bodies. In order to draw the spirits of her
deceased ancestors to take possession of her body, Caterina ordered
singing and dancing to the sounds of musical instruments known as
canzás. Caterina was soon mounted by the spirit and entered her possession, at which time she was dressed in "the skins of wild animals" and
"dyed on the face with a clay," known as *mpemba*. The spirit then used
Caterina's body as a medium to speak "in the language of her homeland."
Caterina's Angolan ancestor proffered remedies to the ailments of her
clients, prompting Caterina to go off into the woods to search for the roots
and herbs that would heal them.[1]

Caterina's ritual and the dance that accompanied it were commonly
referred to in Brazil by their Kimbundu language name, *calundu*, or *lundu*
for short. In Angola, *quilundo* was a generic name for any ancestral spirit
that possessed the living.[2] These spirits intervened in the lives of people
for a variety of reasons, but usually as punishment for a lack of proper
veneration and respect for ancestors. The punishment was believed to
manifest itself in a variety of illnesses that could debilitate and even kill
the person who was possessed. In order to have these *lundus* removed, the

sick person needed to visit a diviner/curer, or *nganga*, who would consult higher spiritual powers to learn how to remove the malevolent spirit.[3]

Among the observers who commented on the ceremonies conducted by the *nganga* in seventeenth-century Angola was an Italian priest, Giovanni Antonio Cavazzi. Cavazzi, who spent seventeen years in Central Africa, described the rituals of the *nganga* in the following manner:

> The man or woman puts himself in the middle of the multitude and orders that all obey him. . . . Meanwhile, the musicians play their instruments and excite those present with appropriate songs and shouting, capable of frightening even the wild beasts. They sing some diabolical songs with invocations, judged efficacious for persuading the Devil to enter into the body of the person. The person, for his part, swears an oath to the Devil and invites him to take possession of him. At the sound of these supplicants, the Devil gives himself to the intervention. . . . Then the fetisher rises with great seriousness, and remaining still for several moments, suddenly begins to agitate, moving his eyes in their sockets, laying himself on the ground, contorting furiously, bending all of his members. . . . The fetisher then begins proffering extravagant words, confused and metaphoric, not without previously having forewarned those present that they are not his words, but of the spirit of the deceased . . . , whose name he then assumes, conserving [that name] until the end of the function. . . . [People] go to this possessed person because they judge that he knows everything that happens in the other life, and they use the forms of respect and reverence that they would use with a demigod, interrogating him and receiving answers as if he were the consulted spirit.[4]

The parallels between Caterina's ritual in Brazil and the one described by Cavazzi in Angola are clear. Just as in Central Africa, Caterina's Brazilian clients consulted her in the hope that she could remove the *calundus* that were causing their ailments. The use of musical instruments like the *canzá* (scraper), *atabaque* (drum), and/or *engoma* (drum) was vital to realizing Caterina's spirit possession and subsequent healing sessions. Indeed, the singing and dancing were explicitly designed to ingratiate the spirits and draw them into the ritual. Other material elements confirmed that the ancestral spirits had taken possession of Caterina. Her animal skin clothing represented a powerful vector to the spirit world, since only the highest-ranking members of Congolese and Angolan societies could wear animal skins.[5] The *mpemba*, or white clay, applied to Caterina's face was symbolic of the underground world of the dead. After spending six to ten months in their coffins, it was believed that the dead crossed over a large body of water (*kalunga*), where they took on the "white" appearance of the clay on the river's bottom. Hence, white clay represented benevolent spirits (as opposed to malevolent ones that roamed the earth) and was used extensively throughout Central Africa as a repellent of evil.[6] Finally, not only were all the tools of invocation distinctly Central African, but also Caterina conducted the ritual in "the language of Angola," probably Kimbundu. Thus, the "grammar" and the substance of Caterina's ritual were clearly Central African.

This description of an Angolan divination and healing ceremony is one of many that appear in the records of seventeenth- and early eighteenth-century Brazil. There is nothing that is exemplary about the case. In fact, what is remarkable is the regularity with which similar cases occurred.[7] Knowledge of Angolan *calundus* was widespread in Brazil, provoking commentary from a variety of observers including priests, poets, and travelers. Catholic clerics, concerned with maintaining religious orthodoxy among the Portuguese, were intolerant of the threat posed by *calundu* and therefore sought to criminalize its practice, especially when whites began consulting African *calundeiros*. In the late seventeenth and early eighteenth centuries, a steady stream of letters flowed from priests in Brazil to their superiors in Lisbon, describing the "scandalous" and "superstitious" *calundus* that were adopted by "many whites" in order to be cured of their illnesses.[8] Poets too were inspired to comment on the "satanic" rituals of Angolans. Gregorio de Mattos, perhaps the most famous poet of colonial Brazil, wrote the following verse describing white adherents of *calundu*:

> All these *quilombos*,
> With peerless masters,
> Teaching by night
> *Calundus* and fetishism
>
> Thousands of women
> Attend them faithfully.
> So does many a bearded man [a Portuguese]
> Who thinks himself a new Narcissus.
>
> This much I know: in these dances
> Satan's an active partner.

Only the jovial master
Can teach such ecstasy.[9]

Finally, the travel narrative of a "pious pilgrim" on his way from Bahia to Minas Gerais at the beginning of the eighteenth century described his encounter with *calundus*. Stopping over one night on the property of a large slave holder, the "pilgrim" was awakened in the middle of the night by what he described as "a horrendous clamor . . . that seemed to be the confusion of hell." When he awoke the next morning, the "pilgrim" complained to his host. The slave master responded that he would order his slaves not to perform their *calundus* that evening. His curiosity piqued, the "pilgrim" asked the master, "What are *calundus*?" The master answered, "they are entertainment or divinations that the slaves are accustomed to making in their homelands . . . for learning various things, like from where illnesses arise; and for divining some lost things; and also for having luck in their hunts and agriculture; and for many other things." The "pilgrim," shocked at these revelations, scolded the master for allowing his slaves to engage in such "superstitious" rituals and urged him to burn all of the *calundu* ritual paraphernalia. The "pilgrim" also implored the master to steer his slaves toward the path of salvation, which the master dutifully did.[10]

Given the overwhelming presence of Central African slaves in Brazil until the 1700s, it should not surprise us that distinct rituals like *calundu* proliferated. Scholars are now suggesting that during the seventeenth century, better than 90 percent of the 560,000 slaves arriving in Brazil were from Central Africa.[11] These Central Africans generally held in common core understandings like religion, language, and so on. Contrary to arguments for the emergence of a "creolized" or "hybrid" African-American culture from the very beginning of the colonial experience, *calundu* and other rituals like it were Central African religion in action.[12] These understandings of *calundu* as a distinct religious ritual probably survived in Brazil well into the nineteenth century, at least among Central Africans and their immediate descendants; however, the Portuguese-language meaning of *calundu* diverged from the Kimbundu by the second half of the eighteenth century, marking a profound shift in Brazilian understandings of the term.

As the "charter generation" of most slave communities in the Portuguese colonial world, Central Africans established the idiom through which some aspects of slave culture would be understood for future generations; however, the ritual terrain of slave communities gradually became more varied and complex over the course of the eighteenth century. During the first two decades of the eighteenth century, the complexion of Brazil's slave population shifted significantly. Large numbers of slaves from the Bight of Benin arrived, especially in the Brazilian northeast.[13] These Africans brought with them new and different rituals that ultimately expanded the Luso-Brazilian meaning of *calundu* to a form that would have been scarcely recognizable to its Central African originators. During this transitional period, Luso-Brazilians generally did not distinguish the cultural shifts that defined the interior worlds of slave communities. Instead, they fell back on the conceptual terms that were most familiar to them. Music and dance of slave communities were *calundu*; scrapers were *canzás*; and drums were *atabaques* and *engomas*, regardless of the origins of the practitioners or the substance of the rituals. Thus, certain Central African forms like *calundu* became associated with a generic form of ritual music and dance in Brazilian slave communities, at least for a brief period of time.

An examination of several cases from the second half of the eighteenth century demonstrates the nature of these shifts. As early as the 1770s, Africans from the Bight of Benin were accused of practicing *calundu*. In Lisbon in 1771, a freed black woman named Teresa de Jesus denounced Maria as a "*calunduzzeira*." In her denunciation, Teresa noted that "the same saints that they worship here, they also worship in the *calundus* of the Costa da Mina."[14] This expansion of *calundu* to include Africans from the Bight of Benin effectively reduced the ritual to a generic African religious form. Similarly, in 1785, a group of six Jeje (Ewe-Fon) slaves were accused of *calundu* in Cachoeira, Brazil. Though singing and dancing were a part of the ritual, the implements used in the ceremony—a feathered arrow, coins, calabashes—were not in keeping with Central African ritual. Moreover, the language of the ritual was Ewe-Fon; not Kimbundu.[15] Again, the specific meaning of *calundu* was lost, as Luso-Brazilian observers conflated Ewe-Fon ritual with the specific Central African ritual that was its historical predecessor.

Complicating matters further was the adoption of *lundu* as a popular music and dance form. Even as *calundu* became associated with African religious ritual, writ large, *lundu* emerged as increasingly palatable for white Brazilians and Portuguese alike. In 1775, Domingos Caldas Barbosa, the Brazilian-born son of an Angolan mother and a white father, performed the *lundu* in the salons of Lisbon's wealthiest elites. Barbosa's music, and the dances that often accompanied it, were considered vulgar by some, but this criticism did not prevent *lundu* from becoming a minor sensation, even at the royal court. Most critics were silenced when Portuguese composers naturalized the musical elements of the *lundu*, rendering it more lyrical and more European in style.[16] This more "refined" form of *lundu* eventually made its way back across the Atlantic to Brazil, where, by 1780, one government official in Pernambuco could claim that *lundu* was a prototypical dance of "whites and pardos," to be distinguished from the "more indecent" dances performed by Africans of various "nations."[17]

Lundu continued as a popular dance form in Brazil well into the nineteenth century; however, its Central African religious roots were long lost on the larger Luso-Brazilian community. When African cultural forms arrived in the Americas, they underwent changes that, over time, could render them mere shadows of what they once were. The relative stability of *calundu* in the seventeenth and early eighteenth centuries split into three different branches by the end of the eighteenth century—one generically African, one Central African, and one Luso-Brazilian. The generic African one quickly fell into disuse. By the turn of the nineteenth century, *calundu* had virtually disappeared from the Luso-Brazilian lexicon, as African dance forms were most commonly referred to as *batuques*.[18] Likewise, the religious associations of *calundu* eventually merged into the more generic *candomblé*, a mixture of Yoruba, Dahomey, and Central African religious forms.[19] The Central African (religious) and Luso-Brazilian (dance) understandings of *calundu/lundu* probably operated in parallel fashion into the nineteenth century. There seems little doubt that the Central African form of *kilundu* survived in Brazil, especially in the southeast. Mary Karasch has shown that at least two-thirds of the Africans in Rio de Janeiro during the nineteenth century were from West Central Africa.[20] And slave trade data suggest that as many as 84 percent of those arriving into Rio between 1776 and 1825 were of Central African descent.[21] Given the continued dominance of Central Africans in the slave populations of southeast Brazil, it seems unlikely that *kilundu* simply disappeared. Rather, the religious basis for the ritual remained hidden behind understandings of it as a Luso-Brazilian dance form that turned "lascivious" when danced by Africans and their descendants. Ultimately, the Portuguese-language transformation of *lundu* rendered it a spiritually impotent homophone of the Kimbundu version. Central Africans may have continued to refer to these rituals as *kilundu* among one another; however, *candomblé* became the preferred way of describing African religious rituals in Portuguese. Ultimately, *calundu* lost nearly all of the distinct Central African religious meaning that it had in its original form in seventeenth-century Brazil.

These transformations in the meanings of *calundu* have had a profound impact on interpretations of culture in Brazilian slave communities, obscuring scholarly understandings of the Central African influences. Though there are sometimes vague understandings that *calundu* had "Bantu" or "Angolan" origins, there is little specificity as to exactly what these origins were or how the rituals connected to Angola.[22] In many cases, Central Africa is completely erased. Several scholars conclude that the origins and definition of *calundu* are "unclear" or "imprecise."[23] Others, who claim to "accentuate the African origins of popular religion," ignore specific African belief systems altogether, emphasizing *calundu* as a peculiarly Brazilian form.[24] Still others "tentatively" accept colonial references to "Ewe (Jeje) *calundus*," cautioning that analyses of African rituals are "approximations," since "African religions transformed themselves over the centuries of slavery and colonialism."[25]

Indeed, it seems that much of the confusion over the definition of *calundu* arises from the chronological limitations of the scholarship. Most of those who study the eighteenth century recognize the religious importance of the ritual, but are confused by the variations in the "*calundus*" performed by "Angolas," "Minas," and "Jejes." This was precisely the period when the ritual was becoming generically "African," at least in Luso-Brazilian eyes. Scholars of the nineteenth century often see only the musical and dance aspects of the ritual in Brazilian slave communities. Thus, *lundu* is interpreted as "a dance tradition from the eastern hinterland of Luanda," with no hint of the ritual's religious underpinnings.[26] Such conclusions are understandable given that the *lundu* had metamorphosed into a mere dance form in nineteenth-century Brazil. The extant documentary record leaves no hint that *lundu* was anything other than a form of entertainment during that period.

The lessons to be learned from longitudinal examinations of specific rituals reveal a great deal about the *process* of creolization and the emergence of African-American culture. To begin with, all inquiries must necessarily start in Africa. Given the advanced state of scholarship on slavery and the slave trade, it is no longer acceptable for scholars to assume that African-American culture begins in the Americas.[27] At the same time, scholars are increasingly aware that the idea of a linear progression of culture from Africa to the Americas is a slippery conceptual slope. Because of warfare, trade, and other forms of human exchange, few parts of Africa were ever culturally or ethnically homogeneous. In the case of Central Africa, "ethnic" signifiers like "Ndembu" and "Ngangela" were very likely products of the slave trade. The peoples who constituted these "ethnic" groups were exiles who fled warfare, famine, and misery to create new peoples *in* Central Africa during the seventeenth century.[28] Thus, the "Dembo" and "Ganguela" that appear in Brazilian documents are not indicators of "traditional" African societies with deep historical or cultural roots. On the contrary, these ethnic designations are indicators of marginal and uprooted status, even in Africa. Brazil represented just one more stop in an arduous and unstable journey where cultural exchange was the norm. Generic rituals like *kilundu* functioned as an anchor of a broadly shared identity, one that emphasized the power of the dead and the importance of ancestor veneration. These beliefs were commonly held across Central Africa, making *kilundu* attractive to numerous Central African peoples, both in Africa and in the Americas.

On the surface, the process of "Africanization" that began in Africa might be seen as destabilizing any claims for the direct retention of African forms in the Americas. But it was precisely the survival of rituals like *calundu*, as well as the accompanying languages, dances, musical instruments, and other implements that illustrate the tenacity of broadly conceived "Central African" cultural forms. During the seventeenth and early eighteenth centuries, the preponderance of Central Africans in Brazilian slave communities resulted in a slave culture that was not peculiarly Brazilian. But nor was it tied to any particular African ethnic group. Rather, Brazilian slave culture is best characterized as "Central African," defined, in part, by a lingua franca like Kimbundu and religious rituals like *calundu*. Only over time were these elements transformed into something that was considered even more broadly "African." In some cases, as with *calundu*, African forms never did become distinctly "Afro-Brazilian." They were either absorbed into other African forms (*batuque, candomblé*) or they were coopted and made new by the colonial power brokers (*lundu*).

The implications of Central African cultural transformation and loss extend well beyond Brazil. Despite constituting nearly 45 percent of all Africans imported to the Americas during the era of the slave trade, Central Africans have largely been ignored in the scholarship on slave culture. Linda Heywood argues that because of the mixed Afro-European cultural heritage of the region, "the Central African input into Afro-Diasporic traditions may have been less dramatic and visible than the Yoruba and Fon elements, which appeared more African (exotic) to researchers and thus merited more attention."[29] Heywood's argument certainly goes a long way toward explaining the absence of Central Africa in studies of slave culture.[30] However, one might also posit that, even where more "exotic" Central African rituals (like *kilundu*) arrived in the Americas, the malleability of the rituals ultimately allowed them to be hidden or subsumed by a larger "African" or creolized culture.

In the case of *kilundu*, there seems to be some tantalizing evidence of its survival and transformation in places as seemingly far-flung as St. Domingue and the United States. Much of this evidence is circumstantial. As such, I merely hope to raise questions and speculate about possible connections between Central Africa and the diaspora beyond Brazil. Admittedly, I do not have a command of the pertinent archival sources for these other regions of the Americas; however, I hope that these suggestions might chart a path for others to follow.

On mission in St. Domingue and other French colonies in the Caribbean in the late 1690s, Dominican priest, Père Labat, was a keen observer of the customs and practices of the African slaves he encountered. Among the "dances" that he described was one known as "*calenda*":

> They have passed laws in the islands to prevent the *calendas*, not only because of the indecent and lascivious postures that make up this dance, but especially to prevent too many blacks from assembling and who, finding themselves gathered together in joy and usually inebriated, are capable of revolts, insurrections or raids. But despite these laws and all of the precautions the masters take, [*calenda*] is almost impossible to suppress, because of all the diversions, this is the one [the slaves] enjoy the most and the one to which they are most sensitive.[31]

Though Labat makes no reference to the potential religiosity of these dances, he makes clear that the master class considered the dances a threat to public order. Indeed, an ordinance of 1704 forbade slaves from "gathering at night under the pretext of holding collective dances." Shortly thereafter a planter was fined 300 livres for having allowed a *calenda* on his property. Finally, in 1765 a military outfit, The First Legion of St. Domingue, was created for the specific purpose of "breaking up Negro gatherings and *calendas*."[32]

Though the precise derivation of the word *calenda* remains unclear, anthropologist, Alfred Métraux, concludes that it "must certainly have meant Voodoo."[33] Historian, Carolyn Fick, also argues that *calenda* "sometimes served as a cover for voodoo gatherings."[34] The description of African religious practices in colonial St. Domingue as "voodoo" is probably anachronistic and ahistorical. Voodoo was a product of post-slave-trade Haiti that continued to transform itself, even in the aftermath of the Haitian Revolution. Nevertheless, both Métraux and Fick were probably on target in describing *calenda* as essentially religious. I would suggest that a deeper inquiry might reveal that *calenda* was, in fact, derived from *kilundu*.

Not only are there obvious linguistic similarities between the two words, but also the physical description of the *calenda* ritual is strikingly similar to *kilundu*. Labat described *calenda* as follows:

To dance the *calenda*, the Negroes make two drums, when possible from the hollow trunk of a single piece of tree. One end is open and they stretch over the other a skin of sheep or nanny-goat. The shorter of these drums is called Bamboula, because it is sometimes made out of very thick bamboo. Astride each drum is a Negro who strikes it with his wrists and fingers, but slowly for one and rapidly for the other. To this monotone and hollow sound is joined a number of . . . calabashes half filled with small stones, or with grains of corn. . . . When they wish to make the orchestra more complete, they add the Banza, a kind of Bass viol with four strings that they pluck. The Negresses, arranged in a circle, regulate the tempo by clapping their hands, and they reply in chorus to one or two chanters whose piercing voice repeats or improvises ditties. For the Negroes possess the talent of improvising, and it gives them an opportunity for displaying especially their tendency to banter. The dancers, male and female, . . . come to the middle of a circle (which is formed on even ground and in the open air) and they begin to dance. . . . This dance, which has its origin on Mt. Atlas, and which offers little variation, consists of a movement where each foot is raised and lowered successively, striking with force, sometimes the toe and sometimes the heel, on the ground, in a way quite similar to the English step. The dancer turns on himself or around his partner who turns also, and changes place, waving the two ends of a handkerchief that they hold. The dancer lowers and raises alternatively his arms, while keeping the elbows near the body, and the hand almost closed. This dance in which the play of the eyes is nothing less than extraordinary, is lively and animated, and an exact timing lends it real grace. The dancers follow each other with emulation, and it is often necessary to put an end to the ball, which the Negroes never abandon without regret.[35]

The symbolic elements of the ritual reveal its likely Central African origin. First, the use of two drums is very similar to the use of larger and smaller drums in Central Africa. In Kimbundu and Kikongo, these drums are known as *ngoma* (the larger) and *atabaque* (the smaller). Interestingly, Labat described the smaller drum as a "Bamboula." *Bambula* is a Kikongo word that means "violin." Either Labat was mistaken in his nomenclature or the names were transformed in the Domingois context. His description of the "Banza" as a violin, however, was on target. In Kimbundu, the violin was *mbanza*, a word that some have argued is the origin of the word "banjo."[36] Second, the "Negresses in a circle" is reflective of the posture taken in *kilundu* rituals. The counterclockwise movement around the circle, in conjunction with the clapping, singing, chanting, and "banter," was all designed to invoke the spirits. Finally, Labat's description of a "dance in which the play of the eyes is nothing less than extraordinary" seems highly suggestive of the trance state that was the culmination of *kilundu* ceremonies.

Clearly, there are elements in Labat's description of the *calenda* dance that suggest little more than entertainment or diversion, but the obvious references to Central African musical instruments, along with other ritual coincidences, would suggest a dance that had its derivation in Central African *kilundu*. The cultural flux that erased the ritual's more overt religious aspects was perhaps similar to the process of transformation that the *kilundu* would later undergo in Brazil. Or, perhaps Labat simply failed to notice the ritual aspects of the dance. Labat's reference to the dance taking place "on even ground and in the open air" would seem to affirm Sterling Stuckey's argument that "since African dance was observed in settings thought inappropriate for worship, the sacred was thereby disguised."[37] Either way, Central African influence in *calenda* is manifest in Labat's description and seems to point to a religious rather than a secular origin.

In the United States, one finds ritual descriptions similar to *kilundu* in the "ring shout" ceremonies of slave communities. The majority of scholarship on "ring shout" concentrates on the second half of the nineteenth century, a period when most slaves had already become firmly "African American." As such, scholars point to the ring shout's mixed cultural heritage—West and Central African—as a signal contribution to the emergence of African-American religion and culture. In his path-breaking book, *Slave Culture*, Sterling Stuckey writes, "the ring in which Africans danced and sang is the key to understanding the means by which they achieved oneness in America."[38] Still, Stuckey emphasizes the Central African contribution when he writes that the "circle ritual imported by Africans from the Congo region was so powerful in its elaboration of a religious vision that it contributed disproportionately to the centrality of the circle in slavery."[39]

This "disproportionate" influence of Central Africa in African-American religion and culture is difficult to pinpoint. Building on the work of Robert F. Thompson, Stuckey draws attention to the symbolic importance of counterclockwise, circular dancing in Bakongo burial ceremonies and "ancestral ritual," but in *Slave Culture* he fails to move far beyond the symbolism of the ring itself in African-American religious rituals.[40] In one of his most recent works, however, Stuckey goes back in time to the eighteenth century and shows more clearly the Central African influence on rituals in upstate New York.

Stuckey describes the rituals of Africans at the annual Pinkster festival in Albany, New York, focusing particularly on one slave man named Charley. Charley was brought to New York from "Angola" as a young child, probably in the first decade of the eighteenth century. In Albany, Charley became a master dancer and drummer. As he drummed, Charley also sang in "some strange African air."[41] Much later in his life, around the age of seventy, Charley acted as the "king" in rituals that included drumming and dancing in the middle of a ring of other dancers. According to one description of this ritual, the drummer beat

> lustily with his naked hands upon its loudly sounding head, successively repeating the ever wild, though euphonic cry of *Hi-a-bomba, bomba, bomba,* in full harmony with the thumping sounds. These vocal sounds were taken up and as oft repeated by the female portion of the spectators not otherwise engaged in the exercises of the scene. . . . Merrily now the dance moved on . . . rapid and furious became their motions . . . copiously flowed the perspiration, in frequent streams, from brow to heal, and still the dance went on in all of its energy and might.[42]

Building on Stuckey's suggestion that these dances were forums for spirit possession, I want to suggest ways that the rituals of the Pinkster festival were related to Central African culture, especially *kilundu*.[43] First, the "strange African air" that Charley sang in was probably Kikongo or Kimbundu. Given Charley's "Angolan" background, we might immediately draw this conclusion, but we can also look to the cry of "*Hi-a-bomba, bomba, bomba*" in the ring dance ritual. Though the evidence is admittedly cryptic, one might suggest "*bomba*" is a reference to Mbumba, the Kongolese rainbow spirit. In eighteenth-century St. Domingue, a similar chant of "*Eh! eh! Bomba, hen! hen!*" was used in rituals that were clearly Kongolese in origin.[44]

Second, Charley's role as "king" of the Pinkster festival may have been a carnivalesque inversion of the social order, but it was also deeply resonant with Central African practices. The Kongolese adopted many of the symbols of Portuguese kingship—titles/hierarchies of nobility, crowns, dress, and so on—by as early as the sixteenth century. Thus, European-style kingship was naturalized in Central Africa very early in the colonial period. At the same time, Kongolese kings were understood to be far more than political leaders. Kings were situated atop a hierarchy of ritual experts who mediated between the worlds of the living and the dead.[45] As those who were closest to the recently deceased, only elders rivaled the king in his ability to access the powers of the dead.[46] As the personification of both the king and the elder in the Pinkster festival, Charley represented the most powerful spiritual force in his community. Thus, it should come as no surprise that African-descended peoples paid "homage to the [Pinkster] king," holding him "in awe and reverence as an African prince."[47]

Finally, Charley's dance in the middle of the ring was probably the forum where he actually received spirits from the other world. As noted above, in *kilundu* ceremonies in Central Africa and Brazil, the song and dance of invocation culminated with the spirit mounting the medium and the medium taking on the traits of the spirit while in the trance state. These traits could include a different voice or a new form of dress. It was not unusual for the medium to be mounted by a former Central African king, even in *calundu* ceremonies in Brazil.[48] Though Charley apparently donned the king's attire of a scarlet coat and yellow trousers before the ring dance, this slight shift in choreography should not divert our attention from his role at the center of the ring dance ritual, the privileged position of the spiritually powerful medium.

In the final analysis, it is very difficult to determine whether Central African *kilundu* survived in St. Domingue or the United States in quite the same way as it did in Brazil. Certainly, there was never the critical mass of Central Africans in either of those places that there was in Brazil.[49] Nevertheless, we can be sure that certain Central African religious influences in the diaspora emanated from a broadly conceived ritual understanding that emphasized, among other things, singing to musical instruments of Central African origin, dancing in counterclockwise formation, veneration of ancestors, and spirit possession—in short, *kilundu*. The key to understanding how these ritual elements evolved into distinctly African-American forms can be determined only through close study of American slave ritual over the *longue durée*. As the Brazilian case shows, ritual meaning can be obscured and erased over the passage of time. When examined over short periods, rituals like *calundu*, *calenda*, and the ring shout appear as little more than historical snapshots, moments in time isolated from their historical pasts and the forces that contributed to their change. By beginning in Africa and tracing change over time and space, we not only see more clearly the elements of African survival, but more important, we better understand the ebbs and flows that led to the formation of African American culture in the Americas.

NOTES

1. Arquivo Nacional do Torre de Tombo (ANTT), Inquisição de Lisboa (IL), Cadernos do Promotor No. 67, Livro 261, ff. 311–320v.

2. Giovanni Antonio Cavazzi, *Descrição Histórica*, 1:209.

3. See Bishop Luiz Simões Brandão, "Ritos gentilicos, e superstições, que observão os negros do gentio do Reyno de Angola desde o seu nascimento athe a morte," in *Boletim da Sociedade de Geografia de Lisboa* 5–6 (Lisbon, 1885): 371–373.

4. Cavazzi, *Descrição Histórica*, 1:204–205.

5. See, for instance, Filippo Pigafetta and Duarte Lopes, *Description du Royaume de Congo et des contrées environnantes* (Louvain, Éditions Nauwelaerts, 1963), 118.

6. Anita Jacobson-Widding, *Red-White-Black as Mode of Thought: A Study of Triadic Classification of Colours in the Ritual Symbolism and Cognitive Thought of the Peoples of the Lower Congo* (Uppsala, Almquist and Wiksell International, 1979), 50.

7. Accusations of *calundu* appear with some frequency in Inquisition cases. See, for instance, James H. Sweet, *Recreating Africa: Culture, Kinship, and Religion in the African-Portuguese World, 1441–1770* (Chapel Hill, NC: University of North Carolina Press, 2003); Laura de Mello e Souza, *O diabo e a terra de Santa Cruz: feitiçaria e religiosidade popular no Brasil colonial* (São Paulo: Companhia das

Letras, 1986), 263–269; and Luiz Mott, "O calundu Angola de Luzia Pinta: Sabará, 1739," *Revista do Instituto de Artes e Cultura* 1 (1994): 73–82.

8. See for instance, ANTT, IL, Cadernos do Promotor No. 59, Livro 256, ff. 130–130v. (1685); ANTT, IL, Cadernos do Promotor No. 82, Livro 275, ff. 421–422 (1715); ANTT, IL, Cadernos do Promotor No. 83, Livro 276, ff. 202 (1715).

9. As quoted from Mattos, in Roger Bastide, *The African Religions of Brazil* (Baltimore: Johns Hopkins University Press, 1978), 134–135.

10. Nuno Marques Pereira, *Compendio Narrativo do Peregrino da America*, 6th edition, 2 vols. (Rio de Janeiro, Publiçaço˜es da Academia Brasileira 1939), 1:123–126.

11. Although most scholars agree on the proportion of Central Africans that arrived in Brazil during the seventeenth century, there is some disagreement on the total number of slave arrivals. David Eltis concludes that 327,000 Africans arrived in Brazil. See Eltis, "The Volume and Structure of the Transatlantic Slave Trade: A Reassessment," *William and Mary Quarterly* 58 (2001), 17–46. Eltis's figures have been contested by Luiz Felipe de Alencastro, who provides a "conservative" estimate of 560,000 arrivals. I find Alencastro's arguments to be more convincing. Alencastro, *O Trato dos Viventes: a formação do Brasil no Atlântico Sul, séculos XVI e XVII* (Rio de Janeiro, Companhia das Letras, 2000), 375–380.

12. The most prominent articulation of the "rapid creolization" model is Sidney Mintz and Richard Price, *The Birth of African-American Culture: An Anthropological Perspective* (Boston: Beacon Press, 1992). Price has retreated somewhat on the speed of the creolization process in some places; however, as the title of his recent article indicates, he continues to see the broader American experience as an exceptional, even "miraculous," break from various African pasts. Price, "The Miracle of Creolization: A Retrospective," *New West Indian Guide/Nieuwe West-Indische Gids* 75 (2001): 35–64.

13. During the first two decades of the eighteenth century, slave exports from the Slave Coast to Brazil surpassed those from Central Africa 153,000 to 129,000. See David Richardson, "Slave Exports from West and West-Central Africa, 1700–1810," *Journal of African History* 30 (1989): 7–22.

14. ANTT, IL, Cadernos do Promotor No. 129, Livro 318.

15. João José Reis, "Magia Jeje na Bahia: A Invasão do Calundu do Pasto de Cachoeira, 1785," *Revista Brasileira de História* 8 (1988): 57–81.

16. José Ramos Tinhorão, *Pequena história da música popular* (São Paulo: Art Editora, 1986), 19. Also see Mary Karasch, *Slave Life in Rio de Janeiro, 1808–1850* (Princeton: Princeton University Press, 1987), 243.

17. As quoted in Tinhorão, *Os Negros em Portugal: uma presença silenciosa* (Lisbon: Editorial Caminho, 1988), 362–363.

18. For more detail on the development of *batuque*, see chapter 2 by João José Reis in this volume.

19. For a provocative rendering of the contribution of *calundu* to *candomblé*,

see Rachel E. Harding, *A Refuge in Thunder: Candomblé and Alternative Spaces of Blackness* (Bloomington: Indiana University Press, 2000), 111.

20. Karasch, *Slave Life*, 15.

21. David Eltis, et al., *The Trans-Atlantic Slave Trade: A Database on CD-ROM* (Cambridge: Cambridge University Press, 1999).

22. One notable exception is Mott, "O calundu Angola de Luzia Pinta."

23. Mello e Souza, *O diabo e a terra*, 265; Daniela Buono Calainho, "Jamba-cousses e Gangazambes: feiticeiros negros em Portugal," *Afro-Ásia* 25–26 (2001): 161.

24. Donald Ramos, "A Influência Africana e a Cultura Popular em Minas Gerais: Um Comentário Sobre a Interpretação da Escravidão," in Maria Beatriz Nizza da Silva, ed., *Brasil: Colonização e Escravidão* (Rio de Janeiro: Editora Nova Fronteira, 1999), 142–162.

25. Reis, "Magia Jeje na Bahia," 59.

26. Karasch, *Slave Life*, 244.

27. For a critique of this approach, see Paul E. Lovejoy, "The African Diaspora: Revisionist Interpretations of Ethnicity, Culture and Religion under Slavery," *Studies in the World History of Slavery, Abolition, and Emancipation* 2 (1997): 1–23.

28. Joseph C. Miller, "Central Africa During the Era of the Slave Trade, c. 1490s–1850s," in Linda M. Heywood, ed., *Central Africans and Cultural Transformations in the American Diaspora* (Cambridge: Cambridge University Press, 2002), 46–47.

29. Heywood, "Introduction," in Heywood, *Central Africans and Cultural Transformations*, 13.

30. Heywood especially emphasizes the Catholic influences in Central Africa. For a more expansive discussion of Central African Catholicism in the Americas, see the essays by John Thornton, Hein Vanhee, and Terry Rey in Heywood, *Central Africans and Cultural Transformations*. Also see Thornton, "On the Trail of Voodoo: African Christianity in Africa and the Americas," *The Americas* 55 (1988): 161–178; "'I am the Subject of the King of Kongo': African Political Ideology and the Haitian Revolution," *Journal of World History* 3 (1993): 181–214; and "African Roots of the Stono Rebellion," *American Historical Review* 96 (1991): 1101–1113.

31. Labat, as quoted in Hénock Trouillot, *Introduction à une histoire du Vaudou* (Port-au-Prince: Imp. De Antilles, 1970), 84.

32. Alfred Métraux, *Voodoo in Haiti* (New York: Shocken Books, 1972), 32–33.

33. Ibid., 33.

34. Carolyn E. Fick, *The Making of Haiti: The Saint Domingue Revolution from Below* (Knoxville, TN: University of Tennessee Press, 1990), 41.

35. Père Labat, *Nouveau Voyage aux Isle de l'Amérique*, vol. 2, 51.

36. Nei Lopes, *Dicionário Banto do Brasil* (Rio de Janeiro: Imprensa da Cidade, 1996), 43.

37. Sterling Stuckey, "African Spirituality and Cultural Practice in Colonial New York, 1700–1770," in Carla Gardina Pestana and Sharon V. Salinger, eds., *Inequality in Early America* (Hanover, NH: University Press of New England, 1999), 163.

38. Sterling Stuckey, *Slave Culture: Nationalist Theory and the Foundations of Black America* (New York: Oxford University Press, 1987), 12. For a fine description of the process of change from African identities to African American identity, also see Michael A. Gomez, *Exchanging Our Country Marks: The Transformation of African Identities in the Colonial and Antebellum South* (Chapel Hill, NC: University of North Carolina Press, 1998).

39. Stuckey, *Slave Culture*, 11.

40. Ibid., 12–13.

41. Joel Munsell, *Collections of Albany* (Albany, NY, 1856), 56, as quoted in Stuckey, "African Spirituality in Colonial New York," 169.

42. James Eights, "Pinkster Festivities in Albany," in *Readings in Black American Music* (New York, 1971), 41, as quoted in Stuckey, "African Spirituality in Colonial New York," 172. Eights' original essay was published in 1867.

43. Stuckey, "African Spirituality in Colonial New York," 173.

44. Carolyn Fick makes a forceful argument that the chant was Kongolese, but then she concludes that the attendant rituals were "voodoo." See Fick, *The Making of Haiti*, 57–58. Original from M.E.L Moreau de St. Mery, *Description topographique . . .* (Philadelphia, 1797).

45. See Wyatt MacGaffey, *Kongo Political Culture: The Conceptual Challenge of the Particular* (Bloomington, IN: Indiana University Press, 2000).

46. In the Kongolese vision of the cosmos, the elderly have attained the greatest knowledge in the temporal world and are at the cusp of entering the world of the dead. They continue moving in a circular motion around the "Kongo cosmogram" until they are reborn. On Kongolese cosmology, see Wyatt MacGaffey, *Religion and Society in Central Africa* (Chicago: University of Chicago Press, 1986). Also see Robert Farriss Thompson, *Flash of the Spirit: African and Afro-American Art and Philosophy* (New York: Vintage Books, 1984), 108–116.

47. Stuckey, "African Spirituality in Colonial New York," 171.

48. See, for instance, ANTT, IL, Cadernos do Promotor No. 91, Livro 284, ff. 41–41v.

49. Although it should be noted that after 1750, Central Africans constituted roughly 60 percent of slave imports into St. Domingue. See Eltis, *Trans-Atlantic Slave Trade: A Database.*

Part II

Memory and Instantiations of the Divine

This section engages the question of religion and the African diaspora, interrogating the multiple ideas of both spirituality and organized religious traditions. The section stretches the spatial framework of issues to be considered, extending from North America to the contemporary Middle East.

Jermaine Archer begins by demonstrating a functional, African-derived spirituality that informed the lives and decisions of the foremost anti-slavery leaders a generation or two removed from African soil. He argues for a cultural transfer that is ongoing but malleable, even unrecognized; his use of slave narratives represents a fresh and innovative reading. Confining the analysis to North America, Archer examines the so-called radical ex-slave narratives from the 1830s through the 1860s, and argues for an "African cultural memory" that is discernible even in those works avowing agnosticism with respect to African antecedents and influences. Taking the secondary literature to task for not recognizing African cultural motifs in these narratives, Archer identifies the constitutive elements of African cultural memory and then locates those elements in the work of Frederick Douglass, William Wells Brown, Harriet Tubman, Harriet Jacobs, Henry Bibb, and others. The case for Douglass and Tubman is particularly striking, as the former's classic struggle with the overseer Covey is reconsidered in light of Douglass's prior consultation with a root worker. The chapter is an effective example of mining well-known texts for heretofore undiscovered insights and is testimony to the benefits of the close read.

Diane Batts Morrow continues with a consideration of the Oblate Sisters of Providence, a Roman Catholic sisterhood that constitutes the first such community made up exclusively of women of African descent. With its origins reaching back to the late eighteenth century, the Oblate sisterhood was officially chartered in Baltimore in 1829. Batts Morrow argues that although ostensibly a Roman Catholic order, values associated with

the Oblate Sisters of Providence reflected African as well as European influences. The author traces the African influences through Saint Domingue
to Dahomey and argues for certain correspondences between Roman
Catholic practices and Dahomean religion and culture as they pertain to
the roles of women. This analysis is quite striking, especially when the
findings of Jermaine Archer regarding an embedded cultural memory of
ex-slaves is placed into juxtaposition. Taken together, these chapters
advance the thesis that African religious influence permeated not only the
subjective, relatively unregulated preserve of the mind, but also the highly
formalized strictures of organized religion. Batts Morrow maintains that
not only did the Oblate sisterhood enjoy certain connections with an
African past, but also that those women who joined the order, by becoming part of the "Holy Slavery of the Mother of God," were in effect stating
their opposition to both the physical institution of racialized slavery and
the stereotypic representations of black women. Their very existence, as an
order of women of African descent espousing values inherited from an
African past, was both an affront to slavery and a challenge to a slaveholding Roman Catholic Church.

In the next chapter of this section, Fran Markowitz draws our attention
to a religious formation similarly related to biblical authority but inhabiting a very different interpretation and manifestation of that authority. Her
examination of the African Hebrew Israelite Community (AHIC) appro-
priates the lens of hybridity and engages a theoretical framework through
which the concept of diaspora is explored as an unresolved collection of
conflicts within both the scholarship and the lived experience. In many
ways in healthy tension with the introduction to this volume ("Diasporic
Africa: A View from History"), Markowitz persuasively points out the
difficulties of embracing complex cultural identities in the face of established racial binaries and social configurations.

The examination of the AHIC allows Markowitz to reinforce notions of
homeland and return as projects of an informed imaginary, themselves
constitutive of the diasporic experience. The embrace of this imaginary, a
"repossessing of the past," provides for a "transcendence of the pain of
diaspora" that begins with the transatlantic slave trade and ends with an
exposure to the tenets of Christianity, a process Markowitz summarizes.
This analysis goes beyond a perfunctory discussion of context, however,
for by establishing the origins of those Africans imported to North America as a process whose historicity can be reconstructed, she is simultaneously laying the groundwork for this particular homeland claim as

something beyond the scope of an organic, intergenerational transfer of memory. Rather, through an introduction of the African-descended to Old Testament literature, a veritable African past is merged with prophetic tradition, and for both the idea of homeland features large. The seeming parallel of the African and Hebrew experiences undergirds a particular reading of holy writ, as does an embrace of millenarianism. Moving to the twentieth century, Markowitz outlines the origins and history of the AHIC and its relations with Liberia, Ghana, and the state of Israel. It is a complicated vision of "homeland," not without its own civilizing mission.

The final chapter of this section engages biblical tradition through an examination of space and architecture. Elizabeth Pigou-Dennis argues that Rastafarian spatial and architectural designs and symbols in Jamaica are laden with meaning and content. As such, they encapsulate and express two extremes—the nadir of separation from and the hope of a return to an African homeland. Combining an analysis of form with an inquiry into intent, Pigou-Dennis demonstrates that Rastafarian architecture metaphysically recreates the homeland of Ethiopia, while it simultaneously represents or symbolizes the disjuncture, loss of memory, and sense of marginality resulting from the transatlantic slave trade. Stated differently, Rastafarian deployment of space and structure represents an attempt to imaginatively reconnect with Africa, to reconcile the homeland with the condition of diaspora. The chapter provides yet another discussion of how the past can be appropriated and deployed in circumstances of displacement and accords well with Archer's discussion of "embedded memory."

4

Bitter Herbs and a Lock of Hair
Recollections of Africa in Slave Narratives of the Garrisonian Era

Jermaine O. Archer

Cultural connections between Africa and the antebellum South are increasingly capturing the interests of scholars across the disciplinary spectrum. Providing an insightful historical and anthropological analysis, Michael Gomez, in his recent discussion of ethnicity formation in precolonial Senegambia, the Bight of Benin, the Bight of Biafra, the Gold Coast, and West Central Africa, sheds light on the continuities and transformations of ethnic associations among southern slaves. While Gomez concedes that many Africans were polyglot and had multiple identities connected to residence, political affiliation, genealogy, religious belief, and occupation, he insists that highly centralized states, like those of the Bambara and Fulbe of Senegambia, often enjoyed regional commonalties based on trade, religion, language, and years of residing in the same geographic area. Gomez argues that the exigencies of the transatlantic slave trade helped to foster the development of African ethnic identities in the South, even among those who arrived from decentralized polities, such as Sierra Leone, where allegiances tended to lie with the familial village groups and towns. Gomez has persuasively demonstrated that arrivals to North America may very well have drawn on the similar notions of the afterlife and ancestral deities that existed among the Igbo, Akan, Bambara, and Bantu-speaking peoples.[1]

Slave narratives in what becomes the United States are among the most compelling sources for examining the slaves' remembrance of Africa, including the incorporation of ancestors into a spiritual worldview that

Gomez touches upon, as well as other not unrelated cultural expressions. While there are over six thousand extant narratives spanning from 1703 to 1944, the most significant literary period of the genre occurred between 1836 and the 1860s. The narratives of the eighteenth and early nineteenth centuries tend to focus on the theme of adventure as the authors were primarily concerned with providing accounts of their own individual escape.[2] With the growth of Garrisonian abolitionism in the 1830s, the tone of the slave narratives shifted. Unlike their more moderate abolitionist predecessors of the late eighteenth century, Garrisonians disagreed with the idea that slavery should come to a gradual end, and since clerical leaders were not fighting for its instant removal, religious institutions became prime targets for criticism. Garrisonians considered slavery a sin and were convinced that the most efficient means to rid the United States of this social wrong was through moral suasion as opposed to political action, the latter only serving to validate a pro-slavery union and its constitution in their view. Since the slave narratives were now being financed and produced by a Garrisonian-influenced anti-slavery press, the authors were given greater leverage to express a class consciousness. No longer did they have to be silent about the hypocrisy of southern religion or minimize the wrongs that had been committed against them.

This period ushered in a new wave of what may be referred to as "radical narratives," as the authors not only called for the preservation of an anti-slavery Christianity and questioned the morality of the slave-owning class, but also impressively recalled the spirit of Africa in ways that were not much different from earlier authors who were actually born there. James Albert Ukawsaw, Olaudah Equiano, and Venture Smith were all African-born slaves and each of their narratives includes references to the religious and spiritual world from which they came.[3] Expressions of cultural memory found in the narratives from both men and women of the latter period suggest that despite the increase in an American-born population and an emerging African-American identity, African culture did not necessarily dissipate with each passing decade of the nineteenth century. In fact, some of the more popular book-length narratives of the antebellum period demonstrate the persistence of memory within the slave quarters.[4]

This chapter explores this mode of remembrance, all too often silenced by the leading scholars of the narratives. Though literary critics and historians have made use of the texts in important ways by examining the different phases of authenticating strategies, the trope of the "talking book," the genre's literary relationship to novels, the emergence of the "trickster" figure in slave autobiography, and the authors' religious conversions or spiritual renewals, there has not been a sustained discussion of the narrators' inclusion of African cultural and spiritual practices within the slave milieu.[5] Root doctoring, divination, and ceremonial dance along with the symbolism of dreams, prophesies, ancestral reverence, and flight are themes that reappear throughout the texts published during the Garrisonian period. The authors, a number of whom were key figures in the abolitionist movement, offer insightful observations and thoughts on these particular expressions of African culture that animated the lives of large numbers of slaves.

Conjuration: Root Working and Protective Amulets

Theologian and literary critic Theophus Smith views the African American magical folk tradition of conjure performance as a language of ritual speech through which slaves were able to communicate with one another. He maintains that this magic is thought of as a way by which one is able to affect and control his or her reality through the form and interpretation of corresponding signs. Smith does not view conjuration as a function of irrational thought and behavior that should be simply assigned to the sphere of the supernatural or the unconventional domain of the occult. Rather, he sees it as a viable system of communication by which the descendants of Africans were able to express themselves through this magical scheme of correspondences. The conjuring culture of slaves was not one that revolved around the sole purpose of witchcraft and malign sorcery. In the African American sense it is defined as the process by which the healing or exacerbating of one's condition is possible through the operation and invocation of exceptional powers. According to Smith, herein lies the distinction of the slave conjure tradition. The dual aspect of the conjure doctor's ability to heal and or harm through pharmacopoeia methods including the use of herbs, roots, and human artifacts reflects the balance that is intrinsic to the African magician and medicinal doctor. Several of those who authored slave narratives revealed the prevalence of this conjuring culture within their communities.[6]

When Frederick Douglass became the victim of the constant floggings for which his overseer Covey was notorious, he heeded the suggestion of local conjure doctor Sandy Jenkins to procure a particular protective root. Sandy told him that if he wore it on his *right* side no white man, including

Covey, could whip him. Initially doubting its effectiveness, Douglass was not inclined to retrieve the talisman, but because Sandy spoke of it with such passion and conviction Douglass, aiming to please the wise elder, decided to test its worth. When Douglass returned to the estate with the roots on his person he was surprised by Covey's cordialness. He reasoned that such an attitude might very well have had something to do with Sandy's prescription. However, Covey's pleasantness was short-lived. The slave breaker took occasion to assault him the following day, at which time Douglass was filled with an unshakeable spirit to fight back. Unlike previous scuffles, Covey was unable to punish Douglass this time. In fact, it was Covey who sustained considerable injuries.

This event was a turning point in Douglass's life. From this moment on he no longer had an incident with Covey or any other person. Moreover, he related how he went through a sort of rites of passage under Sandy's tutelage. "You have seen how a man was made a slave," he says, "you shall see how a slave was made a man."[7] Such were his feelings after defeating Covey while holding on to the roots. Douglass wondered if the spirit within the root was ruled by a divine presence. "How did I know but that the hand of the Lord was in it?" he writes, "with thoughts of this sort, I took the roots from Sandy, and put them in my right hand pocket." He goes on to say, "My religious views on the subject of resisting my master, had suffered a serious shock, by the savage persecution to which I had been subjected, and my hands were no longer tied by my religion."[8] Covey was a class leader in the Methodist church and Douglass was determined to reject the obedient servant motif that was perpetuated by him and other slaveholders. Though Douglass may have not wholeheartedly embraced Sandy's prescription, or at least admit that he had, it still played a significant role in the transformation of his religious views. It should not be lost on us that the talisman that Sandy prescribed affected this social change within Douglass. Sandy's intent was to heal and protect his patient through an African pharmacopeic method, and Douglass was quite candid about the personal spiritual renewal that he underwent as a result of the extraordinary powers that Sandy evoked. His social reality was changed by the belief that Sandy, a gifted conjure doctor, had the ability to effect change through his root remedies.

In William Wells Brown's last published book, *My Southern Home,* he wrote of the close friendship he enjoyed with the slave conjure doctor Dinkie in his Missouri slave community. Dinkie was born in Africa and it was believed that he was the progeny of a royal lineage. Known for wearing a snake skin around his neck and carrying a stiffed frog and dried lizard in his pocket, Dinkie was respected by both blacks and whites. He was the best at his craft in their section of St. Louis.[9] He often proved to be too much to handle for the local overseers and no one could recall an instance in which he was summoned to do any strenuous labor. Whites often "tipped their hats to the old one-eyed Negro," and while other slaves were frequently harassed by the patrollers, Dinkie was left alone. On one occasion Brown queried a gentleman on why people feared Dinkie. The man's response is an example of the slaves' desire to conceal their true opinions about slave culture. He initially indicated that he was not at all afraid of the old conjurer. "He then took a look around and behind," writes Brown, "as if he feared some one would hear what he was saying, and then continued: 'Dinkie's got de power, ser; he knows things seen and unseen, an' dat's what makes him his own massa.'"[10]

While Brown and the other slaves looked favorably upon persons such as Dinkie, Brown thought it "quite extraordinary that well-educated men and women" relied on the oracle.[11] One white lady who visited the Poplar Farm requesting Dinkie's intuitive insights was Martha Lemmy. There was no need for her to inform Dinkie of why she had come, for he already knew the visit was regarding a particular love interest. Dinkie read her palm and assured her that Mr. Scott, a wealthy landowner, would ask for her hand in marriage as long as she held on to the goopher powder that Dinkie had given her.[12] Other whites also knew Dinkie had "de power." Brown informs us of the time when a Mr. Sarpee visited the Poplar Farm and fell victim to the stench of a skunk while out on a hunting excursion. Again, Dinkie prescribed goopher and all were convinced that the remedy worked. Soil from deep beneath the earth served as a key ingredient for the concoction and slaves often relied on dirt from the graveyards when assembling goopher powders.[13]

The narrative of Henry Bibb demonstrates that he too was quite familiar with the role of the slave conjure doctor. In a recent introduction to Bibb's narrative, Charles Heglar concludes that he "deflates and dismisses the love charms of the conjurers." Yet, Bibb admitted to having a firm belief in conjuration while he was held in slavery.[14] When slaves desired to avert the maltreatment of their masters, Bibb says they often relied on "some kind of bitter root," whose effectiveness depended on the person receiving the medicine accurately and spitting the concoction toward their afflicter.[15] A different remedy entailed scattering special powders around the homes of their masters. For a small fee another conjure doctor suggested he combine alum and salt along with some other ingredients to sprinkle in the vicinity of his master. When Bibb tried the doctor's medicines he was allowed to pass without punishment. His faith in the prescriptions began to grow stronger and he became convinced that he was immune to repercussions for insubordination. When he slipped off the following Sunday and did not return until the next morning, he felt quite invincible and impertinently responded to his master's reproach. He was surprised, therefore, when he found himself the victim of a severe flogging for his defiance. Though this incident made him suspicious of conjure doctors he would again try his hand with another elder conjurer who promised to deliver. He was told to combine red pepper, cow dung, and "white people's hair" and plant them around his master's residence and clothing after he burned them to ashes. Bibb followed through with the doctor's recommendation, but because of an unshakeable fear of being found out he decided to suspend his participation in the art of conjuration "for the time being." This was not, however, the last time that he would consult with conjure doctors.[16]

He sought their advice to win the affection of two love interests, and though his conjure potions failed him his detailed descriptions of the prescriptions are insightful. After he paid the first gentleman for his services, Bibb was instructed to rub the bone of a bullfrog on the woman he desired. Another conjure doctor advised him to wear a lock of the woman's hair in his shoes.[17] The slaves who induced Bibb to solicit the aid of these conjure doctors were the elders on the plantation. "I had been taught by the old superstitious slaves, to believe in conjuration," he tells us, "and it was hard for me to give up the notion, for all I had been deceived by them." While Bibb himself might have questioned their authenticity, conjure doctors "among the old superstitious influential slaves" were highly regarded in Shelby County, Kentucky. In fact, according to Bibb these beliefs and practices were held by "the great masses of southern slaves. It is given to them by tradition, and can never be erased."[18]

Harriet Jacobs's memoir *Incidents in the Life of a Slave Girl*, published under the pseudonym Linda Brent, was the first full-length slave narrative authored by a woman in 1861, and it also includes remarkable references to pharmacopoeia methods that mirrored African healing techniques similar to those described by James Sweet in his essay "The Evolution of Ritual in the African Diaspora: Central African *Kilundu* in Brazil, St. Domingue, and the United States, Seventeenth–Nineteenth Centuries."[19] Like most in her condition, Jacobs painstakingly struggled to survive the unforgiving precincts of American slavery. She suffered at the unmerciful hands of her master Dr. Flint. His sexual advances against her will, his decision not to allow her to see the man of her choice, and his unrelenting physical assaults led to Jacobs's decision to leave his quarters and remain hidden for nearly seven years in a diminutive, unhealthy, and poorly ventilated dwelling that was within earshot of where her children slept at night. The lodging was so small that Jacobs was unable to stand fully erect. While discreetly observing those going by her place, on one occasion she saw her master and she recalled having "a shuddering, superstitious feeling that it was a bad omen."[20] Shortly after this she was plagued "by hundreds of little red insects, fine as a needle's point." The assailants worked their way under her skin, giving her an unrelenting burning sensation. Her grandmother prescribed "herb teas and cooling medicines" and Jacobs was no longer burdened by the irritants. Her grandmother's keen understanding of how to deflect harm associated with a bad omen seems to link Jacobs's family to an African healing tradition in which root doctors were thought to have the ability to administer "counter" medicines against "bad magic."[21]

Jacobs also recalled the time that a poisonous reptile of some sort bit her leg. She initially tended to her wound with "a poultice of *warm ashes and vinegar*." This gave Jacobs some relief, but her swelling did not subside. Her friend then "asked an old woman, who doctored among the slaves, what was good for the bite of a snake or a lizard and was told to steep a *dozen coppers in vinegar* to the inflamed part."[22] The reader is led to believe that the prescription worked, for Jacobs gives no indication that the pain failed to subside. Folklorist Newbell Niles Puckett explained that similar remedies could be found among the inhabitants of the Gold Coast: "For a swelling of any sort use mullein tea or a mixture of cream of tartar, *vinegar, and rusty nails* applied as a lotion."[23]

The most well-known Harriet of the nineteenth century from the slave class initially bore the surname Ross, which was changed to Tubman after she was married. Because of her lack of literacy she left no written records. The most extensive nineteenth-century biography of her was written by Sarah Bradford and is often cataloged by scholars as Tubman's slave narrative. Bradford's *Scenes in the Life of Harriet Tubman* was first published in 1869 and appeared again with minor changes as *Harriet Tubman: The Moses of Her People* in 1886 and 1901.[24] Tubman not only worked as an unpaid spy, scout, and recruiter for Union forces during the Civil War, but she also labored as a Union nurse and was known to have come to the aid of many soldiers who suffered from life-threatening ailments in the Port

Royal area of South Carolina. Her remedy often entailed seeking out roots and herbs that were harvested in close proximity to where the disease originated. She had a cunning knack for curing dysentery, small-pox, and malignant fevers—never once acquiring any of the illnesses she treated. In her role as a conjure doctor, Tubman sought to rid her community of the overarching "evil" spirit of slavery which time and again wrought sickness and despair on her people.[25]

Tubman also believed she had a "hand" in the death of her master, Edward Brodess. When rumors around the slave quarters surfaced that Brodess was seeking to sell Tubman to the Deep South to work on a chain gang, she asked God to convert him to a kind-loving Christian gentleman, bestowing upon him a change of heart regarding her sale. When her fears of being sold became a reality she asked God to take Brodess's life if he was not to be proselytized. "Next ting I heard ole master was dead," she says, "and he died just as he had lived, a wicked, bad man."[26] The implication that Tubman had a hand in her master's demise again recalls the nature of the conjure figure who wishes to obliterate malevolent forces.

Divination: Dreams and Premonitions

Diviners appear in the slave narratives as intuitive dreamers, gifted visionaries, and insightful fortunetellers. Much like the conjure doctors, they were vital intermediaries between the slave community and the spirit world and were often times one and the same with their conjurer counterparts. Recall the aforementioned admission in William Wells Brown's narrative that Dinkie had "de power, ser; he knows things seen and unseen, an' dat's what makes him his own massa."

Brown, in his *Narrative of William Wells Brown*, also explained that just prior to his escape from slavery in St. Louis, he solicited the help of Uncle Frank, a highly regarded local diviner in St. Louis who maintained a large black and white clientele.[27] While the number of times Brown went to Uncle Frank is unknown, he did admit that "whether the old man was a prophet, or the son of a prophet, I cannot say; but there is one thing certain, many of his predictions were verified." Uncle Frank was described as a tall gentleman in his seventies with a slim build who was known to have a number of women patrons. Few people questioned his authenticity. "Whether true or not," Brown related, "he had the *name*, and that is about half of what one needs in this gullible age." However, Brown's implication that those who believed in Uncle Frank's gift were naïve is not his definitive stance on the matter. He was quite impressed by Uncle Frank's uncanny perceptivity and despite Brown's claim to be "no believer in soothsaying," he was occasionally baffled by Uncle Frank's prophetic accuracy that came to him from "looking into a gourd, filled with water." That Brown conferred with Uncle Frank before his perilous attempt to run away suggests that he did not take his insight lightly.[28]

Uncle Frank appeared again in *My Southern Home*. When a Mrs. McWilliams, a white lady, was unsure which lawyer she should solicit to aid her in legal matters she sought the advice of "old" Frank, who told her to obtain the services of a John F. Darby. Having faith in his intuitive powers, Mrs. McWilliams hired Mr. Darby and won the case.[29] Similarly, Brown also writes of the white colonel who wanted to know the right horse to bet on: "I went to old Betty, the blind fortune-teller," the colonel disclosed, "to see which horse was going to win; and she said, 'Massa, bet your money on de gray mare.' . . . I bet one hundred dollars on the gray mare, and . . . she won."[30]

We also learn from Harriet Jacobs's narrative that diviners were very much a part of the slave community in Edenton, North Carolina. She quotes one Reverend Pike, recruited by slaveholders to lead the slaves in worship following Nat Turner's insurrection, who provides the insight:

God sees you. You tell lies. Instead of being engaged in worshipping him, you are hidden away somewhere, feasting on your master's substance; tossing coffee-grounds with some wicked fortuneteller, or cutting cards with another old hag . . . and tying up little bags of roots to bury under the doorsteps to poison each other with. . . . you sneak into the back streets, or among the bushes, to pitch coppers.[31]

The slaves were loathe to forsake their diviners or conjure doctors. In fact, Jacobs herself relied on her own visionary insight to predict the future.

She tells us that on one particular evening as she was sitting in her hiding place by the window listening to the sounds of serenaders who were playing "Home, sweet home," she received a vision of her two children. She was well aware that such an experience "reflected the superstition of slaves." The music reminded her of the moaning cries of her children and she witnessed a clear image of them that appeared through a streak of moonlight which reflected off the floor:

They vanished; but I had seen them distinctly. Some will call it a dream, others a vision. I know not how to account for it, but it made a strong impression on my mind, and I felt certain something had happened to my little ones.[32]

Jacobs' vision was later confirmed when she was informed that her children were sold the previous day to their father and were being looked after by her grandmother. Jacobs attributed this good fortune to none other than divine intervention and she was extremely thankful that her children no longer had to remain with her owner. This prophetic vision of hers allows us to see another way in which Jacobs operated within an African cultural tradition.

Harriet Tubman also functioned as a sort of self-proclaimed diviner by interpreting her dreams and visions as premonitions. She often had an uncanny sense of when folk were in danger and needed her assistance. One of her most intriguing premonitions involved the militant anti-slavery advocate John Brown. Just prior to meeting him for the first time Tubman had a dream that she would later come to decipher as a divine warning:

> She thought she was in "a wilderness sort of place, all full of rocks, and bushes," when she saw a serpent raise its head of an old man with a long white beard, gazing at her, "wishful like, jes as ef he war gwine to speak to me," and then two other heads rose up beside him, younger than he,—and as she stood looking at them, and wondering what they could want with her, a great crowd of men rushed in and struck down the younger heads, and then the head of the old man, still looking at her so "wishful." This dream she had again and again, and could not interpret it; but when she met Captain Brown, shortly after, behold, he was the very image of the head she had seen.[33]

Tubman did not fully understand the meaning of the dream until after the disastrous attack on Harpers Ferry. It is fairly well known that Brown's men proved no match for an outfit of U.S. Marines led by Robert E. Lee. Ten of Brown's soldiers were killed including his two sons Watson and Oliver. On the following day Tubman learned the tragic details of the attack from a local newspaper.[34] It was then that she finally understood the meaning of her dream. The serpents represented Brown and his sons.[35]

Writing on the inhabitants of southern Nigeria, Major Arthur Glyn
Leonard found that the dreaming of a snake meant that one's enemies
were seeking to cause tremendous harm and quite possibly death to the
dreamer. It was believed that this was caused by an "evil" or "antipathetic"
spirit who visited the person having the dream.[36] When Susie Branch of
White Bluff Georgia was interviewed in the 1930s, she affirmed that such
dreams held a similar meaning. She divulged that Sukey, one of her
esteemed ancestors, was the head seamstress for the slaves on St. Cather-
ines Island who was stolen "frum off duh beach in Africa wen she wuz a
young miss." When queried on whether or not the dreaming of snakes
bore any significance she responded, "yes, ma'am, dat mean yuh got a
enemy. Not many nights ago I dram bout a snake an uh sho wuz sked wen
uh wake up."[37] Mini Dawson of Pin Point Island Georgia provided a similar account. "Ef yuh dream ub a snake dassa enemy neahby too."[38] While
Harriet Tubman was not specifically targeted at Harpers Ferry, those
responsible for bringing down John Brown and his cohorts in many ways
represented the opposing forces to everything for which she stood. Thus,
her dream of snakes and their association with one's adversary was very
much in sync with others who were also very much influenced by African
culture.

Honoring the Deceased and Ceremonial Dance

While conjure doctors and diviners played a significant role in the slave
community, the good fortune of one's life also had much to do with his or
her relationship to the ancestors. It was a widespread belief that the
improper burial of a family member would engender ill fortune.[39] *A Narrative of the Life and Adventures of Charles Ball, a Black Man* was the first
full-length book narrative published during the Garisonian period. Ball
provides an account of a burial ceremony that took place in South Carolina in which the father of the deceased, who had been a priest in West
Africa, placed a specific talisman around the corpse, which he claimed
would help his son travel back to his countrymen. Ball believed that this
notion of returning to Africa after death was a belief held by a number of
Africans. "They are universally of opinion," he says, "and this opinion is
founded in their religion, that after death they shall return to their own
country, and rejoin their former companions and friends, in some happy

region, in which they will be provided with plenty of food, and beautiful women, from the lovely daughters of their own land."[40]

Harriet Jacobs also maintained a spiritual connection to her parents after they died. In fact, it was at their burial grounds that she vowed to free herself. She believed that "there the wicked cease from troubling, and there the weary be at rest. There the prisoners rest together; they hear not the voice of the oppressor; the servant is free from his master."[41] As Jacobs walked through the graveyard she recalled the blessing her mother had given her before she died and thought about the many times that she heard her voice either chiding her or "whispering loving words." As she prayed for guidance and protection while walking past the old dwelling where the slaves use to worship before the Turner insurrection, she also heard her father's voice emanating from it—encouraging her to push forward until freedom was hers. The burial grounds never seemed so sacred to her as they were on this occasion. "My trust in God," Jacobs says, "had been strengthened by that prayer among the graves."[42]

Slaves honored and invoked the power of their ancestors through the African-influenced counterclockwise dance known as the ring shout. Sterling Stuckey has convincingly demonstrated that the ceremony was largely responsible for strengthening bonds among slaves across ethnic lines.[43] Perhaps Frederick Douglass was referring to the ring shout when he wrote about the songs that he heard while he was a slave in Maryland:

I did not, when a slave, understand the deep meaning of those rude and apparently incoherent songs. I was myself within the *circle*; so that I neither saw nor heard as those without might see and hear. They told a tale of woe which was then altogether beyond my feeble comprehension; they were tones loud, long, and deep; they breathed the prayer and complaint of souls boiling over with the bitterest anguish.[44]

Given the accounts of the ceremony in the urban areas of Maryland by Bishop Daniel Alexander Payne of the African Methodist Episcopal Church during the second half of the nineteenth century, it should not surprise us that Douglass while still a slave would have observed and even participated in the ritual in rural Maryland.[45] The Lloyd plantation was very much an African enclave and Douglass quickly learned that an important spiritual exercise of its inhabitants was the ring shout. It was not uncommon for one to "hear a wild, hoarse *laugh* arise from a circle, and often a song" when the slaves were allowed a brief amount of leisure time following their evening meals.[46] Douglass provided compelling evidence that he might have known that these religious expressions were rooted in an African tradition.

Writing of the ceremonies he observed while traveling in Cairo, Douglass says, "the dancing and howling *dervishes* often spin around in their religious transports till their heads lose control and they fall to the floor sighing, groaning, and foaming at the mouth like madmen, reminding one of scenes that sometimes occur at our old-fashioned camp-meetings."[47] Douglass displayed an interest in the similar phenotypical and cultural traits that existed among Egyptians and blacks in the United States. Never hesitant to exalt the "great" civilization of ancient Egypt, he concluded its inhabitants were a Negroid people. It is quite significant then that Douglass, who was often classified as an integrationist and lacking an African cultural awareness, established a connection between the dances of Egypt and those he observed in the South.

That Douglass did not provide this detailed and explicit description of the ring shout until he published *Life and Times* in 1893 can likely be attributed to his being more comfortable with discussing such practices that were considered heathenish by the upper strata of society well after slavery was abolished. Prior to the end of slavery, Douglass might not have been entirely at ease with society's general unwillingness to value African culture. Yet as a visible proponent for the movement he likely recognized the pragmatic need to convince people that the abject conditions of slavery worked against the cultural genius and moral standards of the slave community. If his reading and listening audience believed that slavery fostered immorality, it could only help to convey the message that the institution should be abolished. While abolitionism remained his primary objective, he was hardly guilty, contrary to conventional thought, of having rejected his Africanness. Nor did he wholeheartedly conform to the idea that blacks were by nature inferior to whites. To do so would only call into question the slave culture to which he gave such important attention.

William Wells Brown also discussed his observations of the ring shout. Consider his rather detailed account of one such gathering in St. Louis:

> The noise was hushed, and the assembled group assumed an attitude of respect. They made way for their queen, and a short, black, old negress came upon the scene, followed by two assistants, one of whom bore a cauldron, and the other, a box. The cauldron was placed over the dying embers,

the queen drew forth, from the folds of her gown, a magic wand, and the crowd formed a ring around her. Her first act was to throw some substance on the fire, the flames shot up with a lurid glare—now it writhed in serpent coils, now it darted upward in forked tongues, and then it gradually transformed itself into a veil of dusky vapors. At this stage, after a certain amount of gibberish and wild gesticulation from the queen, the box was opened, and frogs, lizards, snakes, dog liver, and beef hearts drawn forth and thrown into the cauldron. Then followed more gibberish and gesticulation, when the congregation joined hands, and began the wildest dance imaginable, keeping it up until the men and women sank to the ground from mere exhaustion.[48]

Brown knew that these practices were not uncommon "throughout the Southern states," where one could easily find "remnants of the old time Africans, who were stolen from their native land and sold in the Savannah, Mobile, and New Orleans markets, in defiance of all law." According to Brown, New Orleans was the center of such explicit activity:

Congo Square takes its name, as is well known, from the Congo Negroes who used to perform their dance on its sward every Sunday. They were a curious people, and brought over with them this remnant of their African jungles. In Louisiana there were six different tribes of negroes, named after the section of the country from which they came, and their representatives could be seen on the square, their teeth filed, and their cheeks still bearing tattoo marks.[49]

As many as three thousand onlookers would show up on any given Sunday to observe the "dusky dancers." The dancing was accompanied by banjoes, drums, and shakers and when the participants became aroused by the rhythmic synchronization of the instruments nothing could "faithfully portray the wild and frenzied motions" that caused many to *faint*. After exhaustion overcame one group another would enter the circle. The Igbo, Fulani, Congolese, Mandingos, and Kormantins were some of the groups involved in the ceremonies. "These dances," Brown declared, "were kept up until within the memory of men still living, and many who believe in them and who would gladly revive them, may be found in every state in the Union."[50]

Harriet Tubman became quite fond of the dances she observed at midnight funeral ceremonies in the South Carolina Sea Islands. She recalled

that after a preacher delivered his sermon at one particular funeral ceremony the entire congregation while shaking one another's hand and calling each by name engaged in a circular solemn dance known as the
"spiritual shuffle" at which time they sang:

> My sis'r Mary's boun' to go;
> My sis'r Nanny's boun' to go;
> My brudder Tony's boun't to go;
> My brudder July's boun' to go.[51]

Harriet, a stranger among the faithful, was a participant in this ring shout
ceremony and when it came time for her name to be called during the
song they sang:

> Eberybody's boun' to go![52]

Flying Africans

Harriet Tubman and Henry Bibb seem to have incorporated in their narratives the African notion that certain persons possessed the supernatural
power to fly. The Bight of Biafra contributed significant imports into
North America and Igbo from the region were largely responsible for
spreading the belief.[53] Folktales of "flying Africans" and their frequent
place of departure "Ebo Landing," located off the coast of the Georgia and
South Carolina Sea Islands, are found in the Works Progress Administra-
tion slave narrative collection of the 1930s. It has been suggested that the
comparatively high rate of suicide among Igbo slaves can be attributed in
large part to the idea that through this process they were actually returning to Africa via flight. While we do not have precise numbers of how
many Igbo made their way into Bibb's home state of Kentucky, he does
provide us with evidence that this notion of "flying Africans" did exist
there. After being carted to Louisville after he was captured by four slave-
hunters for an attempted escape, Bibb was briefly left in the care of slaveholder Daniel Lane. The man was notorious for his "slave selling,
kidnapping, and negro hunting." As soon as he turned his back on his
prisoner, Bibb with no hesitation seized the opportunity and took off. Yet
few believed Lane's account of Bibb's escape: "Dan imputed my escape to
my godliness! He said that I must have gone up in a chariot of fire, for I
went off by flying; and that he should never again have anything to do

with a praying negro." That Lane connected flight with the spirituality of slaves can likely be attributed to his familiarity with the customs of Igbo and others who subscribed to their notion of "flying Africans."[54]

Prior to Harriet Tubman's escape, she often dreamt of flying "like a bird" over a variegated landscape which came to signify her flight to the North. In her dream she would approach a barrier either in the form of a huge fence or a river above which she would attempt to soar. "But it' peared like I wouldn't hab de strength," she says, "and jes as I was sinkin' down, dere would be ladies all drest in white ober dere, and de would put out dere arms and pull me 'cross."[55] When she eventually reached the North she came face to face with the places and people she observed in her dreams.[56] It is quite possible that Tubman's reference to flight might have been more than just an allegory for her escape. The motif of the flying African may actually be at work here. Igbo and Akan comprised considerable numbers in Maryland.[57] There is evidence to suggest that the notion of flying Africans would not have been lost on the Akan. Commenting on this phenomenon among the Akan, Anthony Ephirim-Donkor explains that "the Akan people also believe that the soul can be put to flight (*ne kra eguan*)." This would happen when one is incarcerated.[58] While Tubman's encounter with flight occurred only in her dream, that it was a reoccurring dream which eventually came true seems to demonstrate the prevalence of such a belief among Maryland slaves.

This chapter is only a brief illustration of how nineteenth-century slave narratives published after 1836 can be used as a cultural lens for spiritual memory and identity formation in the slave South. Due to the limited sources on African culture predating the twentieth century and the limited synchronic approach of colonial anthropologies on Africa, historians are presented with the formidable task of working with such records, thereby making the process of discerning which cultural patterns originated from what region and among which class an arduous one. Hence, the inferential is often hard to avoid. Nevertheless, Michael Gomez, Sterling Stuckey, Margaret Washington, and others have made rather strong cases for the existence of specific and direct cultural links between Africa and the mainland colonies. My intention here, then, is not to reinvent the wheel but rather show through a comparative textual analysis how ex-slave narratives served as a collective memory of Africans on this side of the Atlantic by pointing to corresponding cultural examples. These narratives not only reflect the individual lives of those few persons fortunate enough to tell their stories but also serve as critical sources for the slave community, as the authors tell of their experiences with slaves across plantations and states, thus making this project more than an intellectual analysis of a select few who had the opportunity to use such mediums. These memoirs are much more than tales of bondage and freedom. Indeed, they are vital tools for all students of African American folklore and should now be considered as texts for uncovering African cultural continuities. When one wonders how slaves endured their condition, an important part of the answer may be found in African spiritual and artistic practices found in the genre of the slave narratives.

NOTES

1. Michael A. Gomez, *Exchanging Our Country Marks: The Transformation of African Identities in the Colonial and Antebellum South* (Chapel Hill: University of North Carolina Press, 1998), 7. Earlier studies on the formation of ethnic identities include LeRoi Jones, *Blues People* (New York: William Morrow and Company, 1963), and Sterling Stuckey, *Slave Culture* (New York: Oxford University Press, 1988).

2. Marion W. Starling, *The Slave Narrative: Its Place in American History* (Washington, D.C.: Howard University Press, 1988), xxvi, 311.

3. James Albert Ukawsaw Gronniosaw, *A Narrative of the Most Remarkable Particulars in the Life of James Albert Ukawsaw Gronniosaw, An African Prince, as Related by Himself* (Leeds: Davies and Booth, 1814); Olaudah Equinao, *The Interesting Narrative of the Life of Olaudah Equiano, or Gustavus Vass, The African Written by Himself*, vol. 1 (New York: W. Duell, 1791); Venture Smith, *A Narrative of the Life and Adventures of Venture, A Native of Africa; But Resident above Sixty Years in the United States of America, Related by Himself* (New London: C. Holt, 1798).

4. Though Harriet Tubman did not write her own narrative she choose what stories to tell to her amanuenses.

5. John Blassingame has written on the subject of authenticity, rehabilitating the narratives' legitimacy as historical sources. See John Blassingame, ed., *Slave Testimony: Two Centuries of Letters, Speeches, Interviews, and Autobiographies* (Baton Rouge: Louisiana State University Press, 1977). Blassingame and others drew largely on Marion Wilson Starling's 1946 dissertation, unpublished until 1982 as *The Slave Narrative*. In *Great Slave Narratives* (Boston: Beacon Press, 1969), Arna Bontemps argues that the genre greatly influenced the style and themes of twentieth-century writers. In addressing authenticity, Robert Stepto, *From Behind the Veil* (Urbana: University of Illinois Press, 1979) connects the slave narratives with Ralph Ellison's *Invisible Man* (1952). Henry Louis Gates, Jr. and Charles T.

Davis echoed these sentiments sixteen years later in their edited volume, *The Slave's Narrative* (Oxford: Oxford University Press, 1985).

6. Theophus H. Smith, *Conjuring Culture* (New York: Oxford University Press, 1994), 4–6.

7. Frederick Douglass, "Narrative of the Life of Frederick Douglass, an American Slave" (1845; repr., in *Douglass Autobiographies* [New York: Penguin, 1994]), 60.

8. Frederick Douglass, *My Bondage and My Freedom* (1855; repr., in *Douglass Autobiographies* [New York: Penguin, 1994]), 282.

9. Williams Wells Brown, *My Southern Home: The South and Its People* (Boston, Mass.: Gregg Press, repr., 1968), 70. Brown also commented on the spiritual importance of reptiles among the Dahomey natives. See William Wells Brown, *The Rising Son; or, The Antecedents and Advancement of the Colored Race* (Boston: A. G. Brown, 1874; repr., Miami, Florida: Mnemosyne Inc., 1969), 108. Leonard found that such practices were more than simply a form of Ophiolatry, that an ancestral spirit was often believed to dwell within the reptile, who would protect its bearer if treated well. See Major Arthur Glyn Leonard, *The Lower Niger and Its Tribes* (New York: Macmillan, 1906), 317. John Pearce describes a similar practice in Africa; see Georgia Writers' Project, *Drums and Shadows* (Athens: University of Georgia Press, 1940), 202.

10. Brown, *My Southern Home*, 70, 71.

11. Ibid., 77.

12. Ibid., 78–79.

13. Ibid., 10–11. Describing the role of the African American root doctor or conjurer, Puckett writes: "Some . . . burn a kind of powder called 'goopher dust,' which represents the person being hoodooed. . . . this causes the conjured individual to lose his personality and to become sick or insane. One must have the power to make up a protecting 'hand' or charm. Another conjurer or hoodo outside the vicinity can work a cure for one so afflicted." Newbell Niles Puckett, *Folk Beliefs of the Southern Negro* (Chapel Hill: University of North Carolina Press, 1926), 215.

14. Henry Bibb, *The Life and Adventures of Henry Bibb: An American Slave*, with an introduction by Charles Heglar (New York: 1849; repr., Madison: University of Wisconsin Press, 2001).

15. Ibid., 25–32. Interestingly, Allan Cardinall observed a similar remedy among the inhabitants of the Gold Coast: "Medical treatment consists generally in charms. There are certain men considered most proficient in the curative art . . . their medicines are drawn from the bush, and are usually *bitter* tasting grasses, herbs, and barks." Italics mine. Allan Wolsey Cardinall, *The Natives of the Northern Territories of the Gold Coast, Their Customs, Religion and Folklore* (New York: E. P. Dutton, 1920), 46.

16. Bibb, 30–31. Ex-slaves who resided off the coast of Georgia also mentioned their belief in the spiritual power of hair, a belief also observed in West Africa. See A. B. Ellis, *The Ewe-Speaking Peoples of the Slave Coast of West Africa* (London:

Chapman & Hall, 1894), 99; C. K. Meek, *A Sudanese Kingdom and Ethnographical Study of the Jukun-Speaking Peoples of Nigeria* (London: Trubner & Co., 1931), 298; Robert Milligan, *The Fetish Folk of West Africa* (New York: Fleming H. Revell Co., 1912), 39.

17. Bibb, 30–31.

18. Ibid., 31.

19. See Sweet's chapter in this volume.

20. Harriet Jacobs, *Incidents in the Life of a Slave Girl: Contexts and Criticisms*, eds. Nellie Y. McKay and Frances Smith Foster (New York and London: W. W. Norton and Company, 2001), 91–93.

21. On the Yoruba and the Malagasy, Farrow comments: "The power of 'medicine' (Ogun) exercised through a certain channel may be neutralized or overcome by a superior power of Ogun through another channel. Van Gennep tells us that in Madagascar fady (the local name for 'taboo') may be broken by one who has a higher power known as hasina. So in Yoruba, a stronger 'medicine' is employed to overcome or counteract, an evil one, or a curse incurred through a broken ewo ('taboo')." Stephen Farrow, *Faith, Fancies and Fetich* (New York and Toronto: Macmillan, 1926), 121.

22. Jacobs, 98. Italics mine.

23. Puckett, *Folk Beliefs*, 388. Italics mine.

24. For this essay I rely on Sarah H. Bradford, *Harriet Tubman, The Moses of Her People* (1886; repr., Auburn, N.Y.: Applewood Books, 1993).

25. Bradford, 95–98.

26. Ibid., 24.

27. William Wells Brown, *Narrative of William W. Brown, a Fugitive Slave, Written by Himself* (Boston: 1847), 91–93.

28. Ibid., 93.

29. Brown, *My Southern Home*, 60.

30. Ibid.

31. Jacobs, 57–58, 62. For further mention of coffee grounds and divination, see Puckett, *Folk Beliefs*, 355. *Drums and Shadows* also provides an account of a root doctor from Brownville, Georgia who was born with the power to foretell the future through the use of coffee grounds. See Georgia Writer's Project, *Drums and Shadows*, 58. Various kinds of seeds were also used to reveal the future in various parts of West Africa. See Melville Herskovits, *Dahomey* (New York: J. J. Augustin, 1938), vol. 11, 209, 210.

32. Jacobs, 87.

33. Bradford, 118.

34. Ibid., 119.

35. Kate Larson, *Bound for the Promise Land: Harriet Tubman, Portrait of an American Hero* (New York: Random House, 2004), 176.

36. Leonard, *The Lower Niger and Its Tribes*, 147.

37. Georgia Writer's Project, *Drums and Shadows*, 77.

38. Bradford, 83.

39. See Sandbury, Georgia resident Emma Stevens's warning about spirits in Georgia Writers' Project, 114. For the West African practice of placing food for ancestors, see Augustus Cole, *A Revelation of the Secret Orders of Western Africa* (Dayton: United Brethren Publishing House, 1886), 39; Robert Nassau, *Fetichism in West Africa* (New York: Charles Scribner's Sons, 1904), 220.

40. Charles Ball, *Slavery in the United States: A Narrative of the Life and Adventures of Charles Ball, A Black Man* (New York: New American Library, repr., 1969), 265.

41. Jacobs, 74.

42. Ibid., 75.

43. Stuckey, *Slave Culture*. Stuckey argues that, contrary to scholarly consensus, Douglass was not far removed from African culture, and that he had captured the African elements of joy and sorrow that were so much a part of the slave spirituals. Stuckey also argues that Douglass paid careful attention to African labor patterns. See Sterling Stuckey, *Going Through the Storm* (New York: Oxford University Press, 1994), 33, 38–39.

44. Frederick Douglass, "Narrative," 24–26.

45. As late as the 1870s Payne, like most black elite and high-ranking clergymen, was unsuccessful in his attempts to rid the ring shout ceremony at various AME churches. Daniel Payne, *Recollections of Seventy Years* (1888; repr., New York: Arno Press, 1968), 254–256.

46. Douglass, "My Bondage and My Freedom" (1855; repr., in *Douglass Autobiographies* [New York: Penguin, 1994]), 188 [italics mine]. Here one is reminded of Thomas Wentworth Higginson's observations of the shout in the Sea Islands during the Civil War: "All over the camp the lights glimmer in the tents, and as I sit at my desk in the open doorway, there come mingled sounds of stir and glee. Boys laugh and shout,—a feeble flute stirs somewhere in some tent, not an officer's,—drums throb not far away in another." This "laugh" is likely a result of the "frenzy" in which the body is mounted by one's ancestors and or other deities. See Thomas W. Higginson, *Army Life in a Black Regiment* (Boston: Lee and Shepard, 1890), 41.

47. Douglass, "Life and Times" (1893; repr., in *Douglass Autobiographies* [New York: Penguin, 1994]), 1013. Douglass's remarks call to mind Sterling Stuckey's analysis of Herman Melville's treatment of Ashantee dance in *Benito Cereno*. See Sterling Stuckey, "The Tambourine in Glory," in Robert S. Levine, ed., *The Cambridge Companion to Herman Melville* (New York: Cambridge University Press, 1998), 57, 63. Thomas Wentworth Higginson's writing on the ring shout echoes Melville and Douglass: "Some 'heel and toe' tumultuously, others merely tremble and stagger on, others stoop and rise, others whirl, others caper sideways, all keep steadily circling like *dervishes*" [italics mine]. See Higginson, 41. Bremer observed similar scenes at a Methodist class meeting in New Orleans during the 1850s.

Fredrika Bremer, *America of the Fifties: Letters of Fredrika*, ed. Adolph B. Benson (New York: Oxford University Press, 1924), 274–276.

48. Brown, *My Southern Home*, 69.

49. Ibid., 121–122. For a broader discussion on the significance of country marks among West Africans see Gomez, *Exchanging Our Country Marks*.

50. Brown, *My Southern Home*, 121–124.

51. Bradford, 104. See *Drums and Shadows* for further commentary on nightly funeral rituals, 182, 192.

52. Bradford, 105.

53. Of the total number of imports that disembarked in what became the United States, at least 13 percent embarked from the Bight of Biafra. David Eltis, Stephen D. Behrendt, David Richardson, and Herbert Klein, eds., *The Trans-Atlantic Slave Trade: A Database on CD-Rom* (Cambridge: Cambridge University Press, 1999). For a discussion of the Igbo presence in America see Gomez, *Exchanging Our Country Marks*, 115.

54. Bibb, 73, 79, 77.

55. Bradford, 25–30.

56. Ibid., 115.

57. Of the total number of those slaves who arrived in Maryland, 10.20 percent embarked from the Gold Coast. The Bight of Biafra was the point of departure for only 2.62 percent of the total number of slaves who arrived in Maryland, yet the region contributed sizeable imports during the earlier period of the slave trade (*The Trans-Atlantic Slave Trade*); Gomez, 149.

58. Anthony Ephirim-Donkor, *African Spirituality: On Becoming Ancestors* (Trenton, N.J.: Africa World Press, 1997), 73.

5

Embracing the Religious Profession

The Antebellum Mission of the Oblate Sisters of Providence

Diane Batts Morrow

Historically, black people in the United States have marshaled their spiritual resources to assert their personal worth. Whether slave or free, black people in the Protestant tradition utilized religion both as individuals and collectively in congregations to counter the onslaughts of a racist society disallowing black humanity. The formation of the Oblate Sisters of Providence provided another incarnation of black religious piety. These sisters distinguished themselves by their collective profession and practice of spirituality as the first women in the world to pursue religious life as an exclusively black community in the Roman Catholic tradition.[1]

This pioneering Roman Catholic sisterhood defined itself as "a Religious society of Coloured Women, established in Baltimore with the approbation of the Most Reverend Archbishop, [who] renounce the world to consecrate themselves to God, and to the Christian education of young girls of color."[2] In the process of living in community, executing their teaching ministry, and defining themselves positively as a black sisterhood, these women utilized religion both as resistance and as community builder in significant ways.

This chapter examines three aspects of the Oblate Sisters' call and response to religious community in the context of the antebellum South. Oblate community building efforts replicated the experiences of diasporic Africans throughout the New World and reflected traditional African as well as European cultural elements. As black women religious, the Oblate Sisters bore witness to the virtue and spirituality of black women that white antebellum society consistently denied. Finally, as educators of children, the Oblate community informed critical dimensions of African American cultural life.

Two streams of immigration that met in Baltimore in the 1790s made possible the formation of the Oblate Sisters almost forty years later. As the see, or official seat, of the first diocese of the Roman Catholic Church formed in the United States in 1789, Baltimore provided a logical haven for Catholics fleeing revolutions in France and the Caribbean. The French Sulpician priests arrived in Baltimore in 1791 to educate young men for the priesthood. Beginning in 1793, black as well as white refugees fled the slave revolution in the French Caribbean colony of St. Domingue—today known as Haiti—to several port cities in the United States.[3] In Baltimore, shared traditions attracted Sulpicians and San Domingan exiles to each other, bound together by their French language and cultural heritage and their profession of the Roman Catholic faith. In 1796, the Sulpician priests organized Sunday religious instruction for the black San Domingan refugees who met in their seminary chapel.

In 1827, Sulpician priest James Joubert assumed direction of Sunday religious training for the black children and proposed a school to improve religious instruction. To staff the school Joubert approached Caribbean emigrants Elizabeth Clarisse Lange and Marie Magdelaine Balas, two educated women of color and experienced teachers who conducted their own school for children of their race in their home. During their first meeting, Lange and Balas informed Joubert of their decade-long desire to become women religious. That these two black Catholic women persisted in their religious vocations for ten years before fulfillment reveals much about them. With neither external acknowledgment nor official encouragement, Lange and Balas relied exclusively on their internalized commitments to their religious vocations, based on their faith that God would provide. After consulting with Archbishop James Whitfield of Baltimore, Joubert concluded that a black sisterhood would suit his purposes as well.[4]

On 2 July 1829, James Joubert received the professions of the four charter members of the Oblate Sisters of Providence: Elizabeth Lange, Marie Balas, Rosine Boegue, and Therese Duchemin. They pledged themselves to a life of service and faithful observance of the vows of poverty, chastity, and obedience. The term "oblate" means "one offered" or "made over to God."[5] Lange served as the first mother superior; Joubert, as the first spiritual director of the Oblate sisterhood they cofounded.

For their habit the sisters adopted a simple dress "of black woolen stuff for winter and summer" and a white cap for housewear, that they exchanged for a black bonnet for streetwear. Only the black band of the cap and the cross suspended from a neck chain adorning the dress of professed sisters distinguished their habit from that worn by the novices.[6] Like the habit of the only indigenous sisterhood preceding them in the United States, the Sisters of Charity of St. Joseph founded in 1809 by Elizabeth Bayley Seton, the habit of the Oblate Sisters of Providence replicated the modest attire of contemporary widows.

The African ancestry and Caribbean provenance of the four charter members of the Oblate Sisters of Providence positioned these women genealogically in a diaspora within a diaspora: from Africa to the Caribbean to the United States, what historian Colin Palmer has identified respectively as the fourth and fifth major African diasporic streams.[7] The standard chronicle of the Oblate experience characterizes the sisters as "French in language, in sympathy, and in habit of life,"[8] in a Eurocentric and proprietary effort to explain their origins. Yet, elements of traditional African cultures plausibly influenced the foundation of the Oblate community in important, if previously unrecognized ways.

From the 1500s, African peoples transported in the Atlantic slave trade to the New World repeatedly demonstrated the complexity, resilience, viability, and dynamism of their traditional cultures in interaction with European peoples. Numerous examples of syncretism occurred between components of traditional African religious beliefs, practices, and icons and corresponding aspects of Roman Catholicism. The practice of *vaudou* that evolved in Saint Domingue constitutes perhaps the single most celebrated example of the syncretic fusion of elements of traditional African religions and Roman Catholicism. Dahomean peoples formed a significant component of the slave population in Saint Domingue and exerted major influence on the development of *vaudou*.[9]

The demographic and cultural prominence of Dahomean peoples in Saint Domingan life proves particularly significant because women—in Dahomean society in particular and throughout West African societies in general—exerted significant agency in their cultures. Historians Sylvia Frey and Betty Wood argue persuasively that, in contrast to Western Christianity, "the participation of women in religious activities was built into the West African cosmological system" and that West African traditional religions "recognized the female as participating in the divine and thus allowed for the parallel and complementary development of male and female ritual leaders."[10] Historian Michael Gomez discusses the Sande, female secret societies widely institutionalized among the peoples of Sierre Leone, that exercised important religious functions. He describes initiation into the Sande as "a celebration of death to life through spiritual rebirth" involving the assumption of new names that symbolize the members' new lives within the society. Gomez further observes that as members of Sande societies "Senufo women in general, 'to a far greater degree than men, assume roles as ritual mediators between humankind and the supernatural world of spirits and deities.'"[11]

In the Dahomean religious belief system the preeminence of Mawu, the Moon Goddess, among the pantheons of gods ascribed both power and divinity to women. In addition to fulfilling customary social functions of reproduction and nurture, Dahomean women also performed vital economic, political, and military functions throughout their society. They controlled local trade markets, served as recorders responsible for memorizing and retaining vital governmental procedures in a preliterate society, supervised male government officials at court, and served as special units in the royal army.[12] Women in European society enjoyed few analogous experiences.

Dahomeans enslaved in the New World transplanted directly to Saint Domingan *vaudou* the prominence of women among devotees to the Dahomean gods, crucial in their service as divine interpreters, mediators, and subjects of possession. This traditional West African antecedent of significant female influence in the religious life of their society corresponded with the vital role European sisterhoods fulfilled in Roman Catholic countries. As Africans and Europeans interacted, black people creatively recast "European forms [to] serve African functions."[13] Certainly, the concept of a group of women engaged in cooperative living and forging a communal identity as "Brides of Christ" resonated in the cultural traditions of West African women from societies that practiced polygyny. Similarly, Roman Catholic ceremonies of religious profession in which women renounced their former lives and received new names symbolizing their rebirth as new members of spiritual communities corresponded to the initiation rites inducting West African women into the Sande secret societies.

West African peoples utilized a panoply of cultural resources in their interaction with French colonists and French culture over time in Saint Domingue. Dahomean and other West African cultural traditions and continuities, incorporating female authority and agency, merged with

French cultural elements, including Roman Catholicism. During the fifth stage of the African diaspora from the Caribbean to Baltimore, women emigrants established the Oblate Sisters of Providence. A synergistic fusion of both African and French traditions contributed the crucial components of faith and female empowerment facilitating their accomplishment.

From 1789 through the 1830s, the church in the South formed the foundation of American Roman Catholicism. Through the nineteenth century, the Catholic Church in the United States retained the imprint of its southern origins. As did their Protestant counterparts, Roman Catholic clergy and women religious not only tolerated the institution of slavery, but they also actively participated in and profited from the ownership and sale of human chattel. Several distinguished prelates, including John Carroll, the first Roman Catholic bishop in the United States, and his colleagues and successors Louis DuBourg of Louisiana, Benedict Flaget of Kentucky, and Samuel Eccleston of Baltimore, owned or had owned slaves. Societies of priests including the Jesuits, the Vincentians, the Sulpicians, and the Capuchins owned slaves. At least nine sisterhoods or congregations of women religious held slave property as well.[14] Not only their racial identity but also their nonslaveholding status distinguished the Oblate Sisters from the other sisterhoods residing in antebellum Baltimore. The antebellum Roman Catholic Church's acceptance of racism and the institution of slavery necessarily affected its attitude and policies toward black people.

In 1835, Louis Deluol, superior of the Sulpician seminary, requested two Oblate Sisters to manage the domestic affairs of the seminary household. Oblate Superior Mary Lange responded to this request with a letter, reflecting her astute grasp of both the promise and the problems of the Oblate community's anomalous position within the antebellum southern Church and society:

> We do not conceal the difficulty of our situation [a]s persons of color and religious at the same time, and we wish to conciliate these two qualities in such a manner as not to appear too arrogant on the one hand and on the other, not to miss the respect which is due to the state we have embraced and the holy habit which we have the honor to wear. Our intention in consenting to your request is not to neglect the religious profession we have embraced.[15]

Oblate experience with clerical disapproval of the concept of a black sisterhood in 1829 had prompted Lange's apprehensions about full recognition of and respect for the Oblate Sisters' religious state at the seminary. Objections to the Oblate foundation expressed within the white Baltimore Catholic community—even among the Sulpician priests—had dismayed the four charter Oblate members. Consequently, Lange insisted on the guaranteed integrity of the Oblate religious state as a precondition to the sisters' employment at the seminary. She further requested seclusion of the sisters from the other seminary servants—slave and free—in an effort to reserve for the Oblate Sisters a distinctive social position, based on their status as women religious, among other people within the seminary household. Lange responded to a routine request for traditional domestic services with a nontraditional manifesto defining the Oblate Sisters' religious, racial, and social positions as they perceived them.

Embracing the religious state and rejecting secular concerns and status could prove both liberating and empowering to black women debased by the worldly social order. In renouncing the world to consecrate themselves to God, the Oblate Sisters of Providence achieved symbolic release from socially ascribed derogation based on their identities as black women. As the Oblate Sisters of Providence, these women of color in the antebellum South utilized their piety and spiritual fervor to defy their socially ascribed inferior status and to act assertively in service to others.

The Oblate Sisters aspired to and realized religious vocations in a slave-holding society that denigrated the virtue of all black women—slave or free. Antebellum United States society ostracized black women beyond the pale of the social construction of gender. From the early days of slavery, white public thought rendered black women the antithesis of women of virtue, the social construct of femininity that defined white gender differences, justified the cult of domesticity, and sanctioned socially ascribed separate spheres for men and women. The image of black women as the sexually promiscuous Jezebel became fixated in the white public consciousness. Negative stereotypes of black women remained so pervasive in American culture that long after the abolition of slavery in 1865 a white observer accurately reflected public sentiment when she asserted in 1904, "I cannot imagine such a creation as a virtuous black woman."[16] Only the equally dysfunctional slave stereotype of black women as Mammy, the asexual caretaker devoted to the nurture of her white family to the detriment of her own, challenged the Jezebel image of black women in the white public mind.

Refusing to internalize such societal disparagement, the Oblate Sisters demonstrated self-empowerment instead, by defining themselves primarily as women of virtue. In dedicating themselves to the religious state, they offered their lives to God. Arrayed in religious garb, the raiment of women of virtue, these black women became "brides of Christ." As teachers, the Oblate Sisters effectively countered the Mammy stereotype's neglect of her own offspring with their collective ministrations to the intellectual, spiritual, and social nurture of black children. As women religious, the Oblate Sisters at least partially transcended their social marginalization in claiming "the respect which is due to the state we have embraced and the holy habit which we have the honor to wear," the same respect, virtue, and honor normally ascribed to white middle-class women exclusively. In a racist society whose restrictions occasionally extended to legal proscription of certain styles or articles of clothing for people of color, overt Oblate acts of religious profession and wearing the religious habit constituted a social challenge, if not subversion.

Humility formed an essential component of the Oblate spiritual identity as it evolved during the first decade of the sisterhood's existence. Spiritual director Joubert frequently charged the Oblate Sisters "to act with all humility and confidence in God" or to comport themselves with "the humility which should characterize religious."[17] On 9 March 1839, Joubert's Sulpician colleague, Edward Damphoux, preached a sermon that "pleased the Director very much, since he tended to inspire us with the virtues which he ceases not to inculcate in us and which he desires to see us practice, chiefly humility."[18]

In a worldly context, humility denotes a demeanor of deference from an inferior toward a superior, a socially hierarchical relationship between people. However, in a religious sense, humility signifies primarily a voluntary submission of self to God, a spiritual relationship between the individual and the divine. In practice, the moral virtue of humility "avoids inflation of one's worth or talents on the one hand, and avoids excessive devaluation of oneself on the other. Humility requires a dispassionate and honest appreciation of the self in relationship to others and to God."[19] Certainly, Oblate Superior Lange articulated the very essence of the challenging practice of humility—framed in reference to Oblate consciousness of their racial identity—in her concern "not to appear too arrogant on the one hand and on the other, not to miss the respect which is due to the state we have embraced and the holy habit which we have the honor to wear."[20] In its focus centered on the divine, humility involves a renunciation of the world, a rejection of secular concerns and status. While distinctions between the secular and spiritual connotations of humility applied generally to all religious congregations, they acquired particular racial significance for the black Oblate Sisters in the antebellum South.

Two aspects of Oblate spirituality established during their first decade resonate with racial meaning. From 1833, the Oblate Sisters claimed St. Benedict the Moor—of both African and slave ancestry—as the fourth special patron of their house, after the Blessed Virgin Mary, St. Joseph, and St. Frances of Rome.[21] This designation represents the only definitive element of African identity in their spirituality, as historian Cyprian Davis has noted.[22]

On 2 July 1830, Oblate spiritual director James Joubert, the four charter Oblate members, and the three Oblate novices enrolled in the Association of Holy Slavery of the Mother of God, receiving the symbolic chain of membership. Future Oblate members were to enroll in the Association the day they received their habits. Oblate affiliation with this devotional society initially appears problematic for black sisters in the context of the antebellum South. However, their allegiance to this devotional society conformed completely to the centrality of devotion to the Blessed Virgin in the Oblate charism. Davis treats this association as a development from seventeenth-century French devotional practices and states that the metaphor "holy slavery" enjoyed widespread usage in church devotional circles. Oblate membership in the Association of Holy Slavery of the Mother of God represented no embrace of slavery as the classic model of the abused of the black community, but rather a conversion—if not subversion—of the specific secular connotations of the institution of slavery in the antebellum South. The spiritual slavery with which the Oblate Sisters associated differed critically from its social analogue of involuntary subjugation to an owner, both in its voluntary nature and sole purpose of personal spiritual benefit. Oblate membership in this devotional society reflected the degree to which these black sisters successfully dissociated themselves spiritually—if not physically—from their immediate social context to divest the term slavery of its dehumanizing connotations.

The Oblate community further sought to divest the institution of slavery of its dehumanizing faculty in their membership policy. Of the forty women who entered the Oblate novitiate in the antebellum period, eight claimed slave origins.[23] The Oblate Sisters of Providence did not consider a candidate's previous condition of servitude a liability for Oblate membership. The Oblate Rule did not explicitly address the issue of slavery.

The general requirement that candidates "be free from debts and detained in the world by no hindrance whatsoever"[24] commonly appeared in the regulations of religious congregations. Only in the context of the racial identity of the Oblate Sisters did this requirement mean that candidates had to be free black women.

It hardly proves surprising that the Oblate Sisters neither expressed abolitionist sentiments nor engaged in anti-slavery activities, whatever their private feelings about slavery might have been. Oblate silence about slavery occurred within the context of an American Roman Catholic Church whose clergy and hierarchy not only frequently and vociferously defended the institution of slavery, but also participated in and profited from it. As a religious society within the Roman Catholic Church, the Oblate Sisters—and all sisterhoods—adhered to official church policy of abstention from public debate about social and political issues confronting antebellum society.

In forming a community of women religious, the Oblate Sisters demonstrated that moral virtue and spiritual fervor among black people occurred not in isolation, but permeated the population sufficiently to motivate a group of black women to claim religious piety as their primary, collective identity. Wearing the distinctive Oblate habit facilitated the sisters' public declaration of their religious state. They utilized their communal profession of piety as currency, to validate and legitimize their claim to public recognition and support to an extent unrealizable by individual, secular black women in antebellum United States society. The Oblate Sisters ministered to the black community with only modest support from white Baltimoreans. The differential levels of support white Catholics provided the black Oblate community and the white sisterhoods in the archdiocese of Baltimore throughout the antebellum period reflected the subordinate position ascribed the Oblate Sisters in the Catholic community, predicated on their racial identity. Nevertheless, the fact that the institutional church and individual white benefactors among both clergy and laity recognized, promoted, and subsidized the Oblate enterprise at all attested to the viability of Oblate virtue as currency in antebellum society. In responding to their call to religious community life, the black Oblate Sisters of Providence defied racial stereotypes to earn grudging white acknowledgment in the antebellum South.[25]

As befitted its reputation as the nineteenth-century free black capital, Baltimore sustained a vital, varied, and self-empowered antebellum black community. Black Baltimoreans created and supported a nexus of religious, social, and educational institutions undergirding their community life.[26] Black and white populations employed different criteria in determining social status. Generally, black people considered not only family wealth but also free lineage, reputation, material possessions, and color in ascribing middle-class status. Baltimore's black community proved exceptional in not privileging color as a criterion of social status. Black barbers, caterers, and tradespeople serving a white clientele exclusively and black people in personal service to important white business, political, or socially elite households formed important elements of the black middle class. Although Baltimore's free black population also supported a small professional elite of physicians, ministers, lawyers, and teachers who served the black community, no evidence documents that Oblate members derived from this portion of the black middle class. Oblate family backgrounds more often included barbers and tradespeople, many of whom achieved a comfortable standard of living in antebellum Baltimore.

Dowries provided a significant source of income for Baltimore's antebellum sisterhoods. Maintaining solvency proved a constant challenge for the Oblate Sisters of Providence. Oblate members consistently enriched their community much more generously with endowments of piety, intellect, and skill than with monetary assets. The Oblate Rule, unlike those of the white sisterhoods, stated a specific dollar amount for the dowry, requiring prospective candidates to advance four hundred dollars. Archbishop James Whitfield had fixed the dowry amount when he approved the founding of the Oblate Sisters. The archdiocese contributed nothing to the maintenance of communities of women religious. Because financial constraints engendered by the racial identity of the Oblate membership and their proposed clientele had threatened the Oblate project from its conception, Whitfield undoubtedly intended to bolster the community's financial self-sufficiency. Depending on the circumstances and qualifications of the candidate, the community could waive this requirement.[27]

The economic assets of the Oblate membership varied. The stipulated $400 dowry could prove prohibitive for black candidates who lacked family affluence and who worked in a society that curtailed their economic options. Five sisters invoked the dowry waiver clause incorporated in the original Oblate Rule during the sisterhood's first decade. Most candidates, however, presented at least a token dowry, if not the full stipulated sum. Some Oblate candidates presenting the full dowry sum had earned the money themselves from working.

The Christian education of young girls of color formed the principal purpose of the Oblate Sisters of Providence, equal to their determination to consecrate themselves to God. This mandate to educate black girls ensured that the Oblate Sisters contributed substantively to the nurture and support of the antebellum black population. The Oblate school engaged in creative financing, tolerated sizeable deficits, offered scholarships, and in general made every effort to work with black families to make the education that was the Oblate mission as affordable and accessible as possible. The black lay community both supported and appreciated Oblate educational and spiritual efforts on their behalf. In financial contributions, patronage of Oblate schools, or in volunteering time, labor, and resources to benefit the Oblate cause, members of the antebellum black community amply demonstrated their conviction of the seminal importance of "our convent."[28]

Previous accounts of the Oblate experience have essentially ignored the complex, nuanced interactions between this pioneering sisterhood and the community they dedicated themselves to serve. The omission of significant instances of lay black initiative from historical accounts of the Oblate Sisters of Providence has distorted the historical record in several ways. It has provided only a partial—in both senses of the term—and therefore inaccurate account of the base of support the Oblate Sisters enjoyed in the Baltimore community. It has disallowed a valid indicator of the seminal importance of the Oblate Sisters to the Baltimore black community: given the smaller numbers, more limited resources, and greater social, economic, and political liabilities of the black population relative to the white, the monetary contributions from black donors represented a proportionally greater financial sacrifice than corresponding contributions from white donors. Finally, the omission of black initiatives to benefit the Oblate Sisters has perpetuated the myth of black people figuring in history primarily as victims or passive recipients of white benefaction.[29]

The Oblate curriculum, advertised in the national Catholic directory for the first time in 1834, offered courses in religion, "English, French, Cyphering and Writing, Sewing in all its branches, Embroidery, Washing and Ironing." The inclusion of washing and ironing as basic courses and the notable omission of such liberal subjects as history, geography, moral and natural philosophy, astronomy, and chemistry as well as music, painting, and drawing distinguished the Oblate curriculum from those of white convent academies.[30] By 1859, the Oblate course of study eliminated washing and ironing from its standard offerings and included catechism, reading, English, French, history, geography, arithmetic, and writing and music.[31]

In addition to common school and domestic instruction, the Oblate teaching ministry obligated the sisters to instill in their pupils "certain principles of virtue becoming their situation: the love of labor and of order . . . a careful attention to avoid the frequentation of persons of a different sex, that innocent bashfulness which is the principal ornament of their sex, and that exterior modesty which is the surest preservative of virtue."[32] The decided emphasis on desirable gender traits in three of the four listed principles of virtue typifies the philosophy informing not only convent school, but also all nineteenth-century education for women. Significantly, the Oblate Sisters inculcated these values of respectability in black girls, in defiance of antebellum American society's exclusion of black women from considerations of gender.

No surviving evidence suggests that the antebellum Oblate school curriculum explicitly addressed the racial identity of its clientele. Nevertheless, in offering a solid Catholic education to black girls, the Oblate Sisters taught their pupils values and ideals beyond those that white society thought either appropriate or possible for black women. Oblate insistence on "the respect which is due to the state we have embraced" for themselves and their pedagogical emphasis on respectability for their pupils conformed to what historian Evelyn Brooks Higginbotham has identified as the politics of respectability:

> By claiming respectability through their manners and morals, poor black women boldly asserted the will and agency to define themselves outside the parameters of prevailing racist discourses. . . . Respectability was perceived as a weapon against such assumptions, since it was used to expose race relations as socially constructed rather than derived by evolutionary law or divine judgment.[33]

The Oblate school, like the white convent academies in the 1830s, readily admitted non-Catholic students. The names of only a minority of the ninety-four documented enrollees in the Oblate school between 1828 and 1834 appeared in Baltimore Catholic baptismal records. This fact suggests that a significant number of these early Oblate pupils were Protestants. Although conversion to Catholicism did not constitute a requirement for admission to the school, during the 1830s seven Protestant Oblate pupils became Catholic.[34]

By 1838, within its first decade, former Oblate students formed fully one-third of Oblate community membership: seven of twenty-one sisters. This circumstance replicated a pattern prevalent among all nineteenth-century students educated in convent schools. The insistent glorification of virginity and the impressive example of the sisters themselves contributed to a high percentage of religious vocations among convent school girls. For a black Oblate pupil and her white convent school counterpart alike, choosing religious life, recognizing and responding to a religious vocation, involved the exercise of personal choice to participate in a divinely sanctioned lifestyle characterized by reduced male interference and control. The limited socially approved alternatives for black women could only have enhanced the intrinsic appeal of religious life and a teaching career for Oblate students.[35] As black women religious, the Oblate Sisters claimed for themselves the traditional entitlements of respectability and societal exemption inherent in the religious state. In community, black women felt empowered to transcend mere social opposition to their divinely mandated mission: their own personal spiritual perfection and the education of black children. To women rejected and scorned by white society because of their racial identity, the appeal of membership in such an organization proved significant.

Nineteenth-century white attitudes denigrated the virtue of all black women and consequently impugned the concept of a community of black women religious. White supporters and detractors of the Oblate cause alike wondered, "Where could be found the pious young women needed for it, who would consent to persevere in virginity and who would be satisfied with the meagre support to be derived from teaching the poorest of the poor?"[36]

The antebellum Oblate Sisters themselves demonstrated no such concern or preoccupation about the pool of prospective Oblate candidates. From their inception the sisters established rigorous and highly selective standards for Oblate membership. They sought quality rather than quantity in their ranks and resisted opportunities to augment membership with candidates less than totally dedicated to the Oblate cause.

Religious vocations prove elitist by definition. Like the Marine Corps in search of a few good women and men, religious communities challenge adherents to live lives of hardship and service, bolstered by their faith and commitment. Attracting a mass membership was not a priority of the Oblate sisterhood. Indeed, amassing sufficient resources to support the significant number of devout women aspiring to Oblate membership remained a major Oblate concern throughout the antebellum period.

By 1859, the influence of the Oblate school had surpassed its immediate impact on its pupils and alumnae. The Reverend John Mifflin Brown, pastor of Baltimore's Bethel African Methodist Episcopal Church and Baltimore correspondent for the New York City black newspaper, the *Weekly Anglo-African*,[37] asserted in that publication:

> The "Sisters of Providence" (Catholic) gave a grand demonstration at the close of their school. I did not witness the literary exercises, but all are abundant in their laudations of these faithful "Sisters." Their pupils number 160. I witnessed their exhibition of needlework. . . . When I left the room I felt deeply impressed that the man who could go there and gaze upon such work from the hands of *colored girls*, and they entirely under the control of *colored teachers*, and hear their sweet music and charming voices, must be either a madman or a fool, if he adopt such silly and uncalled-for sentiments as those published by that Republican paper in Philadelphia and republished by the editor of the New York "Herald" with his remarks. If these Northern editors will come "down South," we will teach them that some of us live otherwise than by *blacking their boots, shaving their faces, and waiting upon their tables.*[38]

In responding to the call of their teaching mission, the Oblate Sisters of Providence nurtured the minds and souls of black folk, the very elements of black existence white society routinely disallowed, in its monolithic focus on the profitable exploitation of black servile labor. Protestant minister John Mifflin Brown's glowing tribute to the sisters' efforts in the *Weekly Anglo-African* reflected how broadly the Baltimore black community recognized these Oblate contributions. The school's established reputation and the competence and commitment of its dedicated staff of teachers came to symbolize for many black people—regardless of their religious affiliation—an affirmation of black humanity in an increasingly hostile environment in the antebellum South.

The Oblate Sisters of Providence remain a vital religious community and celebrated 175 years of spiritual dedication and service in 2004. They maintain ministries in several states, the District of Columbia, Costa Rica, and the Dominican Republic. Ever responsive to the changing needs of the African American community, the Oblate Sisters revised their traditional educational mission in the 1970s and transformed their signature school in Baltimore, St. Frances Academy, from a girls' boarding school to a coeducational day high school, specializing in serving the needs of an inner-city clientele. The dedicated staff of St. Frances Academy, the oldest continuing Catholic school for black youth in the United States, provides more than three hundred students with the necessary skills, discipline, and motivation to attain academic success, to graduate from high school, and to pursue postsecondary education.

Other Oblate ministries serving the inner-city community in downtown Baltimore include the St. Frances Community Center, which hosts programs, parties, and job fairs for all neighborhood residents, and the Mary Elizabeth Lange Center for Girls, which provides residential care for girls in need of temporary housing. The sisters also conduct a tutorial reading center and a day care program at their motherhouse in Catonsville.

The Oblate credal statement, "We believe, as an African American Congregation of multicultured women religious, we are a unique and visible testimony of the church and a constant challenge to its authenticity to be the voice of Jesus Christ to all people," appropriately encapsulates this black sisterhood's historic identity and significance.[39]

NOTES

This chapter is reprinted from *Persons of Color and Religious at the Same Time: The Oblate Sisters of Providence, 1828–1860* by Diane Batts Morrow. (c) 2002 by the University of North Carolina Press. Used by permission of the publisher.

1. Grace Sherwood, *The Oblates' Hundred and One Years* (New York: Macmillan, 1931), 118; John T. Gillard, *Colored Catholics in the United States* (Baltimore: Josephite Press, 1941), 118.

2. The Original Rule of the Oblate Sisters of Providence (hereinafter cited as Original Rule), quoted in Thaddeus Posey, "An Unwanted Commitment: The Spirituality of the Early Oblate Sisters of Providence, 1829–1890" (Ph.D. diss., Saint Louis University, 1993), Appendix I, 314.

3. Gillard, *Colored Catholics in the United States*, 79–80.

4. A Translation of The Original Diary of the Oblate Sisters of Providence, typescript copy (hereinafter cited as Annals), 1, Archives of the Oblate Sisters of Providence (hereinafter cited as AOSP).

5. Cyprian Davis, *The History of Black Catholics in the United States* (New York: Crossroad, 1990), 100; *New Catholic Encyclopedia* (1967), s.v. "Oblates."

6. Original Rule, AOSP; Sherwood, *The Oblates' Hundred and One Years*, 190.

7. Colin Palmer, "Defining and Studying the Modern African Diaspora," *Perspectives: American Historical Association Newsletter* 36, no. 6 (September 1998): 22.

8. Sherwood, *The Oblates' Hundred and One Years*, 5.

9. Albert J. Raboteau, *Slave Religion: The "Invisible Institution" in the Antebellum South* (Oxford and New York: Oxford University Press, 1978), 22–27, 87–89; Melville J. Herskovits, *The Myth of the Negro Past* (Boston: Beacon Press, 1941), 50; Robin Law, "Slave-Raiders and Middlemen, Monopolists and Free Traders: The Supply of Slaves for the Atlantic Trade in Dahomey, c. 1715–1850," *Journal of African History* 30 (1989): 48; David Geggus, "The French Slave Trade: An Overview," Unpublished Paper, September, 1998.

10. Sylvia R. Frey and Betty Wood, *Come Shouting to Zion: African American Protestantism in the American South and British Caribbean to 1830* (Chapel Hill: University of North Carolina Press, 1998), 12.

11. Michael A. Gomez, *Exchanging Our Country Marks: The Transformation of African Identities in the Colonial and Antebellum South* (Chapel Hill: University of North Carolina Press, 1998), 98; quote within quote from Anita J. Glaze, *Art and Death in a Senufo Village* (Bloomington: University of Indiana Press, 1981), 45, cited in Gomez, 96.

12. Raboteau, *Slave Religion*, 9–11; Herskovits, *Myth of the Negro Past*, 61–77; August Meier and Elliot Rudwick, *From Plantation to Ghetto*, Third Edition (New York: Hill and Wang, 1976), 12–19.

13. John W. Blassingame, *The Slave Community: Plantation Life in the Antebellum South*, Revised and Enlarged Edition (New York and Oxford: Oxford University Press, 1979), 20.

14. Richard R. Duncan, "Catholics and the Church in the Antebellum Upper South," in *Catholics in the Old South: Essays on Church and Culture*, ed. Randall Miller and Jon Wakelyn (Macon, GA: Mercer University Press, 1983), 90; Davis, *History of Black Catholics*, 43, 38–39; Barbara Misner, *"Highly Respectable and Accomplished Ladies": Catholic Women Religious in America, 1790–1850* (New York: Garland Publishing, 1988), 75–88.

15. Annals, 38–39, AOSP.

16. Quote cited in Evelyn Brooks Higginbotham, "African American Women's History and the Metalanguage of Race," *Signs* 17, no. 2 (Winter 1992): 256–266, p. 264. For discussions of white society's denigration of black women, see also Angela Y. Davis, "Reflections on the Black Woman's Role in the Community of Slaves," *The Black Scholar* 3 (December 1971): 3–15; Deborah Gray White, *Ar'n't I a Woman?: Female Slaves in the Antebellum South* (New York: W. W. Norton & Co., 1985), 27–61; Elizabeth Fox-Genevese, *Within the Plantation Household: Black and White Women in the Old South* (Chapel Hill: University of North Carolina Press,

1985), 192–241; Patricia Morton, *Disfigured Images: The Historical Assault on Afro-American Women* (New York: Praeger, 1991), 1–25; Gerda Lerner, ed., *Black Women in White America: A Documentary History* (New York: Vintage Books, 1972), 47–53, 150–171; Paula Giddings, *When and Where I Enter: The Impact of Black Women on Race and Sex in America* (New York: William Morrow and Company, 1984), 31–55.

17. Annals, 5, 38.

18. Ibid., 31, 62–63.

19. *Harper Collins Encyclopedia of Catholicism*, 1995 ed., s.v. "humility".

20. Annals, 38.

21. Ibid., 26, 32, 45, 46, 59.

22. Davis, *History of Black Catholics*, 101.

23. "Where He Leads," commemorative pamphlet, n.d., 11, AOSP; Manumission Documents, Box 21, AOSP; Marie Germain: St. Peter's Pro-Cathedral Baptisms, 1812–19, M1511-5, p. 230, Archives of the Archdiocese of Baltimore microfilm, Maryland Hall of Records.

24. Original Rule, AOSP.

25. For a full treatment of the Oblate Sisters's relationship with the institutional Catholic Church and white society, see Diane Batts Morrow, *Persons of Color and Religious at the Same Time: The Oblate Sisters of Providence, 1828–1860* (Chapel Hill and London: University of North Carolina Press, 2002), chapters 5, 6, and 11.

26. For thorough treatments of antebellum black communal institutions in Baltimore, see Carter G. Woodson, *The Education of the Negro prior to 1861* (New York: G. P. Putnam's Sons, 1915), 138–144; James M. Wright, *The Free Negro in Maryland, 1634–1860* (New York: Columbia University Press, 1921), 200–238; Bettye J. Gardner, "Free Blacks in Baltimore, 1800–1860" (Ph.D. diss., George Washington University, 1974), 49–127; Bettye Collier-Thomas, "The Baltimore Black Community, 1865–1910" (Ph.D. diss., George Washington University, 1974), 17–39, 57–61, 74–80; Clarence K. Gregory, "The Education of Blacks in Maryland: An Historical Survey" (Ed.D. diss., Columbia University Teachers College, 1976), 64–103, 131–136; Leonard P. Curry, *The Free Black in Urban America, 1800–1850* (Chicago: University of Chicago Press, 1981), 154–159, 181; Leroy Graham, *Baltimore, the Nineteenth-Century Black Capital* (Washington, D.C.: University Press of America, 1982), 63–85, 93–135, 216; Christopher Phillips, *Freedom's Port: The African American Community of Baltimore, 1790–1860* (Urbana: University of Illinois Press, 1997), 117–176.

27. See the discussion of Oblate dowries in Morrow, *Persons of Color and Religious at the Same Time*, chapter 3; Sherwood, *The Oblates' Hundred and One Years*, 38; Annals, 1; Misner, *"Highly Respectable and Accomplished Ladies."* 70, 252, 255.

28. Montpensier to Toussaint, 23 October 1829, typescript copy, AOSP.

29. For a full treatment of the complex relationship the Oblate Sisters and the black laity forged during the antebellum period, see Morrow, *Persons of Color and Religious at the Same Time*, chapters 4 and 10.

30. *Metropolitan Catholic Calendar and Laity's Directory* (Baltimore: Fielding Lucas, Jr., 1834), 65–71.

31. *Laity's Directory* (1834), 70; (1836), 168; (1840), 72; *The Catholic Mirror* (Baltimore), 26 March 1853, "Colored Schools"; Annals II, 27 July 1859, AOSP; *Laity's Directory* (1859), 272; (1834), 65–71.

32. Original Rule cited in Posey, "An Unwanted Commitment," 323.

33. Evelyn Brooks Higginbotham, *Righteous Discontent: The Women's Movement in the Black Baptist Church, 1880–1920* (Cambridge, MA: Harvard University Press, 1993), 192.

34. Misner, *"Highly Respectable and Accomplished Ladies,"* 8, 11, 189, 251; Annals, 9, 23, 50, 65, AOSP.

35. Annals, 4 (Duchemin); 10 (Bourgoin); 30 (James); 40 (Thomas and Amanda); 44 (Germaine); 54 (Johnson), AOSP; Eileen Mary Brewer, *Nuns and the Education of American Catholic Women, 1860–1920* (Chicago: Loyola University Press, 1987), 123–124, 136.

36. L. W. Reilly, "A Famous Convent of Colored Sisters," in *Annales Congregationis SS. Redemptoris* (Provinciae Americanae, Supplementum, Pars II, 1903), 106.

37. Graham, *Baltimore, the Nineteenth-Century Black Capital*, 133, 253.

38. *Weekly Anglo-African* (New York), 13 August 1859, "Some Correspondence." The author of the letter identified himself merely as Mifflin.

39. Oblate Sisters of Providence, Office of Pastoral Planning Brochure, n.d., AOSP.

6

Finding the Past, Making the Future

The African Hebrew Israelite Community's Alternative to the Black Diaspora

Fran Markowitz

Heralding the analytical shifts that were to occur later in the decade, David Scott (1991) urged ethnographers studying black Americans to change the thrust of their project. Instead of striving to authenticate Africanisms (Herskovits 1941) and slave memories (Price 1983), Scott suggested investigating how black people have built "traditions" that link the trauma of slavery—the inaugural event of diaspora—to contemporary thoughts, memories, and enactments of it.

Writing as the racial categories of "black" and "Negro" gave way to a culture-and-place label of identity in the United States, Scott was prescient in his call for thinking about African-Americans as a diaspora.[1] The concept of diaspora, which "offers a critique of fixed origins while taking account of a homing desire" (Brah 1996:197), has been instrumental in looking beyond primordialist assumptions, and in the particular case of African-Americans, for busting ontological blackness (cf. Anderson 1995). Within the scope of diaspora, African-American culture is reconfigured as a complex, often internally contradictory, bundle of overlapping, sometimes creative, sometimes coercive hybridities that remain linked to remembrances of dispersal—the opening horrors of kidnapping, the Middle Passage,[2] and chattel slavery—while also suggesting ways to overcome and go beyond them (see, for example, Dyson 1993; Gilroy 1993, 2000; Hall 1995; hooks 1990; Howe 1998; Kawash 1997; West 1990).

By contrast, although the people and subgroups who constitute the Black Diaspora have yielded an astonishingly wide array of cultural products and expressions, their hybridity, at least in the United States, has been all but invisible and defied narration.[3] Color, as a legal if not social fact in a racially constituted world, is always manifest when cast into a black/white divide that identifies one shade with the nation while objectifying the "outsidership" of the other (Torres and Whitten 1998:24; Williams 1989). This binary obviates, overlaps, denies, or denigrates mixtures and subverts competing versions of history and identity. The dynamics of the African-American Diaspora—as both a yearning for and critique of anterior origins—have always been animated and deflated in their push against such a relentless color line.

The seemingly impossible meshing of hybridity's fluidity with the fixity of race has constituted among African-Americans a diasporic identity in which homeland has played a tenuous role. Color, stigmatized and objectified through slavery and perpetuated in a starkly racist discourse, put attachments to Africa and an African-American group identity at risk (Thomas 1993, esp. p. 190) as it swallowed up Africa-as-peoples-cultures-places and hid the variety of social forms and cultural expressions that resulted from its mergers with America (Brodkin 1997, esp. Chs, 2 and 3; Dominguez 1997; Kawash 1997).

The power of race to obstruct the central tension of *diaspora*—a term that evokes movement and mergers as it simultaneously conjures up images of prior purity rooted in an originary place (Brah 1996; Young 1995)—is by now well recognized. The Black Atlantic, as Paul Gilroy (1993) has so convincingly explained, has always been a nexus of sites of creolization, yet it had rarely been theorized as such. As a result, although over the centuries fusions of many sorts occurred between Africa and America, these were hardly noticed or recorded as official history, and Africa, the earth's second largest continent, was castigated and deprecated as that dark, pagan land that yielded necessarily black slaves.

Despite its entanglement in a cruelly racist discourse, Africa never disappeared from black people's longings for anterior origins. "The African diasporas of the New World," Stuart Hall (1995:9) explains, "have been one way or another incapable of finding a place in modern history without the symbolic return to Africa." But this return has been uneasy because Africa-as-homeland cannot be singular or pure, and it is contemporary Africa, swathed in layers of prior text and refracted through the trials of modernity, that is being reappropriated as homeland in African-Americans' narratives of authenticity and identity. As primordial or authentic as one may wish it to be, Africa has been cast as cartographic fact and mythographic concept as the result of centuries of hybrid fusions and ruptures, and ambivalence and messiness persist despite the promise of (symbolic) homecoming (Sivanandan 1970:11).

Just as Africa in the twentieth century emerged from the invisibility of hybridity and the bricolage of black American culture, so too did the African Hebrew Israelite Community (AHIC, or more broadly, Black Hebrews) take form through the dynamics of diaspora to become a multi-sited community centered in the Israeli Negev town of Dimona. In fact, according to the group's creation story, it could not have come into being any other way but as a result of exile, sojourns through Africa, and then the ultimate in deracination—the humiliations of slavery and racism in North America.[4] The Black Hebrews explain that experiencing such indignities prepared black people in America to ponder the significance of their plight and motivated those who would to uncover the reasons for it. To do this, they sifted through and fused together all kinds of knowledge, from the most discredited oral traditions passed on over the generations, to those at the hegemonic center of Euro-American culture. This search for identity ultimately led in two mutually dependent directions, back to the past and into the future, for when they looked for origins in Africa, they found their way to Israel, and that is where they discovered the messianic message and social project of their people (see Ben-Yehuda 1975; Gerber 1977; Markowitz 1996; Singer 1979).

The African Hebrew Israelite Community is not the only group of African-Americans to identify with the biblical Israelites or to delineate a special mission for black people (see Crumbley 2000), but it is the first and remains the only one to have established a social program plotted along the circular route of diaspora and return. In this chapter, I demonstrate how the double logic of hybridity—which is itself under assault while animated by an essentializing color line—works its way out in and through the efforts of the AHIC to confront and transcend diaspora, one strand of a complicated story.[5]

Recovering Africa Through the Lens of Modernity

Hybridity necessarily involves ruptures at the same time as it speaks to blendings, but each diaspora's memories and experiences are cast in different ways so that the sides of their hyphenated fusion/divide are differentially weighted. As already noted, for black Americans the inaugural terror of kidnapping and exile followed by the ordeal of chattel slavery overpowered and enveloped homeland in defining their group consciousness (Scott 1991).

The dominance of pain over place in the Black Atlantic has been exacerbated by two interconnected pieces of history. The first is that the Africans shipped to America were men and women from a variety of places who spoke mutually unintelligible languages and held to different traditions. They were not and did not consider themselves one people dispersed en masse from one place. Thus, from the very beginning, what united Africans in America was the violence done to them through slavery and the color of their skin rather than a singular place of origin (Kawash 1997:42). Second, as they developed a collective imagination of Africa-as-homeland, they learned as well that Africa and the Africans were under European control and suffered, as did they, "brutal enslavement, institutional terrorism, and cultural degradation" (West 1990:26). Under such conditions, Africa offered little solace.

By the eighteenth century, Africa was categorically constituted in white discourse as the Dark Continent, a place of savages and heathens, the depraved homeland of black slaves. These images were not simply literary metaphors or inspirations for church sermons; they were also at the heart of political programs and affirmed by science (Young 1995:67). No matter where they turned, even to civil beliefs in the rights to "life, liberty, and the pursuit of happiness," black Americans, slave or free, were bombarded with a total knowledge system that informed them that they deserved to be excluded from America's civil society and condemned to slavery, or at best second-class citizenship, under the domination of whites.

African slaves were introduced to Christianity almost from the moment that they reached America. They received religious instruction and were included in prayer services, usually led by slave owners and in high church denominations. But most blacks did not convert because they perceived Christianity to be the white man's religion, which justified their slavery (Raboteau 1997:89–91). Although one of Christianity's central messages is that God's blessing awaits all humankind, only with the rise of American Evangelical Christianity in the latter part of the eighteenth century did these egalitarian tendencies countermand a divinely sanctioned hierarchy in which whites had exclusive hold on civilization and salvation. In ecstatic revival meetings, charismatic but often unschooled preachers taught that every man and woman, rich and poor, black and white could get the spirit, transcend the woes of the world, and find favor in God's eyes.

Responding to this promise of equality, more African-descended Americans converted as the eighteenth century turned to the nineteenth than in the previous two hundred years. And they made evangelical Christianity their own.

Christianity provided the slaves with at least three overlapping directions for pondering their identity. First, acceptance of the Gospel and receptivity to the Holy Sprit provided a path for transcending earthly woes, temporarily in this world and permanently in the hereafter. Jesus lent solace while furnishing a role model that endowed the slaves' suffering with meaning and assuring them ultimate redemption. Second, complementing the message of transcendence offered by the New Testament, the Old Testament provides rich illustrations of this-worldly deliverance in the personae of Daniel, David, Joshua, Moses, and Noah, and in ways that struck the imagination of the slaves (Levine 1997:78). No single story reverberated with black Americans' embodied experience and utopic vision more than that of Exodus, for it broke the equation between the African and the slave and proved that slavery completely opposes divine will.

Many African-American historians and theologians note that the slaves viewed the deliverance of Israel from Egypt as the "archetype of promise," a universal message, and the ultimate proof that God abhors slavery (e.g., Long 1997:30). Others interpret it as "the prototype of racial and nationalistic development" (e.g., Wilmore 1986:37), which made it ripe for appropriation by American blacks to articulate their own sense of peoplehood. It is difficult to determine if it is "appropriation," which implies strategizing, or "identification," which conveys emotional internalization, that best characterizes the relationship between African-American slaves' yearnings and the history of the biblical Israelites for, as Raboteau (1995:33–34) notes, "In the ecstasy of worship, time and distance collapsed, and the slaves *became* the children of Israel." This often forgotten and severed theme of African-American Christianity later became an important historical source for the Black Hebrews' identity assertions.

The third direction came from a rather obscure Old Testament line. Whereas Exodus captured African-Americans' imagination early on, it was not until the nineteenth century that the verse, "Princes shall come out of Egypt and Ethiopia shall soon stretch forth her hands unto God" (Psalms 68:31), began to circulate with regularity. The line is ambiguous and open to multiple interpretations, but one point is clear: Africa is not doomed to an eternity of depravity. African-Americans grasped this passage as a divine clue for recovering their past and reading their future.

Psalms 68:31 gave to American descendants of African slaves a sacred rejoinder to the dominant discourse of Africa's depraved status. Even white folks could not deny that Egypt, the site of the earliest world civilization, and Ethiopia, the land of King Solomon's consort, the Queen of Sheba, were located on the African continent. Nineteenth-century black Americans identified Ethiopia and Egypt metonymically with their own origins and pointed to these ancient civilizations as indicators of a glorious African past (Raboteau 1995:43).[6] In the twentieth century, these claims have been bolstered by the discovery of fossil evidence, pointing to East Africa as the cradle of *all* human evolution. Biblical verse and science converged once again, but now to refute evidence of Africa's deficiencies.

After Reconstruction, although slavery had ended, "oppression continued, even worsened, and black Americans read their future in Psalms 68:31" (Raboteau 1995:41). Some interpreted this verse as God's commandment for black Christians, who had carried the pain of exile and slavery for 244 years without knowing why, to go back to Africa and convert its people. In so doing, they would redeem their personal suffering and that of Africa, thereby opening the way for princes to come out of Egypt (see Becker 1997; Wilmore 1986, esp. chapter 5). In the 1920s, these themes were at the heart of Garveyism (Burkett 1978; Jenkins 1975) and in modified form reemerged in the 1960s, as central to the program of the African Hebrew Israelite Community.

A different but related version of this story developed within the apocalyptic-millenarian vision of evangelical Christianity. In simplified form, Egypt and Ethiopia are destined to rise again as great civilizations. A new age is quickly dawning, "continuous with a glorious African past accompanied by God's judgment of white society and Western civilization" (Fulop 1997:231). This future golden age will vindicate Africa; the racial order of things will be reversed, and blacks will be on top because of centuries of proven moral superiority. Millenarianism is a powerful charter in the AHIC, where it impels its constituents to educate Africans and African-Americans about their Hebraic origins and urges them to prepare in body and soul for God's judgment and the dawning of a new era.

By the end of the twentieth century, Africa had been reconstituted and reappropriated by African-Americans as both homeland and heritage in a variety of ways, but always as refracted through the lens of modernity. In an unceasing double-bind of acceptance-contestation of white discourse about the lowliness of their origins, blacks in the New World struggled—

and still struggle—to excavate from hegemonic political, scientific, and sacred texts knowledge and counterknowledge that refute the "darkness" of Africa. Competing and conjoining narratives circulate here, there, and back again to remind black Americans (as if they need reminders) that they and Africa are always vulnerable to what Cornel West (1990:26) designates as "the problematic of invisibility and namelessness" as the color line crosses and often blots out hybridity and creativity. Africa has become an overt factor in shaping black American identities, yet the link between Africa and Israel that had been expressed over the centuries through bodily experience, as well as in religious and ethical beliefs, remains open to doubt and under assault by blacks and whites alike. It is here that the African Hebrew Israelite Community ties together its bundle of discursive and programmatic strands to present as essential and enduring, while it also evaluates and amends, its vision for a recovered Africa.

Claiming the Pain, Making a Change

Black Judaic sects, which blend Christian messianic theology with claims for being the chosen descendants of biblical Israel, sprung up in urban America from at least the beginning of the twentieth century (Baer and Singer 1992; Brotz 1964; Chireau 2000; Fauset 1974), but they never challenged the prominence of Christianity or even rivaled Black Muslim groups. According to Ruth Landes (1967:176), "Judaism never became significant in the Negro life of the United States or elsewhere; and it has been hardly more than a curiosity to American (white) Jews. It has made no impact on social institutions or values, though it can matter in some personal lives." The African Hebrew Israelite Community is determined to change this order of things by spreading its message and implementing a return to Israel-as-Africa.

In the 1960s, at the height of the civil rights movement, when a broad array of black pride political and cultural organizations spread across America's urban landscape, the AHIC emerged from an older Hebraic group. In Chicago, the brothers and sisters of the community made manifest strands of discourse that over the centuries had linked the slaves to Israel while fashioning a distinctive form of dress that blends colorful African fabrics with the modesty laws of the Old Testament, and assuming Hebrew names. When peddling incense, oils, and jewelry on street corners—which later grew into restaurants and boutiques—they handed out leaflets and spread the message that the time had come for black people in America to return to Israel and claim their patrimony.

Although the community has changed and grown since then, it remains based on biblical passages that support the "bits and pieces of wisdom" about their origins and destiny carried northward in proverbs by older family members (Markowitz 1996:199–200; Singer 1985).[7] In intimate study groups about the Old Testament, the community's founders probed for the sources of these proverbs and reached the conclusion that the Bible is not only a sacred text but also the chronicle of a people—their people (Prince Gavriel Ha-Gadol 1993:80; cf. Crumbley 2000:15–16). These studies revealed that the Garden of Eden, where life first began, was physically located in Israel, which as both biblical references and geographical evidence indicate, has always extended south into Africa as one continuous landmass.[8] Thus, they concluded that the Hebrew patriarchs and their descendants were dark-skinned Africans.

"But what is history?" they asked as they delved further into the Bible. Noting that the text moves between chronicling events and predicting the future, the Black Hebrews determined that history encompasses prophecy and allegory as well as a linear chart of the past (cf. Harding 2000). Reading and interpreting the book of Deuteronomy from that perspective revealed their Hebraic origins and provided an explanation for why this knowledge had been concealed. Making explicit the once-hidden links between the(ir) historical experience as slaves in the New World and Old Testament predictions of what would befall Israel should its people disobey God, these insights enabled AHIC leaders to understand why African-Americans had been condemned to centuries of pain and namelessness. Most important of all, scriptural exegesis revealed to them a way to end the suffering and provided the key to a future of glory.

During 1998–99, Prince Asiel devoted several Sunday classes in the AHIC's Institute of Divine Understanding in Chicago to a discussion of Deuteronomy 28. In these verses God tells his chosen people of all the rewards that they will reap by following his commandments. But then He warns that should they disobey, they will be "only oppressed and crushed always," and scattered to the four corners of the earth. Once in exile they will "serve other gods . . . of wood and stone. And among these nations shalt thou find no ease" (Deut. 28:64–65). And if that is not punishment enough, the dispossessed people of Israel will be taken away by ships and sold to their enemies to serve forever as slaves (Deut. 28:68). After reading these passages, Prince Asiel stared hard at his audience and asked, "Who *but* our people fit this description?"

The answer is clear to those who have found their way into the community. The AHIC's promotional brochure explains that in the year 70 when the Romans destroyed the second temple in Jerusalem, the majority of the people of Israel fled south into the African continent to escape from the armies that invaded from the north. Over the years these Israelites spread westward across the continent, and in accordance with the prophecies, were swallowed up by other groups and embraced their gods of wood and stone. In the sixteenth century the Portuguese, to be followed by other Europeans, established the slave trade on Africa's West Coast. And there began what is referred to in the AHIC as the painful prophetic link between Israel-Africa and America that could not be severed unless and until the bereft Children of Israel took it upon themselves to study the Bible, rediscover their Hebrew origins, and live according to God's commandments.

In the 1960s, having put together these pieces of the puzzle to explain the futility of black people's endless struggle in America, Ben Ammi, the Black Hebrews' spiritual leader and putative messiah, decided that the time had come to begin anew and reverse his people's history of exile and suffering. Viewing America as the land of chastisement, the exilic equivalent of Egypt and Babylon, in 1967, Ben Ammi led an exodus of some 300 men, women, and children first to Liberia and then to Israel. Although more than half of the original members returned to the United States, the tiny group that settled in Dimona grew throughout the 1970s. As they established a presence through their unique self-governing residential communities in Israel's south, they also attracted attention from the international press and the government of Israel.

A key tenet of the AHIC, as with other black pride and black power groups, is that after centuries of being misplaced and misnamed in the white world, they hold and must assert the power to define themselves. Thus, the Hebrews consider their Africana clothing, vegan-vegetarian diet, "divine families,"[9] and syncretic worship style as direct expressions of their identity and testimony to their origins and mission. Others, however, might view these same characteristics more cynically as "invented traditions," borrowings, or syncretism. The State of Israel, for example, has never accepted the community as descendants of the biblical Israelites, mainly because the AHIC's teachings and practices transgress the boundaries of Judaism.[10] Yet despite denial of the right to settle in Israel under the Law of Return, hundreds of Black Hebrews continued to come from the United States using tourist visas which they allowed to lapse. Although illegal aliens, over the years the men and women of the AHIC became a "tolerated presence" in Israel (Dominguez 1989:178), residents of the land, but not citizens of the state.

After struggling for two decades on their own with no health, education, or welfare services from Israel, in the late 1980s, the AHIC staged a series of demonstrations. Dozens of adults renounced their "second class" American citizenship by marching en masse to the United States embassy in Tel Aviv, where they returned their passports and became stateless refugees who, according to international law, could not be deported. In the United States, the Hebrews rallied support from the Black Congressional Caucus, which paid off in financial assistance for building a school and offering a hot lunch program. Most significant of all is that in 1992, some 1500 long-term residents of the Negev received Israeli temporary residency status, and all the social services that come with that status. Eleven years later, these 1500 men and women were upgraded to permanent residents (see Markowitz, Helman, and Shir-Vertesh 2003).

Many of the Hebrew Israelite men and women with whom I conversed during the 1990s stressed that they joined their fate with the AHIC years ago when they were upwardly mobile college students.[11] Hearing Ben Ammi speak had a profound impact on them because his message about the chastisement of the (black) Children of Israel provided the only reasonable explanation for the sad and painful history of African-Americans and why they felt like "no-identity black Americans." Moreover, it also confirmed their lingering doubts about the effects of the civil rights movement and affirmative action programs: if America was the land of chastisement, improvement in the plight of black people there would never come about. And so they embraced the AHIC, left the United States, and came to Israel. But many more people, black and white, Jews and Christians, react with skepticism, amusement, or ridicule when they encounter the Black Hebrews.

The AHIC—without having read Foucault—learned from experience that the "power to define" is never absolute and has responded to its skeptics by canonizing its teachings. Ben Ammi has published a number of books in which his interpretations of biblical texts are presented as self-evident, and the community has "museumized" its knowledge by constructing the African/Edenic Heritage Museum, a photographic and textual exhibit that documents historical and geographic connections between Israel and Africa. But beyond the specific teachings and texts of the AHIC, which standing alone may constitute a vulnerable, subjugated knowledge system (Foucault 1980b:82), the community has added scientific and historical data from within the orbit of authorized, academic knowledge to its biblical hermeneutics and avidly collects newspaper and magazine articles that document cultural and genetic links between African peoples and the Jews. At the end of May 1999, Moriel, who heads the community's St. Louis extension, informed me that he had just read of a new genetic study that demonstrates a remarkable similarity between the DNA patterns of South Africa's Lemba and Ashkenazi *kohanim*.[12] When I remarked that surely everyone knows that all of us derive from the same source anyway, he smiled and retorted, "You and I know that, but others take a lot more convincing."

And so too did the Black Hebrews. In the 1960s and '70s, responding to the dictum "one people, one state" and the declared desire for their own "land, language and culture," the AHIC echoed the exclusivistic position of several black power movements and earlier Black Jewish sects that "the only true Jews were the blacks, and that white Jews were merely European offshoots of the original black African Hebrews" (Landes 1967:180). Over the years, as their status in Israel changed, the Black Hebrews softened their position from racial absolutism to one of pluralism, if not hybridity, and abandoned the claim that they were the only Original Hebrew Israelite Nation (see Markowitz, Helman, and Shir-Vertesh, 2003). Now they acknowledge that in the wake of the destruction of the temple in Jerusalem some Israelites fled northward into Europe and Asia, where they became the ancestors of today's Ashkenazi and Sephardic Jews. Since the late 1980s, the community has come to accept the sovereignty of the State of Israel and the right of *all* Jewish people to return to its land.

As he discussed these changes in the community's position, Prince Asiel took pride in noting the AHIC leadership's ability to take in new knowledge, ponder it, and move forward. "In 1968," he said, "we were young, we were radical, and no white was going to tell us who we were and what we could do. As we learned more we grew and we changed." Now in the Sunday classes he offers weekly in Chicago, Prince Asiel declares that after centuries of dispersal to the four corners of the earth, the Children of Israel are like a "speckled bird." The Black Hebrews, accordingly, are one branch of the Jewish family, but they are an extraordinary one for only they have fulfilled in its entirety the prophetic wisdom of the Bible. Thus, they hold a special place and bear a special message for black people, Israel, and the entire world.

The AHIC's leaders' reading of the Bible reveals that salvation awaits black people only in Israel-as-Africa. It is therefore the community's responsibility to teach the African diaspora to embrace Hebraic law, reconnect with their origins, break the curse of the past, and usher in a new era. Over thirty years have passed since they established a beachhead for the Kingdom of God in their Dimona residential community, but this small enclave is not nor can it be the end of the story. A huge task remains in bringing all the lost Children of Israel back into the fold, and the sisters and brothers of the AHIC know that this is a long and arduous process that is bound to confront setbacks along the way.

As a starting point, the community has established a presence in three American inner cities, where it offers healthy alternatives to their residents through "Soul Vegetarian" restaurants, health food stores and juice bars, "Afrika" boutiques, and regenerative wellness centers.[13] In Washington D.C., Prince Immanuel stressed that even in the nation's capital, where blacks on the average are better off economically than anywhere else in America, their life expectancy rates, especially for men, are shockingly low (54 years vs. the national average of 76). Pointing to the health food grocery store, restaurant, and holistic health center, he noted that although most will not find their way into the community, the AHIC's duty is to provide Africans-in-America with alternatives that can alleviate the awful conditions with which they have little choice but to contend.

Along with the institutions it operates in America, the AHIC has long been active in exploring business and repatriation opportunities in Africa, thereby documenting what they believe to be their diasporic route and the path of return. They had maintained a small commune and a health food business in Liberia from the late sixties until the military coup of the 1990s, when they moved their African center to Ghana. As we discussed the Ghanaian alternative, Ammi-Kam, executive assistant to Prince Asiel and a community leader in his own right, reminded me that

> Africa is the cradle of civilization, but Israel is the head of Africa. We see Israel as the home of that small chosen remnant, but not everybody wants to go there; for that they need an innate love of the land. Africa is a continent that's never really been developed . . . and it's time to utilize another [divine] structure of government there. We built this society in the Holy Land and it works for anybody, anytime. Africa needs a new breed of lead-

ership that can lead it in a new direction. People have energy and intellect; they just need the correct direction. We're going into the continent to start over again.[14]

Now, as in the nineteenth century, descendants of New World African slaves, having learned important lessons in diaspora, see themselves as returning to Africa with a message of hope and a blueprint for redemption.

Most people in the United States, however, do not give much credence to the Black Hebrews' teachings. Members of the community are philosophical about others' inability to see the truth of their origins and of their mission—after all, it had once eluded them as well. The oft-quoted passages from Deuteronomy, bolstered by mainstream historical evidence of how Europeans deceived and plundered Africa, may convince some blacks of their Hebraic origins and the divine reasons for their plight in the New World. But if it is hard enough to persuade African-Americans that their ancestors were Hebrews, the challenge only increases when facing a white audience, especially when that audience is Jewish.

After attending Sunday class, or just visiting the Soul Vegetarian restaurant in Chicago, I have often been asked, "Can you tell me why the white Jews don't accept us as Jews?" When I offer the *halakhic* (Jewish legal) explanation that they were born and raised as Christians and did not officially convert, I am frequently confronted with the anguished reply, "But we didn't know!" Brothers and sisters of the community then point to the Middle Passage and centuries of slavery. African Hebrews, they stress, were ripped from their traditions and then tossed willy-nilly among other peoples in the New World where they were demeaned, denied literacy, and force-fed Christianity. Recovery of once-lost knowledge is a great source of pride and so it comes as a painful blow when others, particularly Jews, refuse to recognize it as such.

The members of the AHIC were at first incredulous, and then hurt to be rejected by Israel, the people and place that they determined to be their own. Jews stress that their doubts of the Black Hebrews-as-Jews are supported because some of the community's teachings and practices are incompatible with the Jewish religion, especially their use of New Testament scriptures and acceptance of Yeshua ben Yosef (Jesus) and Ben Ammi as messiahs.[15] But due to a long history of being demeaned if not disregarded in America, the Black Hebrews may believe that their attempts to make African-Hebrew-black-Jewish hybridity visible through return are overshadowed and blocked by the color line. Since the AHIC has brought (white) Jews into their historical narrative and acknowledges them as legitimate partakers of Israel's legacy, they can only wonder why—beyond the answer of racism—this acceptance is not reciprocal.

The contrasting American experiences of asymmetrical race and egalitarian religion remain salient and immediate to the Black Hebrews no matter where they may be located. The painful history of racism persists in the present and makes them, as many black people in America, suspicious of being silenced and alert to rejection. But the egalitarian tradition of evangelical Christianity, which accepts one and all and authorizes anyone to preach the word of God (Dyson 1993:230), plays just as influential a role. Unlike the boundaries that confine Judaism to people born of Jewish mothers and rabbinically supervised converts, the AHIC is open to all whose "inner spirit" reveals that they are part of the Hebrew tradition. Ammi-Kam explains, "Hebrew culture and tradition are more than a written tradition. You have to feel who you are, then you look into it, and live it. Do, as the scriptures say, as does Abraham." The Black Hebrews, therefore, follow the egalitarian, anti-racist, individual salvation-oriented example of black Christian churches, while offering an alternative to it.

Religion and ethnicity, however, are different sorts of social categories, and belonging in America or in Israel and anywhere else is not based solely on self-definition or individual acts (see Borneman 1992). Ethnicity, as Emily Miller Budick (1998:3) notes, brings with it "certain ethical and historical responsibilities" which in multiethnic societies "makes inevitable conflict and competition for cultural materials and power" (see also Dunn 1998:19–30). Blacks and Jews both carry cruel and violent histories of pain that predate and overlap with their encounters in twentieth-century America, but their criteria for group membership differ. Jews define themselves as (the descendants of) the people chosen by God to receive and practice His law as revealed to them at Sinai. Black people have been defined as a racial group for centuries by white America's "one drop rule" that assigns any individual reputed to have African ancestry to the category "black," but they may define themselves through "soul," a quality of spirituality and style that while linked to color can also transcend it (see Gilroy 2000). Once tossed together, Blacks and Jews compared and contrasted, mutually constructed and changed each other, while at the same time they examined themselves and ultimately rebuilt or reconfirmed their own group narratives and imperatives.

At the end of the twentieth century, both agreed that the Jews, who in contemporary America have, overall, become white, mainstream, and prosperous (Brodkin 1997), and in Israel an economic and military power, bear little resemblance to the biblical Hebrews enslaved in Egypt or the ghettoized Jewish outcasts of Europe.[16] Nonetheless, Jews in America and Israel hold onto and invoke their centuries-long history of persecution and stay alert to anti-Semitism in the wake of the Holocaust. African-Americans, conversely, are racially marked and are still struggling to have their accomplishments, contributions, and their pain recognized as part of America's heritage and recorded in world history. They may therefore express frustration with and oppose "Jewish history as monopolizing certain tropes of enslavement and genocide, and perhaps privileging them" (Budick 1998:207; also Lerner and West 1995; Salzman and West 1997). Indeed, metaphorically, if not actually, African-Americans may feel that they are the "real Jews" after all.[17]

The Black Hebrews entered Israel from within this American context. Refusal of the Israeli state to grant them the biblically mandated courtesy to love "the stranger as you love yourself," to say nothing of their dashed expectations of a welcome back into the Jewish family, confirmed at least some AHIC brothers' and sisters' fears of racism, which in turn reinforced assertions of an essentialistic black identity that declared them to be the only "real Jews." However, after the initial years in which they attempted (unsuccessfully) to seize Israel's legacy, they have been struggling to dismantle the boundaries dividing Jewish identity claims and diasporic yearnings from their own and directing attention to their contributions to the Jewish "speckled bird." In so doing, the black essentialism, which just thirty years ago was so important for recovering and forging their identity, is now being proved false. In making their "return" to Israel—whether located in Africa's northeast, on Ghana's coast, or in the Soul Vegetarian restaurants of urban America—they defy the power of the white world to define the limitations of race, write African history and determine Africa's geography, name or un-name African-Americans, and steer the course of their future. Likewise, in laying claim to the pain of the violence done them in and by diaspora they piece together a contemporary culture that makes clear links to noble origins, while also highlighting in its multi-stranded hybridity its overlaps and blendings with other Africans, Jews, and Americans that are the necessary results of the dynamics of diaspora and return.

Finding the Past, Making the Future, and Ditching Diaspora?

In order to recover a valorized sense of identity that is recognized and accorded a place in the history of the world, black people in America were faced with the awesome task of first decoding and deconstructing, and then ultimately ditching—or at least redefining—their out of place placement as America's rightfully dispossessed underclass. As originally American as the Jamestown planters and the Massachusetts Pilgrims from England, slaves from Africa were objectified and dehumanized as they cultivated America's crops and served as the in-the-midst Other against which white Americans could constitute themselves as a culture, society, and polity. Ontological blackness, forged into law and reinforced by science and religion, was America's racial reality in the eighteenth, nineteenth, and a good part of the twentieth centuries. The binary of race overpowered the multiplicity of hybridity, and it took a late twentieth-century recasting of blackness as African diaspora to disrupt this order.

In working to recover their origins and culture, the brothers and sisters of the AHIC, like the first slaves who recorded their memoirs, have been restoring subjectivity to peoples of color by highlighting history's hybridities and the multiplicity of black thought and experience. Over the past several decades, they first pieced together and then solidified—while always amending—a master narrative to make their case, and a culture and lifestyle to support it. The AHIC thereby offers a solution to the displacements of diaspora and a promise to revoke the pain that these have caused.

In over thirty years of their existence, the Black Hebrews have claimed the pain as their own. Working through the concept of Christian redemptive suffering on their bodies and in their souls, they converted it from a silent motif of endurance to the impetus for cultural regeneration and self-growth. It is at the heart of their social program and served as the impetus to impel once apathetic or politically radical black brothers and sisters to (re)turn to the Old Testament, find their origins and the key to a future better than the past. Imbuing slavery with positive meaning, and linking that experience to a people whose history is told in the most sacred of texts, enables once "no-identity blacks" to move what had been their shadowy existence into the center of world history. The AHIC's "return" to Israel, their mission in Ghana, and their extensions in major U.S. cities are designed to awaken African Hebrews, who through no fault of their own "don't know" their heritage, and push them to move "beyond"—to what might be when hybridity becomes visible, disrupts, and even overpowers race and the boundaries that set apart nation-states (Bhabha 1994; Gilroy 2000).

It is here that I shall falsely end this story, poised on the verge of utopic realization,[18] where "the 'return,'" as Radhakrishnan (1996:166) reminds us, "takes the form of a cure, or remedy for the present ills of postcoloniality." But if culture is an ever-changing constant, the "return"—even if physically performed—can never be total and has no end. Thus, I will leave the African Hebrew Israelite Community in the present continuous as a transnational black diasporic *and* returning society-in-the-making, still struggling to make its claims for hybridity visible, while pushing against either/or ethnoracial categories, and trying to perfect, while constantly amending, its always authentic but never static culture.

NOTES

Acknowledgments: I am grateful to all the brothers and sisters of the African Hebrew Israelite Community in Israel and in the States, and especially to Prince Asiel, Crown Sister Yoanna, and Brother Ammi-Kam who hosted me in Chicago, and to Prince Rahm who arranged my visit to the Atlanta extension and to Prince Immanuel for his hospitality in Washington, D.C. Funding for this study was provided by the US-Israel Binational Science Foundation.

This chapter is a revised version of "Claiming the Pain, Making a Change: The African Hebrew Israelite Community's Alternative to the Black Diaspora" in *Homelands and Diasporas, Holy Lands and Other Places*, edited by André Levy and Alex Weingrod, (c) 2005 Board of Trustees of Leland Stanford Jr. University, by permission of the publisher.

1. Of course, "African-American" never completely replaced "black," and these terms are often used interchangeably.

2. This is the euphemism for the transport of millions of men and women chained one behind the other in the dank hulls of slave ships, from the West Coast of Africa to America's shores. Estimates of the deaths incurred at sea range from a conservative 10 million to upward of 50–100 million (Davidson 1961:80–81).

3. Earlier voices, most notably W.E.B. Du Bois, Ralph Ellison, and Harold Cruse, called for recognition of the multiplicity of experience, identity, and culture among African-Americans but were met by doubtful, even hostile audiences.

4. This story is told weekly in Sunday classes offered by the AHIC in several American cities and in written form in the books of the community's leaders. See

especially Ben Ammi 1990, Prince Gabriel Ha-Gadol 1993, and the third section of this essay.

5. Other better known directions that this story has taken have been the formation of black churches in the nineteenth century; the twentieth-century developments of pan-Africanism, black nationalism, and scholarly Afrocentrism; Ethiopianism and Rastafarianism, and the Nation of Islam. Marcus Garvey's Universal Negro Improvement Association (UNIA) is often pointed to as the model for other back-to-Africa movements, including that of the African Hebrew Israelite Community.

6. Twentieth-century elaborations of this line would develop into Garveyism and then Rastafarianism and Afrocentrism—all "isms" with definite social programs that emerged from the dynamics of diaspora (Burkett 1978; Howe 1998; Nelson 1994; Smith 1994:65–66).

7. These, like "A small black nation is rising in the east," and "Black people in America are the Children of Israel," are in all probability folk renditions of Psalms 68:31 and the story of Exodus.

8. The promised land of Israel was to have extended from the Tigris and Euphrates Rivers in the north to the source of the Nile in the south and was one land bridge linking Africa to Asia until white Europeans built the Suez Canal in the nineteenth century. See also Mazrui's (1986:29–38) critical analysis of the geography of Africa.

9. Pointing to the marriage arrangements of the patriarchs as well as most African societies, the AHIC condones polygynous marriages, but rejects that term. See Haraymiel Ben Shaleak (n.d.).

10. All of Ben Ammi's books as well as contents of Sunday classes and worship services liberally mix quotations from the New Testament with those of the Old. Furthermore, the rabbinate rejects the claim of the AHIC that Ben Ammi is the(ir) messiah—the latest in the chain of personages from Moses to David to Jesus, who arose to lead the Hebrews from troubles to glory (see Ben Ammi 1994).

11. Since my introduction to the Dimona community in late 1992, I have been meeting over the years with several Hebrew Israelites and attending yearly festivals. I spent the 1998–99 academic year studying the community in Chicago and visiting its branches in Washington, D.C. and Atlanta. See Markowitz 2002 for a discussion of the insider/outsider dilemmas of this fieldwork.

12. The *kohanim* in biblical days were the priests of the temple. Today, though still a Jewish descent group, their ritual functions have been curtailed. In the Black Hebrew Community the kohanim, or priests, mete out spiritual guidance and oversee life passage rituals.

13. The AHIC is institutionally complete in Chicago, Atlanta, and Washington, D.C. It has smaller outreach missions in several other cities.

14. Moreover, Israel certainly does not want hundreds of Black Hebrews to come and settle in Dimona. The Ghana alternative was developed as the AHIC

agreed with the State of Israel to limit, if not end completely, its *aliya* [immigration to Israel].

15. See note 10 and Ben Ammi 1994. In the early 1970s when the first small group of Hebrew men and women arrived in Israel and began studying for official conversion, Ben Ammi ordered them to stop, insisting on the power to define.

16. Of course, because of German racial categorization in the twentieth century, as well as the longue durée of Jewish history (among other reasons), not all Jews accept this felicitous redefinition (see, for example, Azoulay 1997:57–60; Brodkin 1997:182–187; Sunderland 1997).

17. Budick (1998) contends that there is a supercessionist tendency in Black American literature for African-Americans to replace Jews altogether as *the* symbol of exile and homelessness. She links this tendency to Christianity, which teaches that the New Testament supersedes the Old, and that Christian redemptive suffering cancels out the Jewish pain of survival.

18. As does the Chumash, or Pentateuch, of the Old Testament.

REFERENCES CITED

Anderson, Victor
1995. *Beyond Ontological Blackness.* New York: Continuum.
Azoulay, Katya Gibel
1997. *Black, Jewish, and Interracial.* Durham: Duke University Press.
Baer, Hans and Merrill Singer
1992. *African-American Religion in the Twentieth Century: Varieties of Protest and Accommodation.* Knoxville: University of Tennessee Press.
Becker, William H.
1997. "The Black Church: Manhood and Mission." In *African-American Religion,* Timothy E. Fulop and Albert J. Raboteau, eds. Pp. 177–199. New York: Routledge.
Ben Ammi
1990. *God, the Black Man, and Truth,* 2d rev. ed. Washington, DC: Communicators Press.
Ben Ammi
1994. *Yeshua the Hebrew Messiah, or Jesus the Christian Christ?* Washington, DC: Communicators Press.
Ben-Yehuda, Shaleak
1975. *Black Hebrew Israelites: From America to the Promised Land.* New York: Vantage Press.
Bhabha, Homi
1994. *The Location of Culture.* London: Routledge.
Borneman, John
1992. *Belonging in the Two Berlins.* Cambridge: Cambridge University Press.

Brah, Avtar

1996. *Cartographies of Diaspora: Contesting Identities*. London: Routledge.

Brodkin, Karen

1997. *How Jews Became White Folks & What That Says About Race in America*. New Brunswick, NJ: Rutgers University Press.

Brotz, Howard

1964. *The Black Jews of Harlem*. The Free Press.

Budick, Emily Miller

1998. *Blacks and Jews in Literary Conversation*. Cambridge: Cambridge University Press.

Burkett, Randall K.

1978. *Garveyism as a Religious Movement*. Metuchen, NJ: Scarecrow Press.

Chireau, Yvonne

2000. "Black Culture and Black Zion: African American Religious Encounters with Judaism, 1790–1930." In *Black Zion: African American Religious Encounters with Judaism*, Yvonne Chireau and Nathaniel Deutsch, eds. Pp. 15–32. New York: Oxford University Press.

Clifford, James

1994. "Diasporas." *Cultural Anthropology* 9(3):302–338.

Cohen, Robin

1997. *Global Diasporas: An Introduction*. Seattle: University of Washington Press.

Crumbley, Deidre Helen

2000. "Also Chosen: Jews in the Imagination and Life of a Black Sanctified Church." *Anthropology and Humanism* 25(1):6–23.

Davidson, Basil

1961. *The African Slave Trade: Precolonial History 1450–1850*. Boston: Little, Brown and Company.

Dominguez, Virginia R.

1989. *People as Subjects, People as Objects*. Madison: University of Wisconsin Press.

Dominguez, Virginia R.

1997. *White by Definition*, 2nd edition. New Brunswick: Rutgers University Press.

Du Bois, W. E. B.

1939 [1903]. *The Souls of Black Folk*. New York: Henry Holt.

Dunn, Robert G.

1998. *Identity Crises: A Social Critique of Postmodernity*. Minneapolis: University of Minnesota Press.

Dyson, Michael Eric

1993. *Reflecting Black: African-American Cultural Criticism*. Minneapolis: University of Minnesota Press.

Fauset, Arthur Huff

1974. *Black Gods of the Metropolis*. New York: Octagon Books [orig. 1944, University of Pennsylvania Press].

Foucault, Michel

1980a. *The History of Sexuality*. Vol. 1. New York: Pantheon.

Foucault, Michel

1980b. *Power/Knowledge: Selected Interviews and Other Writings, 1972–77*, Colin Gordon, ed. New York: Pantheon.

Fulop, Timothy E.

1997. "The Future Golden Day of the Race:" Millennialism and Black Americans in the Nadir, 1877–1901. In *African-American Religion*, Timothy E. Fulop and Albert J. Raboteau, eds. Pp. 227–254. New York: Routledge.

Gerber, Israel

1977. *The Heritage Seekers: American Blacks in Search of Jewish Identity*. Middle Village NY: Jonathan David.

Gilroy, Paul

1993. *The Black Atlantic: Modernity and Double Consciousness*. Cambridge, MA: Harvard University Press.

Gilroy, Paul

2000. *Against Race: Imagining Political Culture Beyond the Color Line*. Cambridge, MA: Harvard University Press.

Goldberg, David Theo

1997. *Racial Subjects: Writing on Race in America*. New York: Routledge.

Hall, Stuart

1995. "Negotiating Caribbean Identities." *New Left Review* 209.

Haraymiel Ben Shaleak

n.d. *The Holy Art of Divine Marriage*. N.p. Global Images International Press.

Harding, Susan F.

2000. *The Book of Jerry Falwell: Fundamentalist Language and Politics*. Princeton: Princeton Umiversity Press.

Herskovits, Melville J.

1941. *The Myth of the Negro Past*. New York: Beacon.

hooks, bell

1990. *Yearning: Race, Gender, and Cultural Politics*. Boston: South End.

Howe, Stephen

1998. *Afrocentrism: Mythical Pasts and Imagined Homes*. London: Verso.

Jenkins, David

1975. *Black Zion: The Return of Afro-Americans and West Indians to Africa*. London: Wildwood House.

Kawash, Samira

1997. *Dislocating the Color-Line: Identity, Hybridity, and Singularity in African-American Literature*. Stanford: Stanford University Press.

Landes, Ruth

1967. "Negro Jews in Harlem." *Jewish Journal of Sociology* 9(2):175–189.

Lerner, Michael, and Cornel West

1995. *Jews and Blacks: Let the Healing Begin*. New York: G. P. Putnam's Sons.

Levine, Lawrence W.

1997. "Slave Songs and Slave Consciousness: An Exploration in Neglected Sources." In *African-American Religion*, Timothy E. Fulop and Albert J. Raboteau, eds. Pp. 58–87. New York: Routledge.

Long, Charles H.

1997. "Perspectives for a Study of African-American Religion in the United States." In *African-American Religion*, Timothy E. Fulop and Albert J. Raboteau, eds. Pp. 22–35. New York: Routledge.

Markowitz, Fran

1996. "Israel as Africa, Africa as Israel: 'Divine Geography' in the Personal Narratives and Community Identity of the Black Hebrew Israelites." *Anthropological Quarterly* 69(4):193–205.

Markowitz, Fran

2002. "Creating Coalitions and Causing Conflicts: Confronting Race and Gender through Partnered Ethnography." *Ethnos* 67(2):201–222.

Markowitz, Fran, Sara Helman, and Dafna Shir-Vertesh

2003. "Soul Citizenship: The Black Hebrews and the State of Israel." *American Anthropologist* 105(2):302–312.

Mazrui, Ali A.

1986. *The Africans: A Triple Heritage*. Boston: Little, Brown & Co.

Mercer, Kobena

1990. "Black Hair/Style Politics." In *Out There: Marginalization and Contemporary Cultures*, Russell Ferguson, Martha Gever, Trinh T. Minh-ha, and Cornel West, eds. Pp. 247–264. Cambridge, MA: New Museum of Contemporary Art and MIT Press.

Nelson, Gersham A.

1994. "Rastafarians and Ethiopianism." In *Imagining Home: Class, Culture and Nationalism in the African Diaspora*, Sidney J. Lemelle and Robin D. G. Kelley, eds. Pp. 66–84. London: Verso.

Price, Richard

1983. *First Time*. Baltimore: Johns Hopkins University Press.

Prince Gavriel Ha-Gadol and Odehyah B. Israel. 1993. *The Impregnable People: An Exodus of African Americans back to Africa*. Washington, D.C.: Communicators Press.

Raboteau, Albert J.

1995. *A Fire in the Bones: Reflections on African-American Religious History*. Boston: Beacon Press.

Raboteau, Albert J.

1997. "The Black Experience in American Evangelism: The Meaning of Slavery." In *African-American Religion*, Timothy E. Fulop and Albert J. Raboteau, eds. Pp. 89–106. New York: Routledge.

Radhakrishnan, R.

1996. *Diasporic Mediations: Between Home and Location*. Minneapolis: University of Minnesota Press.

Safran, William

1991. "Diasporas in Modern Societies: Myths of Homeland and Return." *Diaspora* 1(1):83–99.

Salzman, Jack, and Cornel West, eds.

1997. *Struggles in the Promised Land: Toward a History of Black-Jewish Relations in the United States*. New York: Oxford University Press.

Scott, David

1991. "That Event, This Memory: Notes on the Anthropology of African Diasporas in the New World." *Diaspora* 1(3):261–284.

Singer, Merrill

1979. "Saints of the Kingdom: Group Emergence, Individual Affiliation, and Social Change among the Black Hebrews of Israel." Ph.D. dissertation, University of Utah.

Singer, Merrill

1985. "'Now I Know What the Songs Mean!': Traditional Black Music in a Contemporary Black Sect." *Southern Quarterly* 23 (3):125–140.

Sivanandan, A.

1970. "Culture and Identity." *The Liberator* 10 (6).

Smith, Theophus H.

1994. *Conjuring Culture: Biblical Formations of Black America*. New York: Oxford University Press.

Stratton, Jon

1997. "(Dis)placing the Jews: Historicizing the Idea of Diaspora." *Diaspora* 6(3):301–329.

Sunderland, P. L.

1997. "'You May Not Know It, But I'm Black': White Women's Self-Identification as Black." *Ethnos* 62(1–2):32–58.

Thomas, Laurence Mordekhai

1993. *Vessels of Evil: American Slavery and the Holocaust*. Philadelphia: Temple University Press.

Torres, Arlene, and Norman Whitten

1998. "General Introduction: To Forge the Future in the Fires of the Past: An Interpretive Essay on Racism, Domination, Resistance and Liberation." In *Blackness in Latin America and the Caribbean*. 2 vols. Arlene Torres and Norman Whitten, Jr., eds. Pp. 3–33. Bloomington: Indiana University Press.

West, Cornel

1990. "The New Cultural Politics of Difference." In *Out There: Marginalization and Contemporary Cultures*, Russell Ferguson, Martha Gever, Trinh T. Minh-ha, and

Cornel West, eds. Pp. 19–36. Cambridge, MA: New Museum of Contemporary Art and MIT Press.

Williams, Brackette
1989. "A Class Act: Anthropology and the Race to Nation Across Ethnic Terrain." *Annual Review of Anthropology* 18:401–444.

Wilmore, Gayrand S.
1986. *Black Religion and Black Radicalism*, 2nd edition. Maryknoll, MD: Orbis Books.

Young, Robert J. C.
1995. *Colonial Desire: Hybridity in Theory, Culture and Race*. New York: Routledge.

7

Spatial Responses of the African Diaspora in Jamaica

Focus on Rastafarian Architecture

Elizabeth Pigou-Dennis

Space and Architecture

From the human point of view, the word *space* encompasses all phenomena from the body to the cosmos. *Social space*, a concept I have developed in an earlier work, may be visualized as a series of concentric spaces which contain each other.[1] The outermost space would be *natural space*, which in turn "contains" *urban or collective space*; the next is *public or institutional space*; and the final, interior space consists of *private or domestic space*.[2] These spaces should not be envisaged as self-contained; rather, they connect with each other. Natural space offers the most general perspective of human organization, private space offers the most fine-tuned perspective.

A human being develops an identity and lives out a lifespan in orientation or relationship to self, others, and nature in each of these concentric "layers" of "reality." The word *reality* is here used in a very wide sense—to include not only what is physically or "objectively" present, but also all aspects of human perception and visualization. On each layer of experience highly significant human transactions take place, and such transactions are made possible in large measure by the instrumentality of *architecture*. Architecture also encodes the meanings of these transactions.[3]

What Is Architecture?

Architecture may be defined as what humans *build*, as opposed to what humans find as "given" in nature, especially on the earth. Yet, in important ways, architecture is also about what is not built. This "not built" aspect occurs on several levels. In the first place, very little of the planet's natural space has escaped human contact. Even without actually building, natural space is modified in human perception, re-created by human thought. This mental or spiritual response to space, which is the beginning of the notion of *place*,[4] is also the initial step toward built architecture. On a second level, where conceptualization begins to take on physical qualities, the mere act of walking across an "empty" or open space has the potential to inscribe an architecture, for certain essential aspects of architecture—path, axis, and connected points[5] have been established. The framing or bounding of such paths and points with built structure constitutes built architecture. Such framing may be rudimentary in architectonic terms, or it may be highly sophisticated and of very durable materials. As far as the capacity to transmit meaning is concerned, there is not necessarily any difference between the rudimentary and the complicated in form. Neither is the "unbuilt" necessarily any less meaningful than the built.[6] In a third way, elements which may not be regarded as structural parts of the "built" object may be highly meaningful—for example, applied ornament or iconography.[7] And finally, the webs of social interaction which occur in and between built structures constitute highly significant loci of meaning—of course, without people, the whole notion of meaning evaporates.[8]

It is interesting to note that the early twentieth-century Functionalist or Modernist architects of Europe and North America went to great lengths to deny the "function" of architecture in terms of transmitting and creating meaning.[9] Rather, they concentrated on the mechanical aspects of function, such as providing shelter or having a logical, readable structural system. In fact, there is no such thing as purely functionalist architecture—even the focus on function is itself a choice in terms of meaning. So, the position taken here is that architecture facilitates, encodes, and transmits meanings concerning human transactions, and that these transactions of necessity take place in a multilayered space, from the personal, individual body to the widest reaches of the cosmos, while encompassing both physical and metaphysical zones of experience.

What Is the African Diaspora?

The *Oxford Dictionary* defines *diaspora* as the Jewish dispersion. A number of dictionaries retain this narrow definition.[10] The Merriam-Webster's online dictionary gives the first meaning as a Jewish experience, with a second meaning of "the breaking up and scattering of a people," as well as migration from an ancestral homeland.[11] The term, in this context, in relation to people of African descent, carries the connotation that even when an ethnic/cultural/religious group has been dispersed from an original source, there is still an underlying unity in identity. During the twentieth century, Marcus Garvey played a pivotal role, from as early as the 1920s, in sensitizing peoples of African descent, on the African continent, in Europe, and the Americas to the notion of a common identity. The American Civil Rights Movement of the 1960s, the Black Power Movement of the 1970s, Alex Haley's *Roots*, the notion of "Afrocentricity," and the international popularity of Reggae music have all contibuted to the greater consciousness among African-American and African-Caribbean persons, and others of the African Diaspora, that somehow, the prefix *African* has the potential to override the distinctions of nationality or social class.[12]

The African-Jamaican Diaspora: Traces of a Personal History

Traditionally, the discipline of history has claimed its authority, via footnotes, from dusty old documents and manuscripts enshrined in archives and libraries and citations from scholarly precedents. Here I break with that tradition, making incursions to sources that cannot be traced to archives, but exist in personal memory. These memories are powerful tools for conveying a significant theme in the experiences of the African Diaspora in Jamaica.

The first memory is of a conversation with my maternal grandfather during the very early 1970s. He would have been in his very late eighties. He was a robust man, who looked much younger than his actual age, with a sharp mind. He was unmistakably African-Jamaican in physical appearance. One day I asked him if any of his ancestors had been slaves. When I asked the question, I already knew that he must have had ancestors who were slaves, but what my childish mind was trying to get at were stories that might have been handed down about plantation life. To my surprise, he became very annoyed and adamantly denied that he was black. He announced that he was of Scottish and French ancestry. He went so far as to roll up his pants leg to his knee to disclose a slightly lighter hue of skin, and he told me that he only looked black because of his exposure to the sun in his farming days. My feelings were complex. Part of me was quite old enough to know what was going on—to understand the denial of African ancestry and the claim on Europe. But another part of me was puzzled, and taken aback, at the extent one would go to deny what seemed objectively obvious.

Another memory is of school days in the 1960s and 1970s. Very frequently, during break times or recess, among groups of schoolgirls, conversations concerning racial ancestry would come up. Girls would disclose elaborate computations which calculated the percentages of English, Scottish, or Irish ancestry, with scant attention paid to African. There seemed to be some sort of contest on to prove who had the most European percentage. Now the whole necessity of such calculations arose from the fact that in appearance, these girls were all evidently mixed. What is significant is the emphasis given to European elements of that mixture, and the denial of the African.

A final memory concerns a cousin, of quite light complexion and long brown hair, who in the 1970s, at the height of the Black is Beautiful Movement, decided to cut her tresses and sport an Afro hairdo instead. That action precipitated a family crisis and provoked discussion and exclamations of shock for months. Relatives could not understand why she had decided to "spoil" her beautiful hair.

I cite these memories because they potently convey what is meant by the words "disjunction" or "dislocation" in terms of African Diaspora experience. Bearing in mind how we defined space at the outset of this chapter, it becomes evident that the spatial experience of African Jamaicans begins with the individual body. It often involves the denial of oneself, one's colour, one's ancestry, and one's history, and purposeful memory loss. It involves not only the remaking of family trees, but also the redrawing of the world map. The dislocated, disjunctive geography reduces the physical size of the African continent. Europe, by contrast, is drawn overlarge.

Martinican writer Edouard Glissant has written extensively on the disjunctive nature of the African-Caribbean experience. He poses the question: "Would it be ridiculous to consider our lived history as a steadily advancing neurosis?"[13] In light of the memories cited above, it would not be considered ridiculous at all. The fact is, the cultural and political imperatives of slavery and colonialism have created behavior which can be labeled neurotic—possibly even psychotic. A peculiar type of neurosis of the Diaspora, which has made black persons look in the mirror and see white and made school children obliterate Africa from the planet. If one does not choose words like neurosis or psychosis to describe these behaviors, then at the least what is evident is a tremendous human capacity to impose the subjective over the objective. To cite Glissant further: "The . . . Caribbean is the site of a history characterized by ruptures that began with a brutal dislocation, the slave trade."[14] What he calls "the dislocation of the continuum" has led to the "inability of the collective consciousness to absorb it all . . . [this characterize[s] what I call a nonhistory." This "non-history" is "the erasing of the collective memory."[15] No more apt examples of this rupture and loss of collective memory—this nonhistory—could be found than my grandfather and my schoolmates in our early years.

Rastafarian Architecture and Caribbean Architectural Discourse

It is in the context of this powerful impetus in Jamaican experience to obliterate Africa and African ancestry, that the focus of this chapter—Rastafarian spatial concepts and architecture—must be considered. For the Rastafarian is the polar opposite of someone like my grandfather. The Rastafarian critiques one's orientation to Europe and reconstitutes and reclaims one's orientation to Africa. But it must be stressed at the outset that this process is not simply one of direct memory or duplication of ancestral forms or practice. It is a reclamation that is largely metaphysical, and mythical, requiring creativity and invention, and is wholly shaped by the Diaspora experience—embodying as it does the disjunctures of the slavery experience. Although the impetus to deny or forget Africa has been strong in Jamaica's history, the counterimpetus to reclaim Africa has also been a potent force of protest. Rastafarian metaphysics can be traced to the early slave experiences, where, it is recorded, enslaved Africans believed that the soul would return to Africa at death. So potent was this belief, that many committed suicide to hasten their return.[16] Rastafarianism thus continues the "return to Africa" theme which has a long history in Jamaican experience, and architectural iconography plays an instrumental role in this "return" or reclamation, which has both physical and objective connotations in terms of repatriation, as well as the metaphysical meanings discussed in this chapter.

The notion of Rastafarian space is something of a novelty in the architectural discourse of the Caribbean. Space in this chapter does not allow a very detailed treatment of the architectural historiography of the Caribbean. However, the overwhelming absence of this subject in the literature may be linked to three reasons. First, there is the overall tendency in the colonial Caribbean to focus on cultural products of Europe, rather than of Africa. Second, there is the low status of Rastafarians in Jamaican society ever since their emergence in the 1930s.[17] And third, there is the low status of the *shack*—which is one of the major modes of Rastafarian architectural expression.[18] In fact, shacks are often forcibly removed from sidewalks and lots. But it will be sufficient to point out that architectural discourse that relates specifically to Jamaica during the twentieth century is coming from a position of orientation toward European precedents and derivations. Thus, Webster, writing in the 1930s, totally disregarded African-derived or "folk" elements in local architecture.[19] McKay, in his memoirs, relates how rural Jamaicans in the early twentieth century, in their quest for upward social mobility, readily abandoned building materials and forms which suggested poverty.[20] Yet, it was these very forms which may have been closest to African precedent. McKay also discloses the fascination with things English, European, and North American in material culture. So powerful has been the influence of things and ideas European that in Haiti today, architectural professionals still refer to their traditional nineteenth-century architecture as "Victorian."[21] This notwithstanding the fact that Haiti was the first independent African-Caribbean nation in the western hemisphere, or that these buildings display some very Haitian interpretations of European precedent. European nomenclature abounds, even in recent studies.[22] Among those writers who have chosen to give credence to the African contributions to Caribbean architecture, there are problems in terms of physical and written evidence of distinctively African or African-derived elements. Green and Voorthuis have argued for a combination of European design with African decorative motifs, but without the provision of hard evidence of the latter.[23] Two studies which have gone the furthest in analyzing African-Caribbean architecture are by Berthelot and Gaume of the French West Indian *kaz* or hut,[24] and Higman's archaeological investigation of Montpelier, Jamaica.[25]

Berthelot and Gaume argue that while discernible African-derived elements do exist in the kaz, these elements always occur in conjunction with European or colonial elements and are outnumbered by the latter two.[26] Higman stressed the difficulties of accurate analysis, given the perishable nature of much slave and post-slavery peasant architecture. The most novel elements he found were two examples of masonry platforms that were reminiscent of Ibibio and Ekoi sleeping platforms.[27] Of the published works on Caribbean or Jamaican architecture, only one exists which deals with the issue of Rastafarianism. This 1999 article by Taylor and Jones of the Caribbean School of Architecture investigates several examples of

Rastafarian layouts in communal dwelling settings, and expressions of Rasta belief in the houses of two Rastafarian men.[28] This study marks a transition in the discourse on Jamaican architecture; however, it is largely descriptive, with little or no overt theoretical input. The major Rastafarian elements described by Taylor and Jones include the typical red, gold, and green colour scheme, emblems of Haile Selassie—late Emperor of Ethiopia—layouts which suggested communal dwelling, and symbols which derived from readings of traditional biblical texts. Also, because of the notions of Repatriation to Africa, materials tend to be impermanent, and because of the tendency to separate themselves from the wider society, construction is of a "do-it-yourself" nature.[29]

From the work of Berthelot and Gaume and Higman, it is possible to draw up a list of the usual African-derived elements in Caribbean architecture. These include:

1. Gable-end entries and gable-end decoration
2. Steeply pitched roofs
3. Timber frame construction methods
4. Preference for solid window shutters
5. Possible yard/compound layouts in villages
6. Possible sleeping platforms

Green argues for the techniques and motifs of fretwork designs being African in origin.[30] Butler, after an exhaustive study, found it difficult to conclude whether these designs were African, European, or local in origin, for the simple reason that abstract designs tend to be quite similar from one culture to another.[31] It is important to bear these "African" elements in mind during the discussion of specifically Rastafarian architecture—for the theme of reinventing memory will be a powerful one.

Rastafarian Space and Architecture

First, it is worthwhile to briefly summarize Rastafarian beliefs. This is a complex subject and cannot be entirely addressed here, as there are a number of distinct Rasta sects such as the Nyabingi, Bobo Shanti, Orthodox, and Twelve Tribes of Israel. There are also many Rastas who claim no official affiliations and maintain their unique constellations of belief. It is useful to have Rasta beliefs expressed in the words of a Rastafarian architect, Najeeb Campbell, a Jamaican, now based in a Miami practice.

A Rastafarian is a person that knows in their heart the importance of the Ethiopian Empire as the heart and soul of what we now know as the African continent. Ethiopia and Egypt are the most mentioned nations throughout the Bible and ever since 1000 B.C. Ethiopia followed the Judaic faith and the emperors and royal family of Ethopia have descended directly from the lineage of King David and Solomon. Ethiopia also has the rightful claim to be the very first Christian nation supported by the historical account of the baptism of the Ethiopian Eunuch, a high official in the court of Queen Candace, by the Apostle Phillip [as recorded] in the Book of Acts in the Bible. Egypt, being the second recipient of Christian faith firmly entrenches the foundation of Christianity as integrally African, not European, as the world has been led to believe.

The existence of this ancient church of Christianity was hidden from the world until the coronation of His Imperial Majesty Haile Selassie I in 1930. The modern world was both shocked and intrigued by the ascendancy of a black African Emperor, directly descended from the line of David, to an ancient Judaeo-Christian throne. . . . Many in Jamaica who knew the importance of Ethiopia saw in the coronation a bright future for the African diaspora in the western hemisphere. Many hailed the Emperor as their saviour and hastily requested through continual correspondence to the Ethiopian government that a branch of the Ethiopian Orthodox Church be sent to Jamaica, as the black majority on the island had never been provided with a church from their own motherland and culture. This was successfully accomplished [with the incorporation of the church] in 1970.[32]

Other aspects of Rastafarian belief, not directly mentioned by Campbell, include the desire to be repatriated to Ethiopia/Africa, and the identification of Rastafarians as one of the tribes of Israel, at present suffering captivity in "Babylon," which signifies the sociopolitical systems of the world, which are perceived as being controlled by whites.[33]

The Rastafarian is thus one who is highly conscious of being a part of a literal Diaspora, of being spatially separated from an ancestral base and a spiritual centre. Disjuncture and fragmentation are critical elements of Rastafarian thought. In the Jamaican context, it is not through literary treatises that these ideas are most often expressed. At the popular level, at the street level literally, the Rastafarian message is powerfully articulated via thousands of roadside shacks and stalls, through architectural iconography. The common emblems are the red, gold and green colours of the Ethiopian flag—either painted on to the structures and/or flown as flags.

Also, the Lion of Judah—a lion with a sceptre in its right paw—a symbol of Selassie; portraits of Selassie himself, portraits of Marcus Garvey, and sometimes portraits of Bob Marley. Graffitti or captions also constitute a potent element of these designs, and may proclaim the rule of Selassie, quote biblical passages, or give the shack a name, such as "African Princess."

To be sure, these elements vary from the African-derived architectural features listed by Berthelot and Gaume and Higman which were discussed above.[34] Neither do the structures resemble traditional Ethiopian architecture.[35] But to dismiss these features on those two accounts would be to miss a wealth of meaning. There are certain well-established "codes" in terms of how architecture is analyzed.[36] Analysis may encompass any or all elements such as:

1. site
2. paths
3. boundaries
4. margins
5. axes
6. openings
7. materials
8. structure
9. services
10. decorative elements
11. symbolism
12. "style"
13. builders/architects
14. occupants

For the purposes of this chapter, we will examine a single shack in the Barbican neighbourhood of Kingston, Jamaica. This shack belongs to a Rastafarian brother by the name of Derek. The accompanying illustrations will show details of the site and Derek's shack.

SITE

Derek's shack is located on an open lot to which none of the occupants have legal tenure. The occupants are all Rastafarian vendors who live in the nearby ghetto. The lot of land is bordered on the east by a storm-water runoff trench called a "gully," and on the south by a main road, and on the

Barbican site.

north by the ghetto settlement. The site consists of many shade trees and shrubs, as well as unpaved earth. It is a very pedestrian-oriented site, with many persons stopping to buy small items—mostly food, drink, and cigarettes—from the vendors. At all times in the day, and late at night, small groups of persons may be seen gathered under the shade trees conversing or relaxing. The immediate surroundings of the site consist of established supermarkets and stores, a service station, and middle- and upper-class residences may be reached via the main road, a short distance away. It is also an overwhelmingly *Rastafarian* site, as each shack bears the typical colour scheme and iconographic details. And, at another level, on the mythical or metaphysical plane, this site is not entirely in Barbican or in Jamaica. With Rasta/Ethiopian flags flying, with proclamations of the sovereignty of His Majesty, Selassie, this site is "lifted" off the ground, so to speak, as it becomes a metaphysical Ethiopia.[37]

Paths, Boundaries, Margins, Axes

These four elements may be considered together, as they all convey meanings concerning spatial interrelationships—both in relation to the overall site, as well as to Derek's shack. Perhaps the most striking visual feature of

Derek's Shack.

the site is that there are strong boundaries and margins. These have not only physical significance, but also social and metaphysical connotations. The gully is one strong boundary, and it is literally a margin, in terms of urban space in Kingston. To inhabit the plots of land that hug the edges of gullies is to be defined as socially and economically *marginal* in the urban society. Barbican is typical of many such squatter sites in Kingston and its environs that contain cramped settlements which claim this "left-over" land, and use the gullies as solid waste disposal systems, as well as paths of entry into other communities or as escape routes, in the case of supposed criminals.[38]

Another strong boundary is a high concrete wall erected to screen off the ghetto settlement. The significance of this wall may be grasped in conjunction with the "For Sale" sign placed on the lot. The wall and the sign highlight the fragile occupancy, the marginal position of those who now use this site. In the near future, this now marginal space will be "reclaimed" as formal commercial space under legitimate ownership. This threat of imminent takeover and forced evacuation is also a typical feature of shack occupants throughout Jamaica's urban areas. This makes them an "other" in the urban space—a force at variance with established authority and concepts of law, order, public cleanliness, and tenure.[39]

The main road is another significant boundary. The shacks, hugging the *roadside*, and relating mainly to the pedestrian traffic using the sidewalks and open ground, have a different meaning compared to the established supermarkets, each of which is sited so as to cater to a driving, parking public. The site as a whole lacks any clearly discernible pathways or axes—even the sidewalks may have vendors on them—so that the path becomes distorted. Movement on the site is casual and rambling. This indefiniteness and lack of obvious, linear "shape" or "plan" is also typical of the shacks themselves, and Derek's shack in particular. Internal space is extremely vaguely defined—one is aware of a clutter of boxes and a small space where Derek could sit inside, if he wanted.

These same words—*boundary, path, margin, axis*—have more than literal meanings, however. In the context of this Rastafarian site, and Derek's shack, they have profound metaphysical meanings which are primarily expressed by the applied symbols. So, to grasp the metaphysical meaning, the words *iconography* and *symbolism* have to be brought into the discussion.

On one side of Derek's shack is a prominent caption, which reads: "Wite Rul" [*sic*]. Derek explained that it should read "W(h)ite Rul(e),

Blacks Must Pool." That is his philosophy, in a nutshell.[40] For him, the most potent element of reality is that blacks occupy marginal positions of power and wealth, as a legacy of colonialism and slavery. As he explained it, his position, squatting on that fragment of land space in his little shack, is a testimony to black marginality. The established supermarkets in the area were not owned by blacks, he said. Chinese and whites, in his estimation, dominated the Barbican economy. On the opposite side of his shack, he has painted images of Jamaican National Heroine, Nanny of the Maroons,[41] and a large caption proclaiming his anger at the killing of Malcolm X. He lamented the fact that blacks, in Jamaica and globally, currently had no viable leader and were so disunited.

Across the front of his shack, Derek has another caption which reads: "Long Live the King, Selassie I." This caption, and a painting of Selassie, establish his connection with Rastafarian beliefs. In his opinion, Ethiopia is the symbol of an ancestral base from which black Jamaicans were forcibly torn by the ravages of colonialism and slavery. He said all the current problems of blacks could be traced to slavery. He stressed that it was the *history* of blacks, as enslaved peoples, that created present-day marginality and disunity. Derek's shack is therefore a quintessential statement concerning the experience of the *African Diaspora*. It is a statement, by architectural iconography of the experience of separation and disjuncture, of wounds not yet healed. The Diaspora/Rastafarian/African-Jamaican is suspended, so to speak, between an ancestral past, a metaphysical geography of Ethiopia, and the "reality" of Jamaican soil. In this suspended space, it is the emperor who is king—Selassie is the sovereign of the metaphysical Ethiopia that Rastas inhabit.

In this context, those words—*paths, boundaries, margins,* and *axes*—relate not only to the physical space on the ground, so to speak, but also to a mythical or metaphysical space, which has charted a path to the ancestral base, has erased the boundary of separation brought about by enslavement, erased the social marginality, by declaring an alterative sovereignty, and established an *axis mundi.* That is, a *centre*—a sacred centre—in Ethiopia.[42] Here, another word is significant—that is, *openings.* On the physical level, Derek's shack is very undefined—there is no clear "door" or "window." There are some irregular gaps in the structure, one or more may be of a size for a person to enter. The shack certainly is not built with a view to the clientele *entering* the crude interior. It is very much of an "exteriorized" structure, with a very vague definition of inside/outside space. But, on the metaphysical level, Derek's shack is all "window" or all "door." The view is "to Africa," so to speak. This view of Ethiopia is above all spawned and shaped in the context of the *Diaspora* experience, which is one of forcible separation and disjunctures in memory and identity. It must be stressed that there is no genetic or literal connection between Jamaica's African Diaspora and the literal Ethiopia. This structure becomes a *threshold* which compensates for the gaps and fragments of the "original" whole. This architecture is, in fact, about "crossing boundaries," returning across the line of separation to an ancestral *centre*. And, in some sense, this ancestral centre is reconstituted in Jamaica via the emblems and icons.

MATERIALS, STRUCTURE, STYLE, SERVICES

These elements may be discussed together, as they all relate to the overall design of the space. It may be stated that the services of Derek's shack—and virtually all shacks—are minimal in the extreme. Fuel for cooking comes from charcoal mainly; there is no installed plumbing and no running water is available in the shacks, although there may be stolen electricity for illumination at night. In terms of materials and structure, the overwhelming impression is of great fragility, and very little care in putting materials together. In form, Derek's shack—like most such shacks—is an *assemblage*.[43] An assortment of odds and ends collected, found, or pilfered from various sources—bits of lattice, sheets of zinc, flattened metal cans, lengths of timber. No particular attention seems to be given to "proper" joints or seams in the structure, little attention appears to have been given to structural qualities at all. The shack tilts at strange angles and appears to have been put up in a great hurry, with no intention of permanence at all. All of which speaks to the socioeconomic status of the builders and occupants. The word *style* may not appear to have any relevance to such a shack—even the word *architecture* may be questioned by some.[44] But there is certainly a "design language," so to speak, that is common to all shacks, whether Rastafarian or not, and it is that of the assemblage. By very nature, there is an inbuilt incoherence, a disjuncture of layers, a kind of unrelatedness of parts.[45] This is so, like all the elements already described, on both the physical and metaphysical levels. Poverty almost dictates the form of the crude assemblage. However, Rastafarian ideology produces an iconography which lifts the odds and ends, through embellishment with specific symbols, to assemble, or *reassemble*, the space lost by forced exile and slavery. The tools of this reassembly include the Rasta/Ethiopian flags, the portraits of Selassie, the red/gold/green colour scheme, the Lions of Judah, the graffitti, and, in Derek's case, portraits of Nanny of the Maroons and Beenie Man, a dance hall DJ. And again, quintessentially, this response is to the Diaspora experience—a powerful urge to reconnect, reconcile, reassemble what was severed.

BUILDER/ARCHITECT, OCCUPANT

Bernard Rudofsky set the precedent for serious analysis of so-called Architecture without Architects.[46] The Rastafarian shack falls into this category of building. Derek built his structure himself and proudly declares that he himself painted the captions and portraits. Derek wears no dreadlocks. He said he cut off his locks because there are too many "false rastas" with locks around. True Rasta, he says, is "from de heart." He said his shack defined him as a Rastafarian and communicated his own worldview. His shack is very much a physical manifestation of his own ideas and feelings about being a member of the African-Jamaican Diaspora. It is doubtful that Derek has much in the way of formal schooling. Derek may never manage to write a treatise on Rastafarian ideology, or spatial responses, nor may he ever get to present his ideas at a conference. The significant thing about him, though, is that he has already presented a treatise in the form of his shack. Concerning the African Diaspora in Jamaica, Derek demonstrates that after more than three hundred years since the inception of British colonization—or even five hundred, including the period of Spanish occupation—the forced exile of blacks from the ancestral continent still sears the subconscious mind. Rastafarian beliefs and icons push what is subliminal out into the open, via built structures, and constitute an element of critique and protest against the current distribution of power and wealth, as well as an attempt to transcend the boundaries of physical separation and lost memory. But there is still something of the suspended, or the unresolved, in the Rastafarian configuration of space. The paradox lies in the fact that these structures and their occupants are distinctively Jamaican, and yet virtually deny their Jamaican-ness in asserting their Ethiopian-ness. In the words of Rastafarian architect Najeeb Campbell, however, "Rastafarian culture really does have a lot to contribute to Jamaican architecture . . . the little shacks with the green, gold and red colours, the stars of David and Ethiopian crosses" constitute "a truly indigenous artistic cultural expression that comes from the heart of a people."[47] It is indeed a legacy of the colonial experience that in the Caribbean, we must so often have to look outside of ourselves to define and find ourselves. This is as true of the slave master as it is of the slave. It

is true that Rastafarian space looks "outside" of Jamaica to establish ancestral roots and a "centre." However, it should be pointed out that in many
of the world's cultures and religions the notion of a journey,[48] or pilgrimage to a sacred "centre" external to one's immediate physical surroundings,
but central to one's sense of identity, is a strong theme.

Derek—like those who share his overall worldview—is quite different
from my grandfather. Both men had the knowledge of their African-ness
embedded in their subconscious. My grandfather felt compelled to bury
his consciousness ever deeper, while Derek discloses and celebrates his.
They represent opposing tendencies within the Diaspora experience—
denial and acceptance. Both responses, however, are configured against the
background of European-derived negations of African worth. The significance is that these matters do not constitute merely attractive embellish-
ments to shacks or stating the worth of the African continent. These
matters begin in the soul of the individual and the body of the individual.
To deny one's ancestors, one's pigmentation, or one's self is surely, as Glissant would put it, a neurosis.

Further Theoretical Musings

Having discussed in some detail Rastafarian spatial/architectural
responses, in particular, through the example of Derek's shack, one key
theme emerges. This is a protest, even rejection, of the local "reality," and
the creation of a metaphysical space which embraces a reconnection or
reenactment of Africa. The "signals" that this metaphysical zone exists are
the emblems, icons, and colours of the Rastafarian Movement. This concluding section seeks to address the need for a coherent theoretical grasp
of this phenomenon. It is not possible in the space of this chapter to
address this in great depth, but rather to suggest possibilities.

Two major lines of approach, which have influenced twentieth-century
thinking and actions regarding societies and cultures, are *Materialism*, as
typified by the thinking of Karl Marx,[49] and *Post-Modernism/Deconstruc-
tivism*, as typified by the thinking of Jacques Derrida.[50] Although superfi-
cially they may be regarded as diametrically opposed ways of interpreting
human life, they are not necessarily mutually exclusive. Human culture is
so complex and multilayered that it is hardly possible for one line of
analysis to sum up all meanings. Certainly, materialism, with its emphasis
on the way economic systems are created and their impact on all aspects

of social activity, helps one to grasp the socioeconomic position of the typical Rastafarian shack-occupant. Materialism also provides the framework for understanding the workings of colonialism—workings which continue to be analyzed currently in the form of post-colonial discourse.[51] The problems of identity, the poverty, the marginality that have followed large numbers of people of African ancestry dispersed around the globe through the workings of colonialism—all this is summed up in Rastafarian discourse.

However, deconstructivism also offers fruitful avenues or trajectories for realizing what is going on. I do not propose to argue for extreme applications of deconstructivist thinking—to deny objectivity, to be lost in a realm of never-knowing and never-understanding, this is of little use. However, there are certain Derridian ideas which do help to lift the veils, probe the corners, peel the layers of reality, ask more questions, and remove the dust from under the carpet. It is proposed, however, that deconstructivism is not the preserve of philosophers and academics. It is a normal human activity—and the point here is not so much to apply deconstructivist ideas to Rastafarianism, but to argue that Rastafarians may be interpreted as being deconstructivists, in certain significant ways.

Derridian terms which appear to have some validity in this context are:[52]

difference—relates to what is suppressed and concealed by objective thought systems and to the impossibility of complete knowledge, which is in fact what the objective thought systems attempt to compensate for. The significance of *absence*—or what is repressed by objective systems of knowledge.
decentering—beginning the process of liberation from the falsities of objective thought.
displacement—the thorough overturning, up-ending, and questioning of so-called objective systems of meaning.

In short, the Rastafarian space up-ends and displaces the worldview of the cultural, political, and economic dominance of European nations over the past 500 years. In Rastafarian terminology, this entire system is "Babylon," and Rastas are quite open in their assertions of nonacceptance of this "system." The significance of this displacement may be grasped by comparison with my grandfather, who suppressed all signs to the contrary, to declare himself a white man, though he was black. So powerful was the impetus to do this in Jamaican colonial society that my grandfather certainly was not an isolated case.[53] By flying Ethiopian/Rastafarian flags, and displaying images of the Emperor Haile Selassie, Rastas challenge what seems to be a simple, commonsense, objective fact—that they are on the terrain of a national entity known as Jamaica. By declaring themselves to be Ethiopians and creating a metaphysical Ethiopia, they dare to assert that objective reality is not all that counts. They place what is absent, in the foreground. Their "real" marginality, objectively obvious in the form of the flimsy, crude shacks, up-ends "official" notions of what Architecture is, and Rastas assertively use these same crude, flimsy structures to proclaim their ancestral lineage and their allegiance to their own royalty and empire.

That a shack should indicate royalty is surely in keeping with the Derridian strategy of uncovering or discovering the suppressed and the repressed in human experience. Thus, the hierarchies of the social order, the racism that has been a part of Jamaica's history, the relationships between who was or is now dominant versus who is subordinate—all this is overturned. Rastafarian ideology, as expressed through architectural iconography, critiques and rewrites the scripts for conventional understandings of geography and society. As such, it is surely a highly significant phemomenon in the realm of African Diaspora experience. Of course, if one is to be true to the most far-reaching implications of Derrida's arguments, then further questioning may be applied to the "system" which Rastas have created. No doubt, lines of weakness could be disclosed—the major one being that they have simply replaced one system with another, and replaced one set of dogmatic assertions with another. Yet, Derrida himself did not advocate deconstruction for the sake of pure chaos, but rather that the process of displacement would reveal recompositions and fresh insights. And in this aspect, it would seem possible to argue that Rastafarian space does exactly this, by displacing the hierarchy of dominance and subordination instilled in the relationships and meanings between Europe and Africa, while creating a uniquely and distinctively "Rastafarian" space that overrides those historical and spatial distinctions.

To reinforce concepts raised at the beginning of this chapter concerning the layers of space, as well as the transmission of meaning beyond the physical form, it can be summarized that Rastafarian space demonstrates these concepts. The concept of Rastafarian space begins with the individual body—its blackness, or African-ness, is accepted—and the major signal of this acceptance is the dreadlocked hairstyle. This self-awareness is extended in many cases to domestic space, which displays the red, gold, green colour scheme, Ethiopian flags, and other Rastafarian emblems. At the institutional level, Rastafarianism has produced its own institutions— such as the Twelve Tribes, Bobo, or Nyabingi—as well as an alternative sovereign, Selassie. At the same time, it has developed an ideology and iconography which critiques existing "establishment" institutions. On the level of the collective/urban space, typical Rastafarian space occupies quite distinct sites, which relate to physical, economic, and social marginality if one considers the criteria of building materials, services, tenure, and location. Yet, in an apparent contradiction, Rastafarian spaces are dominant— they are easily the most eye-catching and visible spaces in a given setting because of their bright colours and recognizable icons. They are the only spaces in Jamaica where such an assertive iconographic statement of identity is made. Where natural space is concerned, Rastafarians have distinct ideas about the environment and claim a special kinship with what is natural or "ital." Rasta space is very close to the earth, so to speak. Occupying a segment of natural space with a national boundary known as "Jamaica," Rastas nevertheless cross this boundary to establish Ethiopia. Thus, the twin levels of meaning are apparent in Rasta space—the physical as well as the metaphysical—and this metaphysical space is pivotal to an understanding of its physical manifestations.

NOTES

1. Beverley Elizabeth Pigou, "The Social History of the Upper and Middle Classes in Jamaica, 1914–1945," Ph.D. diss., Department of History, University of the West Indies, Mona, 1995. Based on the phenomenological theory of architectural theorist Christian Norberg-Schulz, *The Concept of Dwelling*, Rizzoli, New York, 1984, and the materialist theory of Karl Marx. See Max Eastman (ed.), *Capital: The Communist Manifesto and Other Writings*, Modern Library, New York, 1932.

2. The names of the four spaces derive from Norberg-Schulz, materialism contributes the ideas of base and superstructure, translated in this formulation to mean that however humans organize themselves in natural space, it will be reflected in all other spaces.

3. See for example, Roxana Waterson, *The Living House: An Anthropology of Architecture in South-East Asia*, Thames and Hudson, London, 1997.

4. Christian Norberg-Schulz, *Genius Loci*, Rizzoli, New York, 1984.

5. Francis D. K. Ching, *Architecture: Form, Space and Order*, John Wiley & Sons, New York, 1996.

6. For instance, Japanese Shinto shrines may consist of beautiful natural settings, marked only by a free-standing gate or *torii*. It is the natural space which is imbued with sacred meaning. Myrtle Langley, *Religion*, Dorling Kindersley, London, 1996.

7. See, for example, Keith Critchlow, *Islamic Patterns: An Analytical and Cosmological Approach*, Thames and Hudson, London, 1995; Gary N. van Wyk, *African Painted Dwellings: Basotho Dwellings of Southern Africa*, Harry N. Abrams, New York, 1998.

8. An example of the social history of architecture is Mark Girouard's *Life in the English Country House: A Social and Architectural History*, Penguin, London, 1980.

9. This is discussed in Edward R. Ford, *The Details of Modern Architecture*, MIT Press, Cambridge, Mass., 1997. In this connection the argument of nineteenth-century architect and theorist, Gottfried Semper, to the effect that ornament is the most significant aspect of architecture is relevant. Harry Francis Mallgrave, *Gottfried Semper: Architect of the Nineteenth Century*, Yale University Press, New Haven, Conn., 1996; Hanno-Walter Kruft, *A History of Architectural Theory*, Princeton University Press, Princeton, N.J., 1994.

10. *The Little Oxford Dictionary*, Clarendon Press, Oxford, 1998.

11. *Merriam-Webster's Collegiate Dictionary* http://www.yourdictionary.com/cgi-bin/mw.cgi

12. Rupert Charles Lewis, *Marcus Garvey: Anti-Colonial Champion*, Africa World Press, Trenton, N.J., 1988; Maureen Warner-Lewis and Rupert Lewis (eds.), *Garvey: Africa, Europe, the Americas*, Africa World Press, Trenton, N.J., 1994; Molefi Kete Asante, *The Afrocentric Idea*, Temple University Press, Philadelphia, 1998; *The Black Scribe* http://www.high-ground.com/blackscribe/openbooks.html covers issues such as the inclusion of African-American history in school curricula, and the adoption of African holidays like Kwanzaa, by African-Americans; Carolyn Cooper, "Chanting Down Babylon: Bob Marley's Song as Literary Text," *Jamaica Journal* Vol. 19, No. 4, 1987, pp. 2–18.

13. Edouard Glissant, *Caribbean Discourse: Selected Essays*, Charlottesville, University Press of Virginia, 1999, p. 65.

14. Glissant, 1999, p. 61.

15. Glissant, 1999, pp. 61–62; Trinidadian author V. S. Naipal has stressed the disjunctive, hollow nature of Caribbean culture in *The Mimic Men*, Penguin, London, 1973; Edward [Kamau] Brathwaite has, on the other hand, sought to restore the loss of memory through the medium of poetry, *The Arrivants*, Oxford University Press, Oxford, 1973. For discussions of this loss and compensation of memory, see João José Reis's chapter "*Batuque*" in this volume.

16. John Taylor, ". . . *Life and Travels in America . . . description of the Island of Jamaica*," 1689, Manuscript, National Library of Jamaica, p. 544 and quoted in Beverley Elizabeth Pigou, "Attitudes to Death in Jamaica between the Seventeenth Century and the Twentieth Century," M.Phil. thesis, Department of History, University of the West Indies, Mona, 1985.

17. For example, *Planters Punch*, edited by H. G. DeLisser and published in Kingston between 1914 and 1945, completely eliminated African-Jamaicans from its features on social activities and individual biographies. "Howard Hamilton Reasons with Rasta at Flamingo Beach," *The Gleaner*, Thursday, June 1, 2000, p. A2—this report refers to the recent media controversy over public official Hamilton's support for the Rastafarian movement.

18. "Shacks Demolished," *Jamaica Gleaner Online*, Saturday, June 3, 2000, p. A1. http://www.go-jamaica.com/gleaner/20000603/Lead/Lead1/html

19. Burnett Webster, "The West Indian Home: The House," *West Indian Review* Vol. 1, No. 5, 1935, pp. 37–42; "The West Indian Home: The Garden," *West Indian Review* Vol. 1, No. 7, 1935, pp. 20–24; "The West Indian Home: The Interior," *West Indian Review* Vol. 1, No. 8, 1935, pp. 29–33.

20. Claude McKay, *"My Green Hills of Jamaica,"* Heinemann Caribbean, Kingston, 1979.

21. Conversations with Haitian MA students, Universidad de Pedro Henriques Urena (UNPHU), Santo Domingo, DR, November 1999. See *Gingerbread Houses: Haiti's Endangered Species*, Anghelen Arrington Phillips, Haiti, 1975.

22. Edward Crain, *Historic Architecture in the Caribbean Islands*, Gainesville, Florida, University Press of Florida, 1994, adheres to conventional European nomenclature. Jacob Voorthuis, "Style and Nomenclature in Jamaica," *Axis, Journal of the Caribbean School of Architecture* No. 2, July 1998, pp. 62–73, argues for inventing a new nomenclature.

23. Pat Green, "Small Settler Houses in Chapleton: Microcosm of the Jamaican Vernacular," *Jamaica Journal* Vol. 17, No. 3, 1984, pp. 39–45; Jacob Voorthuis, "What Makes Jamaican Architecture So Special?" *The Jamaican*, 1998, pp. 9–15, 30.

24. Jack Berthelot and Martine Gaume, *Kaz Antiye: The Caribbean Popular Dwelling House*, Paris, Editiones Caribbeane, 1982.

25. B. W. Higman, *Montpelier Jamaica: A Plantation Community in Slavery and Freedom, 1739–1912*, Kingston, The Press, University of the West Indies, 1998.

26. Berthelot and Gaume, *Kaz*, 1982, pp. 15ff.

27. Higman, *Montpelier*, 1998, pp. 139, 185.

28. Andrea Taylor and Shawn Jones, "Rastafari: An Architecture of Self-Reliance," *Axis: Journal of the Caribbean School of Architecture*, 3/4, 1999, pp. 58–83.

29. Taylor and Jones, 1999, pp. 82–83.

30. Green, "Small Settler Houses," 1984.

31. Natalie Butler, "The Significance of Fretwork in Jamaican Heritage," The Edna Manley School for the Visual Arts, Kingston, 1993.

32. Architect Najeeb Campbell, e-mail dated June 6, 2000. Quoted with permission.

33. Sources of Rastafarian beliefs include conversations with Rastafarians Najeeb Campbell, Mikheal Vernon, the Barbican brethren, and the following texts: Barry Chevannes, *Rastafari: Roots and Ideology*, Syracuse University Press, Syra-

cuse, N.Y., 1995; Neville Garrick, *A Rasta's Pilgrimage: Ethiopian Faces and Places*, Pomegranate, San Francisco, 1998; M. G. Smith, Roy Augier, and Rex Nettleford, *The Rastafari Movement in Kingston, Jamaica*, Kingston, Institute of Social and Economic Research, University of the West Indies, Mona, 1978; Barbara Makeda Lee, *Rastafari: New Creation*, Kingston, 1981; Taylor and Jones, "Rastafari," 1999.

34. Berthelot and Gaume, *Kaz*, 1982; Higman, *Montpelier*, 1998. For an analysis of African architecture see, Nnamdi Elleh, *African Architecture: Evolution and Transformation*, McGraw-Hill, New York, 1997.

35. Jill Last, *Ethiopians and the Houses They Live In*, Ethiopian Tourism Commission (undated). However, it is of interest to note that some Ethiopian houses, built with corrugated iron roofing material and timber walls, incorporating verandahs and fretwork, closely resemble the traditional Jamaican cottage, Barbadian chattel house, or French West Indian kaz. See Last, p. 30. Similarities in climate and materials may be the underlying reasons for this similarity.

36. Francis D. K. Ching, *A Visual Dictionary of Architecture*, Van Nostrand Reinhold, 1995. A single shack is chosen to explore these elements, although several shacks and individuals have been researched by the author. The choice of one is not to deny the fact that there are nuances and variations in how specific Rastafarians and Rasta communities construct their spaces. See different descriptions in Taylor and Jones, "Rastafari," 1999, for example. However, the main themes of honoring Selassie, the metaphysical qualities of Ethiopia, and the consciousness of being "African" are common to virtually all. In architectural history and criticism, it is well established that a single structure may be analyzed and is valid on its own terms.

37. Garrick, *A Rasta's Pilgrimage*, 1998—in the foreword, Prof. Teshome H. Gabriel refers to Ethiopia as a "dream landscape" (p. 4) with both physical and spiritual dimensions, playing an important role in reconstituting the "collective memory" of Rastafarians (p. 6). Some Rastafarians, such as Mikheal Vernon, and the Rasta community he belongs to, consider themselves to be literal Ethiopians. Taylor and Jones, "Rastafari," 1999, p. 66.

38. "Death cuts path across city," report in *The Gleaner*, Saturday, August 12, 2000, p.1, refers to the body of a murdered man found in the Sandy Gully, Kingston.

39. "Shacks Demolished," *Gleaner Online*, 2000.

40. Conversation with Derek, July 2000.

41. Mavis Campbell, *The Maroons of Jamaica*, Africa World Press, Trenton, N.J., 1988; Richard Price, *Maroon Societies in the Americas*, Johns Hopkins University Press, Baltimore, 1996.

42. A. T. Mann, *Sacred Architecture*, Element Books, Dorset, Gt. Britain, 1993; Colin Wilson, *The Atlas of Holy Places and Sacred Sites*, Dorling Kindersley, London, 1996; Garrick, *A Rasta's Pilgrimage*, 1998.

43. *The Thames and Hudson Dictionary of Art Terms*, Thames and Hudson,

London, 1995, p. 22, "the use of three-dimensional found materials to create art objects." Artlex, http://www/artlex.com Assemblage—"a three-dimensional composition made of various materials, such as found objects, paper, wood and textiles."

44. Bernard Rudofsky, *Architecture Without Architects*, Prentice Hall, New York, 1969; Paul Oliver, *Encyclopedia of Vernacular Architecture of the World*, Cambridge University Press, Cambridge, 1998, are important precedents in the analysis of types of architecture which have been traditionally overlooked.

45. Interestingly, these elements bear some similarity to contemporary deconstructivist architecture, such as work by Frank O. Gehry. See Peter Gossel and Gabriel Leuthauser, *Architecture in the Twentieth Century*, Benedikt Taschen, 1991, Köln, Germany, p. 360.

46. Rudofsky, *Architecture Without Architects*, 1969.

47. Architect Najeeb Campbell, e-mail dated June 28, 2000. Quoted with permission.

48. Thomas Barrie, *Spiritual Path, Sacred Place: Myth, Ritual, Meaning in Architecture*, Shambhala, Boston, 1996. Such sites of pilgrimage include the Kaaba, Mecca; Teotihuacan, Mexico; Santiago de Campostela in medieval Spain; Chartres Cathedral in medieval France; and Jerusalem. Garrick's *A Rasta's Pilgrimage* underscores the role of Ethiopia as a sacred center.

49. Max Eastman (ed.), *Capital*, 1932.

50. Robert Mugerauer, "Derrida and Beyond," in Kate Nesbitt (ed.), *Theorizing a New Agenda for Architecture: An Anthology of Architectural Theory, 1965–1995*, Princeton Architectural Press, 1996; Jacques Derrida, "Point de Folie—Maintenant l'Architecture," in Neil Leach (ed.), *Rethinking Architecture: A Reader in Cultural Theory*, Routledge, New York, 1997, pp. 324–336.

51. Edward Said, *The World, the Text and the Critic*, Harvard University Press, Cambridge, Mass., 1983, is an example of post-colonial discourse.

52. Mugerauer, "Derrida and Beyond," 1996; Derrida, "Point de Folie," in Leach, 1997.

53. Pigou, Ph.D. diss., 1995, discusses this theme in detail.

Part III

Reconfiguring the Political/Contesting the Conceptual

This third and final section explores the experiences of the African-descended in relation to the state or to international political processes broadly conceived. With the exception of the eighth chapter, the subject matter pertains to the twentieth century.

Chouki El Hamel's investigation of "race" and slavery in Morocco seeks to follow the process by which "racial" attitudes developed in this part of North Africa by the latter part of the seventeenth century. Examination of these phenomena has been impeded by interpretations of Islam and Arab nationalism and culture, a silencing whose practical effect is not unlike the myth of racial democracy in Brazil. In rupturing this silence, El Hamel marshals evidence suggesting that the enslaving of a particular group within Moroccan society, the *haratin*, was a watershed event in that it stimulated widespread debate over the fact that those enslaved were Muslim, an apparent violation of Islamic law. That they were also "black," however, a characterization that the author contextualizes, indicates the existence of a social value system at least partially informed by differences of color. The source of such values is not to be found in the teachings of Islam itself, but in the particular way in which empire created dislocations that in turn resulted in contestations over land and resources, a process that began in Morocco as early as the twelfth century. The subsequent enslavement (in perpetuity) of the Haratin in the late seventeenth century served to strengthen the valuation of color distinctions, but it was also challenged by certain of the leading scholars of the day. Thus, we have in El Hamel's contribution an opportunity to observe the origins and trajectory of racialized thought and practice that, as was true of the Americas, were fundamentally tied to the expansion of the institution of slavery. Its inclusion in this volume is an argument for the existence of diasporas within Africa itself, and underscores the need for more inquiry into the experiences of Africans and their descendants in the Islamic world.

One implication that flows from El Hamel's work is that Moroccan identity and culture were also tied to the enslavement of the Haratin; that is, the creation of the Haratin as a discrete and stigmatized group helped to define what was acceptably "Moroccan." What is implicit in El Hamel's chapter is made explicit in Tyler Stovall's contribution regarding the role of race in the emergence of modern French nationalism and identity. Noting that concepts of "blackness" were current in Europe long before the transatlantic slave trade, such that Europe made its own contributions to the unfolding of race as an ideational category, Stovall advances the argument that the concept of the "nation" in France was shaped to some degree by the existence of blacks, and that in turn blackness was shaped by the national project in France, an interaction extending from the eighteenth into the twentieth centuries. In this way, both Stovall and El Hamel make the case for the importance of a black experience bounded by the nation-state, notwithstanding the usefulness of the transnational perspective.

Beginning with the eighteenth century, Stovall presents metropolitan France as mired in a series of contradictions with respect to the African presence. Many Enlightened minds were nonetheless occluded by their involvement in and profits from the transatlantic slave trade and slave-based plantation agriculture in the Caribbean. The contradictions between the pronouncements and the practices of the *philosophes* were most notable during the French Revolution and its aftermath, and especially during the reign of Napoleon, who reestablished slavery in the French empire. His decision parallels the enslavement of the Haratin in Morocco in that in both instances, persons who would have otherwise qualified as citizens of the state were excluded solely on the basis of race. The French nationalist project was therefore racially configured very early on.

Although not as well studied as the eighteenth and twentieth centuries, blackness in nineteenth-century France was nevertheless critical in the development of French nationalism. This was a period in which the French nation was further clarified by both French expansion and colonialism in Africa, and by class antagonisms in the metropole, where workers were increasingly characterized in racialized terms. Of course, the twentieth century introduced a number of changes that seemingly worked to undermine the conditionalities of preceding periods, alterations that included world war, decolonization, and an influx of immigration from former colonies. In the face of such massive upheaval and transformation, notions of blackness, further complicated by the Algerian experience, continue to serve emblematically as sites of confusion and irreconcilability between French "citizenship and culture."

From "Old World" cultures of France and Morocco, the ensuing chapters shift the focus to the Americas, where Erik McDuffie introduces a much-needed corrective into the historiography of pan-Africanist and leftist activity in the early twentieth century. McDuffie excavates the roles and contributions of black women radicals during the period, who struggled not only against the racism and imperialism of the age, but also against black nationalist and pan-Africanist movements as decidedly phallocentric enterprises. One consequence of these ideological interactions is the emergence of feminisms, internationalisms, and radicalisms that combine variously and creatively.

Focusing on such principals as Amy Jacques Garvey, Amy Ashwood Garvey, Henrietta Vinto Davis, Grace Campbell, and Maymie Turpeau De Mena, McDuffie initially examines the circumstances of the earlier, pre-radical lives that help to explain their gravitation to such organizations as the Universal Negro Improvement Association, the African Blood Brotherhood, and the Socialist and Communist parties. For example, and although not true of all female radicals, a number were from middle-class backgrounds and were therefore well educated. In addition, a number hailed from either the Caribbean or Central America.

Engaged in a variety of related movements all calling for an end to European colonialism in Africa, these women visionaries diverged in their particular brands of feminism. The relationship between women's rights and socialism was one site of disagreement, as was the degree to which organizations should give tangible support to female activist agendas. Amy Jacques Garvey is an example of a woman who struggled to expand the prerogatives of women in the public sphere while holding on to a more conventional conceptual framework regarding the private sphere. While Amy Jacques Garvey advocated for her position from her column in the *Negro World*, Grace Campbell chose a form of community activism that saw her engage with a number of community-based projects, as well as run for political office on the Socialist Party ticket. As another example of the divergence mentioned above, Campbell and Jacques Garvey would view the role and value of capitalist enterprise very differently (at least the 1940s for Jacques Garvey). McDuffie expounds upon other such differences and examines the reasons for these divisions.

McDuffie's chapter has the effect of demonstrating the global reach and internationalist perspective of women thinkers. They were clearly involved in articulating visions of an African diaspora that included Africa, if the latter was not entirely central to their parties' and organizations' everyday activities. The same can be said of the radicals of the 1960s, discussed by Rose Thevenin, to whom we transition from McDuffie's radicals of the 1920s. Thevenin writes about a specific "episode" in the unfolding of diasporic history; namely, ventures involving Black Panther Party members going into exile in Cuba. Here we again encounter divergence, this time between the expectations of such individuals as Eldridge Cleaver and Huey Newton, and the realities of a Castro-led Cuba. The Black Panthers were not a nationalist organization (in fact, they presented themselves as unalterably opposed to black nationalism, which they maintained was far too narrow-minded), nor did they espouse a reorganization of the world along the coordinates of prior bondage, dispersal, and race. Yet the thrust of their arguments for revolution called for a global realignment of power and privilege that would directly address race-based inequalities. Indeed, the Panthers never denied their interest in the plight of black people, both local and international, a focus enshrined in their ideology and in their very name.

That race was central, at least to Cleaver's way of thinking, became clear in his own description of his experience in Cuba. Frustrated that his plans to launch guerrilla warfare in the United States did not receive Castro's backing, Cleaver became increasingly disillusioned with what he saw in Cuba and concluded that the Castro regime was racist. William Lee Brent, another Panther, became equally exasperated with his treatment in Cuba, as did Huey Newton. Assata Shakur's experience stands in some contrast, but as a whole, the Panther saga in Cuba points to the observation that visions of diaspora are just as multiple as the realities, with theory and substance often in tremendous tension. The experience also highlights the fact that even when individuals and groups from different parts of the diaspora all subscribe to it as an idea, they do not necessarily understand each other's conception of diaspora, nor do they necessarily appreciate the local manifestations of a globalized imaginary.

Perhaps a remedy to the foregoing, to the degree that it is desired, is to be found in the realms of the discursive. This is certainly one implication of Wendy Walters's chapter on black international literature, a contribution that is clearly descriptive but potentially prescriptive as well. In some contrast to Markowitz's contribution in which hybridity is a principal mechanism of organization, Walters sees a critical association between race and diaspora. She further argues that writing about the diaspora is an important means of achieving an "alternative homeland." Citing examples of such writing as early as Olaudah Equiano, and tracing the diaspora impulse through the luminaries of the Harlem Renaissance, Walters notes that such writers often refused to confine their vision to any one physical location, but rather frequently incorporated Africa and the Caribbean into their work. This was equally true of the Black Arts Movement of the 1960s. It is the author's argument that the condition of diaspora, not unlike exile, is a vantage point that allows for both a healthy assessment of the "homeland" and a dynamic envisioning of new, reconstituted sites of coalescence. As such, "diaspora identity is performed in writing, even as it also precedes the act of writing itself."

After establishing the concepts central to the analysis, Walters proceeds to define diasporic writing as a "political act" that is "counter-hegemonic" in effect. Unsatisfied with the binary of home-diaspora, Walters offers the argument that "black international prose writing itself performs a home in diaspora." Accepting the critique of essentialism, Walters nonetheless rehabilitates notions of (forced) migration, slavery, and empire as embedded in the memories (à la Jermaine Archer) of those in diaspora and culturally expressed. That is, far from some residual of the blood, such memories flow from demonstrably historical processes that continue to reverberate; the quote from Booker T. Washington on this point is particularly poignant (and all the more so considering it was Washington who wrote it).

Walters is after something. She is attempting to redeem the concept of "home" from the dustbin of certain theorists. Rather than discarding it, Walters calls for a redefinition, a reconceptualization, that allows for a multiplicity of locations and a rejection of boundedness. Home then becomes "an enacted space" and diaspora an "alternate community." Walters concludes the chapter with ruminations on the problematic of "wholeness" in relation to diaspora.

The final chapter moves decidedly into the contemporary and brings to the fore the implications of diaspora for the here and now. While in some ways a continuation along the trajectory of the theoretical established by Walters, the piece in other ways calls into question both the conceptual underpinnings and conventional understandings of diaspora. Establishing the distinction between the otherwise related worlds of diaspora and transnational studies, Asale Angel-Ajani qualifies her use of the former, indicating her uneasiness with the concept while emphasizing the need to differentiate between and within diasporas. With regard to transnationalism, Angel-Ajani cautions that in paying particular attention to the porous nature of the nation-state, we should not lose sight of the fact that it still plays a significant role. This caution is offered in support of her own project, as is the observation that gender and women and the realities of the quotidian are woefully underrepresented in diaspora studies.

With such observations in hand, Angel-Ajani moves to the focus of the work, imprisoned African women in contemporary Rome, Italy. Citing the scholarly consensus that the violation of women's rights is deplorably underreported, the author engages with tensions in the literature on displacement, calling for both "a more nuanced understanding" of the relationship between displacement and transnational movements, and for centering the experiences of women in the literature. Angel-Ajani then introduces an interview with a Nigerian woman imprisoned in Rome, who along with so many others had been "trafficked" there by the unscrupulous as drug couriers and prostitutes. The plight of such women has heretofore been largely ignored by transnational studies. More than simply adding gender to the variables of analysis, Angel-Ajani calls upon transnationalism to pay heed to the "lived experiences" of the everyday.

8

Blacks and Slavery in Morocco

The Question of the Haratin at the End of the Seventeenth Century

Chouki El Hamel

On the Question of "Race" and Slavery in Morocco: Theory versus Practice

Several tenets of the dominant culture in North Africa—namely, the uni-
fying concepts of one Islam, one Arab nation, one culture and language—
have effectively prevented North African historians from honestly
examining the region's history of race and slavery.[1] And this silence, perhaps unpredictably, has also characterized the work of non-African historians of slavery, who have generally ignored the issue of race in North
African slavery. But a new generation of scholars, in Africa and abroad,
has now broken these silences from the southern edge of the Sahara[2] to
the Atlas mountains and beyond to the sea.[3] It is the principle of silence
that effectively precludes North Africans from discussing attitudes about
slavery and racial attitudes. In North Africa, topics of race and slavery are
politically sensitive and are concealed internally in the name of Arab-
Islamic hegemony. It should be noted that a similar silence could be found
in Europe as well. Jacques Heers, a specialist of European history, in his
study of slavery in medieval Europe, has written that this silence reflects
an embarrassment felt collectively throughout the centuries.[4] The North
Africans must have felt a similar embarrassment, especially on the official
level, vis-à-vis the challenges to interpretations of the sacred codes of
Islam in relation to the ethics of slavery. It has also been professionally
unsafe for a North African scholar to research slavery issues in an
unapologetic way.[5]

Using Morocco as a model, this work will be useful in enhancing our understanding of the wider political, economic, social, and cultural dimensions of the North African societies and in establishing a foundation for further, more comparative inquiries into how attitudes toward slavery have changed through the cultural exchange endemic of the whole Mediterranean region.

The case of Moroccan slavery is a useful starting point for a historical discussion of slavery in North Africa for three reasons. In the first place, Morocco has significant historical connections to several different subregions, which extend beyond the Mediterranean to include strong bonds to regions in subsaharan Africa as well. Second, the slave community in Morocco has played an active and continuous role in Moroccan society over the course of history. And last, from a historiographic perspective, Morocco possesses extraordinarily rich and accessible archival sources, which consist of collections of legal opinions called *fatawi* (Ar. sing. *fatwa*), slave registers called *dafatir* (Ar. sing. *diftar*), royal correspondences, biographical dictionaries, and chronicles.

There has been a tendency among Western historians to argue that Islamic slave holders harbored no racism and generally took a benign attitude toward their slaves. The French historian E. Levi-Provençal stated in his famous book on Muslim Spain: "Thus in the 10th century, like present-day Morocco, there was no lack of mulattos in the Muslim bourgeoisie and aristocracy, among which we must acknowledge that color prejudice has never existed, no more in the Middle Ages than today."[6] This view asserts that such a nonracist attitude toward slaves reduced the potential for economic and political subjugation as well as social marginalization based on categories of skin color. In effect, this nonracist attitude forestalled the emergence of a more humiliating and oppressive slavery, such as the racial slavery of North America, in Islamic societies like Morocco.

I argue, however, that such an understanding of the politics and the practice of slavery in Morocco ignores important historical evidence and derives from gross generalizations deduced from Islamic legal treatises regarding the status and practice of slavery. Slavery is by definition an exploitative system[7] and evidence that I present below strongly suggests that in the late seventeenth century Morocco did in fact possess/demonstrate the ideological foundation for a society divided by skin color.

The main legal schools of Islam all sanction the enslavement of non-Muslims regardless of skin color, race, or ethnicity. The counterpoint of this ruling was that Islamic law explicitly forbade Muslims to enslave fellow Muslims. Historical events, however, point to instances where Muslims did in fact enslave other Muslims. The enslavement of the *Haratin*—a problematic term whose meanings and significations will be addressed below—during the reign of the 'Alawi Sultan Mawlay Isma'il (r. 1672–1727) is one particularly poignant example. The enslavement of the Haratin by the Sultan for the purposes of forming an army consisting solely of "black slaves" (known in Arabic as *'Abid al-Bukhari*) and the debate that it stimulated marked a crucial turning point in the history of social relations between groups of different skin colors in Morocco, and what have more recently been articulated as "racial" relations.

Morocco during the reign of Sultan Mawlay Isma'il was a complex society that could be divided according to a variety of overlapping social categories. Prior to the French protectorate period, linguistically, Morocco consisted of Arabic-speakers[8] and Berber-speakers.[9] Religiously, there were Muslims and a Jewish minority. Among Muslims, there were the followers of various Sufi orders, some of which conflicted openly with the teachings and practices of the others. There were the descendants of the Prophet Muhammad, the *shurafa'* (Ar. sing. *sharif*), who possessed certain privileges, which might relate to material or political benefit. There were the religious scholars (*ulama*) and Sufi masters (*shuyukh*); sometimes the two were one and the same. There were also the transhumant pastoralists, nomads, sedentary agriculturalists, urban merchants, and artisans. And then there were the social groups known as Haratin and slaves (Ar. sing. *'abd*; pl. *'abid*). Physical characteristics and other means of categorizing the latter subaltern groups constituted another cluster of markers that could be used in defining Moroccan society. The complexity of the category of the Haratin is what we will consider here.

Physical characteristics, and skin color in particular, were a crucial factor in identifying at least one group in Morocco, the freed black people or so called ex-slaves (sing. Hartani; pl. Haratin). The term Haratin referred to a group of people who occupied an intermediary position between slaves and free Muslims, and thus their social status was at times unclear. However, in addition to being identified as freed slaves, the Haratin were invariably recognized in the historical documents as having been black. The episode of their reenslavement during the reign of Sultan Mawlay Isma'il begs a series of questions: Who were these Haratin and why were they enslaved? What was their status before their enslavement? How did their status change after they were freed? What conditions precipitated their reenslavement in the Mawlay Isma'il episode under consideration here and what role did skin color play in the decision to categorically reenslave them? The line of inquiry that develops out of this event is twofold: to investigate how the image of "black" as a social category was constructed and how this changed diachronically, and to explore the contrast between Islamic theories on slavery and the practice of slavery during Mawlay Isma'il's era.

The Etymological and Social Meaning of Haratin

Etymologically speaking, the meaning of Hartani very likely derives from the Berber word *ahardan*, which is connected with skin color. It means "dark color" (either black or reddish), and the earliest known use of the term was among the Berbers of Sanhaja and Zanata before the coming of the Banu Hassan in the thirteenth century.[10] Among the Tuareg (Berber-speaking people inhabiting the western and central Sahara and western Sahel of northwest Africa), a similar word is used to designate a person of both black and white parentage: *achardan*.[11] According to L. Mezzine, in his dissertation about the region of Tafilalt, the Arabic-speaking population of Tafilalt used the term Hartani to designate the enslaved black. But this term has no such significance in the Arabic language, and among the mountain-dwelling Berbers of Sanhaja origin, it designates a person with a black skin, "*Aherdan*," in contrast with the white "*Amazigh*." So the term Hartani used by the Arabic-speaking population of Tafilalt to designate the enslaved black is not an Arabic term. The word Haratin, however, has produced diverging interpretations: for some it is an Arabic word of two possible meanings. Certain scholars suggest deconstructing the term into "*hurr*" and "*thani*," literally "the second free man," but more likely meaning "a free person of a second class."[12] It could be also derived from the Arabic verb "*haratha*" that signifies "to cultivate." The reason for the latter meaning is possibly because the Haratin were known to be cultivators in the south of Morocco, mainly in the Draa region.[13] The famous Moroccan historian an-Nasiri (1835–1893) accepted the first meaning. In his book, *al-Istiqsa'*, he said that the word Hartani meant in the common Moroccan language "freed," in opposition to a person of a free origin. Through a long usage of the two words "*hurr*" and "*thani*" together it was transformed into Hartani.[14] These different interpretations concerning the term Haratin are very important because they indicate that there are difficulties in defining the identity of blacks in Morocco.[15]

There is also a commonly used term among the Berbers, especially in the Sus valley region in southern Morocco. This term is *asuqi* (black). Berbers had generally two terms to designate black people: *asuqi* and *aharadani* (Hartani). *Asuqi* could have been used as a neutral term to mean all blacks, but currently the two are used interchangeably. Or it could be that originally Berbers used the terms to differentiate between a free black (Hartani) and a black slave (*Asuqi*) or (*Ismkhan*).[16]

It is commonly believed that the Haratin were originally slaves who had been freed under different circumstances through time. However, the Haratin were not of slave origin from Black West Africa, as Mawlay Isma'il claimed in his legal defense to enslave them but, rather, at least a group of them were natives of southern Morocco, as Jacques-Meunié, in her book *Le Maroc saharien des origines à 1670*, suggested when she wrote that the Haratin were the descendants of the black people who inhabited the Draa valley since time immemorial. These people were black, sedentary agriculturists, thus lending credence to the etymological argument that Haratin derives from the Arabic *haratha*.[17] With the advance of the Romans into the Moroccan interior, the Jazula Berbers may have been forced to move toward the south and competed with the blacks in the oases of the Draa. As Stéphane Gsell in *Histoire ancienne de l'Afrique du Nord* suggests: "Thus these fugitive Berbers became conquerors."[18] They may have entered into an interdependent or clientele relationship with the Haratin, with the Berbers assuming the patron's role. This claim is also congruent with the local oral traditions of the Tata area in southern Morocco: that the Haratin were in the region hundreds of years ago and had always been free. That is to say that they were in this region long before the coming of the Berbers and later on the Arabs.[19]

Slavery and the Islamic Law: A Critical Examination

Mohammed Ennaji is among the few scholars to have published on the issue of slavery in Morocco.[20] His study of Moroccan slavery in the nineteenth century closely addresses some issues related to the tragic experience of black slaves.

Prior to Ennaji's work, the bulk of scholarship on slavery in Islam was undertaken by European and American scholars, who presented a different, if not altogether orientalist, perspective. Statements made by scholars like the early twentieth-century British historian, Arnold Toynbee, argued that properly Islamic lands were free of racial discrimination:

> White Muslims were in contact with the Negroes of Africa and with the dark skinned-peoples of India from the beginning and have increased that contact steadily, until nowadays Whites and Blacks are intermingled, under the aegis of Islam, through the length and the breadth of the Indian and the African continent. Under this searching test, the White Muslims have demonstrated their freedom from race-feelings by the most convincing of all proofs: they have given their daughters to Black Muslims in marriage.[21]

In addition to being laden with orientalist overtones, the charged comparison of twentieth-century Muslims with medieval Christians and the assumption that Islam has the sole role in explaining the societies of the Islamic world, make this argument overly simplistic. Not much more convincingly, Bernard Lewis, in *Race and Slavery in the Middle East*, wrote:

> We thus have two quite contradictory pictures before us—the first contained in [Toynbee's] *Study of History*, the second reflected in that other great imaginative construction, *The Thousand and One Nights*. The one depicts a racial egalitarian society free from prejudice or discrimination; the other reveals a familiar pattern of sexual fantasy, social and occupational discrimination, and unthinking identification of lighter with better and darker with worse.[22]

Although Lewis discusses the latter characterization as an "imagined construct," he maintains that Arabs had a preconceived notion that blacks were of an inferior and lesser breed, so much so that the latter were "almost entirely missing from the positions of wealth, power, and privilege."[23] His main analysis focuses on racial prejudice toward blacks, a particular aspect of reality that to him obviously became institutionalized, particularly through the practice of slavery. Historically, it is plausible that each of these varied conceptions existed at one time or another in North Africa, and in Morocco in particular.

The advent of Islam first in the Arabian Peninsula, and then in the North African lands, brought crucial changes regarding the practice of slavery. Although Islam asserted that the basic human condition was to be free,[24] after the codification of Islamic law (*shari'a*) in the ninth century, Islamic law "recognize[d] only one category of slaves, regardless of their ethnic origin or the source of their condition."[25] The *Qur'an* itself in a way presumes the existence of slavery and then regulates its practice, by actually discouraging the institution of enslavement, although it does not utterly abolish it. While all official Islamic schools made slavery legal under Islamic law, the *Qur'an* and the Prophet urged kindness toward slaves and recommended that masters free their slaves in time. The *Qur'an* speaks of the merits one will receive for emancipating a slave.[26] The advent of Islam greatly changed the position of enslaved persons. Essentially, Islam assumed that the natural condition of humankind is freedom, and slavery thus could lawfully result from only three conditions. The first condition is being born to slave parents, and the second is being captured during war, as long as the captive was not already a Muslim. The third way slaves could be acquired was through purchase. Islam eradicated some long-standing practices by making it unlawful for a freeman to sell himself or his children into slavery, and by forbidding persons to be enslaved as punishment for debt or crime.[27]

Islam encouraged manumission as an act of great piety and it was recommended under the same category as almsgiving, and many wealthy slave owners did free slaves on certain religious holidays. There existed several ways under Islamic law for an enslaved person to be emancipated, although for the most part manumission remained a unilateral act that could only be initiated by a master or by a judge in the case of maltreatment. The first was through manumission, "a formal declaration on the part of the master and recorded in a certificate given to the freed slave."[28] In this case the slave's offspring would be freed as well. The second way was through a written agreement by which the master granted freedom to the slave in return for a certain amount of money. This agreement could only be annulled by the slave, and not by the owner. In this case, only the children born after the slave entered into the contract were free. Third, the master could bind himself to liberate a slave at a specific future date, or he could bind his heirs to liberate the slave after the master's death. A fourth method was through a legal judgment made by a Muslim judge (*qadi*) if a master failed to meet his moral obligations toward his slave.[29] The fifth manner of liberation occurred when a female slave gave birth to a child of her owner. The child would be free and thereby the slave mother acquired certain legal rights. It should be noted, as we shall see from the example of the Haratin in the Moroccan context, that there was a difference between a freeborn Arab or Berber and a freed slave or a freeborn black (e.g., the Haratin case). The freeborn was free in theory and practice. But for a slave who was freed through one of the above means, even though he or she was legally free, it was nonetheless difficult to entirely sever the master-slave bond. John Hunwick rightly describes this relationship as clientship (*wala'*), explaining that it "provided a social context for the freedman, providing him [or her] with an ersatz family, with a family name, and even, in time, a fictive lineage."[30]

The institution of slavery in eighteenth-century Morocco seems, however, to be not all that different from premodern and early modern notions of slavery held in the Mediterranean basin in general. It seems that the scriptures of the three major religions of the Mediterranean all contained passages that could be interpreted as condoning slavery; several legal aspects of the practice of slavery in the Mediterranean point to commonalities. For example, at least in the thirteenth century, Spanish slavery was nondiscriminating. In fact, the regulation of slavery in the *Siete Partidas* (*The Seven Divisions*) is very similar indeed to Islamic law regarding slaves and perhaps points to a shared Mediterranean concept of slavery, relative to both religion and law. The *Siete Partidas* was the Spanish manifestation of the thirteenth-century renaissance of Roman law that swept across Europe. Instituted by Alfonso X in the mid-thirteenth century in order to replace the prevailing feudal custom-law of Castile, it became the legal foundation throughout the ensuing Hispanic empire from Asia to Africa to the New World. Similar to Islam's position vis-à-vis slaves in personal status law, the *Siete Partidas* rectified the status of slavery from what it was in ancient Roman law. In Roman law, the slave is specifically an object, a possession, and not a person.[31] Furthermore, reflecting the somewhat resigned attitude toward slavery that has often been described as characteristic of the Islamic world, the *Siete Partidas* declared that "servitude is the vilest and most contemptible thing that can exist among men."[32] Such a statement underscores the degree to which slavery was considered in religious terms as much as in legal terms relating to property rights. Additional examination of the *Siete Partidas* demonstrates further similarities between Christian and Islamic positions on slavery. The *Siete Partidas* proclaims:

> We also decree that slavery is something that men naturally abhor, and that not only does a slave live in servitude, but also anyone who has not free power to leave the place where he resides. Learned men have also declared that a party whose irons have been removed is not free, or liberated from restraint, if he is still held by the hand, or guarded in a courteous manner.[33]

The Blacks in Arabic and Islamic Perceptions

Neither in the *Qur'an* nor in the *Hadith* (sayings of the Prophet) is there any indication of racial difference among humankind.[34] But as a consequence of the Arab conquest, a mutual assimilation between Islam and the cultural and the scriptural traditions of Christian and Jewish populations occurred. Racial distinction between humankind with reference to the sons of Noah is found in the Babylonian Talmud, a collection of rabbinic writings that date back to the sixth century. According to this tradition "the descendants of Ham are cursed by being black, and [it] depicts Ham as a sinful man and his progeny as degenerates."[35] This contradicts B. Lewis's conclusion that seems to attribute this tradition to the Arabs.[36] In all likelihood, these racial attitudes toward black Africans were a common perception on the southern lands of the Mediterranean, and this tradition in the Talmud appears to be an articulation of racial divisions in a religious voice.

One of the early Arabic writers who addresses the issue of racial distinction among individuals is Ibn Qutayba (d. 276/889) of Baghdad. He wrote:

> Wahb b. Munabbih said that Ham b. Nuh was a white man having a beautiful face and form. But Allah (to Him belongs glory and power) changed his colour and the colour of his descendants because of his father's curse. Ham went off, followed by his children. . . . They are the Sudan.[37]

Al-Ya'qubi (d. 897 in Egypt) assumed in his *Tarikh* the same Hamitic theory,[38] and al-Mas'udi (d. 956) also followed suit, as he reported in his *Akhbar az-Zaman*:

> The traditionalists say that Nuh, peace upon him, cursed Ham, praying that his face should become ugly and black and that his descendants should become slaves to the progeny of Sam. . . . They are the various peoples of the Sudan.[39]

Ibn Hawqal (d. after 988), in his geographical work, *Kitab Surat al-Ard* (The Picture of the Earth), assumed the previous Hamitic theory and added that different shades of color resulted from the intermixing between light-skinned Berbers and the blacks in North Africa.[40]

One of the first historians to reinterpret these traditions was ad-Dimashqi (d. 1327). He wrote:

> But in truth, the fact is that the nature of their country demands that their characteristics should be as they are [black], contrary to those connected with whiteness, for most of them inhabit the south and west of the earth.[41]

Ibn Battuta, traveling in West Africa in 1353, made critical observations that sharply stigmatized what he considered pagan attitudes: bare breasts, sexual freedom, and bad manners. He wrote in his *Rihla* about the black people of West Africa: "These people have remarkable and strange ways. As for their men, they feel no [sexual] jealousy [. . .]. The women there have friends and companions among the foreign men [e.g., not a kinsperson]."[42] He also said: "One of their disapproved acts is that their female servants and slave girls and little girls appear before men naked, with their privy parts uncovered."[43] His reaction to local customs can be summarized in the following statements: "At this I repented at having come to their country because of their ill manners and their contempt for white men."[44] "When I saw it [their trivial reception gift] I laughed, and was long astonished at their feeble intellect and their respect for mean things."[45]

Though Ibn Battuta sometimes renders his judgments in terms of race, he does not adhere to any consistent "racist" ideology. His criticisms of the blacks are by and large reserved to the subject of social customs. For Ibn Battuta, the ultimate determinant of a people's worth was not skin color but rather their adherence to Islam or lack thereof. Ibn Khaldun (d. 808/1406), one of the best-known Arab historians and thinkers, was the first to treat fully the Hamitic theory and to dispel it as myth or as a "silly story."[46] Ibn Khaldun was a truly Mediterranean figure, coming from a prominent Andalusian family and having spent his entire career along the southern shores of the Mediterranean, from Fez to Tunis to Cairo. In *The Muqaddimah*, he wrote:

> To attribute the blackness of the Negroes to Ham, reveals disregard of the true nature of heat and cold and the influence they exercise upon the climate and upon the creatures that come into being in it. The black skin common to the inhabitants of the first and second zones is the result of the composition of the air in which they live, and which comes about under the influence of the greatly increased heat in the south [. . .]. People there go

through a very severe summer, and their skins turn black because of the excessive heat.[47]

Ibn Khaldun disputed the traditionalists' claim that the black-skinned people of the Sudan are descendants of Ham because of the color of their skin. Some traditionalists incorporated a body of *hadith* known as the *isra'iliyyat*, derived from reports of Jews in the Arabian Peninsula at the time of the Prophet, thus explaining the incorporation of the account of the sons of Ham into Arab-Islamic history. Ibn Khaldun broke with the traditionalists on this and many other issues and asserted that the peoples of the Sudan were black-skinned because of the intense heat of the climate in which they lived. Likewise, the peoples of the north were white-skinned because of the intense cold of their particular climate. Furthermore, the strange practices and customs of these peoples can be attributed to their climates and are not genetic in origin. It is important to ask why the Arabs or light-skinned North Africans did not use color to denote themselves. Ibn Khaldun explained:

> The inhabitants of the north are not called by their colour because the people who established the conventional meanings of words were themselves white. Thus, whiteness was something usual and common to them, and they did not see anything sufficiently remarkable in it to cause them to use it as a specific term.[48]

It must be noted that the Arabs were not the first to use this conventional word *Sudan* (e.g., black people) to designate Africans south of the Sahara. Classical documents indicate that the ancient Greeks were the first people to use a similar denotation "Ethiopia," which meant "a burnt faced person," to call Africans south of Egypt.[49] The Greek concept of color was clearly based on the environment just like Ibn Khaldun's theory. Ibn Khaldun was clearly familiar with the Greeks notion of color regarding the Africans.

But Ibn Khaldun was not concerned to correct the negative image of the blacks; in fact, he held similar views to Ibn Battuta's. Ibn Khaldun described the blacks of subsaharan West Africa as inferior and submissive human beings living at an inferior level of social organization.[50] This tradition had left a negative impact on how the blacks were perceived among the light-skinned Arab-Berber people in North Africa. These consistent perceptions of the blacks as a different people with inferior and bad customs created this image of blacks in the North African ideology to justify their enslavement and this image continued to exist until modern times. As contemporary historian William McKee Evans concludes:

> By studying the shifting ethnic identifications of the "sons of Ham," by following their journey in myth from the land of Canaan to the land of Guinea, we can perhaps learn something about the historical pressures that shaped modern white racial attitudes.[51]

Blacks in Berber Perceptions

Before Islam came to Morocco, the concept of freedom was based on human bonds, on the connection and the protection that a certain tribe could provide. Freedom, then, was established through tribal solidarity. Blacks interacted with Berbers both through trade and war. Individual blacks living in the land of the Berbers were either in a marginalized status (servants or slaves) or a dependent status (intermarriage or clientele). Berber racial attitudes toward black people could have dated back to before the Arab conquest, when the Berbers of Sanhaja and Masmuda were forced to leave their homeland because of external invasions. The Berbers, victims of successive invasions by the Romans, the Vandals, and the Byzantines, were forced to move south and into areas predominantly inhabited by black people. Technologically superior, as a result of their contact with different cultures and the use of the camel, the Berbers most likely conquered the black populations of the Sahara and assumed for themselves a superior status, placing the blacks in lesser, subordinate status. Because the blacks were different in their cultural and physical characteristics, the racial binary was in the making. Simultaneously, these groups of Berbers may have started to preserve their identity by rallying around family kin groups based on egalitarian concepts. The kin group was a creative way to coexist after the dispossession and the dispersal of the Berbers by the external invaders. Those who migrated developed a sense of kin solidarity that did not allow intermixing with outsiders. The blacks were not only outsiders but also perceived as lower class. Intermarrying with them became taboo and shameful.

The following story of Abu Madyan, a North African Sufi figure (1115–16/1198) is a particularly salient illustration of black-Berber social relations, in this case, from the Sanhaja:

Abu Madyan used to tell his companions that Shaykh Abu Ya'za informed him that he would be given an "Abyssinian" (*habashiyya*—i.e., black African) slave girl as a gift and that she would bear him a son who, if he lived, would be great. A merchant gave him a black slave girl and she bore him a son, whom he named Muhammad. Then Abu Madyan ceased having sexual relations with her and signs of distress appeared upon him. He was asked about this [by his disciples] and said, "I have no desire for this slave girl. If Shaykh Abu Ya'za had not told me that I would have a son by her I would never have approached her. No desire for her is left in me. Yet if I abandoned her I would be committing a sin and if I married her I would be embarrassed at having a son by her."

"Then [said Abu Madyan] Abd ar-Razzaq [al-Jazuli] said to me, 'I will marry her and care for your son.'" Abu Madyan replied, "Would you do that, even though marriage with a black woman is shameful among the Masmuda [Berbers]?" "I would do it for your sake," said Abd ar-Razzaq.

So he married her and cared for the son of Abu Madyan, who memorized the Qur'an in a very short period of time and began to give evidence of clairvoyance (*firasat*). But death carried him off while he was still young and Abd ar-Razzaq moved to the East.[52]

The late American anthropologist David Hart also confirmed and explained similar resentment toward the Haratin by the rural Berbers in the Draa region that was still existing in the twentieth century. He explained that the Ait Atta Berbers of the Draa region were egalitarian among themselves but vis-à-vis the Haratin they were ethnocentric. In this sense the Ait Atta are without question the biggest racists in the Moroccan South. They, white tribally organized, transhumant Berbers, who traditionally always bore arms, despise the Haratin for being (1) negroid, (2) nontribal, (3) sedentary and agricultural, and (4) inexperienced in bearing arms.[53]

When Islam came to the land of the Berbers, it transformed the land of the blacks into the land of the "infidels" or "pagans." The marginalized status of blacks was reduced further to slave status. Only "infidels" were normally legally allowed to be enslaved. Therefore, the best place to obtain slaves was across the closest borders of the "infidels," in the Sudan. This borderline, with the contrast in physical type, contributed to the connection of skin color with slavery. So, the ancient rivalry between nomadic Berbers and sedentary blacks that led toward cultural and racial prejudice took an Islamic form after the conversion of the Berbers to Islam during the seventh and eighth centuries.

These perceptions, along with condescending spoken and unspoken assumptions in urban Arab and rural Berber circles, must have had some influence on public opinion and must have paved the way for Sultan Mawlay Isma'il and the *ulama* who supported him to legitimize the enslavement of the free blacks and to undermine any opposition to this project. The enslavement of the free blacks and the emphasis on their permanent slave status perpetuated these assumptions and reinforced the racial attitudes of Arab-Berbers toward blacks, as "black" (*aswad*) became interchangeable with "slave" (*'abd*).

The Isma'ili Operation

Around 1673, when Mawlay Isma'il went to fight against his nephew Ibn Mahraz who had revolted agaist him,[54] a local government official named Abu Hafs 'Umar b. Qasim al-Murrakushi, also known as 'Alilish, presented Mawlay Isma'il with a register containing the names of black slaves who served in the army of al-Mansur as-Sa'di, who had reigned in Morocco from 1578 to 1603. He also informed the Sultan that a lot of their descendants still existed and were to be found in Marrakech and in its vicinity. Then he added: "if my lord ordered me to bring them to him I would do it."[55]

It appears that this register inspired Mawlay Isma'il to build an army of black slaves. Consequently, he gave orders to enslave all blacks including the Haratin, thus generating a heated debate that involved the enslavement of people based on color. But the debate that was generated was as much about defending a specific group of people from being enslaved as much as defending one of the Islamic tenets that says that it is illegal to enslave a fellow Muslim. This was a crucial turning point in Moroccan history that shaped the future of racial relations and the black "identity." Official texts were created to justify the legality of the compulsory buying of slaves from their owners and the enslavement of the Haratin. Every register of slaves was annexed by a long list of names and signatures of the learned men and another list of notaries.

The Haratin, being conscious of their social conditions, refused to accept the servile status attributed to them and hence they refused to submit to the order of the Sultan. This self-perception is expressed in the protests of the Haratin of Fez in the year 1110/1699.[56] Similarly in other regions, the Haratin of Tetouan to the north of Fez, for example, contested the project of the Sultan and took refuge in the sanctuary of Ibn Mashish.[57] These protests slowed down the process of the Sultan's project, yet they were not strong enough to counteract it.

When he came to power in 1672, Mawlay Isma'il had to face a fragmented society and political instability in many areas of Morocco. The southern provinces that controlled the trans-Saharan trade routes frequently revolted against the central authority. In the north, the towns also desired some, if not all, of the autonomy that they had gained during the decline of the previous Sa'di dynasty in the middle of the seventeenth century. In central Morocco, the Sufi group of the Zawiya Dilaiyya challenged the young 'Alawi dynasty and its claims of sharifian descent. In addition, the European occupation of some coastal towns such as Larache by the Spaniards and Mogador by the Portuguese, and the threat of the Ottomans from Algeria, urged the Sultan to strengthen the authority of the Makhzen (e.g., Moroccan central authority) and the unity of the territory under his control.[58] Traditionally, the strength of the royal power was negotiated and relied upon a clientele system—the political support of tribal groups and *turuq* (Sufi orders) in return for royal favors. Sultans mustered their soldiers from specific tribal groups or rural Sufi orders in return for exemption from taxes and rights to land owned by the Sultan. Mawlay Isma'il was convinced that this "clientele system" was not reliable enough for the maintenance of a strong central government. The soldiers provided to the state by a certain tribe were not completely free of their obligations toward their tribes and those conscripted from Sufi orders still pledged their allegiance to the heads of their orders. In one of the letters that he wrote to justify his need to establish a professional army, he said: "the soldier doesn't forget from where he came from. He cannot wait to go back to his flock or land and if the opportunity is offered he would leave the army and join his tribe again after he has been paid for his unfinished job."[59]

Az-Zayani, a twentieth-century Moroccan chronicler, in his book *at-Turjuman al-Mu'rib*, said that Sultan Isma'il gave the order to collect all black people of all ages and both sexes. No black person was spared, whether the person was slave or free black or Hartani. In one year, 3,000 blacks were gathered from the area around Marrakech alone.[60] There, the color of the skin was reason enough for a person to be enslaved: that is, forcibly bought and forcibly enrolled in the army of the Sultan.

Regardless of the nature of Mawlay Isma'il's intent, his decree was in some way unusual in the history of Islamic Morocco. It posed a challenge to the fundamentals that Islam had introduced to reform pre-Islamic slavery. Cognizant of a potential confrontation with Morocco's *ulama*, Mawlay Isma'il had prepared a legal defense of his actions based on interpretations of *shari'a* precedents.

The change in the meaning of Hartani into a synonym for "freed slave" could have developed with Mawlay Isma'il's project. At the very least it was certainly reinforced at that time. This new meaning was an ideological construct to justify the subjugation of the free/freed blacks and was buttressed by documents that sought to advance the Makhzen's agenda by demonstrating that the Haratin were of slave origin and therefore creating a racialized caste. The *fatwa* of Ibn an-Naji,[61] which represents the Makhzen's official opinion during the reign of Mawlay Isma'il, was set against the dissenting opinion of the *ulama* of Fez. Fez was the most important intellectual center in Morocco, owing to its famous al-Qarawiyyin Mosque-University. Through the annually renewed oath of investiture (*al-ba'ya*), it was the *ulama* who ensured that a ruler remained within the scope of accepted Islamic practice. It was these learned men who challenged the order of the Sultan to reenslave the freed slaves. But some *ulama*, who traditionally benefited from the patronage of the rulers in exchange for the legitimacy they offered them, backed his project. Thus, state officials meticulously wrote registers of slaves to document the legality of the steps taken in buying the slaves and enslaving the Haratin.[62] The *Jany al-Azhar wa Nur al-Abhar* was compiled in 1117/1705 under the order of Mawlay Isma'il to summarize all the documents concerning the acquisition of slaves.[63] This official document reports that a total of 221,320 slaves, free blacks, and Haratin were gathered in Morocco.[64] According to the historian an-Nasiri (1835–1893), the total was 150,000 persons. Obviously, not all of them served in the army. The French Consul in Morocco Louis de Chenier (1722–1795), author of the book, *Recherches historiques sur les Maures, et histoire de lÕempire de Maroc,* reported that at the death of Mawlay Isma'il about 100,000 blacks had served him as soldiers.[65]

Mawlay Isma'il consulted and frequently corresponded with the *ulama*. Correspondence between the *ulama* of Fez and the Sultan demonstrates that some of the *ulama* supported the Sultan's proposal to conscript all black people in Morocco into his army. These letters represent the official opinion and are preserved in the archives of Morocco. Some of these letters were compiled and published by Muhammad al-Fasi, the president of the Qarawiyyin during the 1940s and 1950s.[66] No texts or documents that give us a clear description of the Haratin's opposition to the Isma'ili decree have yet been found, except for a few comments concerning the opposition to the Sultan's project found in official texts. In other words, thus far, pending the location of other documents, or the application of oral histories, opposition to the Sultan's proposal to reenslave the Haratin can only be assessed through the arguments put forth by the official record to countermand any opposition the proposal faced. There is a record, however, of one instance in which an *'alim*, 'Abd as-Salam Jassus, issued a *fatwa* against this operation, but he was quickly imprisoned. When the Sultan was unable to persuade him of the legality of his actions over the Haratin, he ordered Jassus to be executed.[67]

To gain more support of the *ulama* of Fez, Sultan Mawlay Isma'il sent a letter to the *ulama* of al-Azhar in Cairo, a renowned center of Islamic scholarship, seeking their legal opinion regarding his desire to establish an army of black slaves or, in this case, of black freed slaves.[68] In order to convince the learned men of the al-Azhar to issue him a favorable legal opinion, he prepared his text carefully. He added somewhat disingenuously that he had already consulted the Moroccan learned men and that they had given him their full support and the support of the *shari'a*. He explained that the economic and political crisis in Morocco was so disastrous that the only means of salvation and staving off further European incursions on Islamic lands was to build a strong, servile army. He stated in his letter that free [Arab and Berber Muslim] men were irresponsible, lazy, weak, envious, and opportunistic, but slaves, and he emphasized black slaves, were different. They were content, satisfied, patient, and strong. These were necessary qualities to have in a person to be trusted to defend the coastal cities and to protect the land of Islam.

Mawlay Isma'il explained that these black people originally came to Morocco through trade from subsaharan Africa, thus indicating that they were of slave origin. He continued to say that, at the time being, the majority of the black people had been separated from their masters either by running away or because their masters were forced to abandon them during times of drought and famine. After years and even centuries, they had come to form their own families and groups. Among the Makhzen's records of the event and ensuing debate, it appears that a negative image of blacks as restless, thieves, and rebels was revived in order to legitimate their subjugation. These characteristics seem contradictory to those qualities stated above, but in fact, they were not. Rather, they imply that blacks have natural, good qualities as long as they are in a servile status. Once free, they would return to their natural state of corruption and irreligion. These texts therefore tacitly imply that the blacks are natural slaves!

Archival sources further indicate that there was a precedent for using blacks in the armies of the Makhzen, to the point of entire garrisons consisting solely of black soldiers. The first ruling dynasty in Morocco to use a large number of black slaves in the army during the Islamic era was the Almoravids (al-Murabitun). The fourteenth century historian of the Maghrib and al-Andalus, Ibn 'Idhari, said that the Almoravid ruler Yusuf Ibn Tashfin "bought a body of black slaves and sent them to al-Andalus."[69] Another dynasty that used a large army of blacks was the Sa'di dynasty who invaded the Songhay Empire (present-day Mali) in 1591 under the rule of Mawlay al-Mansur, which gave them direct access to acquiring black slaves as recruits for the army.

Mawlay Isma'il's decision to forcibly enlist all black people in his army seems to have been political. What is more, his policy seems to have determined the future image of the blacks in Morocco. His initiatives gave rise to cruel practices and racial conceptions that affected how Islam was heard and interpreted with respect to black people. He did not use the ideals of Islam to create a diverse army in a truly diverse society, but he manipulated Islam politically to serve materialistic needs to increase his power. He needed people whom he could trust in the military, soldiers who owed their allegiance solely to him and not to another tribal solidarity as well. The decision to favor certain black individuals in the palace, some of whom had reached a very high status in power, caused many tribes to envy them. The power of some blacks surpassed that of some Arab dignitaries.[70]

An unsurprising response to Mawlay Isma'il's decree was that he was perceived to have placed himself above the inviolable tenets of Islamic law—namely, that a Muslim must not enslave a fellow Muslim. As a result, he usurped or at least circumvented the political domain of the *ulama*, those who ostensibly interpreted and regulated Islamic practice and to whom the Sultan was to answer in his actions as the leader of the country's Muslims. By creating an army loyal only to his person, Mawlay Isma'il affected a separation between the sultanate and the community of Muslims that he ruled. After his death in 1727, the individuals in the black army became the most powerful economic and political members of the society and in effect became free agents and "Sultan-makers." In 1757, a new Sultan, Sidi Muhammad b. 'Abd Allah, inherited the scepter and decided to put an end to the political instability presumably created by the black garrisons. He dissolved the black army and substituted Arabs to whom he gave the right to enslave the black soldiers and to seize their possessions; only a few blacks remained in the army of the 'Alawi dynasty.[71]

Conclusion

Three main points arise from this narrative. First, Islam was politically manipulated to serve some materialistic needs in specific situations. In other words, the socioeconomic and political factors proved to be more imperative than the precepts of the *Qur'an*. Second, the social context in which this textual edifice was created had a long lasting negative effect on the status of black people. The religious message, characterized by the belief in equal political, economic, social, and civil rights for all peoples of Islam, proved at times difficult to identify and put into practice. Lastly, class and cultural prejudices were intertwined in the process of constructing the Haratin identity. The ruling and living arrangements of Mawlay Isma'il's were such that the words "*'abd*" (slave), "*aswad*" (black), and "Hartani" became fused. Mawlay Isma'il's project ultimately altered the status of the free blacks and obscured the origin of the Haratin people.

NOTES

1. This is a thoroughly revised version of my article, "'Race,' Slavery and Islam in the Maghrebi Mediterranean Thought. The Question of the Haratin in Morocco," published in *The Journal of North African Studies*, 2002, volume 7 (3): 29–52, and printed here by permission of the publisher, Taylor and Francis, http://www.tandf.co.uk/journals. My gratitude to my colleagues and research assistant were omitted in that version for technical reasons and here I must say that I am so grateful to all my colleagues and friends, especially at the Schomburg Center. I like to thank particularly Kim Butler, Collin Palmer, and the Center's research assistant, Geof Porter, for their contributions, corrections, and suggestions. Many thanks also go to Tim Cleaveland, Barry Gaspar, Monica Green, and Sarah Shields, and all the librarians who assisted me here in the United States, in France, and in Morocco.

2. See, for instance, Tim Cleaveland, "The Kinship between Master and Slave: Concubinage, Race and Contested Identity in the Sahara and the Sahel," *American Historical Review*, forthcoming, and Urs Peter Ruf, *Ending Slavery, Hierarchy, Dependency and Gender in Central Mauritania*, Bielefeld: Transcript Verlag, 1999.

3. See, for instance, John Hunwick and Eve Trout Powell, editors, *The African Diaspora in the Mediterranean Lands of Islam*, Princeton: Markus Wiener, 2002, and Mohammed Ennaji, *Soldats, Domestiques et Concubines. L'esclavage au Maroc au XIXe siècle*, Casablanca: Editions Eddif, 1994. There are also unpublished works such as Allan Meyers, "The 'Abid 'l-Buhari: Slave Soldiers and Statecraft in Morocco, 1672–1790," Dissertation: Thesis (Ph.D.), Cornell University, 1974.

4. J. Heers, *Esclaves et domestiques au Moyen Age dans le monde méditerranéen*, Paris, Fayard, 1981, 10 and 14.

5. On this issue, see Bernard Lewis, *Race and Slavery in the Middle East: An Historical Enquiry*. New York: Oxford University Press, 1990, vi.

6. E. Levi-Provençal, *Histoire de l'Espagne musulmane*, Paris, G.-P. Maisonneuve, 1953, Vol. 3, 178.

7. Regarding the definition of slavery, see Suzanne Miers and Igor Kopytoff, editors, *Slavery in Africa, Historical and Anthropological Perspectives*, Madison: University of Wisconsin Press, 1977; Paul Lovejoy, *Transformations in Slavery: a History of Slavery in Africa*, Cambridge: Cambridge University Press, second edition, 2000, and Claude Meillassoux, *Anthropologie de l'esclavage: le ventre de fer et d'argent*, Paris: Presses universitaires de France, 1986.

8. The Arab people of Arabia were ambitious to extend their sphere of influence under the new religion of Islam and invaded North Africa in 640s. Since then North Africa became vastly linguistically and biologically arabized and Islamized.

9. Berbers are a linguistic group and were the first inhabitants of North Africa.

10. L. Mezzine, *Le Tafilalt, contribution à l'histoire du Maroc au XVII et XVIII siècle*, Rabat: Publications de la Faculté des Lettres et des Sciences Humaines, 1987, 193, fn. 34.

11. Charles de Foucauld, *Dictionnaire Touareg-Français*, Paris: Imprimerie Nationale de France, 1951, tome I, 134. "Mulâtre: né d'un père blanc et d'une mère négresse, ou d'une mère blanche et d'un père nègre."

12. Mezzine, 1987, 193–94.

13. See David Hart, "The Tribe in Modern Morocco: Two Case Studies," in *Arabs and Berbers. From Tribe to Nation in North Africa*, ed. Ernest Gellner and Charles Micaud, London: Lexington Books, 1972, 27.

14. An-Nasiri, *al-Istiqsa'*, Casablanca: Dar al-Kitab, 1997, vol. 7, 58.

15. Mezzine, 193, 198, and 210 fn. 10.

16. On *Ismkhan* see the article of Cynthia Becker, "'I am a real slave, a real Ismkhan': Memories of the trans-Saharan slave trade in the Tafilalet of southeastern Morocco," *Journal of North African Studies*, 2003 (4), 97–121.

17. D. Jacques-Meunié, *Le Maroc saharien des origines à 1670*, Paris: Librairie Klincksick, 1982, tome I, 180–81.

18. Stéphane Gsell, *Histoire ancienne de l'Afrique du Nord*, 2ème édition, Paris: Librairie Hachette, 1929, tome V, 3.

19. For more information on this subject, see Hsain Ilahiane, "The Power of the Dagger, the Seeds of the Koran, and the Sweat of the Ploughman: Ethnic Stratification and Agricultural Intensification in the Ziz Valley, Southeast Morocco," Ph.D. dissertation, University of Arizona, 1998.

In June 1998, I met a historian from Tata, an oasis region in the Moroccan Sahara south of anti-Atlas between the western Bani and Oued Draa, who told me: "I am a Hartani and I live in the area of Tata and all my villagers are completely black and that the Haratin were not imported from Black West Africa but they were always native of this great region of Draa." This is an expression of self-perception and a self-reflection of the black community of this village.

20. Mohammed Ennaji, *Soldats, Domestiques et Concubines. L'esclavage au Maroc au XIXe siècle*, Casablanca: Editions Eddif, 1994.

21. Arnold Joseph Toynbee, *A Study of History*, Oxford University Press, 1934, v. 1, p. 226.

22. Bernard Lewis, 1990, 20.

23. Ibid., 61.

24. R. Brunschvig, *The Encyclopedia of Islam*, Leiden: E.J. Brill, CD-ROM edition, 2001, v.1.1, article: 'Abd.

25. Brunschvig, 2001, art. 'Abd.

26. *Al-Qur'an*, 2:177; 90:13.

27. See Brunschvig, 2001, art. 'Abd.

28. Lewis, 1990, 8.

29. Brunschvig, 2001, art. 'Abd.

30. John Hunwick, "African Slaves in the Mediterranean World: A Neglected Aspect of the African Diaspora," in *Global Dimensions of the African Diaspora*, ed. Joseph Harris, 2nd ed. Washington, D.C.: Howard University Press, 1993, 293. In this scholarly article, John Hunwick summarizes well some of the cases in which the slave was treated as half of a free man.

31. Raymond Monier, *Manuel élémentaire de droit romain*, Paris: Les Éditions Domat-Montchrestien, 1938, tome I, 276–77.

32. *Las Siete Partidas*, trans. Samuel Parsons Scott, New York: Commerce Clearing House, 1931, 901.

33. Ibid., 1478.

34. Racial distinction and racism are not a part of Islam, and the *Qur'an* clearly states all peoples are equal in the sight of God. "We have created you from a male and a female, and made you into nations and tribes, that you might get to know one another. The noblest of you in God's sight is he who is most righteous. God is all-knowing, and wise." *The Koran*, 49:13.

35. See Edith Sanders, "The Hamitic Hypothesis: Its Origin in Time," in *Problems in African History*, ed. by Robert O. Collins, Princeton: Markus Wiener, 1994, 9.

36. He says in *Race in Slavery in the Middle East*, 1990, 55: "The slaves of the

Arabs were not Canaanites but Blacks—so the curse was transferred to them, and blackness added to servitude as part of the hereditary burden."

37. Abu Muhammad 'Abd Allah b. Ibn Qutayba al-Dinawari, in J. F. P. Hopkins and Nehemia Levtzion (eds.), *Corpus of Early Arabic Sources for West African History*, Fontes Historiae Africanae, Cambridge University Press, 1981, 15.

38. Ahmad b. Abi Ya'qub b. Ja'far b. Wahb b. Wadih known as al-Ya'qubi, in Hopkins and Levtzion, 1981, 21.

39. Al-Mas'udi (attrib.), *Akhbar az-Zaman*, in Hopkins and Levtzion, 1981, 34.

40. Abu 'l-Qasim Ibn Hawqal al-Nusaybi, *Kitab Surat al-Ard*, in Hopkins and Levtzion, 1981, 50–51.

41. Shams ad-Din al-Ansari ad-Dimashqi, in Hopkins and Levtzion, 1981, 212.

42. In Hopkins and Levtzion, 1981, 285.

43. Ibid., 296.

44. Ibid., 284.

45. Ibid., 289.

46. Ibn Khaldun, *The Muqaddimah*, trans. by Franz Rosenthal, Princeton: Princeton University Press, 1969, 61.

47. Ibn Khaldun, 1969, 59–60.

48. Ibid., 60–61.

49. See Frank M. Snowden, Jr., *Before Color Prejudice. The Ancient View of Blacks*, Cambridge: Harvard University Press, 1991, 7.

50. See Ibn Khaldun, 1969, pages 59 and 117.

51. William McKee Evans, "From the Land of Canaan to the Land of Guinea: The Strange Odyssey of the 'Sons of Ham,'" *American Historical Review*, Vol. 85, No. 1. (Feb., 1980), 16.

52. At-Tadili, *at-Tashawwuf ila rijal at-tasawwuf*, établi et annoté, par Ahmed Toufiq, Rabat: Université Muhammad V, Publication de la Faculté des Lettres et des Sciences Humaines de Rabat, 1404/1984, 328. Trans. by Vincent Cornell in *The Way of Abu Madyan*, Cambridge, Eng.: Islamic Texts Society, 1996, 14.

53. David Hart, 1972, 53–54. Hart had extensive field work knowledge on the Ait Atta. He died in 2002.

54. 'Abd al-Karim b. Musa ar-Rifi (d. in 1780's), *az-Zahr al-Akamm*, ed. by Asia Ben'dada, Rabat: Matba'at al-Ma'arif al-Jadida, 1992, 153.

55. An-Nasiri, 1997, vol. 7, 56.

56. Ahmad Ibn al-Hajj, *ad-Dur al-muntakhab al-mustahsan fi ba'd ma'athir amir al-mu'minin mawlana al-Hasan*, Rabat: Bibliothèque Royale, ms. 12184, v. 6, 339 and 396. For more information about the *haratin* of Fez, see the scholarly article of Aziz Abdalla Batran, "The 'Ulama' of Fas, M. Isma'il and the Issue of the Haratin of Fas," in J. R. Willis, *Slaves and Slavery in Muslim Africa*, ed. John Ralph Willis (London, Eng.; Totowa, N.J.: Frank Cass), 1985, vol. 2, 1–15.

57. Muhammad Dawud, *Tarikh Titwan*, Titwan: al-Matba'a al-Mahdiya, 1963, II, 38.

58. See Mohammed Kenbib (ed.), *La Grande Encyclopedie du Maroc: Histoire,* Rabat, GEM, 1987, 121–26.

59. Muhammad al-Fasi, "A special issue on the Sultan Mawlay Isma'il," *Hespéris Tamuda,* Rabat: Editions Techniques Nord-Africaines, 1962, 49.

60. Ahmad az-Zayani, *at-Turjuman al-mu'rib 'an duwwal al-mashriq wa 'l-Maghrib,* Rabat: Bibliothèque Générale, D 1577, 32.

61. I own a copy of this document of 48 pages which came from a private collection in Rabat.

62. Unknown author, *Jany al-Azhar wa Nur al-Abhar,* Rabat: Bibliothèque Royale, ms. 11860, 10.

63. Ibid., 8.

64. Ibid., 18–19.

65. Louis de Chenier, *Recherches historiques sur les Maures, et histoire de lÔempire de Maroc,* Paris: Chez l'auteur [etc.] 1787, tom. III, 226. This work is also available in English translation: *The Present State of the Empire of Morocco,* trans., New York: Johnson Reprint Corp., 1967, vol. I, 297.

66. Muhammad al-Fasi, "Rasa'il Isma'iliyya," in *Majallat Titwan,* special issue, Maroc, 1962.

67. Muhammad al-Karkudi, *ad-Dur al-Munaddad al-Fakhir bima li-abna' Mawlay 'Ali ash-Sharif mina 'l-Mahasin wa 'l-Mafakhir,* Rabat: Bibliothèque Générale, ms. D 1584, folio 174a. An-Nasiri, 1997, vol. 7, 94.

68. *Lettre de Mawlay Isma'il aux 'ulama' al-Azhar,* Rabat: Bibliothèque Royale, ms. 12598, 60–63.

69. Hopkins and Levtzion, 1981, 229.

70. For more information on the story of the black army, known as 'Abid al-Bukhari and their role in the success of Mawlay Isma'il's efforts to reform the state, see Meyers, "The 'Abid 'l-Buhari: Slave Soldiers and Statecraft in Morocco, 1672–1790."

71. An-Nasiri, 1997, vol. 8, 47–49.

9

Race and the Making of the Nation
Blacks in Modern France

Tyler Stovall

In the summer of 1996, 300 "illegal" African immigrants in France took refuge in the church of Saint Bernard in Paris, claiming that the right of sanctuary should prevent them from being expelled. Their struggle for the right to stay in France received wide public attention and support before their final ouster and deportation by French police two months later. Shortly afterward the Disney animated film version of *The Hunchback of Notre Dame* opened in Paris theaters. In light of the recent expulsions from Saint Bernard, several Parisian writers and commentators seized upon the film's story of a gypsy seeking asylum in the cathedral of Notre Dame as a powerful metaphor for contemporary issues of tolerance, ethnicity, and bigotry.[1] Stunningly, this anecdote reveals that the plight of a marginal group of black African men had such a dramatic impact upon French national consciousness that it led a number of leading intellectuals to comment approvingly upon, of all things, a Disney cartoon version of a French literary classic.

This story, with its illustration of complex negotiations between ideas of immigration, race, and national identity, speaks to some key themes in the concept of diaspora. As the field of African diasporic studies has developed and grown, scholars have wrestled with the question of how to conceptualize the relationship between blacks in different parts of the world. Some, especially those writing from an Afrocentric perspective, have responded to this issue by asserting the unity of blackness, whether social, political, or cultural in a kind of unchanging African essentialism.[2] Others, especially black British writers like Stuart Hall, Paul Gilroy, and Hazel

Carby, have championed the diversity of the black experience, embracing diaspora as a kind of countervailing identity to essentialist nationalism.[3] For all their differences, both have tended to reject the nation-state as a primary locus of the black experience, preferring to see those patterns that transcend it as the essence of diaspora.

More recently, some have challenged these perspectives, contending that the heterogeneity of the African diasporic condition is in part grounded in diverse national cultures and histories. In a path-breaking article, Tiffany Patterson and Robin D. G. Kelley discuss the neglect of non-Anglophone black diasporas, and give several examples from recent historical literature of responses to that neglect.[4] At the same time, while arguing for a more inclusive global vision is extremely important, one must also note how diasporic black cultures both respond to and indeed shape the modern nation-state. As Asale Angel-Ajani points out in her chapter on imprisoned black women in Italy later in this book, both diasporic and transnational studies tend to underestimate national institutions in the lives of black migrants, thereby neglecting an important aspect of the politics of displacement.[5] In other words, discussions of diaspora cannot simply ignore the nation or posit it as an unproblematic Other but must rather devote the same critical focus to its interaction with blacks as with other important components of hybrid identities.

Such a perspective is especially important in considering the Afro-European diaspora. The study of blacks in Europe presents a series of paradoxes that pose both problems and opportunities. Populations of African descent in European nations have generally been very small,[6] only recently beginning to achieve the kind of critical mass encountered in many areas of the Americas.[7] This demographic fact contributes to a broader conceptual issue, the widespread perception of Europe as the white continent, racially homogeneous and naturally counterposed both to the dark continent of Africa and to the melting pot of America. References to courses about European history as the study of dead white males are only one common manifestation of this belief. At the same time, one cannot claim that Europeans have had no contact with blacks until recent years: whether or not Africans existed in Europe, Europe certainly has played a major role in Africa. It is not merely true that the central aspect of the African diaspora, the transatlantic slave trade, was largely a European creation, or that European nations colonized large parts of Africa in the modern era. More fundamentally, Europeans to a significant extent created the very notion of what it means to be black in the modern world.[8]

Ideas of blackness cannot of course be separated from ideas of whiteness, so that European meditations upon the African Other also shaped the self-identity of the "white" continent. Long before large numbers of peoples of African descent settled in Europe during the twentieth century, blackness existed as a part of the European imagination.[9]

This paradox between a small demographic presence and a significant cultural impact suggests, I would argue, certain methodological imperatives for the study of the African diaspora in Europe. In order to comprehend this phenomenon to the fullest, one must consider both the lives and experiences of blacks in different European societies, and the representations of blackness created by other Europeans based upon a wide variety of experiences, personal, cultural, and political. In short, the techniques of both social history and cultural studies must be brought to bear upon this subject. Moreover, as is the case with the African diaspora, in general, the experiences of blacks in Europe suggest both parallels and contrasts with the experiences of blacks in other parts of the world. European black populations have often been unusually diverse, bringing together peoples from Africa, the Caribbean, and the United States. In exploring such diversity scholars must examine how black cultures have been shaped both by their origins and by their contemporary circumstances. The very notion of blackness will therefore differ from place to place, creating divergent perspectives upon the nature of the African diaspora.[10]

The presence of blacks on French soil can be traced back to the Roman era, although virtually nothing is known about their history before the eighteenth century.[11] Most of France's black history has centered around two essential themes: (1) colonial encounters and representations, from the slave trade and Caribbean plantations of the seventeenth and eighteenth centuries to the colonization of sub-Saharan Africa in the nineteenth and twentieth, and (2) postcolonial migrations and settlements, primarily (but not only) during the twentieth century and especially after 1945. Yet it is not enough simply to chronicle the story of black life in France. In order to contribute significantly to the study of the African diaspora one must investigate what is unique about that experience in comparative perspective. Or, to put it another way, given the importance of national cultures in the modern age, what is particularly French about blacks in France?[12]

There are many ways to approach such a question. I have chosen to do so here by focusing on one characteristic of French life not only important for blacks but also key to national identity. That is, the concept of the nation itself. The French have probably done more than any other people in the Atlantic world to develop the idea of the modern nation. This concept has been both civil and juridical, emphasizing the nation as a legal, contractual entity, and organic, portraying it as a linguistic, historical, and cultural presence.[13] In considering the history of blacks in modern France, this chapter will briefly explore it over three centuries, from the eighteenth to the twentieth. It will argue that the ambivalence between civil and cultural constructs of the nation so key to the modern French experience has not only shaped black life in France, but also to an important degree arises out of France's black history. Furthermore, this ambivalence has intertwined concepts of nation and race in such a way as to give France's peoples of African descent a distinctive racial profile in the context of the broader African diaspora.

I do not see this approach as trivializing the black experience or reducing it to a subset of national history. On the contrary, I argue that students of the black diaspora should not only ask how blackness has been shaped by a variety of experiences in the modern world, but also how the variable meanings of blackness have themselves determined what it is to be modern, in this case how one interprets national identity. For example, one should respond to issues of African American exceptionalism not only by studying non-U.S. black experiences, but also by interrogating the ways in which blackness and American identity have mutually shaped each other.[14] To return to the anecdote that opened this chapter, the analogies between the African immigrant experience and canonical French literature reconfigure both. Ultimately, to write about the African diaspora is to consider the ways in which blackness both transcends and reaffirms the nation, underscoring the polyvalent nature of racial identity in the modern world.

The Eighteenth Century

From the standpoint of France's black history, the eighteenth century is one of paradoxes. The era of the Enlightenment also witnessed the birth of scientific racism. The triumphant crusade against feudalism went hand in hand with the high point of the African slave trade. In addition, whereas the black population in metropolitan France only amounted to a few thousand people, during the eighteenth century, the nation extended its control over large populations of African descent in the Caribbean. Moreover, blackness itself became a subdued yet significant issue in the creation of French identity, as France began its difficult transition from a kingdom of subjects to a nation of citizens.[15]

Well before the age of Enlightenment, the French had developed widespread, overwhelmingly negative images of Africans. Stereotypes inherited from the ancient Greeks and Romans, and travelers' tales like those of Leo Africanus in the sixteenth century, created a generally accepted view of Africans as people whose black skins denoted stupidity, depravity, and barbarism. French interest in blacks increased sharply during the eighteenth century, part of the fascination displayed by French intellectuals, in particular with non-European cultures. Although the *philosophes* of the Enlightenment paid more attention to Asians and native Americans, they also began to investigate the condition of blacks. Yet since very few French intellectuals actually traveled to Africa, they tended to base their views of that continent upon preexisting stereotypes. This is not to say, however, that the Enlightenment contributed nothing new to French images of blacks. On the contrary, this intellectual movement gave a new foundation to racial thinking, systematically developing ideas about the biological bases of different human races. In particular, the Enlightenment transformed the notion of the Great Chain of Being into a racial hierarchy, with Europeans at the top and Africans almost always at the bottom of the evolutionary scale. For example, in 1797, the biologist Georges Cuvier wrote that blacks resembled monkeys, arguing that the black race had "always remained in the most complete state of utter barbarism."[16]

The heightened interest of eighteenth-century French men and women arose less from scientific curiosity and more from expanded contact and conquest. Although less so than the British, the French participated extensively, and profitably, in the Atlantic slave trade. During the 1700s, more than three thousand French ships transported over a million men, women, and children from Africa to slavery in the Americas. By the end of the century, roughly one out of every eight people in France earned their living from the colonial slave trade.[17] One of the nation's leading port cities, Nantes, was widely known as the city of slavers.[18] The development of the French slave trade was intimately linked with the rise of a plantation slave economy in the French Caribbean. Although France had begun its imperial expansion there in the seventeenth century, it was not until the beginning of the eighteenth century that the islands of Martinique, Guadeloupe, and above all Saint Domingue became full-fledged plantation economies based upon African slavery. For the first time in French history, the French flag flew over territories where all aspects of economic, social, and political life were governed by considerations of racial difference.[19]

In spite of their distance from metropolitan France, the profitability and extent of the slave trade and the Caribbean plantation economy gave race an undeniable significance in eighteenth-century French life. A century before the nation's revolutionary Declaration of the Rights of Man, France issued one of the most extensive official documents on race, slavery, and freedom ever drawn up in Europe. The Black Code of 1685 spelled out in detail the duties and conditions of black slaves in France's American possessions, including proscriptions against assembly, alcohol use, flight, and interracial sexual relations. But the Black Code went beyond regulating slave life to defining the very nature of blackness in France. Although in theory black freedmen were equal to whites, interpretations of the Code during the eighteenth century tended to restrict their freedoms, at times making their status little better than that of slaves. Such interpretations also gradually defined the mixed race, or colored, population as more akin to blacks than whites, a shift from the early years of French settlement. The Black Code thus represented one of the first major examples of the conflict between legal equality and racial discrimination that would prove a key determinant of black life in France.[20]

In different ways, the condition of blacks in metropolitan France during the eighteenth century also reflected this tension between equality and difference. France's population of African descent was very small in the eighteenth century, no more than 5,000, of whom less than 1,000 lived in Paris. It was a diverse group of people, including individuals at all levels of society. One of the most notable was Joseph de Saint Georges, a mixed race man from Guadeloupe who became one of the leading classical musicians in Paris, and later formed a battalion of blacks to fight for the French Revolution.[21] Most blacks lived in much more humble circumstances. The majority consisted of young men from the Caribbean, who generally worked as servants or skilled tradesmen. The single most important determinant of black life in eighteenth-century France was the so-called Freedom Principle, according to which slavery did not exist in metropolitan France. Although on the face of it this principle seemed clear enough, in reality it was fraught with tensions and ambiguities. One could use it to argue either that setting foot upon French soil automatically made slaves free, or that slaves (and for that matter blacks in general) had no right to live in France. As Sue Peabody has recently demonstrated, during the

1700s, a number of Caribbean slaves successfully petitioned French courts for manumission based upon their presence in France, so that the very existence of the black community in France constituted part of the struggle against slavery. At the same time, the royal government attempted to restrict the arrival of blacks in France, fearing not only for the pristine whiteness of the French population, but also possible subversion of the slave societies of the Caribbean. This tension between courts and monarchy both reflected and contributed to critiques of despotism which would erupt at the end of the century in the French Revolution.[22]

The Revolution itself pushed the contradiction between freedom and race to its logical extreme. One of its most important contributions to French life was to make the idea of liberty central to national identity: the Declaration of the Rights of Man was at the same time a statement of universal values and an assertion of French greatness. Under the banner of universal liberty France did not hesitate to impose its revolutionary civilization upon all of Europe by force of arms.[23] However, setting a pattern that would occur time and time again in French colonial history, first the colored freedmen then the African slaves of Saint Domingue interpreted the value of French liberty for themselves, producing the most massive and successful slave insurrection in Caribbean history. In 1794, the revolutionary government did abolish slavery, but largely because the Haitian revolution had already destroyed it in practice. In 1802, Napoleon, who would conquer Europe in the name of the Revolution, reestablished slavery in the French empire.[24] In doing so, he introduced a racial dimension to the notion of French citizenship; whites could be citizens of the nation, but most blacks remained slaves and subjects. Not until 1848 would France abolish both monarchy and slavery once and for all, and even then the idea of unequal citizenship based upon race endured.[25] As the French Revolution demonstrated conclusively, during the eighteenth century ideas of liberty and of race both became part of French national identity, underlining the contradiction between two very different concepts of the nation.

The Nineteenth Century

For France as a whole, the years between 1815 and 1914 were dominated by the development of an industrial economy and society, and by the gradual dissemination of liberal democratic structures throughout the country. The revolutionaries of 1789 may have proclaimed the ideal of the nation, but only during the course of the nineteenth century did it become a reality for most French people. Advances in literacy, education, transportation, and many other fields of French life effectively tied the country together, creating a nation that represented not only a civil status but also a defined culture, one in which the value of liberty as formulated by the Revolution became paramount.

The black history of nineteenth-century France is far less developed than that of either the eighteenth or the twentieth centuries. The loss of Saint Domingue and the decline of Caribbean plantation society diminished the significance of African labor and life to the metropole. Although small black communities existed in France, they have rarely come to the attention of either contemporaries or historians. A few people of African descent, notably the novelist Alexandre Dumas, achieved some recognition, but in general the history of France between the great Revolution and the Great War seems bereft of black subjects.[26]

However, it does not therefore follow that blackness had no place in this crucial period of French national identity formation. In two important respects questions of racial difference played a determining role in the history of nineteenth-century France. First, in this period race emerged as a key marker of social difference, in general, so that distinctions based upon class, gender, and region were often framed in racialized terms. Second, during these years France vastly expanded its position in sub-Saharan Africa, not only bringing millions of blacks under French rule but also creating a new empire with paradoxical implications for the very notion of national identity. In a century bracketed by the withdrawal from Port-au-Prince and the conquest of Timbuktu, concepts of blackness helped define both the shape of French society and France's place in the world.

As elsewhere in western Europe, the industrialization of French society in the nineteenth century created a large, disenfranchised working class that posed a major social and political challenge to the established order.[27] Historians have only recently begun to explore the ways in which discourses of class and race intersected in Europe during the Industrial Revolution, using racial imagery to characterize and understand the new laboring population. Bourgeois commentators in France frequently referred to workers as savages, regarding them as brutish, primitive, and uncivilized.[28] That classic statement of nineteenth-century French racism, Count Arthur de Gobineau's *Essay on the Inequality of the Human Races* (1853), was inspired largely by aristocratic fears of the French Revolutionary mob, which it perceived as essentially a different species and a racial threat to national purity and survival.[29] Gender and regional differences also took on a racialized tone during the 1800s. Discourses of bourgeois domesticity created images of women as hysterical and uncontrollable. Lacking in restraint, their passionate and irrational behavior could threaten the foundations of civilized society.[30] Peasants and residents of underdeveloped regions were also portrayed as savages. As Eugen Weber has shown, in the early nineteenth century Parisian intellectuals frequently viewed the French provinces as little different from darkest Africa.[31] Even the Paris suburbs were often seen as an encampment of barbarians surrounding and threatening to overwhelm urban civilization.[32] The processes that gradually integrated all such groups into the nation at the same time highlighted their marginality in racialized terms.

In the nineteenth century national integration went hand in hand with imperial expansion. In place of the old American colonial possessions, France carved out a new empire in Asia and Africa. Starting with Algeria in 1830, the French took control of Tunisia and Morocco, Indochina, Tahiti, and Madagascar. Expansion into sub-Saharan Africa was particularly rapid. Starting from outposts along the coast of Senegal, by the end of the century France controlled much of western and central Africa.[33] The creation of a vast new overseas empire produced a new wrinkle in the contrast between civil and cultural aspects of the nation. France became in effect an imperial republic, an empire without an emperor, the very idea of which was a contradiction in terms.[34] A nation based upon universal citizenship now ruled millions of subjects, people deprived of the basic rights of man. According to the theory of assimilation, colonial subjects could in theory become French citizens by demonstrating a mastery and love of French culture, yet in practice only a tiny minority could take advantage of this possibility.[35] Consequently, by the dawn of the twentieth century, the French flag flew over an enforced alliance of white citizens and nonwhite subjects. In 1910, for example, French politicians and soldiers debated whether or not the army should enlist African soldiers. In spite of the revolutionary tradition of a citizen army, the government decided that military needs outweighed liberal principles and began to sign up black recruits.[36] In general, therefore, discourses about difference in nineteenth-century France, both at home and in the empire, revealed that the concept of the nation was in practice, if not theory, inflected by concepts of race.

The Twentieth Century

If the nineteenth century brought the triumph of the liberal ideal of the nation, the twentieth century produced new, global challenges to traditional concepts of French identity.[37] From the two world wars, which reshaped relations with Europe and America, to the decolonization of the French empire and the rise of a new postcolonial population in the metropole, certainties about what it means to be French have been questioned and transformed in the modern era. Such changes have made the twentieth century the preeminent era for black history in France, so much so that some believe the nation has no significant black history before 1914. While this chapter has been at pains to demonstrate the inaccuracy of that belief, it is nonetheless true that the recent past has brought an entirely new level of significance to France's black experience.

This shift began abruptly with the First World War. Thanks to the fact that much of the fighting took place on French soil, the nation became a gathering place for peoples from the world over. If one totals the numbers of blacks from Africa, the Caribbean, and the United States who served the Allied war effort, one arrives at a figure of nearly 500,000 people of African descent who spent time in France during the war.[38] Virtually all left after the Armistice, but enough remained to create small, enduring black communities. In these years certain urban areas, like Barbés-Rochechouart in Paris or the old port in Marseilles, first assumed their character as black neighborhoods. The wartime black experience in France was notable not only for its size but also its diversity, and consequently during the interwar years the nation became a preeminent site for African diasporic encounters.[39] The history of the *négritude* literary movement, for example, should be read not only as an assertion of black cultural unity, but also as an experience in diversity, fostering debates between intellectuals from the Caribbean, Africa, and the United States.[40] At the same time, the war helped generate a tremendous vogue for African culture in France, especially among writers and artists. This interest reflected not so much the intrinsic qualities of that culture but rather disenchantment with traditional European civilization and an increased modernist impulse. At a time when blacks played a greater part in the life of metropolitan France than ever before, blackness was attractive precisely because it seemed non-French, an embodiment of the Other.[41]

This contradiction between increased importance and greater marginality intensified during the Second World War and the process of decolonization that followed it. The resistance to Nazism revived a tradition of popular struggles for national liberty that went straight back to the French Revolution. Yet it could only work as a movement to reaffirm the nation's commitment to liberty if it was seen as a *French* movement, and therefore excluded those who were not French. Consequently, even though many members of the French resistance were foreigners, and the majority of free French troops were colonial subjects, they were largely ignored in both contemporary and historical accounts of the national struggle for liberation during World War II.[42] Given this exclusion from the national polity, it is not surprising that the end of France's antifascist war gave way to a series of uprisings in the empire, as colonial subjects took the values of national liberty so dear to the French and applied them to their own strivings for independence and freedom.[43]

Yet it is also true, interestingly enough, that the old ideal of assimilation into French liberal civilization retained considerable force after the war, especially for blacks in the French empire. In 1946, the Caribbean colonies of Martinique, Guadeloupe, and Guiana opted against independence and for departmental status, the French equivalent of statehood.[44] France's sub-Saharan colonies achieved formal independence in 1960, for the most part, yet chose to retain substantial economic, military, and cultural links to the metropole. These links have remained powerful to the present day, so that Francophone Africa can be considered one of the world's leading examples of neocolonialism.[45] The conviction that one can be a part of French culture, even if not a French national or resident of the metropole, clearly still appeals to many French-speaking blacks. This belief offers a new perspective on distinctions between civil and cultural views of the nation, subverting traditional paradigms of racial exclusion by suggesting that those born far away from Paris also have the right to determine what and who is French.

Since World War II, racial difference has emerged as one of the key issues in French social and political life. This is primarily due to the immigration of a massive North African population to the nation since the 1960s. France is now home to over 5 million Muslims, giving it the largest Islamic population in Europe. In many parts of France, ranging from central Marseilles to the Belleville neighborhood of Paris, the sights, sounds, and smells of life remind one of Algiers or Casablanca. For a variety of reasons, ranging from fears of Islam dating back to the Crusades, to bitter memories of the Algerian war, no group in France has suffered harsher treatment at the hands of the majority than North Africans. This has had a complex impact on the situation of blacks in contemporary France: on the one hand, perhaps benefiting them in comparison with a group that is even more despised; on the other, by increasing racism in general.[46]

The end of the formal empire also had the effect of creating a major new postcolonial black population in France. The postwar need of the French economy for labor, and the economic dislocations caused by decol-onization in both Africa and the Caribbean, created an unprecedented level of immigration to the metropole from those areas. By the end of the twentieth century, France had roughly a million residents of sub-Saharan African descent, ranging from newcomers to those who had lived in the country for generations.[47] Geographic origins also make a difference. Those from the Caribbean are French citizens, natives of territories that have been French for several centuries.[48] Most French blacks from Africa have much more recent contacts with French culture. Many are also illegal immigrants and generally live at the bottom of French society.[49] According to traditional notions of French nationality, the two groups would have little in common, and distinctions certainly do exist. Yet one can also detect a process of racial convergence between the two groups. Young people of Caribbean origin in particular are frequently lumped together with young Africans and Arabs under the category of dangerous, suspect non-white delinquents.[50] They are frequently referred to as immigrants, even though they were born French citizens on French territory. In response, many young blacks have embraced a racial identity, often one directly copied from American models. The use of the English word *black* to refer to themselves is a case in point.[51] Such attitudes represent both a certain investment in the concept of African diaspora, and a challenge to the French idea of the nation, color-blind in theory, racially coded in practice. French hostility toward American culture and ideology, so much a part of the nation's experience of modernity in the twentieth century, is in part shaped by its conflicted attitudes toward blackness.

In general, therefore, conceptualizations of the nation and national identity have played a central role in the history of the African diaspora in modern France. The French pioneered the idea of the nation as a civil contractual entity, one to which all people who agreed to certain legal ground rules could belong. However, this universalist idea of the nation became in fact intertwined with culture and heritage as part of French identity, creating a contradiction between global and particularist perspectives on citizenship. From the era of the Enlightenment down to the present day, blacks in France have pushed the envelope of what was French, subscribing to French values and making important contributions to French civilization, yet also frequently judged as not quite French. In response, blacks have pursued a variety of strategies, including an embrace of assimilation and struggles for separation. Most important, they have sought to resolve this contradiction between citizenship and culture, seeking to make the values inscribed in the Declaration of the Rights of Man truly universal.

This critical yet loyal engagement with universalism is perhaps a key component of French black culture. In striving to make a place for themselves within France, blacks have also challenged and shaped ideas of French nationhood. Contemporary debates about the role of race in French life spring in large part out of the black experience there, yet at the same time reflect new uncertainties about France's place in the world as a whole. In posing such questions, French blacks can point the way toward a new national identity, one with global implications and yet one that will remain at the same time very much French.[52]

NOTES

1. Craig Whitney, "A Disney Cartoon Becomes a Morality Play for Paris," *New York Times*, January 5, 1997.

2. On Afrocentrism see Wilson Moses, *Afrotopia: The Roots of African American Popular History* (Cambridge: Cambridge University Press, 1998).

3. Stuart Hall, "Cultural Identity and Diaspora," in Jonathan Rutherford, ed., *Identity, Community, Culture, Difference* (London: Lawrence and Wishart, 1990); Hazel Carby, *Race Men* (Cambridge, MA: Harvard University Press, 1998); Paul Gilroy, *The Black Atlantic: Modernity and Double Consciousness* (Cambridge: Harvard University Press, 1993).

4. Tiffany Ruby Patterson and Robin D. G. Kelley, "Unfinished Migrations: Reflections on the African Diaspora and the Making of the Modern World," *African Studies Review*, vol. 43, 1 (April 2000).

5. Asale Angel-Ajani, "Displacing Diaspora: Trafficking, African Women, and Transnational Practices," in this volume.

6. One partial exception to this pattern was Portugal during the early modern period. From the fifteenth to the seventeenth centuries, the nation which launched the transatlantic slave trade played host to a considerable African population. Lisbon alone counted over 10,000 African slaves among its population in 1620. Nonetheless, even here the black population came nowhere near that in the Amer-

icas. Hans Werner Debrunner, *Presence and Prestige: Africans in Europe* (Basel: Basler Afrika Bibliographien, 1979), 36–45; A. C. Saunders, *A Social History of Black Slaves and Freedmen in Portugal* (Cambridge: Cambridge University Press, 1982).

7. No single individual has contributed more to the historiography of blacks in Europe than Allison Blakely, who should be regarded as the father of this genre. See Blakely, *Blacks in the Dutch World: The Evolution of Racial Imagery in a Modern Society* (Bloomington: Indiana University Press, 1993); *Russia and the Negro: Blacks in Russian History and Thought* (Washington, DC: Howard University Press, 1986).

8. Allison Blakely, "European Dimensions of the African Diaspora: The Definition of Black Racial Identity," in Darlene Clark Hine and Jacqueline McLeod, eds., *Crossing Boundaries: Comparative History of Black People in Diaspora* (Bloomington: Indiana University Press, 1999).

9. See, for example, George Mosse, *Toward the Final Solution: A History of European Racism* (New York: Howard Fertig, 1978). Also, Martin Bernal's *Black Athena: The Afroasiatic roots of classical civilization* (New Brunswick: Rutgers University Press, 1987) has raised a spirited discussion about the influence of blacks on ancient Greece. See *Black Athena Writes Back: Martin Bernal Responds to His Critics* (Durham, NC: Duke University Press, 2001).

10. Patterson and Kelley, "Unfinished Migrations"; Robin D. G. Kelley and Sidney J. Lemelle, eds., *Imaging Home: Class, Culture, and Nationalism in the African Diaspora* (London: Verso, 1994); Aubrey Bennett and Watson Llewellyn, eds., *Emerging Perspectives on the Black Diaspora* (New York: University Press of America, 1990).

11. Jacques Dupaquier, et al., *Histoire de la population française*, vol. 1 (Paris: Presses Universitaires de France, 1988), p. 78; Michel Gayraud, *Narbonne antique: des origines à la fin du III siècle* (Paris: Diffusion de Boccard, 1988).

12. The only real overview of the history of blacks in France is Shelby T. McCloy, *The Negro in France* (Lexington: University of Kentucky Press, 1961), a useful but dated survey.

13. Stanley Hoffman, "Thoughts on the French Nation Today," *Daedalus*, vol. 122, no. 3 (Summer 1993); Brian Jenkins, *Nationalism in France: Class and Nation since 1789* (London: Routledge, 1990). On questions of race and national identity in France, see Tzvetan Todorov, *On Human Diversity: Nationalism, Racism, and Exoticism in French Thought* (Cambridge, MA: Harvard University Press, 1993); Etienne Balibar and Immanuel Wallerstein, *Race, Nation, Class: Ambiguous Identities* (New York: Verso, 1991); Maxim Silverman, *Deconstructing the Nation: Immigration, Racism, and Citizenship in Modern France* (London: Routledge, 1992); Maxim Silverman, "Citizenship and the Nation-State in France," *Ethnic and Racial Studies*, vol. 14, no. 3 (July 1991).

14. See on this point Earl Lewis, "To Turn as on a Pivot: Writing African Americans into a History of Overlapping Diasporas," Darlene Clark Hine and Jacque-

line McLeod, eds., *Crossing Boundaries: Comparative History of Black People in Diaspora* (Bloomington: Indiana University Press, 1999).

15. Useful overviews of race in eighteenth-century France include Emmanuel Chukwudi Eze, ed., *Race and the Enlightenment: A Reader* (Cambridge, MA: Blackwell, 1997); Sue Peabody, *"There Are No Slaves in France": The Political Culture of Race and Slavery in the Ancien Regime* (New York: Oxford University Press, 1996).

16. Cited in Eze, *Race and the Enlightenment*, 105. See also William Cohen, *The French Encounter with Africans: White Response to Blacks, 1530–1880* (Bloomington: Indiana University Press, 1980); Pierre Pluchon, *Nègres et Juifs au XVIIIe: le racisme au siècle des lumièresi* (Paris: Tallandier, 1984).

17. Lynn Hunt, ed., *The French Revolution and Human Rights: A Brief Documentary History* (Boston: Bedford, 1996), Introduction, 9.

18. Robert Louis Stein, *The French Slave Trade in the Eighteenth Century: An Old Regime Business* (Madison: University of Wisconsin Press, 1979); Philip Curtin, "The French Slave Trade of the Eighteenth Century," in Curtin, ed., *The Atlantic Slave Trade: A Census* (Madison: University of Wisconsin Press, 1963).

19. Clarence J. Munford, *The Black Ordeal of Slavery and Slave-Trading in the French West Indies, 1625–1715* (Lewiston, N.Y.: Edwin Mellen Press, 1991); Pierre Dessalles, *Sugar and Slavery, Family and Race: The Letters and Diary of Pierre Dessalles, Planter in Martinique, 1808–1856*, edited and translated by Elborg Forster and Robert Forster (Baltimore: Johns Hopkins University Press, 1996); Dale W. Tomich, *Slavery in the Circuit of Sugar: Martinique in the World Economy, 1830–1848* (Baltimore: Johns Hopkins University Press, 1990); Richard Burton, *La famille coloniale: la Martinique et la mère patrie, 1789–1992* (Paris: Harmattan, 1994).

20. Louis Sala-Molins, *Le code noir, ou le calvaire de Canaan* (Paris: Presses Universitaires de France, 1988).

21. Alain Guédé, *Monsieur de Saint-Georges: le nègre des limières* (Grenoble: Actes Sud, 1999).

22. Peabody, "There Are No Slaves in France."

23. David Geggus, "Racial Equality, Slavery, and Colonial Secession during the Constituent Assembly," *American Historical Review*, vol. 94, no. 5 (December 1989); Alyssa Goldstein Sepinwall, "Eliminating Race, Eliminating Difference: Blacks, Jews, and the Abbé Grégoire," in Sue Peabody and Tyler Stovall, eds., *The Color of Liberty: Histories of Race in France* (Durham, NC: Duke University Press, 2003); Anna Julia Cooper, *Slavery and the French Revolutionists (1788–1815)* (Lewiston: Edwin Mellen Press, n.d.); Shanti Marie Singham, "Betwixt Cattle and Men: Jews, Blacks, and Women and the *Declaration of the Rights of Man and Citizen*," in Dale Van Kley, ed., *The Rights of Man: Its Origins* (Stanford: Stanford University Press, 1994).

24. C. L. R. James, *Black Jacobins: Toussaint L'Ouverture and the San Domingo*

Revolution (New York: Vintage Books, 1963); Joan Dayan, *Haiti, History, and the Gods* (Berkeley: University of California Press, 1995); David Geggus and David Barry Gaspar, eds., *A Turbulent Time: The French Revolution and the Greater Caribbean* (Bloomington: Indiana University Press, 1997); Aimé Césaire, *Toussaint Louverture: La Révolution française et le problème colonial* (Paris: Presence Africaine, 1981); Carolyn E. Fick, *The Making of Haiti: The Saint Domingue Revolution from Below* (Knoxville: University of Tennessee Press, 1990); John D. Garrigus, "White Jacobins/Black Jacobins: Bringing the Haitian and French Revolutions Together in the Classroom," *French Historical Studies*, vol. 23, no. 2 (Spring 2000).

25. See Lawrence Jennings, *French Anti-Slavery: The Movement for the Abolition of Slavery in France, 1802–1848* (Cambridge: Cambridge University Press, 2000).

26. On Alexandre Dumas see Mercer Cook, *Five French Negro Authors* (Washington, DC: Association Publishers, 1943); Claude Schopp, *Alexandre Dumas: Genius of Life*, translated by A. J. Koch (New York: Franklin Watts, 1988).

27. There is a very large historical literature on French workers in the nineteenth century. Probably the best single source is Michelle Perrot, *Les ouvriers en grève: France, 1871–1890*, 2 vols. (Paris: Seuil, 1974). See also Lenard Berlanstein, *The Working People of Paris* (Baltimore: Johns Hopkins University Press, 1984); and Mark Traugott, editor and translator, *The French Worker: Autobiographies from the Early Industrial Era* (Berkeley: University of California Press, 1993). For a series of revisionist accounts, see Lenard Berlanstein, ed., *Rethinking Labor History: Essays in Discourse and Class Analysis* (Urbana: University of Illinois Press, 1993).

28. Ann Stoler, *Race and the Education of Desire: Foucault's History of Sexuality and the Colonial Order of Things* (Durham: Duke University Press, 1995). In particular, scholars of Ireland and Irish labor have mapped the racial dimensions of class in the nineteenth century. See Richard Ned Lebow, *White Britain and Black Ireland: The Influence of Stereotypes on Colonial Policy* (Philadelphia: Institute for the Study of Human Issues, 1976); Noel Ignatiev, *How the Irish Became White* (New York: Routledge, 1995).

29. Arthur de Gobineau, *Essai sur l'inégalité des races humaines* (Paris: Firmin-Didot, 1922); Michael D. Biddis, *Father of Racist Ideology: The Social and Political Thought of Count Gobineau* (New York: Weybright and Taley, 1970).

30. See Joan Scott, *Gender and the Politics of History* (New York: Columbia University Press, 1988); Kristin Ross, introduction to Emile Zola, *The Ladies Paradise* (Berkeley: University of California Press, 1992); Debora Silverman, *Art Nouveau in Fin-de-Siècle France: Politics, Psychology, and Style* (Berkeley: University of California Press, 1989).

31. Eugen Weber, *Peasants into Frenchmen: The Modernization of Rural France, 1870–1914* (Stanford: Stanford University Press, 1976).

32. Tyler Stovall, "From Red Belt to Black Belt: Race, Class, and Urban Marginality in Twentieth Century Paris," *L'esprit créatur*, vol. 41, no. 43 (Fall 2001).

33. Interest in the history of French colonialism has skyrocketed in recent years.

An excellent introduction to this literature is Robert Aldrich, *Greater France: A History of French Overseas Expansion* (New York: St. Martin's Press, 1996).

34. On the concept of France as an imperial republic, see Gary Wilder, *The French Imperial Nation-State: Negritude and Colonial Humanism between the Two World Wars* (Chicago: University of Chicago Press, 2005); Tyler Stovall, "'The Oldest Negro in Paris': A Postcolonial Encounter," in K. Steven Vincent and Alison Klairmont-Lingo, eds., *The Human Tradition in Modern France* (Wilmington, DE: Scholarly Resources, 2000).

35. See Raymond Betts, *Assimilation and Association in French Colonial Theory, 1890–1914* (New York: Columbia University Press, 1961); Alice Conklin, *A Mission to Civilize: The Republican Idea of Empire in France and West Africa, 1895–1930* (Stanford: Stanford University Press, 1997).

36. Charles Mangin, *La force noire* (Paris: Hachette, 1910); Charles John Balesi, *From Adversaries to Comrades in Arms: West Africans and the French Military, 1885–1918* (Waltham, MA: Crossroads, 1979).

37. An excellent survey is James F. McMillan, *Twentieth Century France: Politics and Society, 1898–1991* (London and New York: E. Arnold/Routledge, 1992).

38. Balesi, *From Adversaries to Comrades in Arms*; Marc Michel, *L'appel à l'Afrique* (Paris: Publications de la Sorbonne, 1982); Joe Harris Lunn, *Memoirs of the Maelstrom: A Senegalese Oral History of the First World War* (Portsmouth, NH: Heinemann, 1999); Myron Echenberg, *Colonial Conscripts: Tirailleurs Sénégalais in French West Africa, 1857–1960* (Portsmouth, NH: Heinemann, 1992); Arthur E. Barbeau and Florette Henri, *The Unknown Soldiers: Black American Troops in World War I* (Philadelphia: Temple University Press, 1974).

39. Philippe Dewitte, *Les mouvements nègres en France pendant les entre-deux-guerres* (Paris: Harmattan, 1989); Tyler Stovall, *Paris Noir: African Americans in the City of Light* (Boston: Houghton Mifflin, 1996); Craig Lloyd, *Eugene Bullard: Black Expatriate in Jazz-Age Paris* (Athens: University of Georgia Press, 2000); William Shack, *Harlem in Montmartre* (Berkeley: University of California Press, 2001).

40. On *négritude*, see Lilyan Kesteloot, *Black Writers in French* (Washington, DC: Howard University Press, 1991); James Arnold, *Modernism and Negritude: The Poetry and Poetics of Aimé Césaire* (Cambridge, MA: Harvard University Press, 1981); Belinda Elizabeth Jack, *Negritude and Literary Criticism: The History and Theory of "Negro-African" Literature in French* (Westport: Greenwood Press, 1996); Colette Michael, *Negritude: An Annotated Bibliography* (Cornwall: Locust Hill Press, 1988).

41. Phyllis Rose, *Jazz Cleopatra: Josephine Baker in Her Time* (New York: Doubleday, 1989); Petrine Archer Shaw, *Negrophilia: Avant-Garde Paris and Black Culture in the 1920s* (New York: Thames and Hudson, 2000); Elizabeth Ezra, *The Colonial Unconscious: Race and Culture in Interwar France* (Ithaca: Cornell University Press, 2000); James Clifford, "Negrophilia," in Denis Hollier, ed., *A New History of French Literature* (Cambridge, MA: Harvard University Press, 1994); Jody

Blake, *Le Tumulte noir: Modernist Art and Popular Entertainment in Jazz-Age Paris, 1900–1930* (University Park: Pennsylvania State University Press, 1999).

42. On the French resistance, see Henri Noguëres, *Histoire de la Résistance en France,* 5 vols. (Paris: R. Laffont, 1967–1981); H. R. Kedward, *In Search of the Maquis: Rural Resistance in Southern France, 1942–1944* (Oxford: Clarendon Press, 1993); John F. Sweets, *The Politics of Resistance in France: A History of the Mouvements Unis de la Résistance* (DeKalb: Northern Illinois University Press, 1976). For a consideration of wartime France from the point of view of the colonies, see Eric Jennings, *Vichy in the Tropics: Petain's National Revolution in Madagascar, Guadeloupe, and Indochina, 1940–1944* (Stanford: Stanford University Press, 2000).

43. On French decolonization, see Raymond Betts, *France and Decolonization, 1900–1960* (Basingstoke: Macmillan, 1991); Anthony Clayton, *The Wars of French Decolonization* (London: Longman, 1994); Kristin Ross, *Fast Cars, Clean Bodies: Decolonization and the Reordering of French Culture* (Cambridge, MA: MIT Press, 1996); Jacques Dalloz, *The War in Indochina, 1945–1954* (Dublin: Gill and Macmillan, 1990); Irwin M. Wall, *France, the United States, and the Algerian War* (Berkeley: University of California Press, 2001).

44. David Macey, *Frantz Fanon: A Life* (London: Granta Books, 2000); Robert Aldrich and John Connell, *France's Overseas Frontier: Départements et territoires d'outre-mer* (New York: Cambridge University Press, 1992).

45. Prosser Gifford and William Roger Louis, *The Transfer of Power in Africa: Decolonization, 1940–1960* (New Haven: Yale University Press, 1982); Dorothy S. White, *Black Africa and de Gaulle: From the French Empire to Independence* (University Park: Pennsylvania State University Press, 1979); John Chipman, *French Power in Africa* (Oxford: Blackwell, 1989).

46. On North Africans in France, see Tahar Ben Jelloun, *French Hospitality: Racism and North African Immigrants* (New York: Columbia University Press, 1999); Alec Hargreaves, *Immigration, "Race," and Ethnicity in Contemporary France* (London: Routledge, 1995); Gilles Kepel, *Les banlieues d'Islam: naissance d'une réligion en France* (Paris: Editions du Seuil, 1987).

47. On blacks in contemporary France, see Bennetta Jules-Rosette, *Black Paris: The African Writers' Landscape* (Urbana: University of Illinois Press, 1998); Brigitte Tallon and Maurice Lemoine, "Black: Africains, Antillais . . . Cultures noires en France," *Autrement,* no. 49 (April 1983); Felix Bankara, *Black Micmacs* (Paris: Éditions Robert Laffont, 1988); Calixthe Beyala, *Le Petit Prince de Belleville* (Paris: Éditions Albin Michel, 1992).

48. Alain Anselin, *L'Emigration antiallaise en France: Du Bontoustan au Ghetto* (Paris: Éditions Anthropos, 1979); Stephanie Condon and Philip Ogden, "Emigration from the French Caribbean: The Origins of an Organized Migration," *International Journal of Urban and Regional Research,* vol. 15, no. 4 (September 1991).

49. On Africans in France, see Bernard Dadié, *An African in Paris,* trans. Karen C. Hatch (Urbana: University of Illinois Press, 1984); Brigitte Dyan, *L'Afrique à*

Paris (Paris: Rochevignes, 1984); Mar Fall, *Les Africains noirs en France: des travailleurs sénégalais aux* . . . *blacks* (Paris: Harmattan, 1986); na, *La France et les migrants africains* (Paris: Éditions Karthala, 1997); Janet MacGaffey, *Congo-Paris: Transnational Traders on the Margins of the Law* (Bloomington: Indiana University Press, 2000); Albert Nicollet, *Femmes d'Afrique noire en France—la vie partagée* (Paris: Harmattan, 1992); Christian Poiret, *Familles africaines en France: ethnicisation, ségrégation et communalisation* (Paris: Harmattan, 1996).

50. Maria Llaumet, *Les Jeunes d'origine Étrangère. De la marginalisation à la participation* (Paris: Harmattan, 1984); Harlem Desir, *Touche pas à mon pote* (Paris: B. Grasset, 1985); Jean-Paul Brunet, ed., *Immigration, vie politique et populisme en banlieue parisienne (fin XIXe–XXe siècles)* (Paris: Harmattan, 1995).

51. See Steve Cannon, "Panama City Rapping: B-Boys in the *Banlieues* and Beyond," in Alec G. Hargreaves and Mark McKinney, eds., *Post-Colonial Cultures in France* (London: Routledge, 1997); Hugues Bazin, *La Culture hip-hop* (Paris: Desclée de Brouwer, 1995).

52. See, for example, Édouard Glissant, "La culture française face à la créolisation," in Tyler Stovall and Georges van den Abbeele, eds., *French Identity and its Discontents* (Lanham, MD: Rowman and Littlefield, 2003).

10

"[She] devoted twenty minutes condemning all other forms of government but the Soviet"

Black Women Radicals in the Garvey Movement and in the Left during the 1920s

Erik S. McDuffie

World War One, the Great Migration, intense postwar, global labor unrest, racial violence in the United States, the Russian Revolution, and anti-colonial nationalist revolts immediately after the war, helped to ignite a black revolt across the diaspora that became known in the United States as the "New Negro Manhood Movement."[1] Harlem became the center of this new, militant racial consciousness in the United States and the headquarters of the Universal Negro Improvement Association (UNIA) and the African Blood Brotherhood (ABB), the most important black leftist group during the 1920s.[2]

The Jamaican-born Amy Ashwood Garvey and Amy Jacques Garvey were critical in leading and building the UNIA into the largest, black mass organization in history. At its peak between 1919 and 1923, the Garvey movement claimed 6 million members in the United States, Canada, Cuba, England, Nigeria, South Africa, and other communities throughout the diaspora and Africa. The organization was a pro-capitalist, masculinist movement that promoted race pride, Pan African unity, economic self-sufficiency, and the redemption of Africa from European imperial powers.[3]

Although not as well known as their counterparts in the UNIA, Grace Campbell, Elizabeth Hendrickson, and Maude White Katz were major figures in left-wing movements in the United States during the 1920s. Campbell was a key figure in the African Blood Brotherhood for African Liberation and Redemption. Cyril Briggs and Richard Moore, veteran Caribbean-born Harlem left-wing radicals, along with Campbell, formed the ABB by early 1919. The New York City–based group initially promoted a revolutionary nationalist program that resembled the UNIA's, calling for the redemption of Africa, armed self-defense, race pride, black cooperative economics, and alliances with anti-colonial nationalist movements world-wide.[4] The ABB counted fewer than 10,000 members, mostly in New York, Oklahoma, and in scattered "lodges" across the United States and the Caribbean. The group became an important gathering place for left-wing radicals with strong black nationalist, anti-imperialist sympathies, who had become disillusioned with the Socialist Party's ambivalence toward the Russian Revolution and its program that continued subordinating race to class. By the early 1920s, the ABB had gradually aligned itself with the nascent Workers (Communist) Party.[5] The organization's leaders, includ-ing Campbell, joined the Workers Party by 1924. At the same time, the ABB—and other New York-based black leftists—became increasingly crit-ical of the UNIA, seeking to move it toward the Left. Black leftists and the UNIA became bitter, legendary political rivals.[6]

Uncovering the history of black female leftists during the interwar years is a formidable task. There is considerably less material on the first genera-tion of black female leftists who came into the Workers Party in the 1920s than there is for the second cadre who joined the Party during the Depres-sion.[7] Like most of their male counterparts, the first generation of black Communist women did not write autobiographies.[8] In addition, these women rarely penned articles for left-wing periodicals. This chapter pieces together existing information from oral interviews, the ABB's *Crusader* newspaper, Communist Party files, A. Philip Randolph's *The Messenger*, and secondary texts to produce a sketch—albeit an incomplete one—of black women in the Left during the 1920s.[9]

The task of reconstructing the histories of leading female Garveyites is not as difficult. Writings by Amy Jacques Garvey frequently appeared in the UNIA's newspaper, *The Negro World*. She also wrote a memoir, *Garvey and Garveyism* (1963). In addition, several recent studies by Ula Taylor, Barbara Bair, and E. Frances White, Winston James, Irma Watkins-Owens, and Karen Adler have shed important light on black women's involvement in the UNIA and on the importance of gender in shaping the organiza-tion's ideology and program.[10]

This piece joins a growing body of literature on feminism, radicalism, and internationalism in the African diaspora.[11] However, since there is little comparative work on black women in the Left and the Garvey movement, this chapter points us in new directions. We can see parallels and contrasts in the social backgrounds, the events that radicalized these women, and the black feminist politics and global visions that women of African descent in the UNIA and the Left embraced. An appreciation of these women's politics has important implications for the study of twentieth-century black feminism, black internationalism, and black radicalism as a whole. Both the Garvey movement and left-led groups were important sites for the development of black feminist thought and activism. Women played important roles in leading black radical organizations during the interwar period. At the same time, black feminist and black internationalist discourses of the early twentieth century were hardly monolithic. Indeed, as black feminist scholar Joy James admonishes, black feminism is too often conflated as "ideologically unified and uniformly 'progressive.'"[12] Black women in the UNIA and the Left developed distinct positions on women's issues, highlighting the multiple origins of and the different configurations that black feminism took during the 1920s.

The strong record of movement back and forth between women in the Garvey movement and the Left during and after the Depression suggests a common set of ideological assumptions about black liberation embraced by female radicals of African descent. This suggests that we ought to be cautious about viewing black nationalism, black feminism, Pan Africanism, communism, and socialism as mutually exclusive political categories. My intention in this chapter, then, is to provide a more complete understanding of the multiple strains of black feminism, black internationalism, and black radicalism within the African diaspora in the years immediately before World War One to the Depression.

The Social Origins of Black Women Radicals

Several of the major black female figures in the UNIA and left-wing movements were children of a new middle-class that emerged throughout the African diaspora during the late nineteenth and early twentieth centuries.[13] Both Amy Ashwood Garvey (1896–1969) and Amy Euphemia Jacques Garvey (1897–1973) were born into elite Jamaican families.[14] (Madame) Maymie Leona Turpeau De Mena (1891–1953), one of Garvey's most effective organizers during the mid-1920s, was born in San Carlos, Nicaragua, the daughter of the nation's minister of lands.[15] Henrietta Vinton Davis (1860–1941), a leading U.S.-born Garveyite, who in 1922 was elected fourth assistant president of the UNIA, was reared in an elite African American family in Baltimore.[16]

There is significantly less biographical information about the early years of New York-based, black leftist women than there is for prominent female Garveyites. For example, information on the class and national origins of Helen Holman and Anna Brown, two prominent Harlem left-wing stepladder orators and women's rights advocates before and after World War One, is sparse. It is certain, however, that Hermina (Dumont) Huiswood and Elizabeth Hendrickson, who were actively involved in Communist-led tenants rights campaigns during the late 1920s, were originally from Guyana and the Danish Virgin Islands, respectively.[17]

Grace Campbell (1882–1943), the leading black female leftist in Harlem from before World War One through the 1920s, was born in 1882 in Georgia to a Jamaican father and an African American mother from Washington, D.C. She spent some of her early childhood years in Georgia and then later in Texas before her family relocated to Washington. From there, she migrated to New York City in about 1905.[18]

Not all major black female left-wing radicals of the early twentieth century, however, emerged from middle-class backgrounds. For instance, Ethel Collins, who served as acting secretary of the UNIA in 1929, was reared in a humble family in Jamaica.[19] Likewise, Maude White Katz, an African American who joined the Communist Party in 1927 and remained in it for most of her adult life, grew up in a poor, working-class black family near Pittsburgh.[20] Williana (Jones) Burroughs (1882–1945), who enlisted in the Workers Party in the mid-1920s and became a radio announcer for Soviet radio in Moscow during the late 1930s and World War Two, was the daughter of a slave woman in Virginia.[21]

The Making of Black Female Radicals in the Early Twentieth Century

How do we explain the rise of black radicalism in the early twentieth century, especially among middle-class women of African descent who arrived in New York? Historian Kevin Gaines has argued that black American cultural elites espoused a "racial uplift ideology" in an effort to assert their leadership over the masses of black people and acquire status and respectability during a virulently racist moment in American life. According to Gaines, racial uplift ideology promoted self-help, racial solidarity, race pride, temperance, charity, thrift, chastity, and respectability as strategies to counter racist perceptions of African Americans and secure dignity, security, and the economic well-being for the entire race and the black elite in particular. Uplift ideology accepted dominant racist beliefs that viewed impoverished blacks as pathological and primarily responsible for their own poverty. Uplift proponents promoted patriarchal authority and Victorian mores to counter white supremacist perceptions of blacks and to build African American community institutions. Although black American elites contested the ideology's meanings, they nevertheless subscribed to its main premise that the black middle-class was primarily responsible for the well-being of the black masses and for uplifting the race.[22]

Amy Jacques Garvey's memoir *Garvey and Garveyism* illustrates that she and her husband subscribed to uplift ideology.

> In 1914, he [Marcus Garvey] returned to Jamaica, and for nearly two years he struggled to unite Jamaicans to a consciousness of race—a gigantic task, as educated, well-off blacks ignored the cause of the black masses. . . . This was done to weaken the black majority economically and intellectually. The ambition of blacks when they got money and education was to "lift up the color" of their children by marrying whites or near whites. They argued that these children would be accepted in society and get better business opportunities and jobs; this was a social and particularly an economic expedient, but it created a color-of-skin bias. Garvey tried to show them the falsity and trickery of it . . . prejudice based on "class" was an English institution, and to ape the English and be snobbish made blacks feel "high and mighty." This is one of the phases of "divide-and-rule" policy of imperialism in colonial countries, to reduce the people of a particular country—the real owners of the land—to impotence in thinking as a group, and acting in their own interests.[23]

Her recollections highlight how Garvey sought to uplift the masses of people of African ancestry by building a race-conscious movement under his leadership. Jacques Garvey did not question whether her husband had the right to lead such a movement in the first place. She—like her husband— believed that this racially conscious segment of the black middle-class had a natural right to do so. It seems that this militant segment of the African diasporic middle-class may have embraced radicalism in part to assert its racial identity and maintain its control over the black masses.[24]

Knowledge of global affairs also played a central role in helping to radicalize a segment of women of African descent in the diaspora during the early twentieth century. For example, Amy Jacques Garvey's father, George Samuel Jacques, who spoke Spanish and had lived in Cuba and Baltimore, actively encouraged her to read foreign newspapers as a child. He often discussed international news with her. She credited him with helping to "learn how to think independently on world affairs and to analyze situations."[25]

The recollections of Audley "Queen Mother" Moore (1898–1997), a lifelong Garveyite and a major figure in both Communist and African American nationalist movements during much of the twentieth century, provide excellent insight into how the global upheavals of the early twentieth century in the diaspora and beyond affected her understanding of her place in the larger world. In her oral testimonies from the 1970s, she recollected that "[her] first encounter with the real struggle" occurred during World War One. She learned that African American army recruits in her hometown of New Orleans were denied food and herded into freight cars as they headed off to training camps in Alabama in preparation to serve in France. Outraged by this humiliation, Moore and her sisters decided to follow the troops from New Orleans to Alabama to ensure their wellbeing. The women established a recreation center for black troops near their base at Anniston, Alabama, since neither army facilities nor whiteowned civilian restaurants would serve them.[26]

According to Moore, these events made her receptive to Garveyism. She claimed to have first heard Marcus Garvey speak at a black union hall in New Orleans sometime in the early 1920s. In a fiery speech, Garvey extolled the glories of ancient black civilizations, and he impressed upon the audience to be proud to be black. She credited this event for first bringing "the consciousness to me."[27] In about 1923, Moore and her husband left New Orleans for New York with the intention to help Garvey launch the Black Star Line, the UNIA's premier commercial venture intended to serve as a symbol of race pride and initiate black economic self-sufficiency. They were part of the Great Migration, the mass movement that brought nearly 1.5 million African Americans out of the South to the urban, industrialized North between 1900 and 1930. Harlem's black population grew exponentially from 91,709 in 1910 to 152,467 in 1920. By the time Moore arrived in New York, close to 175,000 people lived in a highly segregated, overcrowded, impoverished Harlem.[28] The grinding poverty and overt racial discrimination that she found in Harlem appalled her, prompting her to become involved in tenants rights struggles and in Republican Party organizing by the beginning of the Depression.[29]

The sense of confinement within the existing racial and gender status quo played a role in making women like Amy Jacques Garvey search for a life beyond the restrictive confines of her formative years. For example in 1972, she wrote that her father, George Samuel Jacques, "trained [her] as if she were a boy," since her parents had no "son and heir."[30] However, he discouraged her from pursuing a career as a law clerk, asserting that such a profession was best suited for a man. Instead, he saw a career in nursing as a more suitable path for her. Even though her father's untimely death enabled her to work in a near-by law office, the job did not assuage her sense of "restless," as she described it. In search of better opportunities for herself, she departed Jamaica for England in 1917. After a brief stay there, she left Great Britain for the United States "to see this land which according to my father's description, was one mixed of opportunity and restriction."[31]

Traveling also played an important role in making women leaders in the UNIA and left-wing movements aware of their place in the larger world. Like Marcus Garvey, who had traveled extensively as a young man through the Caribbean, Central America, and England, Amy Ashwood Garvey, Amy Jacques Garvey, Henrietta Vinton Davis, and Maymie Leona Turpeau De Mena also either had lived outside of their native countries or had toured the Caribbean and in some cases Europe before they joined the UNIA.[32] As Ula Taylor points out, New York City "provided a freedom zone" for Jacques Garvey when she first arrived in the United States in 1917. She was one of approximately 40,000 people of Caribbean origin to migrate to the United States during what Winston James calls the "peak years" (1913–1924) of West Indian migration to the United States.[33] Living in New York allowed her to interact with a broad range of people from throughout the diaspora and to encounter new ideas that challenged the "aristocratic values she had learned during her formative years."[34] Migrating from the Caribbean to New York City most likely had similar effects on Elizabeth Hendrickson and Hermina Huiswood, key figures in left-wing movements in Harlem during the 1920s. Soon after enlisting in the American Communist Party, Maude White attended the University of the Toilers of the East, the Marxist-Leninist institute in Moscow that trained future Communist leaders from ethnic national minority groups in the Soviet Union and from the colonial world, from 1927 to 1930.[35] These kinds of encounters were powerful transformative experiences for these women.

Black Feminist Thought and Activism

Black women radicals involved in the Universal Negro Improvement Association and in smaller left-led groups like the African Blood Brotherhood developed a kind of black feminist praxis. Few of these women would have identified themselves as "Feminists."[36] Yet we can see in these women's journalistic writing, speeches, and organizing what black feminist scholar Beverly Guy-Sheftall identifies as an attempt "to articulate their understanding of the complex nature of black womanhood, the interlocking nature of the oppressions black women suffer, and the necessity of sustained struggle in their quest for self-definition, the liberation of black people, and gender equality."[37] Their activism shows that they believed that empowering women of African descent and improving their status in society were in inextricably linked to uplifting the race as a whole. Like their counterparts in black movements of the nineteenth century and from the Civil Rights–Black Power era, women of African descent were key players in building and sustaining the UNIA and left-led groups.[38] They also developed a transnational feminist perspective that saw the struggle for women's equal rights in a global context that transcended national (and colonial) boundaries.[39] However, we can see important differences in the thought of black female radicals of the 1920s, namely, on the relationship between socialism and women's equality and the different ways the UNIA and left-wing groups provided formal institutional support for women's activism. Their views reveal the divergent ideological origins, political underpinnings, and permeations of black feminism.

Amy Ashwood Garvey's involvement in the UNIA highlights both the critical role that black women played in building the organization and the masculinist, nationalist ideology of the group that could thwart women's efforts to gain equal power within the organization. In July 1914, Ashwood and Garvey cofounded the UNIA in Kingston, Jamaica. She served as the organization's first secretary and first board member, lectured at UNIA meetings, and raised funds for the group. She was critical in starting the UNIA's official newspaper, *The Negro World*.[40] As Ula Taylor points out, it was upon Ashwood's initiative that the UNIA created a "system in which women could enjoy equal participation" that was very different from black organizations of the time.[41]

As stipulated by the UNIA constitution, local divisions elected a male and female president and vice president. Ashwood Garvey also formed the "ladies division," which developed later into the Universal African Black Cross Nurses (Black Cross Nurses). The Black Cross Nurses carried out vital community services such as running soup kitchens, old age homes, and shelters.[42]

Despite the unprecedented power women enjoyed in the organization, as scholar Barbara Bair points out, the socially constructed roles for women and men in the UNIA were "separate and hierarchical."[43] The UNIA promoted dominant notions of separate spheres and socially constructed notions of women's and men's proper roles, which Ula Taylor refers to as "helpmate ideology." This ideology defined the home and family as the primary sphere for women. Men were to protect their families from violence and economic despair and be independent and assertive in leading their households and communities.[44] Garveyites—as had other black movements before and after them—equated the redemption of black manhood rights with the uplift of the entire race. Hence, as scholar E. Frances White points out, black nationalism "can be radical and progressive in relation to white racism and conservative and repressive in relation to the internal organization of the black community."[45]

The Garveys' brief, volatile marriage illustrates the unequal gender politics within the UNIA. The couple separated only three months after their wedding on Christmas Day 1919. Garvey accused Ashwood Garvey of infidelity, financial impropriety, and excessive drinking, while she accused him of infidelity and poor political judgment. As Ula Taylor suggests, Marcus Garvey seems to have been infuriated by Ashwood Garvey's attempts to continue leading the movement, socializing with men, and drinking in public after they were married. In other words, her refusal to remove herself from the public spotlight and assume a more traditional role as a submissive housewife appears to have been the source of contention between the two. In 1922, they were divorced. Garvey married Jacques soon afterward.[46] (Similarly, Jacques Garvey encountered resistance from George Weston, William Sherrill, and other male UNIA leaders, who questioned the appropriateness of a married woman publicly taking part in efforts to free Garvey from government persecution during the mid-1920s.)[47] Despite the acrimonious end of their marriage, Ashwood Garvey remained true to the cause of Pan Africanism, anti-colonialism, black nationalism, and black feminism for the rest of her life.[48]

Amy Jacques Garvey's column in the *Negro World*, "Our Women and What They Think," from 1924 to 1927 stands as one of her most important contributions to the movement. She wrote nearly two hundred editorials. Her writings highlight what Ula Taylor calls Jacques Garvey's "community feminism." Community feminism enabled her "to balance her commitment to Garveyism and Pan-African ideas, and her commitment to her own personal development and feminist interests." In this sense, "community feminists are undeniably *feminists* in that their activism discerns the configuration of oppressive power relations, shatters masculinist claims of women as intellectually inferior, and seeks to empower women by expanding their roles and options." Her feminism also embraced a "politics of respectability," which promoted middle-class morality and virtues. Despite her call for women's participation in the public sphere, she nevertheless did not call into question socially constructed, gender-specific roles that women should be self-sacrificing wives and nurturing mothers and that men should be the primary providers for their families.[49]

Jacques Garvey's column often mirrored prevailing gender conventions by excoriating black men for not protecting women of African ancestry. At the same time, her column shows how she sought to challenge women's exclusion from the public sphere. In an era when most women's columns focused exclusively on fashion, weddings, and social events, her writings discussed women's involvement in politics and UNIA affairs. She saw the struggle for women's equality through a global perspective. As Taylor notes, Jacques Garvey's articles often linked the destinies of women of African descent in the metropoles with those in India, Egypt, and other sites in the colonial world. "Our Women," in short, illustrates how the UNIA created a platform from which women of African descent could actively build a mass, diasporic movement.[50]

Like their Garveyite counterparts, agitating on behalf of black women was a key part of the activism of left-wing female militants of African descent. No one's politics and community service better exemplified this tendency than Grace Campbell's. In the years before World War One, she became close to a small group of Harlem leftists, including Cyril Briggs, Richard B. Moore, W. A. Domingo, Otto Huiswood, Frank Crosswaith, and A. Philip Randolph, and, most notably, Hubert Harrison, known by his contemporaries as the "father of Harlem radicalism."[51] All of them with the exception of Briggs joined the Socialist Party prior to World War

One. By the end of the war, Campbell had distinguished herself as a leading radical and as a well-respected community organizer in Harlem. A.
Philip Randolph and Chandler Owens's newspaper *The Messenger* attributed her popularity to "her pioneer [*sic*] social service work for colored
girls."[52] Her community-based activism showed a strong concern for the
well-being of black women and youth. As Winston James's recent research
has discovered, she worked for the Association for the Protection of Colored Women, a forerunner of the National Urban League. Beginning in
1915, she was employed by the City of New York as a parole officer. She
continued working as a civil servant in numerous capacities until her
death in 1943. While working for the City of New York, she continued to
participate in radical activities. In 1919 and in 1920, she ran on the Socialist
Party (SP) ticket for New York state representative to the 19th Assembly
District in Harlem. In an article on the coming 1920 election, *The Messenger* placed Campbell's photograph prominently in the center of the page
that contained the photographs of four other black Socialist candidates,
including Randolph's. In the election, Campbell won nearly 2,000 of a
total of 18,000 votes, more votes than any of the other SP candidates. In
the same year, she along with A. Philip Randolph, Richard Moore, Otto
Huiswood, and Cyril Briggs founded the People's Educational Forum, an
organization that hosted radical political events in Harlem.[53] In 1921, using
mostly her own earnings, Campbell established the Empire Friendly Shelter, a settlement home for unwed black mothers and their children. In
light of her concern for women's issues and her long-standing involvement with the Socialist Party, it is likely that Campbell identified herself as
a "Feminist," when, as historian Nancy Cott has observed, the "merging of
and blending of feminist and socialist politics" was possible before the
Communist movement and the National Woman's Party became mutual
adversaries by the early 1920s.[54]

We can see in the activism of other black female left-wing radicals their
special interest in women's issues. For instance, Socialist Party member
Helen Holman was a well-known, fiery street corner speaker for women's
suffrage in Harlem during the war. She enlisted in the New York Woman
Suffrage Party. During the mid-1930s, her name was listed on the advisory
board of the Communist Party's *Woman Today* magazine, suggesting that
she had enlisted in the CPUSA.[55] In addition, Danish Virgin Islander, Elizabeth Hendrickson, also a well-known street orator, devoted special attention to black women' issues. For example, she served as president in 1924
and again during the Depression of the American West Indian Ladies Aid

Society (AWILAS), a benevolent society formed around 1915, which participated in efforts to build A. Philip Randolph's Brotherhood of Sleeping
Car Porters and Maids trade union. By 1929, she served as the vice president of the Communist-affiliated Harlem Tenants League. Her affiliation
with this organization put her into direct contact with Richard Moore and
Grace Campbell, who served as president and secretary of the group,
respectively. In addition, Hendrickson's involvement in tenants organizing
invariably put her into close contact with women who often took the lead
in struggles around housing and consumer issues.[56] During the early
1930s, she participated in Communist-led mass actions to free the Scottsboro boys, nine African American adolescents, who were falsely charged
with raping two white women on a freight train near Scottsboro, Alabama
in 1931—eight of whom were sentenced to death.[57] Her involvement with
these activities suggests that she may have joined the Communist Party.[58]

In the years immediately after the war, Campbell concentrated her political activities in the flagging American Communist movement. A Bureau of
Investigation informant reported that she was one of the "prime movers of
the African Blood Brotherhood" in Harlem.[59] She was the only woman to
help found the group and sit on its Supreme Council as Director of Consumer Co-operatives. Her residence served as a meeting place for the ABB's
leadership. She also helped form the Friends of the Negro Freedom, a short-
lived group formed primarily to oppose Garvey. She attended its opening
convention in May 1920 in Washington and served as its vice-chair. After she
joined the Workers Party by 1924, she worked closely with the ABB's successor: the Party-affiliated American Negro Labor Congress (ANLC) formed
in 1925. Along with Cyril Briggs, Richard Moore, Otto Huiswood, and Hermina Huiswood, who served as the ANLC's office manager, Campbell
helped organize community forums on lynching, trade unionism, and segregation in Harlem through the end of the decade.[60]

Grace Campbell's feminism and internationalist perspectives bore
striking differences from women in the UNIA. Her feminism contained a
strong anti-capitalist component. During her 1920 bid for the New York
Assembly, an informant for the Bureau of Investigation reported that she
"made a few remarks upon the need of women waking up to the fact that
they are being driven to prostitution and other evils by the low scale of
wages. She promised to work hard among the women, not only of her race
but all of the women." Her alleged statements charged that capitalism was
largely responsible for women's oppression. Another government informant reported that at a New York City left-wing forum "[she] devoted

about twenty minutes condemning all other forms of government but the Soviet, which she claims is the only hope of the workingman."[61] These statements and her Communist political affiliations indicate that she viewed the USSR as a model not only for liberating the working class— black and white—but also all women from capitalist exploitation and drudgery. She adopted a kind of socialist feminist perspective that viewed capitalism as inherently antithetical to the well-being of all women.[62]

Amy Jacques Garvey and Grace Campbell's positions on the Soviet Union illustrate stark differences in their feminisms. Jacques Garvey drew contradictory conclusions about the Soviet Union. For example, in a February 2, 1924 obituary on V. I. Lenin in her column "Our Women and What They Think," Jacques Garvey bluntly called Soviet Russia's economic experiment "a failure." But she went on to lament "the death of Nickolai Lenin, the wonder man of Russia who with one blow, deposed the Czarist despots of Russia."[63] In a 1926 editorial, she praised how

> the much despised Soviets challenge the white world to exemplify equal
> rights of women in politics and industry. . . . The Reds have sense enough to
> realize that if the mothers of men are not treated fairly men are but limiting
> their own progress and development.[64]

These statements illustrate that Jacques Garvey followed developments related to women in the Soviet Union. She recognized that Soviet family policy provided rights to women that were absent in the West and that she admired the USSR for challenging the Western (white) imperial powers. On these two points, Grace Campbell would have undoubtedly agreed.[65] Jacques Garvey's positive remarks about women's rights in the Soviet Union, however, should not be construed to indicate that she advocated socialism. This certainly was not the case. The UNIA was a pro-capitalist organization.

These subtle but important differences between Jacques Garvey's and Campbell's positions on the USSR reveal the different ideological origins and underpinnings of their feminisms. The former's transnational feminist perspective was grounded in a Pan African, black nationalist, pro-capitalist discourse, while the latter's was based in both a revolutionary black nationalist *and* a Communist internationalist discourse. In this sense, Campbell's global vision speaks to how Tiffany Patterson and Robin Kelley contend "that black internationalism does not always come out of Africa, nor is it necessarily engaged with pan-Africanism or other kinds of black-isms. Indeed, sometimes it lives through or is integrally tied to other kinds

of international movements—socialism, Communism, feminism, surreal-
ism, religions such as Islam, and so on."[66] The grounding of Campbell's
black feminism partially in a Communist international discourse, then,
helps explain how and why black women in the Left and in the Garvey
movement diverged sharply on political matters during the 1920s.

As a member of the ABB and later the Workers Party, Campbell was
part of a global, multiracial Communist movement that called for world
revolution. The positions of the Communist International (Comintern)
on the "Woman" and the "Negro" questions were critical to framing the
activism and political affiliations of Campbell and the first cadre of female
Communists of African descent in the United States.[67] The International
Women's Secretariat (IWS) founded in 1920 as an arm of the Comintern
sought "the complete and all-sided liberation of women."[68] The 1920 *Theses of the Communist Women's Movement* issued by the Comintern in conjunction with the IWS called on national Communist parties to recruit
women "into all branches of active struggle of the proletariat . . . on the
basis of equality and independence."[69] As historian Elizabeth Waters contends, the *Theses* "suggested that the Woman Question was central to the
socialist project, that the liberation of women was cause as well as effect of
socialist change."[70] In the Soviet Union, new legislation granted full and
equal citizenship to women, legalized divorce and abortion, and gave
women far-reaching equal protections in property and labor rights. In
addition, a small group of Bolshevik feminists such as Aleksandra Kollontai advocated that the sexual emancipation of women, "withering away of
the family," and creation of a new system of morals were essential to realizing women's liberation *and* socialism.[71] It is not certain if Campbell went
so far as to advocate these radical positions on women's emancipation, but
she believed that capitalism was anathema to women's well-being.

It is uncertain how Campbell, who appears to have never married or
have had children, may have implemented Communist positions on the
Woman Question into her private life. However, it is clear that the eradication of sexism within their private lives was important to black Communist women such as Louise Thompson Patterson and Esther Cooper
Jackson, who came into the Left during the 1930s. These women not only
devoted special attention to mobilizing and addressing the special needs of
African American women. Inspired by Soviet family policy and discussions around the Woman Question within the American Left, Thompson
Patterson and Cooper Jackson and their husbands made conscious decisions to share housework and child-rearing. They saw the eradication of

sexism within their personal lives as an important piece in fighting against women's subordination in the public sphere. These women and their partners sought to redefine socially constructed gender-specific roles for women and men.[72] On the other hand, as Ula Taylor observes, Amy Jacques Garvey did not question culturally constructed gender-specific roles for women as self-sacrificing wives. In this sense, the Communist movement's gender politics encouraged black female leftists to think and act differently on gender matters than their counterparts in the UNIA.[73]

The Comintern's evolving positions on the Negro Question were also important in directing Campbell's political activism during the 1920s. The Comintern initially saw the African American freedom struggle as subordinate to the class struggle.[74] However, in search of new allies after the defeat of Bolshevik-inspired revolutions in Western Europe and in the aftermath of the Russian civil war (1918–1921), the Comintern sought allies in the colonized and semicolonized world.[75] As Robin Kelley points out, the 1922 resolution on the Negro Question issued at the Fourth Congress of the Comintern in Moscow called on Communists to view African Americans "as a nationality oppressed by world-wide imperialist exploitation."[76] This new position prompted Communists to gain a new—although qualified—respect for the UNIA and black nationalist traditions of resistance. The 1922 *Theses* allowed for Pan African, anti-imperialist cultural and political expressions reminiscent of Garveyism within the Communist movement. It was in this context that black left-wing radicals like Grace Campbell disbanded the ABB, organized the American Negro Labor Congress, and enlisted in the Workers Party by the mid-1920s in an effort to bring black people into the global, anti-capitalist, anti-imperialist struggle.[77]

Real and imagined ties to the global Communist movement had profound implications on the activism of Harlem black radicals during the 1920s. As British Marxist historian Eric Hobsbawm has noted, for the women and men who joined Communists parties during the Old Left period, the Soviet Union represented "the beginning of the new world" and "the proof both of the profundity of the contradictions of capitalism . . . and of the possibility—the *certainty*—that socialist revolution would succeed" [italics in original].[78] This faith in the inevitability of world socialist revolution helps to explain the source of the zeal with which Campbell and her comrades in the ABB assailed Garvey and sought to steer the UNIA to the Left.

Affiliation with the Communist movement also created direct links between black leftist and white radicals in New York. As scholar William

Maxwell points out, the Communist Left of the 1920s enabled downtown white and Harlem-based black radicals unique opportunities to interact politically and socially as equals. These left-wing, bohemian communities were often receptive to alternative sexual lifestyles, free thought, and forms of leisure that challenged middle-class, Victorian morals and conventions. For example, Maxwell points out that in 1922 Campbell was the main organizer of a fundraiser featuring a basketball game between white and black teams for the *Liberator*, a New York-based, left-wing newspaper edited by Jamaican novelist Claude McKay and white radical Mike Gold. These interracial political and social circles in which Campbell traveled were significantly different from those in which Amy Jacques Garvey and other high-profile female Garveyites moved.[79]

The 1928 resolution on the Negro Question issued at the Sixth Comintern Congress, however, marked a key turning point in the Communist movement's relation to black communities. The Comintern called for the "self-determination for the Black Belt." The "Black Belt thesis" not only sparked considerable theorizing on the Negro Question within the American Communist movement, but the resolution was also a central component of the new "Third Period" line, which contended that global capitalism was facing its final crisis. The Black Belt thesis generated a frenzy of Communist organizing in black communities in Harlem, Chicago, Birmingham, and other U.S. cities, centering on housing, segregation, lynching, and unemployment. In Harlem, the new initiative encouraged Grace Campbell, Hermina Huiswood, and other Harlem Communists to take part in tenants struggles during the late 1920s. Indeed, the 1928 resolution created unforeseen opportunities for black women Communists to build mass movements in the United States and across the world to free the Scottsboro boys and to fight for black equality during the Depression.[80]

Although Grace Campbell and Elizabeth Hendrickson attained leadership positions within left-wing organizations, they were exceptional to the movement as a whole. There appear to have been no black female national leaders in the Socialist and Workers parties during the 1920s. Women of African descent comprised a tiny minority in the Socialist Party and in the smaller, clandestine, fractured Communist movement. In addition, the ABB, which paled in size to the UNIA, claimed to have counted approximately 2,000 female members out a total of 8,700 members in 1923.[81]

The absence of institutionalized support for black women's issues in the early Communist movement helps explain why women like Grace

Campbell were exceptional. The ABB did not develop a politically orien-
tated women's column like Amy Jacques Garvey's column. Rather, the
short-lived "Helpful Hints for Women and Home" column in *The Crusader* featured articles mainly about beauty aids, recipes, health tips, fashion, and child rearing.[82] Even though the Comintern prioritized the
African American freedom struggle as an important component of the
global Communist movement, the Workers Party developed no formal
mechanisms to bring black women systemically into or to elevate them to
formal leadership positions during the 1920s—or after.[83] For instance,
black left-led groups did not create lady president positions or women's
auxiliaries like the UNIA.[84] (Throughout the entire Old Left period, the
Communist Party viewed racially and gender exclusive organizations with
suspicion and as antithetical to building working-class unity.)[85] The
absence of these formal structures prevented the ABB from carrying out
the kinds of community work that the Garvey movement initiated
through such organizations as the Black Cross Nurses. This may explain
why during the early and mid-1920s Campbell's women's shelter and position as a civil servant were the two main sites—outside of left-wing movements—for her community-based activism. Moreover, the helpmate
ideology embraced by the Garvey movement may have spoken more
directly to the concerns of women of African descent than the more radical positions on gender advocated by the nascent American Communist
movement. It seems, then, that the UNIA—despite its tendency to privilege male authority—was more effective in providing black women with
formal leadership positions and opportunities to take part in community-
based movements than the ABB and Communist Party.[86]

The Journeys of Garveyites into the American Communist Party during and after the Depression

The movement of black women from the Garvey movement into left-wing
movements during the Depression and after suggests a kind of fluidity in
political affiliation and political thought. For example, Audley "Queen
Mother" Moore came into the Left through Party-led mass actions to free
the Scottsboro boys. She attended a large Scottsboro rally brimming with
Garveyite rhetoric in Harlem in November 1933. Fiery black Communist
speakers demanded the freedom of Scottsboro youths and denounced Jim
Crow and imperialism. After witnessing this spectacle, she recalled think-

ing: "If they got a movement like that, and they're conscious of this thing that Garvey has been talking about, then this may be a good thing for me to get in to help my people." She signed on with the Party soon after.[87] Her recollections indicate that she saw in the Communist Party a continuation of the Garvey movement, which, by the early 1930s, had splintered into several competing factions that lacked coherent programs to alleviate suffering in black communities devastated by the Depression.[88]

For nearly the next twenty years, Moore became one of the Party's most effective grassroots organizers in Harlem. She involved herself in the Scottsboro movement, tenants struggles, labor organizing, and efforts to elect African Americans to political office. However, she broke from the CPUSA in 1950, claiming that it no longer prioritized black self-determination. After leaving the Party, she reinvented herself into a radical black cultural nationalist. From the early 1960s until her death, she became a vocal proponent of reparations and a promoter of Garveyism. She worked closely with several nationalist organizations, including the Revolutionary Action Movement (RAM). In the early 1970s, she was bestowed with the title "Queen Mother" upon a visit to Ghana. Despite her decision to break from the Communist Party, she continued to acknowledge late in life how it provided her with a clear understanding of the "science of society" and how it taught her to organize.[89]

Moore was not the only ex-Garveyite to move into the Communist Party. Her good friend, Bonita Williams, also became a leading figure in the Harlem Section. Although little is known about her earlier years, Williams was born to a modest family in the British West Indies, and she migrated to New York City by the beginning of the Depression if not sooner. She signed on with the Communist Party in the early 1930s due to its efforts to free the Scottsboro boys. She held leadership positions on the New York and national boards of the Party-affiliated League of Struggle for Negro Rights. Williams was a remarkable speaker, who articulated Communist politics in a language that everyday Harlemites could easily understand. She is best known for leading "flying squads" of black working-class housewives against high food prices during the Depression in Harlem. She remained active in the Party through the Second World War.[90]

Claudia Jones, the most important black woman in the CPUSA of the Old Left period, arrived in the Party through nationalist organizations. Born in 1915 in Trinidad and migrating to New York in 1924, she was reared in a poor yet politically informed family with strong nationalist sentiments. Her mother's death coupled with the frenzy of political activity in Harlem around Scottsboro and the Italo-Ethiopian War (1935–1936) made Jones aware of her place in a larger world. In 1935, she signed on with the African Patriotic League, a Harlem-based, nationalist organization led by former-Garveyites, Ira Kemp and Arthur Reid. Attracted to the Communist movement's antifascist, antiracist politics, she joined the CPUSA in 1936.[91]

Over the next ten years, Jones became head of the Young Communist League, and she was elected in 1945 to the CPUSA's National Committee. She also became an important theoretician on the Negro and Woman questions. By the late 1940s, however, she fell victim to McCarthyism. She was deported from the United States to Great Britain in 1955. In London, she continued to immerse herself in radical political movements until her death in 1964. Highlighting the convergence between Garveyites and black leftists, in 1958, Jones founded and coedited, *The West Indian Gazette*, a radical, anti-colonialist, anti-imperialist newspaper, with Amy Ashwood Garvey, who had also relocated to London.[92]

Although Amy Jacques Garvey never joined a Communist party, her politics, as Ula Taylor persuasively shows, became more aware of working-class issues in her later years. During World War Two, she gradually moved out of the UNIA. She became close to a younger generation of radical, anti-colonial thinkers and activists from the continent and diaspora, including Nnamdi Azikiwe and Kwame Nkrumah. She served as a coconvener with veteran activist/intellectual W.E.B. Du Bois of the historic Fifth Pan African Congress in Manchester, England in October 1945. In the years leading up to Jamaican independence in 1962, Jacques Garvey consistently criticized the People's National Party and Jamaican Labour Party, the two major political organizations on the island, for ignoring the issues of working people. Indeed, Taylor suggests that by the end of her life Jacques Garvey had developed a more sophisticated understanding of black liberation on a global scale than her late husband.[93]

The movement of former-Garveyite women into the Left suggests that they continued to search for new sites of struggle to realize black self-determination, build Pan African and Third World unity, decolonize Africa, and promote race pride. As Moore's experiences indicate, she never forgot what she had learned in the UNIA. She attempted to synthesize her nationalist politics with those of the American Communist Party. Her break from the Communist Party and Amy Jacques Garvey's gradual separation from the UNIA poignantly show that when Garveyites no longer felt comfortable within a particular organization they moved on. But they were profoundly changed by what they had learned through all of their political affiliations. These women's changing political affiliations illustrate how women and men of African descent could move in and out of nationalist and left-wing organizations sometimes with relative ease.

Conclusion

This chapter has provided a preliminary comparative sketch of the origins and activism of black radical women in left-wing organizations and the UNIA during the 1920s, demonstrating the multiple origins of black feminism and the distinct political trajectories that black women radicals followed in the UNIA and Left, respectively. Much of the history of black women's involvement in these movements before 1930, however, still remains shrouded. Future research on Grace Campbell and other first-generation black female Communists will surely provide a more complete picture of their black feminist politics, community-based activism, and political journeys. Additional studies need to probe how gender along with race, class, and culture operated within the African Blood Brotherhood. Similarly, as Winston James has noted, biographies on Maymie Leona Turpeau De Mena, Henrietta Vinton Davis, and other key female Garveyites are desperately needed.[94] Scholars will need to critically compare the ways in which gender, race, class, age, culture, and sexuality defined women's and men's proper place within black radical organizations from the interwar years with those from the Civil Rights–Black Power era. Such work will invariably shed new light into the multiple identities, political discourses, the movement of ideas and people, and the formation of alliances (real and imagined) that peoples of African ancestry formed across and beyond the diaspora during the entire twentieth century. In light of the profound challenges that continue to confront people of African descent on a global scale, it is critical for scholars and activists to better understand how black female and male militants often embraced multiple political identities and programs during their lifetime in order to uplift and liberate black people.

NOTES

1. Quote in title from Robert A. Hill, ed., *Marcus Garvey and the Universal Negro Improvement Association Papers* (Los Angeles: University of California Press,

1983), 4:688. I rely on Winston James's definition of black radicalism, but for my purposes, "black radicalism" includes Marxism, socialism, revolutionary nationalism, Pan Africanism, anti-colonialism, and separatism. I therefore group the UNIA, ABB, and other left-wing organizations under the rubric of radicalism. I readily concede that my definition contains its own set of contradictions and weaknesses. See, Winston James, *Holding Aloft the Banner of Ethiopia: Caribbean Radicalism in Early Twentieth-Century America* (London: Verso, 1998), n. 1, 292.

2. As Tyler Stovall argues in this volume, the migration of colonial subjects from French colonies in Africa and the Caribbean during and immediately after World War One was critical in birthing *negritude* and a vibrant diasporic community in Paris. Also see Robin D. G. Kelley, "'But a Local Phase of a World Problem': Black History's Global Vision, 1883–1950," *Journal of American History* 86, 3 (December 1999): 1045–1077; Oscar Berland, "The Emergence of the Communist Perspective on the 'Negro Question' in America: 1919–1931," part one, *Science and Society* 63, 4 (Winter 1999–2000): 411–422; Rod Bush, *We Are Not What We Seem: Black Nationalism and Class Struggle in the American Century* (New York: New York University Press, 1999), 83–120; James, *Holding Aloft the Banner of Ethiopia*, 9–49, idem., "Being Red and Black in Jim Crow America," *Souls* 1, 4 (Fall 1999): 45–63; Mark Solomon, *The Cry Was Unity: Communists and African Americans, 1917–1936* (Jackson, MS: University of Mississippi Press, 1998), 7–17; Cedric J. Robinson, *Black Movements in America* (New York: Routledge, 1997), 67–122; idem, *Black Marxism: The Making of the Black Radical Tradition* (London: Zed Books, 1983), 290–296.

3. Tony Martin, *Race First: The Ideological and Organizational Struggles of Marcus Garvey and the Universal Negro Improvement Association* (Dover, MA: Majority Press, 1976); Ula Y. Taylor, *The Veiled Garvey: The Life and Times of Amy Jacques Garvey* (Chapel Hill: University of North Carolina Press, 2002); Ula Y. Taylor, "'Negro Women Are Great Thinkers As Well As Doers:' Amy Jacques-Garvey and Community Feminism in the United States, 1924–1927," *Journal of Women's History* 12 (2): (Summer 2000); Lionel M. Yard, *Biography of Amy Ashwood Garvey, 1887–1969: Co-Founder of the UNIA* (Washington, DC: Associated Publishers, 1980); Tony Martin, "Women in the Garvey Movement," in *Garvey: His Work and Impact*, ed. Rupert Lewis and Patrick Bryan (Trenton, NJ: Africa World Press, 1991), 67–72; Honor Ford-Smith, "Women and the Garvey Movement in Jamaica," in *Garvey: His Work and Impact*, 73–83.

4. The ABB and the UNIA were hardly the only black protest organizations that sought to forge alliances with people in the colonized and semicolonized world. Rose Thevenin's chapter in this volume highlights the international activities of the Black Panther Party during the late 1960s and early 1970s.

5. Formed in 1919, the Workers Party, which had the endorsement of the Communist International in Moscow, was the most significant of the three major (rivaling) Communist factions that formed immediately after the war. It was also

the organization that most leading black radicals joined. In 1930, the Workers Party renamed itself the Communist Party USA. When discussing its activities prior to 1928, I will use both Communist and Workers Party. For the history of the early years of the American Communist movement, see William Z. Foster, *History of the Communist Party of the United States* (New York: International Publishers, 1952), 186–195.

6. The Brotherhood's 1920 "Program and Aims" outlined a nine-point program for black liberation:

1. A Liberated Race
2. Absolute Race Equality—Political, Economic, and Social
3. The Fostering of Racial Self respect
4. Organized and Uncompromising Opposition to Ku Kluxism
5. A United Negro Front
6. Industrial Development
7. Higher Wages for Negro Labor, Shorter Hours, and Better Living Conditions
8. Education
9. Cooperation with the other Darker Peoples and with the Class Conscious White Workers.

In "Summary of the Program and Aims of the African Blood Brotherhood (Formulated by 1920 Convention)," Communist Party USA Records, Russian State Archive of Social-Political History (RGASPI), Moscow, Russia, fond 515, opis 1, delo 37 in the Library of Congress, Washington, D.C. (hereafter CPUSA/RGASPI); *The Crusader* (November 1920), 904, (July 1921), 1181; Cyril Briggs to Theodore Draper, 17 March 1958, James, *Holding Aloft the Banner of Ethiopia*, 155–184; Bush, *We Are Not What We Seem*, 102–112; Philip S. Foner, *American Socialism and Black Americans: From the Age of Jackson to World War II* (Westport, CT: Greenwood Press, 1977), 288–336; Martin, *Race First*, 221–272; Sally M. Miller, "The Socialist Party and the Negro, 1901–1920," *Journal of Negro History* 61, 3 (July 1971): 220–229; For the first full-length study of the ABB see, Minkah Makalani, "For the Liberation of Black People Everywhere: The African Blood Brotherhood, Black Radicalism, and Pan-African Liberation in the New Negro Movement, 1917–1936" (Ph.D. diss., University of Illinois, Urbana-Champaign, 2004).

7. The second generation of black women to join the CPUSA included Louise Thompson Patterson, Claudia Jones, Esther Cooper Jackson, Audley (Queen Mother) Moore, Bonita Williams, and Dorothy Burnham. Most of them played an active role in the Left through the early 1950s and in some cases beyond. See Erik S. McDuffie, "Long Journeys: Four Black Women and the Communist Party, USA, 1930–1956" (Ph.D. diss., New York University, 2003); Robin D. G. Kelley, "Louise Thompson Patterson," in *Black Women in America: A Historical Encyclopedia* (Brooklyn: Carlson Publishers, 1984); idem, "The Left," in *Black Women in America*, ed. Hine, 708–714; Louise Patterson, interview by Ruth Prago, 16 November 1981, Oral History of the American Left (OHAL), Tamiment Library Collection,

New York University, New York; Maude White Katz, interview by Ruth Prago, 18 December 1981, OHAL.

8. Nor did any black women who came into the Communist Party during the Depression pen their memoirs. Long-time CPUSA activist Louise Thompson Patterson failed to complete her autobiography before her recent death in September 1999. Copies of the manuscript, however, are in the Louise Thompson Patterson Papers, Box 18, Special Collections Department, Robert W. Woodruff Library, Emory University, Atlanta. Angela Davis is the only major black woman Party member to have authored an autobiography. See Angela Davis, *Angela Davis: An Autobiography* (New York: International Press, 1974).

9. James, *Holding Aloft the Banner of Ethiopia*; Irma Watkins-Owens, *Blood Relations: Caribbean Immigrants and the Harlem Community, 1900–1930* (Bloomington, IN: Indiana University Press, 1996).

10. Taylor, *Veiled Garvey*; James, *Holding Aloft the Banner of Ethiopia*; Karen Adler, "'Always Leading Our Men in Service and Sacrifice': Amy Jacques Garvey, Feminist Black Nationalist," *Gender and Society* 6, 3 (September 1992): 358–361; Barbara Bair, "True Women, Real Men: Gender, Ideology, and Social Roles in the Garvey Movement," in *Gendered Domains: Rethinking Public and Private in Women's History: Essays from the Seventh Berkshire Conference on the History of Women* (Ithaca: Cornell University Press, 1990); idem., "Pan-Africanism as Process: Adelaide Casely Hayford, Garveyism, and the Cultural Roots of Nationalism," in *Imagining Home: Class, Culture and Nationalism in the African Diaspora*, ed. Sidney Lemelle and Robin Kelley (London: Verso, 1994), 121–144; Martin, "Women in the Garvey Movement," in *Garvey: His Work and Impact*, 67–72; Ford-Smith, "Women and the Garvey Movement in Jamaica," in *Garvey: His Work and Impact*, 73–83; E. Frances White, "Africa on My Mind: Gender, Counterdiscourse, and African American Nationalism," *Journal of Women's History* 2, 1 (Spring 1990): 73–97; William Seraile, "Henrietta Vinton Davis and the Garvey Movement," *Afro-Americans in New York Life and History* 7, 2 (July 1983): 7–24; Okonkwo Rina, "Adelaide Casely Hayford: Cultural Nationalist and Feminist," *Phylon* 42, 1 (March 1981); Mark D. Matthews, "'Our Women and What They Think,' Amy Jacques Garvey and *The Negro World*," *Black Scholar* 10, 9 (May/June 1979): 2–13.

11. Tiffany Patterson and Robin D. G. Kelley, "Unfinished Migrations: Reflections on the African Diaspora and the Making of the Modern World," *African Studies Review* 43, 1 (April 2000): 43, 1, 27; Gerald Horne, *Race War: White Supremacy and the Attack on the British Empire* (New York: New York University Press, 2004); Brent Hayes Edwards, *The Practice of Diaspora: Literature, Translation, and the Rise of Black Internationalism* (Cambridge: Harvard University Press, 2003); McDuffie, "Long Journeys"; Katherine A. Baldwin, *Beyond the Color Line and the Iron Curtain: Reading Encounters Between Black and Red, 1922–1963* (Durham: Duke University Press, 2002); Fanon Che Wilkins, "In the Belly of the Beast: Black Power, Anti-Imperialism, and the African Liberation Solidarity Move-

ment" (Ph.D. diss., New York University, 2001); Peter Linebaugh and Marcus Rediker, *The Many-Headed Hydra: Sailors, Slaves, Commoners, and the Hidden History of the Revolutionary Atlantic* (Boston: Beacon Press, 2000); William Maxwell, *New Negro and Old Left: African American Writing and Communism Between the Wars* (New York: Columbia University Press, 1999); Robin D. G. Kelley and Betsy Esch, "Black Like Mao: Red China and Black Revolution," *Souls* 6 (Fall 1999): 6–41; Kevin Gaines, "African-American Expatriates in Ghana and the Black Radical Tradition," *Souls* 1, 4 (Fall 1999): 64–71; Theodore Kornweibel, *"Seeing Red": Federal Campaigns Against Black Militancy, 1919–1925* (Bloomington: Indiana University Press, 1998); Penny M. Von Eschen, *Race Against Empire: Black Americans and Anticolonialism, 1937–1959* (Ithaca: Cornell University Press, 1997); Brenda Gayle Plummer, *Rising Wind: Black Americans and U.S. Foreign Affairs, 1935–1960* (Chapel Hill: University of North Carolina Press, 1996); Julius Scott, "The Common Wind: Currents of Afro-American Communication in the Era of the Haitian Revolution" (Ph.D. diss., Duke University, 1986).

There is a growing number of works that theorize and discuss black feminist thought and black women's activism. Some examples include Barbara Ransby, *Ella Baker and the Black Freedom Movement: A Radical Democratic Vision* (Chapel Hill: University of North Carolina Press, 2003); Dayo Folayan Gore, "To Light a Candle in a Gale Wind: Black Women Radicals and Post World War II US Politics" (Ph.D. diss., New York University, 2003); Bettye Collier Thomas and V. P. Franklin, eds., *Sisters in the Struggle: African American Women in the Civil Rights Struggle* (New York: New York University Press, 2001); Patricia A. Schechter, *Ida B. Wells-Barnett and American Reform, 1990–1930* (Chapel Hill: University of North Carolina Press, 2001); Chana Kai Lee, *For Freedom's Sake: the Life of Fannie Lou Hammer* (Urbana, IL: University of Illinois Press, 1999); Angela Y. Davis, *Blues Legacies and Black Feminism: Gertrude "Ma" Rainey, Bessie Smith, and Billie Holiday* (New York: Pantheon, 1998); idem, *Women, Culture, and Politics* (New York: Random House, 1989); Deborah Gray White, *Too Heavy a Load: Black Women in Defense of Themselves, 1894–1995* (New York: W.W. Norton, 1999); Hazel Carby, *Race Men* (Cambridge: Harvard University Press, 1998); Joanne Grant, *Ella Baker: Freedom Bound* (New York: John Wiley and Sons, 1998); Tera W. Hunter, *To 'Joy My Freedom: Southern Black Women's Lives and Labors after the Civil War* (Cambridge: Harvard University Press, 1997); Belinda Robnett, *How Long? How Long? African-American Women in the Struggle for Civil Rights* (New York: Oxford University Press, 1997); Vicki L. Crawford, "Race, Class, Gender, and Culture: Black Women's Activism in the Mississippi Freedom Movement," *Journal of Mississippi History* 56 (Spring 1996): 1–21; Stanlie M. James and Abena P. A. Busia, eds., *Theorizing Black Feminism: the Visionary Pragmatism of Black Women* (New York: Routledge & Kegan Paul, 1994); Elsa Barkley Brown, "Negotiating and Transforming the Public Sphere: African American Political Life in the Transition from Slavery to Freedom," *Public Culture* 7 (1994): 107–146; Evelyn Brooks Higginbotham, *Righteous*

Discontent: The Women's Movement in the Black Baptist Church, 1880–1920 (Cambridge: Harvard University Press, 1993); idem, "African American Women's History and the Metalanguage of Race," *Signs* 17 (Winter 1992): 261–276.

12. Joy James, "Radicalizing Feminism," in *The Black Feminist Reader*, ed. Joy James and T. Denean Sharpley-Whiting (Malden, MA: Blackwell Publishers, 2000), 246.

13. Robinson, *Black Marxism*, 251–265, 266–301; Judith Stein, *The World of Marcus Garvey: Race and Class in Modern Society* (Baton Rouge: Louisiana State University Press, 1986), 7–23; James, *Holding Aloft the Banner of Ethiopia*, 9–49; Watkins-Owens, *Blood Relations*, 11–29; Bush, *We Are Not What We Seem*, 85–93.

14. Taylor, *Veiled Garvey*, 6–17; Ula Y. Taylor, "Intellectual Pan-African Feminists: Amy Ashwood-Garvey and Amy Jacques-Garvey," *Abafazi: The Simmons College Women's Journal* 9 (1998): 10–18; Yard, *Biography of Amy Ashwood Garvey*, 6–7; Adler, "Amy Jacques Garvey, Feminist Black Nationalist," 349; Robert A. Hill and Barbara Bair, eds. *Marcus Garvey: Life and Lessons* (Berkeley, CA: University of California Press, 1987), 358–359.

15. Hill, ed., *Marcus Garvey*, 6:117–118.

16. Seraile, "Henrietta Vinton Davis," 7–21; Stein, *The World of Marcus Garvey*, 150–151; James, *Holding Aloft the Banner of Ethiopia*, 137–138, 154; Hill, ed., *Marcus Garvey*, 6:375–376; Bair, "True Women, Real Men," 161, Martin, "Women in the Garvey Movement," 68.

17. Watkins-Owens, *Blood Relations*, 202n.7; Solomon, *Cry Was Unity*, 3, 61, 97; W. Burghardt Turner and Joyce M. Turner, eds., *Richard B. Moore: Caribbean Militant in Harlem, Collected Writings, 1920–1972* (Bloomington, IN: University of Indiana Press, 1988), 55–56, 165–166, 217. Otto and Hermina Huiswood left the United States during the 1930s, where they settled in Paris and later in Amsterdam. See Harry Haywood, *Black Bolshevik: An Autobiography of an Afro-American Communist* (Chicago: Liberator Press, 1978), 470, 583; Foner, *American Socialism and Black Americans*, 266.

18. James, *Holding Aloft the Banner of Ethiopia*, 173–175. For incorrect statements that Campbell was Caribbean-born, see Mark Naison, *Communists in Harlem during the Depression* (New York: Grove Press, 1983), 5; Watkins-Owens, *Blood Relations*, 26.

19. Bair, "True Women, Real Men," 165–166.

20. White Katz, interview by Prago; Haywood, *Black Bolshevik*, 217.

21. Williana Burroughs, "Miniatures of Our Militant Women," n.d., from private collection Carola Burroughs; Harvey Klehr, et al., *The Secret World of American Communism* (New Haven: Yale University Press, 1995), 199–203.

22. Kevin Gaines, *Uplifting the Race: Black Leadership, Politics, and Culture in the Twentieth Century* (Chapel Hill, NC: University of North Carolina Press, 1996), 1–99; Cedric Robinson makes a similar argument, see *Black Marxism*, 251–301.

23. Ibid., 12.

24. Robinson, *Black Marxism*, 251–265, 266–301; Bush, *We Are Not What We Seem*, 85–93.

25. Quoted in Amy Jacques Garvey, "The Role of Women in Liberation Struggles," *Massachusetts Review* 13 (Winter–Spring 1972): 110; Amy Jacques Garvey, *Garvey and Garveyism* (New York: Collier Books, 1970), 39.

26. Quoted in Moore, interview by Ruth Prago, 23 December 1981, OHAL, 4.

27. Queen Mother Audley Moore, interview by Mark Naison, 1972, OHAL, 5; McDuffie, "Long Journeys," 21–40.

28. Manning Marable, *Race, Reform, Rebellion: The Second Reconstruction in Black America, 1945–1990* (Jackson: University of Mississippi Press, 1991), 10; Darlene Clark Hine, "Black Migration to the Urban Midwest: The Gender Dimension, 1915–1945, in *The New African American Urban History*, ed. Kenneth W. Goings and Raymond Mohl (Thousand Oaks, CA: Sage Publications, 1996), 256; Jacqueline Jones, *Labor of Love, Labor of Sorrow: Black Women, Work, and the Family from Slavery to the Present* (New York: Basic Books, 1985), 156; Gilbert Osofsky, *Harlem: The Making of a Ghetto*, 2nd ed. (1966, 1971; rpt. Chicago: Elephant Paperbacks, 1996), 128.

29. "Audley (Queen Mother) Moore," interview by Cheryl Townsend Gilkes, 6, 8 June 1978, in *The Black Women Oral History Project*, vol. 8, ed. Ruth Edmonds Hill (Westport, CT: Meckler, 1991), 130–133.

30. Amy Jacques Garvey, "The Role of Women in Liberation Struggles," *Massachusetts Review* 13 (Winter–Spring 1972), 109–110.

31. Jacques Garvey, *Garvey and Garveyism*, 112–113.

32. Yard, *Biography of Amy Ashwood Garvey*, 13–14, 10; Hill and Bair, eds., *Marcus Garvey: Life and Lessons*, 358; Seraile, "Henrietta Vinton Davis," 8–21.

33. James, *Holding Aloft the Banner of Ethiopia*, 12.

34. Taylor, *Veiled Garvey*, 38.

35. White Katz, interview by Prago; Haywood, *Black Bolshevik*, 154–165, 217, 281; Woodford McClellan, "Africans and Black Americans in the Comintern Schools, 1925–1934," *International Journal of African Historical Studies* 26, 2 (May 1993): 370–391; Solomon, *Cry Was Unity*, 89–91.

36. Historian Nancy Cott has provided the best discussion of the origins, meanings, and applications of the term "Feminism," which was commonly capitalized during the early twentieth century. See Cott, *The Grounding of Modern Feminism* (New Haven: Yale University Press, 1987), quoted 15, 3–50; idem, "What's in a Name? The Limits of 'Social Feminism': of Expanding the Vocabulary of Women's History," *Journal of American History* 76, 3 (December 1989): 809–829.

37. Beverly Guy-Sheftall, *Words of Fire: An Anthology of African-American Feminist Thought* (New York: New Press, 1995), xiv.

38. Ransby, *Ella Baker and the Black Freedom Movement*; Collier Thomas and V. P. Franklin, eds., *Sisters in the Struggle*; Gray White, *Too Heavy a Load*; Kimberly Springer, "'Our Politics Was Black Women': Black Feminist Organizations,

1968–1980," Ph.D. diss., Emory University, 1999; Chateauvert, *Marching Together: Women of the Brotherhood of Sleeping Cars* (Urbana: University of Illinois Press, 1998); Tracye Matthews, "'No One Ever Asks What a Man's Place in the Revolution Is': Gender and Sexual Politics in the Black Panther Party, 1966–1971," Ph.D. diss., University of Michigan, 1998; Hunter, *To 'Joy My Freedom*; Robnett, *How Long? How Long? African-American Women in the Struggle for Civil Rights*; Crawford, "Race, Class, Gender, and Culture: Black Women's Activism in the Mississippi Freedom Movement"; Brooks Higginbotham, *Righteous Discontent.*

39. Recently, some feminist scholars have adopted the term "transnationalism" to describe feminist practices and to critique the use of the terms such as *global feminism* and *global sisterhood*, which according to them, universalizes women's experiences and promotes the western women's liberation model. These scholars use the term *transnational feminism* to provide an analysis that examines the intersections between the local and the global. For these reasons, I have chosen the term transnational. See Asale Angel-Ajani, "Displacing Diaspora: Trafficking, African Women, and Transnational Practices" in this volume; also see Nancy A. Naples and Manisha Desai, eds., *Women's Activism and Globalization: Linking Local Struggles and Transnational Politics* (New York: Routledge, 2002); Jacqui Alexander and Chandra Mohanty, eds. *Feminist Genealogies, Colonial Legacies, Democratic Futures* (New York: Routledge, 1997); Inderpal Grewal and Caren Kaplan, eds. *Scattered Hegemonies: Postmodernity and Transnational Feminist Practices* (Minneapolis: University of Minnesota Press, 1994); Cynthia Enloe, *Bananas, Beaches, and Bases: Making Sense of International Politics* (London: Pandora, 1990).

40. Ashwood Garvey's participation in the UNIA was hardly unique. Historian Winston James notes that three of the six directors of the UNIA at one time were women, and eight of the fifteen original members of the African Communities League, the UNIA's political and commercial wing incorporated in July 1918, were women. James, *Holding Aloft the Banner of Ethiopia*, 138; Yard, *Biography of Amy Ashwood Garvey*, 44–50; Hill and Bair, eds. *Marcus Garvey: Life and Lessons*, 356, 362–363.

41. Taylor, *Veiled Garvey*, 44.

42. Taylor, *Veiled Garvey*, 44–45; James, *Holding Aloft the Banner of Ethiopia*, 140; Martin, "Women in the Garvey Movement," 67–70; Ford-Smith, "Women and the Garvey Movement in Jamaica," 77–82.

43. Bair, "True Women, True Men," 154–157; see also Taylor, *Veiled Garvey*, 44.

44. Taylor, *Veiled Garvey*, 1–2.

45. E. Frances White, "Africa on My Mind," 76–77.

46. Yard, *Biography of Amy Ashwood Garvey*, 51–63, 75–79; Taylor, "Intellectual Pan Africanists," 12–13; "Affidavit of Amy Ashwood Garvey," 30 August 1920, in Hill, ed., *Marcus Garvey*, 2:634–642.

47. Taylor, *Veiled Garvey*, 66–69.

48. After her marriage dissolved, Ashwood Garvey led an active life, moving to

London in 1924, traveling extensively through the Caribbean, joining the International African Service Bureau in the 1930s, working with the Council of African Affairs in the 1940s, serving as chair to a panel at the Fifth Pan African Congress in Manchester, England in 1945, and traveling to Ghana that same decade in search of her ancestral roots. During the 1950s, she associated with Caribbean and African student and community organizations in London. By the late 1960s, she was revered by a new generation of young black nationalists. See Yard, *Biography of Amy Ashwood Garvey*, 108–219; Hill and Bair, *Marcus Garvey: Life and Lessons*, 359.

49. Quoted 64 in Taylor, *Veiled Garvey*, 1–3, 64–90; For an insightful discussion of "politics of respectability," see Brooks Higginbotham, *Righteous Discontent*, 14–15, 185–229.

50. Taylor, *Veiled Garvey*, 64–90; Matthews, "Amy Jacques Garvey and *The Negro World*," 4–12.

51. Marcus Garvey credited Harrison for introducing him to Harlem's political scene when he first arrived in 1916. Hubert Harrison, "Socialism and the Negro," *International Socialist Review* (July 1912): 65–68; Jeffrey B. Perry, *A Hubert Harrison Reader* (Middletown, CT: Wesleyan University Press, 2001), 1–30; Jeffrey Babcock Perry, "Hubert Henry Harrison, 'The Father of Harlem Radicalism': The Early Years—1883 Through the Founding of the Liberty League and *The Voice* in 1917" (Ph.D. diss., Columbia University, 1986), 1–40; James, *Holding Aloft the Banner of Ethiopia*, 122–134; James, "Being Red and Black in Jim Crow America," 51–54. See, Cyril Briggs to Theodore Draper, letter, 17 March 1958, Theodore Draper Papers, Box 31, Folder Negro-Briggs, Cyril, Hoover Institute on War, Revolution, and Peace, Stanford University, Stanford.

52. *The Messenger* (November 1920), 138.

53. James, *Holding Aloft the Banner of Ethiopia*, 173–175, 271; *The Messenger* (November 1920), 139.

54. Cott, *Groundings of Modern Feminism*, 74.

55. Watkins-Owens, *Blood Relations*, 79. 93; Holman's name appears in issues of *Woman Today* from June through December 1936. It is very likely that she had developed ties to the magazine before this time. Grace Campbell was also noted as an advisory board member during this time.

56. Annelise Orleck, *Common Sense and a Little Fire: Women and Working-Class Politics in the United States, 1900–1965* (Chapel Hill: University of North Carolina Press, 1995), esp. 215–249.

57. James Goodman, *Stories of Scottsboro* (New York: Vintage, 1994); Dan T. Carter, *Scottsboro: A Tragedy of the American South*, rev. ed. (Baton Rouge: Louisiana State University Press, 1979).

58. *The Negro Champion*, 20 April 1929, 2; *The Liberator*, 21 December 1929, 3; 24 December 1929, 1; 28 December 1929, 1; 1 February 1930, 3; *Amsterdam News*, 16 January 1929, 3; 5 June 1929, 1, 2; Turner and Turner, *Richard B. Moore*, 55, 65, 217; Watkins-Owens, *Blood Relations*, 70–71, 74, 84, 92, 99, 108, 202n. 7.

59. Bureau of Investigation report quoted in Hill, ed., *Marcus Garvey and the UNIA Papers*, vol. 4, 688.

60. *The Messenger* (April–May 1920), 3; "Resolutions of the Convention of the Friends of the Negro Freedom," CPUSA/RGASPI, 515/1/37; 515/1/2024; Solomon, *Cry Was Unity*, 9–21, 52–67; James, *Holding Aloft the Banner of Ethiopia*, 155–184; Bush, *We Are Not What We Seem*, 102–112; Kornweibel, *"Seeing Red,"* 151; Naison, *Communists in Harlem*, 13–14.

61. Hill, ed., *Marcus Garvey*, 4:688.

62. For discussions of socialist feminism, see Karen V. Hansen and Ilene J. Philipson, eds., *Women, Class, and the Feminist Imagination* (Philadelphia: Temple University Press, 1990); Sheila Rowbotham, *Women, Resistance, and Revolution: A History of Women and Revolution in the Modern World* (New York: Vintage, 1972), esp. 59–169; idem, *A New World for Women: Stella Browne—Socialist Feminist* (London: Pluto Press, 1977); Sherma Gluck, "Socialist Feminists between the Two World Wars: Insights from Oral History," in *Decades of Discontent: The Women's Movement, 1920–1940*, ed. Lois Scharf and Joan M. Jensen (Boston: Northeastern University Press, 1987), 279–298; Zillah Eisenstein, ed., *Capitalist Patriarchy and the Case for Socialist Feminism* (New York: Monthly Review Press, 1979).

63. *The Negro World*, 2 February 1924, 10. Soon after Lenin's death, Marcus Garvey telegraphed a message to the Soviet government, expressing his condolences; he wrote: "To us Lenin was one of the world's greatest benefactors. Long life to the Soviet government." Quoted in Martin, *Race First*, 252; Jacques Garvey, *Garvey and Garveyism*, 96.

64. *The Negro World*, 6 January 1926, 7.

65. Other black women leftists drew similar conclusions about Soviet family policy, in particular Louise Thompson, who visited the USSR for nearly six months in 1932. See, McDuffie, "Long Journeys," 71–72, 93–126; *New York Amsterdam News*, 23 November 1932, 5; see also White Katz, interview by Prago.

66. Patterson and Kelley, "Unfinished Migrations," 27.

67. For histories of the Communist International, see Fernando Claudín, *The Communist Movement: From Comintern to Cominform, Part One, The Crisis of the Communist International*, translated by Brian Pearce (New York: Monthly Review Press, 1975); Franz Borkenau, *World Communism: A History of the Communist International* (Ann Arbor, MI: University of Michigan Press, 1962); C.L.R. James, *World Revolution, 1917–1936* (Atlantic Highlands, NJ: Humanities Press, 1993; orig. 1937).

68. "Kollontai Writes of Third International and Working Women," *Worker*, 11 March 1922, 4, quoted in Lynn Shapiro, "Red Feminism: American Communism and the Women's Rights Tradition, 1919–1956" (Ph.D. diss., American University, 1996), 51.

69. "Women and the Communist International: Thesis Adopted at the Third Congress," *The Communist* 1, 5 (November 1921): 31.

70. Elizabeth Waters, "In the Shadow of the Comintern: The Communist Women's Movement, 1920–43," in *Promissory Notes: Women in the Transition to Socialism*, ed. Sonia Kruk, et al. (New York: Monthly Review Press, 1989), 33.

71. Wendy Z. Goldman, *Women at the Gates: Gender and Industry in Stalin's Russia* (Cambridge: Cambridge University Press, 2002), 33–42; idem., *Women, the State and Revolution: Soviet Family Policy and Social Life, 1917–1936* (Cambridge: Cambridge University Press, 1993), 1–13, 111–113, 254–336; Waters, "In the Shadow of the Comintern," 31–46; Elsa Dixler, "The Woman Question: Women and the American Communist Party, 1929–1941" (Ph.D. diss., Yale University, 1974), 20–24; Goldman, *Women at the Gates*, 33–42; Gail Warshofsky Lapidus, *Women in Soviet Society: Equality, Development, and Social Change* (Berkeley: University of California Press, 1978), 54–94; Barbara Clements, *Bolshevik Feminist: The Life of Aleksandra Kollontai* (Bloomington: Indiana University Press, 1979).

72. McDuffie, "Long Journeys," 361, 378–383; Robin D. G. Kelley, *Hammer and Hoe: Alabama Communists During the Great Depression* (Chapel Hill: University of North Carolina Press, 1990), 206–207. Although it deemphasized the "withering away of the family" line by the early 1930s, the American Communist movement continued to promote and debate gender politics that were often more progressive than the political mainstream. See Kate Weigand, *Red Feminism: American Communism and the Making of Women's Liberation* (Baltimore: Johns Hopkins University Press, 2001), 28–45; Shapiro, "Red Feminism," 55–95, 213–255; Mary Inman, *In Woman's Defense* (Los Angeles: The Committee to Organize the Advancement of Women, 1940); Avram Landy, "Two Questions on the Status of Women under Capitalism," *The Communist* 20, 9 (September 1941): 818–833.

73. Taylor, *Veiled Garvey*, 2, 64–90; McDuffie, "Long Journeys," 361, 378–383; Weigand, *Red Feminism*, 97–113.

74. For instance, Bolshevik leader, V. I. Lenin, briefly mentioned in his speech, "Theses on the National and Colonial Question," that "communist parties must give direct support to the revolutionary movements among the dependent nations and those without equal rights (e.g., in Ireland, and among the Americans Negroes), and in the colonies." Jane Degras, ed., *The Communist International, 1919–1943, Documents Vol. 1, 1919–1923* (London: Frank Cass and Company, 1971), 142; Claudín, *The Communist Movement: From Comintern to Cominform*, 250–253; Solomon, *Cry Was Unity*, 40.

75. Borkenau, *World Communism*, 221–237.

76. Robin D. G. Kelley, *Race Rebels: Culture, Politics, and the Black Working Class* (New York: Free Press, 1994), 107.

77. Ibid., 105–121.

78. Qtd. in Eric Hobsbawm, *Revolutionaries* (New York: New Press, 1973), 3.

79. Maxwell, *New Negro, Old Left*. See also Rachel Scharfman, "Freethought and New York City's Radical Public Sphere, 1890–1917" (Ph.D. diss., New York University, forthcoming); Mari Jo Buhle, *Women and American Socialism,*

1870–1920 (Bloomington: Indiana University Press, 247–287); Kevin J. Mumford, *Interzones: Black/White Sex Districts in Chicago in the Early Twentieth Century* (New York: Columbia University Press, 1997); Christine Stansell, *American Moderns: Bohemian New York and the Creation of a New Century* (New York: Metropolitan Books, 2000); Ann Douglas, *Terrible Honesty: Mongrel Manhattan in the 1920s* (New York: Farrar, Straus, and Giroux, 1995); George Chauncey, *Gay New York: Gender, Urban Culture, and the Making of the Gay Male World, 1890–1940* (New York: Basic Books, 1994).

80. Solomon, *Cry Was Unity*, 68–91; James A. Miller, Susan D. Pennybacker, and Eve Rosenhaft, "Mother Ada Wright and the International Campaign to Free the Scottsboro Boys, 1931–1934," *American Historical Review* 106, 2 (April 2001): 387–430; Goodman, *Stories of Scottsboro*; Kelley, *Race Rebels*, 103–121; idem., *Hammer and Hoe*, 78–116; Carter, *Scottsboro*; Naison, *Communists in Harlem*, 57–94.

81. Kornweibel, "*Seeing Red*," 151; Shapiro, "Red Feminism," 62; Dixler, "The Woman Question," 33–34.

82. *Crusader*, 1, 1 (September 1918), 28–29; 1, 2 (October 1918), 64–65; 1, 3 (November 1918), 100–101; 1, 7 (March 1919), 236–237; 1, 8, (April 1919), 272–273; 1, 9 (May 1919), 308–309; 1, 10 (June 1919), 344–345; 1, 11 (July 1919), 380–381; 1, 12, (August 1919), 416–417.

83. This is not to say that black women did not become high-ranking formal leaders in the Party and CPUSA-affiliated groups during the 1930s, 1940s, and 1950s. They did. For example, Louise Thompson Patterson, sat on the executive board of the International Workers Order, a Party-affiliated fraternal group, from the late 1930s through the late 1940s. Esther Cooper served as executive secretary of the Southern Negro Youth Congress, a Birmingham-based, progressive civil rights group, during World War Two. In 1945, Claudia Jones was elected to the CPUSA's National Committee. Audley Moore sat on the state committee of the New York State Communist Party during most of the 1940s. However, the Party did not establish a systematic process to elevate black women to high-ranking, formal leadership positions. McDuffie, "Long Journeys," passim.

84. There is no mentioning of women's divisions of auxiliaries in the Friends of the Negro Freedom or ANLC constitutions. See, "Summary of the Program and Aims of the African Blood Brotherhood"; "Constitution of the African Blood Brotherhood," *Crusader*, 6, 4 (4 June 1922), 1155–1157; "Constitution and Program of the American Negro Labor Congress," 1925, CPUSA Records, 515/1/575, 35–54.

85. The low numbers of black women in the rank-and-file and leadership, as well its inability to address the special concerns of African American women, was a source of bitter contention within the CPUSA during the Depression and later years. See Louise Thompson, "Negro Women in Our Party," *Party Organizer* 10 (August 1937): 25–27; Claudia Jones, "An End to the Neglect of the Problems of the Negro Woman!" *Political Affairs* 28, 6 (June 1949): 51–67.

86. Bush, *We Are Not What We Seem*, 93–116; James, *Holding Aloft the Banner of Ethiopia*, 134–184; Solomon, *Cry Was Unity*, 3–67.

87. Qtd. in Cheryl Townsend Gilkes, "Interview with Audley (Queen Mother) Moore," 6, 8 June 1978, in *The Black Women Oral History Project*, 145, 132; McDuffie, "Long Journeys," 154–171.

88. Stein, *The World of Marcus Garvey*, 248–255; E. David Cronon, *The Story of Marcus Garvey and the Universal Negro Improvement Association* (Madison: University of Wisconsin Press, 1955), 138–156, 160–161.

89. Moore, interview with Gilkes, 135; McDuffie, "Long Journeys," 233–251, 323–340, 484–489; Robin D. G. Kelley, *Freedom Dreams: The Black Radical Imagination* (Boston: Beacon Press, 2002), 77–78, 119–120.

90. Audley Moore, Rose Gaulden, Bonita Williams, and Helen Samuels to Earl Browder, Earl Browder Papers, Reel 5, Series 2, Item 118, Negroes, 1929–1945, Manuscript Reading Room, Library of Congress, Washington, DC; George Charney, *A Long Journey* (Chicago: Quadrangle, 1968), 34; Naison, *Communists in Harlem*, 136, 149; Queen Mother Audley Moore, interview with Mark Naison, 1972, OHAL, 12.

91. Jones to Foster, 3; McDuffie, "Long Journeys," 33–36, 52–63, 220–233; Buzz Johnson, *"I Think of My Mother": Notes to the Life and Work of Claudia Jones* (London: Karia Press, 1985), 1–7; Roi Ottley, *"New World A-Coming": Inside Black America* (Cambridge: Riverside Press, 1943; reprint, New York: Arno Press, 1968), 105–106, 110–111; William R. Scott, *Sons of Sheba: African-Americans and the Italo-Ethiopian War, 1935–1941* (Bloomington, IN: University of Indiana Press, 1993), 106–120; Shapiro, "Red Feminism," 262–266; Cheryl Lynn Greenburg, *Or Does It Explode? Black Harlem in the Great Depression* (New York: Oxford University Press, 1991), 114–139; Naison, *Communists in Harlem*, 135, 155–158.

92. For the best discussion of Jones's years in Great Britain, see Marika Sherwood, *Claudia Jones: A Life in Exile* (London: Lawrence and Wishart, 2000); Foster, *History of the Communist Party of the United States*, 392, 517–520; Claudette Williams, "We Are a Natural Part of Many Different Struggles: Black Women Organizing," in *Inside Babylon: The Caribbean Diaspora in Britain*, ed. Winston James and Clive Harris (London: Verso, 1993), 155–156; McDuffie, "Long Journeys," 482–483; Yard, *Biography of Amy Ashwood Garvey*, 194, 222–223; Johnson, *"I Think of My Mother,"* 64–90.

93. Taylor, *Veiled Garvey*, 91–237.

94. James, *Holding Aloft the Banner of Ethiopia*, 137.

11

"Boundaries of Law and Disorder"

The "Grand Design" of Eldridge Cleaver and the "Overseas Revolution" in Cuba

Rose C. Thevenin

I was an outlaw still out,
the gap could not be bridged.   —Eldridge Cleaver[1]

Huey P. Newton and Bobby Seale founded the Black Panther Party (BPP) for Self-Defense in Oakland, California in 1966 to demand self-determination through their Ten Point Platform and Program. By 1968, the organization dropped self-defense from its name and by 1969, the BPP boasted nationwide and international support. BPP members considered themselves revolutionaries who challenged institutional racism and capitalism.[2] In November 1969, the BPP had twenty-nine chapters nationwide and opened an International Section of the BPP led by BPP Minister of Information Eldridge Cleaver in Algiers in 1970.

The BPP's international activities have been probed in some works, including Kathleen Rout's biography of Eldridge Cleaver, an essay by Kathleen Neal Cleaver, and Ruth Reitan's examination of Cuba and African-American leaders in the 1960s.[3] Eldridge Cleaver has also elaborated on his international activities in his second autobiographical account and in numerous interviews. However, specific details concerning Cleaver's "overseas revolution" in Cuba have not been probed to evaluate his leadership and BPP attempts to mobilize an international chapter of the BPP in Cuba.

Together with the experiences of such individuals as Robert F. Williams, Huey P. Newton, and Stokely Carmichael, William Lee Brent and Assata Shakur, such an examination affords an opportunity to probe the context within which the BPP attempted to define "diaspora." It is significant to the discourse on definitions, applications, and contextualizations of diaspora based on a "radical" organization's strategies during one of the most turbulent periods of its history. The BPP's definition of "diaspora" was not based on remembrances of dispersal, religion, ethnicity, color, or "hybridity." Instead I argue that the BPP defined "diaspora" within the context of "revolution," which connotes a redefinition of power rooted in a redistribution of wealth to compel transformations in the existing power hierarchy.

This research is a case study highlighting the successes and failures of the BPP's application of "diaspora" to Cuba in an attempt to internationalize its concept of liberation. Utilizing letters, published interviews, and newspapers, this chapter appraises Cleaver's leadership to illuminate the strengths and weaknesses in launching what he termed the "overseas revolution" in Cuba. Reviewing the conditions which brought Cleaver to Cuba illuminates the context within which Cleaver arrived in Cuba, and his expectations of the Cuban government.

BPP Minister of Information Eldridge Cleaver and BPP Treasurer seventeen-year-old Bobby Hutton's outrage two days after the assassination of civil rights leader Martin Luther King Jr. prompted a shootout with Oakland police on April 6, 1968. Cleaver viewed King's assassination as an acrimonious and fatal repudiation of nonviolence and a signal for black people to "fight fire with fire," to commence a "terrible and bloody chapter" of what he termed a "holocaust."[4] He was insulted by President Lyndon Baines Johnson's call for calm and argued that America had committed suicide by killing King.

During the ensuing gun battles, Hutton was killed by police gunfire and Cleaver was arrested.[5] The California Adult Authority (CAA) revoked Cleaver's parole status.[6] Shortly after his attorneys secured a writ of habeas corpus, ordering his release from prison and reinstatement of his parole status, the State Appellate Court affirmed the CAA's earlier decision ordering Cleaver's return to prison on November 27, 1968.

Determined never to return to prison, Cleaver contemplated two scenarios, including taking over Merritt College as a fortress to force "a final shoot-out scenario" with police, and a possible hijacking immediately vetoed by BPP founder Newton from prison.[7] "I wanted to hole up there with some fellow Panthers and tell the white power–police pig structure to come and get me," he resolved.[8] Newton notified the Central Committee, the ruling body of the BPP, to assist Cleaver with other plans to jump bond and leave the country.[9]

Cleaver jumped his $50,000 bail and escaped to Cuba, claiming he would have been killed if he returned to prison.[10] The BPP heralded Cleaver's departure as the realization of the "revolutionary suicide" espoused by Newton.[11] Newton asserted, "the revolutionary must always be prepared to face death and hope because it symbolizes a resolute determination to bring about change."[12] In its newspaper, the BPP proclaimed that Cleaver represented the international solidarity which had been at the core of the BPP's self-determination ideology chronicled in its Ten Point Platform and Program.[13] Given that the BPP revered revolutionary countries such as Cuba, Vietnam, China, and various African countries, the organization boldly announced that Cleaver had taken the "revolution" underground.[14] Such an assertion was a realization of Newton's 1968 essay "On the Correct Handling of Revolution." Newton and the BPP asserted that the vanguard party's activities would necessarily be short-lived because it must exist aboveground until it is forced into secrecy underground, whereupon the masses would then continue the resistance struggle.[15] Thus, the organization subscribed to a vision of "collective identity," based on political, economic, and social oppression and resistance.

Cleaver's assertion of the "overseas revolution" reflected his political ideology of "community imperialism."[16] He asserted that the black community was effectively excluded from the economic process because it neither owned nor controlled sources of wealth such as land, natural resources, manufactured goods and products.[17] He called for the creation of "organizational machinery" to combat U.S colonialism and imperialism reinforced by international organizations.[18] The "overseas revolution" mirrored what Newton later termed "revolutionary intercommunalism" in 1971, based on the principle that the world was a collection of dispersed communities which must be united against common oppressors. Such a view epitomized the BPP's attempt to define "diaspora" in a global context rooted in a redefinition of existing power relations.

Newton argued that technology created a "global village," mandating sharing all wealth produced. He urged "world communities" to seize power from the small ruling circle and "expropriate the expropriators" by extricating members from the pinnacles of power for the equitable distribution of the fruits of labor.[19] Cleaver sought to mobilize international groups to launch an offensive against the U.S government. Cuba's history contextualized the ideal site for initiating the BPP's "overseas revolution." The BPP extolled Fidel Castro and the Cuban revolution as great "revolutionary" achievements that established an "island of socialism" amid "capitalist exploitation, imperialist aggression and fascist suppression."[20] Tensions between Cuba and the United States increased during the early 1960s due to the Cuba–Soviet Union alliance, the failed Bay of Pigs invasion in 1961, the Cuban missile crisis of 1962, alleged Cuban involvement in President Kennedy's assassination in 1963, American attempts to return the favor by targeting Castro, and the American embargo of Cuba.[21] Cuba's resilience under Castro attracted advocates of black power who extolled its "revolutionary" fervor and visited the island to express endorsement and respect.

BPP Minister of Education George Murray visited Cuba on September 7, 1968. He boasted that he was well received by the Cuban people and that Cuban "revolutionary ambassadors" pledged support for the black liberation struggle in the United States.[22] A week later, the BPP also proclaimed that the Cuban people pledged unlimited assistance and recognized the BPP as the vanguard of the "revolution" in America because of its powerful revolutionary force, courage, and strength.[23] The organization also claimed that Fidel Castro's triumphant revolution fomented national consolidation and sweeping social changes. The BPP also proclaimed that the socialist world's embrace of Cuba had not become a "suffocating bear hug," stifling its independence, agency, and self-determination.

It was in this context that Cleaver went to Cuba, expecting to receive a "brotherly welcome" from the Cuban government. Such anticipation was also rooted in Fidel Castro's 1962 Second Declaration of Havana expressing support for armed revolutions in Latin America and endorsing the struggle of the masses to combat imperialism. Most persuasive was Castro's assertion that "the duty of every revolutionary is to make the revolution."[24]

The Cuban government granted Cleaver an apartment in Havana and assigned to him two security men from the Cuban Ministry of the Interior, one black and one white. He described only one man in great detail, "Captain Toro," a "zealous young black Cuban Army officer,"[25] Cleaver was also assigned "an elderly lady" and a political party member to "cook and look after domestic things."[26] He acknowledged, "on physical comforts, I was going first class," yet, he remained dissatisfied.[27] His "grand design" in Cuba was "of a building or units surrounded by acres of revolutionary camps and personnel, all working rigorously for the glorious invasion of America."[28]

He aspired to establish a center in the Caribbean to prepare and mobilize "revolutionary cadres" to "slink back" into the United States, blend with the urban scene, and "function as guerillas on that sidewalk level."[29] Cleaver planned to dispatch two guerrilla units. One would not engage in confrontation with police or the U.S. army but would create "much disruption and chipping away" at the existing power structure.[30] Another cadre of "trained and equipped forces" would be strategically based in the mountains of North America to function as "small mobile units that could shift easily in and out of rural areas, living off the land and tying up thousands of troops in fruitless pursuit."[31] He sought to replicate guerrilla warfare methods formerly employed by Fidel Castro at Sierra Maestra during the Cuban revolution to ensure victory in America. Cleaver interpreted antagonisms and existing tensions between the two countries as indicative of a signal for political and collective transformation of the masses.

Cleaver's plan was reminiscent of Ernesto "Che" Guevara's 1961 Guerrilla Warfare manual. Guevara argued that all conditions for revolution would not necessarily be created through impulses of guerrilla activities unless and until the people were convinced that all possibilities for peaceful struggle had been exhausted. Guevara extolled the characteristics of an "agrarian revolutionary" who is first and foremost a "social reformer" intent on breaking the mold of oppressive institutions. Cleaver and the BPP failed to acknowledge the differences in the environmental, social, political, and economic conditions between Cuba or Bolivia and the United States, and did not make the pivotal distinction between the agrarian environment of Cuba and the urban United States; rather, they argued that just as "Che" and Fidel Castro succeeded in Cuba, the BPP would prevail in the United States. Cleaver overlooked Guevara's assertion that guerrilla warfare tactics and methods predominantly applied to "wild places of small population," wherein the struggle for reform is concentrated on the "peasant masses" whose main concerns centered on the ownership of land and the means of production.[32]

Cleaver convinced himself that the BPP would duplicate Guevara and Castro's guerrilla warfare. He also assumed that conditions of racial, political, and economic oppression and exploitation would necessarily mobilize the masses to destroy "Babylon." The inherent flaw of his plan was that despite the turbulence of the 1960s, including conflicts and tensions over Vietnam, voting rights, desegregation, political, economic, and social disparities, Americans remained unconvinced that the complete overthrow of the U.S. government would remedy all inequities and that all means of effecting changes had been exhausted by the BPP.

Cleaver attempted to internationalize the BPP's "revolution" based on class struggle, and years later he admitted that his "grand design" was both "ridiculous" and "unreal."[33] Although relations between Cuba and the United States were tense and politically charged, Cuba did not plan to invade the United States. Ruth Reitan argued that national security concerns interspersed with self-preservation limited Cuba's commitment to international solidarity with African-American militants during the 1960s.[34] Cleaver assumed that the hostility between the two countries meant Cuban support of his "grand design." The quid pro quo Cleaver anticipated from the Cuban people and government never developed and his training camps never materialized. Cleaver could not persuade the Cuban people that waging war on the United States was the most viable alternative for eliminating inequities. When Cuban endorsement of his grand design was not forthcoming from either the Cuban government and the Cuban people, Cleaver questioned the feasibility of his plans, "I sat in my apartment wondering if I was the enemy in the eyes of nervous Cuban security guards."[35]

Although Cleaver developed better rapport with Captain Toro, he was suspicious of him because of his criticisms of Castro, "I thought perhaps he was part of a government plot to test me or set me up."[36] Captain Toro curbed visits to Cleaver's apartment, never came alone, and later stopped coming as the white security guard roamed freely.[37] Cleaver noticed "immediate tension" when he confronted both men, because Captain Toro remained silent as the white security guard spoke and answered for him.[38]

Cleaver's encounters with Captain Toro convinced him of pervasive racism in Cuba, which he confirmed after reading volumes of Cuban history seven months later. He challenged official government accounts, claiming that José Martí was the "father of the Cuban revolution," as Antonio Maceo, a black man who also liberated Cuba, was lesser known. Thus, he began questioning Cuba's commitment to racial solidarity.

Cleaver surmised that he would be accorded privileges similar to Robert F. Williams, a former president of the North Carolina NAACP who founded the Deacons for Self-Defense in response to the menace of the Ku Klux Klan (KKK). Williams went to Cuba in 1961 after the FBI issued warrants for his arrest, stemming from a shoot-out with police officers in Monroe, North Carolina. Williams broadcasted "Radio Free Dixie" from

Havana and used the air waves to denounce racism in the United States and the hypocrisy of the U.S. government. Cleaver's expectation of his own Havana radio program from the Cuban government, broadcasted to the United States from Cuba, remained unfulfilled.[39]

Cleaver described his life in Cuba as "a wretched and restless existence—sort of a San Quentin with palm trees, an alcatraz with sugar cane."[40] Cleaver later admitted, "we kind of went there very naive—open-minded and idolizing Cubans."[41] Cleaver's statement reflected his realization that even as Castro supported the Black Power movement in the United States, the Cuban government did not promote "cultural manifestations" of black power.[42]

Cultural expressions such as African daishikis, boubous, afros, and the natural hair style, were ascribed to homosexuals and other anti-social elements in Cuba.[43] They were strongly discouraged as those sporting them were summoned to either police stations or to the Cuban Ministry of the Interior where they were urged to cut their hair and change their clothing.[44] Furthermore, "Cuban men were clean shaven and wore their hair close-cropped, except in the case of a few top Cuban leaders, beards and long hair did not fit in with Cuban custom, women office workers were not allowed to wear pants, men were fined for walking around the streets baring their chests in public."[45]

Such details elucidate differences between American and Cuban culture and demonstrate that although Castro seemingly endorsed the "Afro-American liberation struggle," he did not completely embrace its cultural manifestations in Cuba. Castro's actions cannot be simplistically construed as evidence of racism, but confirmed his attempts to cement Cuban identity devoid of western influences and standards.[46] A photograph in a 1969 BPP paper shows Cleaver wearing daishikis and boubous, which implies that he may have worn such clothing in Cuba in defiance of and resistance to Cuban custom. It is also possible that he was not aware of its Cuban cultural interpretations.

Cleaver complained that the Cuban government rebuffed his expectation of other Panthers to visit and join him in Havana to help him "man these facilities." He blamed such rejection for the southern California deaths of Alprentice "Bunchy" Carter, BPP Deputy Minister of Defense, and John Huggins, BPP Deputy Minister of Information.[47] Cleaver maintained that his encouragement of both men to join him in Cuba was rejected by the Cuban government. He reasoned that had both men left the combative environment of the BPP in Los Angeles to come to Cuba they would not have been killed. Although he was encouraged by the Cuban government to maintain a low profile, Cleaver violated Cuban recommendations by "sneaking out" of his apartment regularly and making weekly visits to the Chinese and Vietnamese embassies.[48] He adopted the name of Bobby Hutton and befriended a blonde woman from Georgia he alternately referred to as "Kitty" and "Bunny Hearne," who years after writing "fan mail" to Castro believed that she was in love with Cleaver and expected him to marry her.[49] Although Cleaver claimed a platonic relationship with her, his true identity unraveled during an evening visit to her apartment whereupon he encountered Commandante Pinato, responsible for managing his case in Cuba. Pinato's immediate recognition of him and further inquiries prompted "Kitty" or "Bunny Hearne" to reveal his whereabouts to Reuters reporter James Pringle of the British news service. Pringle notified the national news media of Cleaver's presence in Cuba, which violated official Cuban recommendations to Cleaver to maintain a low profile.[50]

Determined to mobilize a cadre of recruits in Cuba, Cleaver befriended and actively sought former friends and comrades of the BPP in Cuba, further damaging his relationship with the Cuban government. He embraced many who hijacked planes to Cuba, including current and former members of the BPP. Unlike Cleaver, hijackers such as William Lee Brent, a captain of the BPP's Oakland chapter, were not readily embraced by the Cuban government. Brent arrived in Cuba in 1969, following his formal expulsion from the BPP for his involvement in a 1969 shoot-out which injured two police officers. Brent's Cuban experience paralleled that of other BPP members and Americans in Cuba who joined Cleaver there. Such actions indicate Cleaver and the BPP's attempts to build an immigrant community of dispersed "revolutionaries" in Cuba and highlights the strengths and weaknesses of the BPP's strategy.

Brent's autobiography offers detailed accounts of American revolutionaries in Cuba and of the treatment they received.[51] As Brent's U.S. trial date for a variety of felony and misdemeanor charges drew near, Brent reasoned that going to Cuba was a "logical revolutionary response" to his "extremely difficult predicament."[52] Brent hijacked Trans World Airlines (TWA) flight number 154 and diverted the seventy-six passengers aboard the Boeing 707 to Havana, Cuba.[53] Brent's actions were reminiscent of previous hijackings by Cleaver's former prison mates Byron Booth, Clinton Smith, and Raymond Johnson. All three men assumed that their "revolutionary actions" would be embraced by the Cuban government. However, upon landing in Cuba, they were surprised at the Cuban government's response. Similarly, Brent stated, "the reception I received left a hell of a lot to be desired, straight from the airport to a foul-smelling jail cell, no food that day, and only a hunk of bread with cold coffee and milk the next morning."[54]

Brent quickly became disillusioned with "revolutionary Cuba" when his "long boring days in isolation" extended to twenty-two months of frustration, solitary confinement, investigation, and continuous interrogations by Cuban officials. Such procedures were employed by the Cuban government as a security measure to ferret operatives from the States who might be informants or agents of the FBI or CIA.[55] An anonymous black expatriate to Cuba explained that he was treated as someone who came without permission, which mandated investigation and interrogation to determine his trustworthiness, willingness, and ability to contribute to the development of the revolution. Such a process allowed Cuban officials to also determine whether he was an agent, "some nut or someone who might be dangerous or harmful."[56]

Life in a Cuban prison was "degrading." As "an uninvited guest" imprisoned in a foreign country, Brent explained, "you don't know what to expect, and if you don't know the language, you can't ask questions or understand what your jailers are talking about, you're always uptight because you're a complete outsider, you feel stupid and alone and sometimes afraid."[57] After interrogations, persons were later released and the government provided for their basic food, clothing, and shelter needs. The housing shortage in Cuba required sharing a room with others or residence in hotels and apartments when available. The Cuban government assigned Brent to what he referred to as a "skyjack house" where he resided with other hijackers. The crowded conditions and shortages of toiletries led to conflicts among those whom the government detained.

Brent and others before him were assigned to work collective farms, construction work, or sugarcane cutting to escape the idleness of their residence and to express support for the Cuban revolution. Of all the positions, sugarcane cutting was perhaps the most difficult, requiring the use of a "mocha," a heavy machete with a short wide blade, in the sugarcane fields, which often resulted in bleeding and stinging fingers along with "blisters, sore muscles, body aches and headaches."[58] The rigors of such labor were similarly and voluntarily experienced by University of California professor and BPP supporter Angela Davis, who visited Cuba in 1969 as part of a delegation.[59] Brent described his experience working in the village of La Granja Cervantes: "cutting burnt cane . . . left our entire bodies covered with a fine black ash and gave us the sensation of being covered up with fire ants, the more you rubbed or scratched, the more it itched."[60]

Brent and other hijackers were later assigned to construction work on a hog farm and worked ten hours a day, six days a week and often completed voluntary work on Sundays to exercise "revolutionary zeal."[61] Brent immediately dubbed the place "Plan Pig" and remarked, "I'm going from fighting two-legged pigs in Stateside to building pens for four-legged ones in the Cuban countryside."[62] Similar handling of "revolutionaries" incensed Cleaver, who vehemently opposed such treatment, perceiving it as a betrayal and negation of Castro's assertion in a speech urging revolution in Latin America and that the Cuban government would recognize "only revolutionaries as representatives of the people."[63] Cleaver's residence became a haven for those who escaped from the prison work camps. He stated, "when they got to my pad, I would baptize them . . . and make them Black Panthers."[64] He housed eleven people in his apartment including the newly "baptized" members.[65]

Booth and Smith escaped from the prison work camps to join Cleaver at the Libre Hotel after receiving a clandestine message from him. He stubbornly defended their actions because of their willingness to commit "revolutionary suicide" by escaping from a minimum security prison in the United States, and eluding the clutches of a Cuban government which infringed upon the privileges that their "revolutionary" status entailed. To Cleaver, the men exemplified desired recruits necessary for launching the "overseas revolution" against the U.S. government.

Kathleen Neal Cleaver cited Eldridge Cleaver's assistance to Byron Booth and Clinton Smith as the root of his difficulties with the authorities because he "pressured Cuban authorities to treat both men as revolutionaries rather than criminals."[66] Cleaver did not elaborate on the activities of the men in his apartment; however, he wrote in a published article, "so what if we're disorderly, like a bunch of toughs . . . through disorder we will put the pigs in order and in the process create a new order that we can relax in."[67]

Cleaver's apartment was soon under siege when he adamantly refused to release the men to Cuban officials. He also refused to turn over machine guns kept at his apartment.[68] Cleaver and his recruits adopted a "siege frame of mind" which he termed an "Afro-American Custardism—LAST STAND." "We were all in this together, we would go down together," he explained.[69] In fulfillment of the "revolutionary suicide" doctrine, all of the men in Cleaver's apartment authored their last will and testaments on tapes sent to the United States via "some Puerto Rican who was from New York."[70]

Cleaver's defiance of Cuban government restrictions rendered him a disruptive American element attempting to fracture Castro's government. Cuban officials persuaded Cleaver to travel to Algiers to reunite with his wife Kathleen Neal Cleaver, who had remained in Oakland and expected the couple's first child. Eldridge Cleaver was later informed by Cuban officials that he would also travel to Amman, Jordan to visit Palestinian camps. Cleaver remarked, "I was supposed to go to some goddamn camp with a wife who was about to have a baby, by this point I didn't trust those slippery Cubans."[71] Realizing the Cuban government's plans to effectively relocate him anywhere other than Cuba, Cleaver decided to remain in Algiers where his wife and Emory Douglas joined him.

After leaving Cuba, Cleaver sent a tape to friends in the United States condemning Castro's Cuba as "more insidious and dangerous for black people than that of South Africa," based on his conversations with Captain Toro.[72] Cleaver claimed Captain Toro repudiated Cuban military assistance to African nations, and viewed Castro as "the last white hope of the traditional ruling class," who deliberately reduced the historical significance of "the great black hero of Cuban independence" General Antonio Maceo.[73] Given that Cleaver later named his son Maceo, he was likely ascribing his personal views to the national media through Captain Toro.[74] Cleaver's bitter denunciations also reflected his disillusionment with the Cuban government at large and Fidel Castro in particular. He admitted, "the Cuban disaster was still eating me."[75] Cleaver's experience in Cuba mirrored that of other advocates of black power including Robert F. Williams.[76]

Examination of African-American leaders in Cuba, including other BPP members, provides a comparative lens to contextualize experiences there, including similarities and differences. Robert F. Williams was revered by the Cuban government and like Cleaver, he too received an apartment, two guards, and a chauffeur-driven Cadillac.[77] His broadcast program, "Radio Free Dixie," was very successful and rendered him a folk hero among Cubans. However, Williams longed to return to the United States, especially since his political views were not in accord with those of the Cuban government. Williams left Cuba in August 1966 and later renounced Castro and Communist USA members in Cuba for perpetuating racism. He concluded that the "white petit-bourgeoisie" ruled in Cuba at the expense of Afro-Cubans.[78]

In 1967, Stokely Carmichael, chairman of the Student Nonviolent Coordinating Committee (SNCC) and the field marshal of the BPP, attended the Organization of Latin-American Solidarity (OLAS) meeting in Havana as an observer and later as an honorary delegate. During his visit, Carmichael expressed international solidarity with the Cuban government and called for armed revolution against the U.S. government. Historian Clayborne Carson maintained that whereas Castro endorsed Carmichael's enthusiasm, the Cuban press "played down" his condemnation of the complicity of the CIA and his implied call for African-American people to exact vengeance on American political leaders for the deaths of African-American leaders.[79] Such reaction reflected the Cuban government's reluctance and ambivalence about being presented as a platform from which aggressive and subversive American revolutions could be launched.

Carmichael's statements provoked the wrath of Congressional leaders who demanded his immediate imprisonment upon his return to the United States, resulting in Castro's announcement welcoming Carmichael to remain in Cuba. Carmichael relayed that Castro had personally given him a tour of strategic positions from which he launched the revolution at Sierra Maestra. Months later, Carmichael later condemned communism as a coherent strategy for black liberation because it did not address racism in all its forms.[80] Such a pronouncement may have been due to his dissatisfaction with Castro over the existence of racism in Cuba, according to Julius Lester, who coordinated Carmichael's press relations. The Cuban government rebuked both Williams and Carmichael as "persona non grata" CIA operatives and spies.[81]

Long after Cleaver's departure, the BPP continued to praise Fidel Castro and the Cuban people for their "revolutionary heroism," and for igniting the "revolutionary fire" of the oppressed masses throughout the world.[82] Cuba continued to be a haven for BPP members such as Huey P. Newton, who went there in 1974 to avoid criminal prosecution in the United States for allegedly murdering a prostitute. Assata Shakur, also known as Joanne Chesimard, a New York Black Liberation Army (BLA) member who escaped from a New Jersey prison, was also exiled in Cuba. Newton's experience in Cuba paralleled that of Eldridge Cleaver but differed from that of Shakur and William Lee Brent. Although Newton did not elaborate on his experience in Cuba, Elaine Brown, the only chairwoman of the BPP appointed by Newton, visited him there and relayed details of her visit in her autobiographical account. Similarly, Brent provided details of his visit with Newton while living in Cuba.

In addition to bringing $10,000 in cash, Brown also brought Newton leather pants and silk shirts.[83] The necessity of these items illuminated Newton's financial difficulties in Cuba. He never learned Spanish and briefly worked at what Brown described as a "sweatshop."[84] Brent stated that Newton briefly worked as a mechanic's helper.[85] Newton never assumed another job after two and a half years in Cuba mainly due to his assertion in his autobiography that he "could not deal with work on a permanent basis."[86] Brown noted that the concept of work to Newton was "as foreign to him as Spanish would remain."[87] Newton's main source of support was his wife, Gwen, who worked as an English tutor for nurses and doctors in Cuba. As part of their daily rations, the Cuban government gave Newton and his wife a "live chicken." Neither of them knew what to do with it. Brent noted, "I was surprised to find the leader of the Black Panther Party didn't know how to wring the neck of a chicken and cook it for dinner."[88]

Newton and his family also experienced housing difficulties in Cuba. His wife Gwen and their two children lived in "shifting locations" at the Capri Hotel, then in Havana for six months, Las Villas for another six months, then back to Havana for a year, followed by six months in Alamar.[89] Newton complained of his failure to secure a face-to-face meeting with Castro as a personal affront, since his predecessors in Cuba, Robert Williams and Stokely Carmichael, were accorded such a privilege.[90]

Like Cleaver, Newton was discouraged from becoming involved with any hijackers or former members of the BPP, but he ignored such restrictions.[91] He attempted to regroup the BPP in Cuba by reestablishing contact with former BPP members and asked Brent to rejoin the BPP. His efforts did not reinvigorate the BPP in Cuba, although he maintained contact with the BPP in Oakland through a series of long distance phone calls and visitors to his apartment from abroad.

It is unknown whether Assata Shakur experienced any interrogation or imprisonment upon her arrival in Cuba.[92] She contends that she arrived in Cuba in 1984 and that it was difficult to adjust to Cuban society because she missed American people, music, culture, verbal interchange, and "ebonics."[93] Shakur maintained that she was treated "very well." She found that Cuban officials were most interested in her projects and that "the Cuban attitude was one of solidarity with respect."[94] Nevertheless, she had to learn both a new language and adapt to a different culture. She received, "a dictionary, an apartment, and she was also guided to historical places" before branching out on her own. Shakur praised free medical care and education and the absence of federal, city, or state taxes in Cuba, and concluded that the Cuban government was "completely committed" to eradicating all forms of racism in Cuba.

Shakur denounced U.S. foreign policy and endorsed Cuba's humanitarian policies concluding, "I respected the Cuban government, not only for adopting nonracist principles, but for struggling to put those principles into practice."[95] Her positive statements may have been due to the fact that she was convicted of murder and other charges, despite her claims to innocence, and had managed to escape from an American prison after enduring multiple indignities. Assata Shakur continues to reside in Cuba despite former New Jersey Governor Christine Todd Whitman's efforts in sponsoring a bill in the late 1990s demanding her extradition back to the United States.[96] Cuba's refusal to return Shakur and others continues to irk conservatives, politicians, and other government officials.

The experiences of some BPP members in Cuba and that of Cleaver, in particular, elucidate some BPP expectations of Castro and the Cuban government in general. Cleaver and others expected the Cuban government to honor its commitment to international solidarity by supporting subversive activities against the United States. Cleaver, Newton, Brent, and BPP hijackers to Cuba assumed that BPP affiliation was a passport and license for "revolutionary" status abroad. All BPP members came to Cuba to escape from the American criminal justice system. Most African-Americans who came to Cuba translated hostilities between the United States and Cuba as an endorsement of "revolutionary activities." Cleaver, in particular, expected fulfillment of his "grand design." He believed that such hostilities would lead to Cuban mobilization of guerrilla forces and overthrow of the U.S. government.

Overall, Cleaver's "overseas revolution" was unrealistic because he strongly believed that a loosely organized group of fifteen to thirty self-proclaimed "revolutionaries" would destroy one of the most, if not the greatest, army in the world in 1968. However, it would be erroneous to conclude that the BPP's concept of "diaspora" was ambiguous. The case study of the BPP further complicates notions and definitions of "diaspora" by transcending the interconnected strands of race and gender but specifically roots itself in class struggle to demand fundamental changes in existing power relationships. The BPP's definition of "diaspora" was firmly grounded in its demand for self-determination through overt forms of violent resistance. Both Cleaver and Newton sought the implementation of the "intercommunalism" Newton espoused but failed to realize that the collective identity consciousness and transformation of the masses that they envisioned would not necessarily be internalized by the Cuban government and its people.

Cleaver's "grand design" of "Afro-American Custardism" lacked a concrete strategy for effecting substantive changes in the economic, political, and social strata in Cuba. When his plans never materialized, Cleaver concluded that Cuba was a "farce" and labeled Castro a "cigar store revolutionary," whose own "grand design" after the Cuban revolution was tainted with "brutal accomplishments."[97] He maintained that despite some economic and employment gains, "even my thick skull could perceive and understand the new misery that saturated Castroland: the unrelieved suffering of mind and spirit that comes from living under a dictatorship."[98]

Although the BPP revered international resistance movements and sought to emulate and replicate similar movements in the United States, the BPP failed to persuade the masses that its organization offered the best and most viable alternative to domination by the existing power structure.[99] Whereas "Che" and Fidel Castro successfully rallied the masses during the Cuban revolution, the BPP could not generate similar support to compel the masses to pick up the gun to overthrow the existing American government. The BPP failed to convince the masses that violent revolution was the only recourse for ending social, political, and economic oppression.

Examination of the experiences of African-Americans who sought refuge in Cuba, especially Eldridge Cleaver, reveals that "revolutionary" underpinnings did not transform into substantive actions, yielding fundamental changes in either Cuban or American society. Moreover, oppression, exploitation, and resistance in and of themselves did not create a collective consciousness or identity between African-American "radicals" and the Cuban people. Refuge in Cuba did not translate into offensive action against the U.S. government, nor did it yield local mobilization of the Cuban people. Thus, class struggle, which served as the basis of the BPP's contextualization of "diaspora," did not yield substantive transformations of identity. Cleaver's treatment was not extended to every American who came to Cuba under similar circumstances. Eldridge Cleaver and Robert Williams were both exceptions rather than the norm in terms of how the Cuban government received African-American "revolutionaries."

It is also important to note that the Cuban people did not embrace or endorse Cleaver's "overseas revolution" because Cleaver never really embraced them or the Cuban government. After some years, neither

Cleaver nor Newton attempted to acclimate to the Cuban environment. Neither man learned Spanish, and Cleaver did not work (unlike others who sought refuge in Cuba), while Newton worked only briefly. Both were disillusioned with Cuba and later denounced Fidel Castro.

An anonymous expatriate in Cuba disapproved of these denunciations and charged that self-proclaimed American "revolutionaries" "could not live up to the front they had presented to the Cuban revolution."[100] Cleaver admitted, "I had lived defiantly for so long in such seething hatred of all governments, people in power, people in charge, that when I came under the shelter of Communist powers, I sadly discovered that their corruption was as violent and inhuman as the people they victoriously replaced."[101]

NOTES

1. Eldridge Cleaver, *Soul On Fire* (Waco, Texas: Word Books, 1978), 171.

2. The Ten Point Platform and Program of the Black Panther Party.

3. Kathleen Rout, *Eldridge Cleaver* (Boston: Twayne Publishers, 1991), 101–111; Kathleen Neal Cleaver, "Back To Africa: The Evolution of the International Section of the Black Panther Party, 1969–1972," in Charles E. Jones, ed., *The Black Panther Party Reconsidered* (Baltimore: Black Classic Press, 1998), 211–256; Ruth Reitan, *The Rise and Decline of an Alliance: Cuba and African-American Leaders in the 1960s* (East Lansing: Michigan State University Press, 1999), 63–67; Ruth Reitan, "Cuba, the Black Panther Party, and the U.S. Black Movement in the 1960s," in Kathleen Cleaver and George Katsiaficas, eds., *Liberation, Imagination and the Black Panther Party* (New York: Routledge, 2001), 172–173.

4. "The Death of Martin Luther King: Requiem for Nonviolence," in *Eldridge Cleaver: Post Prison Writings and Speeches*, edited and with an Appraisal by Robert Scheer (New York: Random House, 1969), 75.

5. "Cleaver Shootout Damages Granted," *San Francisco Examiner* (hereinafter cited as *SFE*), 8 August 1972, 10. Two women, eighty-two-year-old Nellie Pere and her daughter fifty-nine-year-old Ella Wade, cowered on their kitchen floor for 90 minutes during the gunfire exchange with police, leaving 189 bullet holes in their home. After a civil trial, Superior Judge William Brailsford awarded both women $16,000 for damages to their home, concluding that the police assault with bullets and tear gas was "unreasonable."

6. Cleaver was on parole after serving nine years at San Quentin, Folsom, California MenÕs Colony East and Soledad prisons for rape.

7. In 1968, Huey P. Newton was convicted of voluntary manslaughter for the death of police officer John Frey, which occurred on October 28, 1967.

8. Cleaver, *Soul On Fire*, 137.

9. Cleaver also expressed interest in an escape scenario in which he would ride to the Rockies on horseback then flee to Canada. Some BPP sympathizers offered to hijack a plane to the islands which Cleaver and Central Committee members rejected. Ibid., 141.

10. Gordon Parks, "Eldridge Cleaver In Algiers: A Visit With Papa Rage," *Life*, 6 February 1970, 22.

11. The phrase "revolutionary suicide" was employed by Huey P. Newton, who argued that "a revolutionary must realize if he is sincere death is imminent due to the fact that the things he is saying and doing are extremely dangerous." Ibid., 21.

12. Huey P. Newton, *Revolutionary Suicide* (New York: Black Classic Press, 1995), 7.

13. "On Eldridge Cleaver By Kathleen Cleaver," *The Black Panther* (hereinafter cited as *TBP*), 9 August 1969, 5–6. The BPP contributed $5000 to the bonding company. The signatures of Dr. Jane Aguilar, Godfrey Cambridge, Dr. Phillip Shapiro, and Ed Keating served as collateral for the $50,000 bail which all had to collectively pay when Cleaver jumped bond.

14. "About Eldridge," *TBP*, 31 December 1968, 2; "Eldridge Cleaver: Takes Revolution Underground," Editorial By Brother Dynamite, *TBP*, 7 December 1968; "Where's Eldridge?" *TBP*, 7 December 1968; "Soul On The Lam," *Newsweek*, 9 December 1968, 31.

15. Huey P. Newton, "In Defense Of Self-Defense, The Correct Handling Of A Revolution," *TBP*, 18 May 1968, 8.

16. Eldridge Cleaver, "Community Imperialism," *TBP*, 18 May 1968, 10.

17. Ibid.

18. Ibid.

19. Huey P. Newton, "Intercommunalism: In Conversation at Yale University," in David Hilliard and Donald Weise, eds., *The Black Panther Party Reader, Selected Writings of Huey P. Newton* (Oakland, California: Huey P. Newton Foundation, 1998), 11.

20. "On Criticism of Cuba," *TBP*, 27 December 1969, in Eric Foner ed. *The Black Panthers Speak* (New York: J.B Lippincott, 1970), 37–38; "Cuban Revolution Is Ten Years Old," *TBP*, 2 February 1969. On Castro and Cuban history, see Carla Anne Robbins, *The Cuban Threat* (New York: McGraw-Hill, 1983); Hugh Thomas, *Cuba: The Pursuit of Freedom* (New York: Harper & Row, 1971); Robert E. Quirk, *Fidel Castro* (New York: W.W. Norton, 1993); Carlos Moore, *Castro, the Blacks and Africa* (Los Angeles: Center for Afro-American Studies, 1988); Thomas G. Moore, *Contesting Castro: The United States and the Triumph of the Cuban Revolution* (New York: Oxford University Press, 1994).

21. Warren Hincle and William W. Turner, *Deadly Secrets: The CIA-Mafia War against Castro and the Assassination of JFK* (New York: Thunder's Mouth Press, 1992).

22. "Late News Brief," *TBP*, 7 September 1968, 7; "Cuban Revolution Is Ten Years Old," *TBP*, 2 February 1969.

23. "Freedom Fighters," *TBP*, 14 September 1968, 6.

24. Martin Kenner and James Petras, eds., *Fidel Castro Speaks* (New York: Grove Press, 1969), 93–117.

25. Eldridge Cleaver, "Fidel Castro's African Gambit," *Newsweek*, 3 May 1976, 13.

26. Curtis Taylor, "Eldridge Cleaver," *Rolling Stone*, 11 September 1971, 40.

27. Ibid.

28. Cleaver, *Soul On Fire*, 107.

29. Ibid.

30. Ibid., 108.

31. Ibid.

32. Ernesto "Che" Guevara, "General Principles of Guerilla Warfare," quoted in Daniel Castro, ed., *Revolution and Revolutionaries, Guerrilla Movements in Latin America* (Wilmington, Delaware: Scholarly Resources, 1999), 65–86.

33. Cleaver, *Soul On Fire*, 107.

34. Reitan, *The Rise and Decline of an Alliance*, 4–5.

35. Cleaver, *Soul On Fire*, 108.

36. Ibid.

37. "Cuban Experience: Eldridge Cleaver On Ice," Interview by Skip Gates, *Transition* (1975), 33.

38. Ibid.

39. Ibid., 32.

40. Eldridge Cleaver, *Soul On Fire*, 143.

41. Gates, "Cuban Experience," 35.

42. Moore, *Castro, the Blacks and Africa*, 259.

43. Ibid.

44. Ibid., 259–260.

45. William Lee Brent, *Long Time Gone* (New York: Times Books, 1996), 178.

46. Reitan, *The Rise and Decline of an Alliance*, 112.

47. Alprentice Bunchy Carter and John Huggins were both killed on the campus of UCLA by two members of Ron Karenga's U.S. organization on January 17, 1969.

48. Cleaver, *Soul On Fire*, 149.

49. Ibid., 49.

50. Taylor, "Eldridge Cleaver," 42; "Cleaver Turns Up In Havana," *SFE*, 25 May 1969, 1.

51. Brent, *Long Time Gone*, 190–196.

52. Ibid., 131.

53. "TWA Jet Left S.F., Diverted," *SFE*, 17 June 1969, 1; "Hijacked Oakland Jet Lands Safely In N.Y.," *SFE*, 19 June 1969, 3; "Bay Area Skyjacker Identified As Panther," *SFE*, 20 June 1969, 4; "Skyjacker Linked To Cleaver," *SFE*, 21 June 1969, 5.

54. Brent, *Long Time Gone*, 147. Brent surmised that his imprisonment was particularly unusual as Eldridge Cleaver did not share his similar experience. He therefore concluded that Cleaver convinced Cuban officials that he was an agent, thereby causing his long imprisonment.

55. Black Scholar Interviews, "A Black Expatriate in Cuba," *The Black Scholar*, February 1973, 49–55.

56. Ibid., 49.

57. Brent, *Long Time Gone*, 148.

58. Ibid., 190–196.

59. Angela Davis, *Angela Davis, An Autobiography* (New York: Random House, 1974), 208–209.

60. Brent, *Long Time Gone*, 193–194.

61. Ibid., 205–206. Brent continued to work in Cuba and later earned a degree. He remained in Cuba and resides there to this day.

62. Ibid., 205–206. Brent blamed Cleaver for his twenty-two months of imprisonment, claiming Cleaver maligned him to the Cuban government. It is unknown whether Cleaver exercised any control over Brent's fate, as he was released months after Cleaver's departure from Cuba.

63. Kenner and Petras, eds., *Fidel Castro Speaks*, 146.

64. Gates, "Cuban Experience," 32.

65. Ibid., 38.

66. Kathleen Neal Cleaver, "Back To Africa," 222.

67. "Eldridge On Weatherman," *TBP*, 22 November 1969, 5.

68. Cleaver, *Soul On Fire*, 143.

69. Gates, "Cuban Experience," 49.

70. Ibid.

71. Taylor, "Eldridge Cleaver," 44.

72. Eldridge Cleaver, "Fidel Castro's African Gambit," 13.

73. Ibid.

74. "The Revolutionary Spirit Of Antonio Maceo Lives On Today In The People's Revolutionary Vanguard, The Black Panther Party And In Our New Revolutionary Warrior Named After Him," *TBP*, 16 August 1969, 3.

75. Cleaver, *Soul On Fire*, 144.

76. Timothy B. Tyson, *Radio Free Dixie, Robert F. Williams and the Roots of Black Power* (Chapel Hill: University of North Carolina Press, 1999), 291–294.

77. Ibid., 291.

78. Ibid., 291–294; Moore, *Castro, the Blacks and Africa*, 254–255.

79. Clayborne Carson, *In Struggle: SNCC and the Black Awakening of the 1960s* (Cambridge: Harvard University Press, 1981), 274–275.

80. Moore, *Castro, the Blacks and Africa*, 254–262.

81. Julius Lester, "Black Revolution Is Real: Stokely in Cuba," *Movement*, September 1967, 1–4; Moore, *Castro, the Blacks and Africa*, 261–262.

82. "Message Of Solidarity To Our Cuban Comrades," *TBP*, 9 August 1971.

83. Brown, *A Taste of Power: A Black Woman's Story* (New York: Pantheon Books, 1992), 377–400.

84. Ibid.

85. Brent, *Long Time Gone*, 236.

86. Newton, *Revolutionary Suicide*, 95.

87. Brown, *A Taste of Power*, 390.

88. Brent, *Long Time Gone*, 236.

89. Brown, *A Taste of Power*, 390.

90. Ibid., 383–384.

91. Brent, *Long Time Gone*, 232.

92. Assata Shakur, *Assata: An Autobiography* (Westport, Connecticut: Lawrence Hill and Company, 1987), 267–268; "A Survivor, Former Black Panther Assata Shakur," *Emerge*, May 2000, 32–36.

93. "A Survivor," 35.

94. Christian Parenti, "Assata Shakur Speaks from Exile" from http://lists.village.virginia.edu/lists_archive/sixties-1/1724.html, 1–8.

95. Shakur, *Assata*, 272.

96. Editorial, "Playing Chesimard with Cuba," *New York Post*, 9 May 1998, from http://www.rose-hulman.edu/~delacova/cuba/playing-chesimard.htm, 1–2.

97. Cleaver, *Soul On Fire*, 144.

98. Ibid.

99. Jon Lee Anderson, *Che Guevara, A Revolutionary Life* (New York: Grove Press, 1997); Daniel Castro, ed., *Revolution and Revolutionaries*.

100. "A Black Expatriate in Cuba," 54.

101. Cleaver, *Soul On Fire*, 97.

12

Writing the Diaspora in
Black International Literature
"With Wider Hope in Some More Benign Fluid . . .":
Diaspora Consciousness and Literary Expression

Wendy W. Walters

In 1940, W.E.B. Du Bois described his books *The Souls of Black Folk* and *Darkwater* as "written in tears and blood." *Dusk of Dawn*, he said, "is set down no less determinedly but yet with a wider hope in some more benign fluid" (2).[1] In this reference to ink in the opening "Apology" to *Dusk of Dawn: An Essay Toward an Autobiography of a Race Concept*, Du Bois calls our attention to writing as a hopeful space where concepts of race and identity can be expressed. Studying African diasporic literature shows us how ink, and the varieties of narrative forms which have made up African-American, Caribbean, and Black[2] European literatures, are important sites where contemporary writers continue Du Bois's project of tracing "a race concept" which may be called diaspora. The history of African-American literature alone has evidenced a shift between writers claiming an American identity, experiencing a form of racialized exile in their American homeland, and seeking diaspora in their writing as a way to construct an alternative homeland.

The written story of diaspora is certainly not new. We can see international leanings and longings in the eighteenth-century slave narratives of Olaudah Equiano and Mary Prince, and in the nineteenth-century abolitionist writings of Frederick Douglass. Early novels by Sutton Griggs and Martin Delany take up this project. The Harlem Renaissance of the 1920s was an international movement whose guiding spirit was never confined to the neighborhood for which it was named. Langston Hughes, Alain

Locke, Claude McKay, Zora Neale Hurston, Countee Cullen, all looked beyond the borders of the United States, frequently toward Africa and the Caribbean for a cultural identity for black people, an identity which they claimed in their narrative practices. In the early 1950s, Richard Wright, James Baldwin, Chester Himes, and other African-American writers physically displaced themselves from the racial discrimination they experienced in the United States, relocating to Europe and yet consistently "writing back" to U.S. political life, African-American urban life, as well as African independence movements. Black Aestheticism or the Second Black Renaissance of the 1960s also looked to Africa and the Caribbean, seeing in those places guiding examples of resistance and opposition to racist exclusion. Contemporary writers such as Paule Marshall, Michelle Cliff, Audre Lorde, and Caryl Phillips use their writing to construct Caribbean identities which are not bounded by the borders of the Atlantic or the islands which dot its waters.

Focusing on the link between displacement and narrative, this chapter suggests that displacement allows a distance by which writers encode critiques of their "homelands," construct new homelands, and envision new communities.[3] This displacement can be physical as in the case, for example, of Chester Himes, who migrated permanently to Europe in 1953, and yet never stopped writing to and about the United States. Or the displacement may be generational, as in the case of Audre Lorde, child of Caribbean-born parents, whose writing in many ways seeks routes back to the islands where her parents were born, in order to construct new *identities in diaspora* for the first-generation writer—identities which are both more than and part of African-American identities. And yet what this generational or physical distance enables, via the double displacement of both racial exclusion and exilic or diasporic travel, is a distance which allows critique. Jamaican-born Michelle Cliff, for example, writing novels about Jamaica in the United States, is able to articulate a Caribbean feminism that acknowledges homophobia in her homeland, social stratifications in Jamaica based on race or skin color, as well as the transnational corporate politics that contribute to the dire pollution of the island. Distance, then, couples the longing of nostalgia with the liberty of critique. These entanglements and complications are fruitfully articulated in literary narratives.

The principal claim of this chapter is that diaspora identity[4] is performed in writing, even as it also precedes the act of writing itself, in the less benign fluids of tears and blood which Du Bois references. Indeed, the articulation of diaspora identity in writing is more than a literary performance and is in fact a political act. Speaking specifically of the importance of writing by black women, Abena P. A. Busia states, "*In its very existence* . . . our literature can be read as a political body of works, and we have a contingent need for a criticism to read and interpret it" (5 original emphasis). Nation-state categories of identity are at odds with the social practices of migratory/diasporic communities as delineated in their cultural production. Lisa Lowe and David Lloyd's "Introduction" to *The Politics of Culture in the Shadow of Capital* urges us to pay attention to culture in a transnational era as a key site for political contestation, the expression of resistance to exploitation. They argue for the expansion of the concept of political agency and the need "to reconceive the 'social'—as the terrain in which politics, culture, and the economic are related, in terms radically other than those given by post-Enlightenment rationalizations of Western society" (3). Literature still carries the weight of cultural capital, and as such it represents an important location for the staging of resistant identities. Writing a counterhegemonic story about identity is staking a claim through the medium of ink, as opposed to tears and blood.

One way to approach the relationship between diaspora and literature is to state that the condition of exile/diaspora is the material condition that produces particular (perhaps repeated) literary responses. There are many important works which delineate certain themes taken up by diasporic writers. Another way to view the topic is to say that the condition of exile/diaspora is itself constituted in literature via these themes.[5] Though my argument is informed by this work, the central claim I want to make about diaspora identity is that it is revised in the works of black international writers. Studying writing by black authors living in the West, perhaps in exile or expatriation, or one generation removed from a perceived cultural homeland, enables us to unsettle and complicate the typical construction of home and diaspora as binary opposites. That is, in general usage one cannot be at home and in diaspora at the same time. Here I want to argue that black international prose writing itself performs a home in diaspora.

The circulation of texts in transnational markets, the traveling capacity of the fluid ink, means also that a diasporic community is created through these literary acts. This community is often not recognized by nation-states or by traditional models of literary study, yet it exists as a resistant social practice. For example, when Chester Himes, living in permanent exile in Paris, writes a detective novel set in Harlem, this work is read by many disparate audiences, from black European novelists to continental

African critics. The conversations which Himes's texts create can be seen as a diasporic network. This is not to suggest that the concept of diaspora allows black writers to live outside either the hegemonic powers of nation-states, or the nation-bound categorizing of literary audiences, publishers, reading communities, etc. Rather, their work can be read as resistance to this hegemony and thereby presents us ways to think beyond both the nation-state and transnational capital as organizing forces of identity. In that the imaginative work of writers like Richard Wright and Chester Himes has taken them to places where they materially conceive of themselves as extranational, they are creating and describing a "third space" which can be called diaspora. Citing Fanon's chapter "The Fact of Blackness" (from *Black Skin, White Masks*), Homi Bhabha claims that this "is a space of being that is wrought from the interruptive, interrogative, tragic experience of blackness, of discrimination, of despair" (1994b 238). Yet we can also see the ways in which writing allows diasporic authors to transform these experiences into oppositional identities that move beyond the tragic and against the despair that Bhabha cites.

An analysis of diasporic texts can (and should) encompass an emphasis on both the "evidence of experience" and the discursivity of race and the performativity of identity. That is, in discussing racial discrimination and exclusion, we must never lose sight of the tears and blood behind Du Bois's hopeful prophecy. Bhabha asks, "How do strategies of representation or empowerment come to be formulated in the competing claims of communities where, despite shared histories of deprivation and discrimination, the exchange of values, meanings and priorities may not always be collaborative and dialogical, but may be profoundly antagonistic, conflictual and even incommensurable?" (1994b 2). Like Stuart Hall, Paul Gilroy, and others, Bhabha warns against using shared experiences of discrimination to expect generalizable or consistent articulations of diaspora identities. It is this marking of a ground between essentializing diaspora as a unified or seamless identity, and being able to instead analyze perhaps shared strategies of resistance through fiction that readers must successfully negotiate. I am arguing for seeing literary narratives as crucial ongoing sites where these diaspora claims are made, unmade, contested, or reinforced.

The Politics of Diaspora: Writing and Location

Literary studies, as a discipline, has for a long time defined its subjects in national terms, characterized by a cartographic ordering of cultural production: Japanese Literature, British Literature, American Literature, and so on. A project of comparative cultural studies would intervene in this geographic ordering and instead privilege a nexus of movement over one of stasis, migration over dwelling. It is important to hold sight of the multiple tensions in both dwelling and traveling, studying the ways that black international writers both construct a home, via their writing, and critique the exclusions of home(s). For example, Michelle Cliff uses her fiction to both embrace and critique the gendered politics of her island homeland; in her biomythography, *Zami*, Audre Lorde attempts to dwell in New York City as a lesbian via the eroticization of her mother's homeland, brought into New York spaces. Barnor Hesse's work in redefining notions of "settling" in relation to diasporic communities is very important as he argues that "the contours of Black settlements are, however, always more than residential, they are cultures of movement. . . . The articulation of community itself is a discursive investment in time-spatial constitutions within and beyond the nation-state" (177). This discursive investment is articulated in literature, though clearly literary narratives are not the only sites where diaspora discourses emerge. Several recent cultural studies works have focused on multiple sites where this "discursive investment" can be seen.[6] Wolfgang Iser writes about the noise which literature still provides in late twentieth century cultures: "For a technocratically organized culture [cf. the U.S.], the noise of literature carves out a space for the unpredictability and invention that allows an unfettered imagination to impinge on cultural circulation" (18). When we listen to the noise produced by literature, we can hear the diverse (sometimes messy and entangled) ways that prose narratives perform diaspora identifications.

What happens when we focus on the work of African diasporic writers who do not live in their "home" country? Such writers may be said to be triply displaced—first, they may be seen as displaced by the discrimination suffered by people of color in any country which is organized either explicitly or implicitly around principles of white supremacy; second, by an actual movement out of that country, away from a place they may have once called home; and third, by a generational displacement from a homeland whose culture is retained by the writer's community and/or family.

Studying these writers unsettles the binary between home and diaspora, opening up both terms for redefinition. One understanding of the term diaspora implies a collective cultural identification in which Africa represents a putative original home or pure origin. But contemporary critical discourse has taught us to be skeptical of concepts like purity, authenticity, and even home itself. Paul Gilroy, for example, warns that "there isn't any anterior purity—there isn't any anterior, first of all, and there isn't any purity either" (cited in Lott 54). What then does it mean to identify either a writer or her cultural expression as African diasporic? Given that there is not a unitary, recoverable, originary meaning to the term Africa, what kinds of qualities can such work be said to possess in common with the work of other diasporic writers? It is important to avoid essentializing either the writers or their work by referring back to a monolithic notion of blackness or even African "diasporic-ness."[7] In their seminal work on women's diaspora literatures, both Abena P. A. Busia and Gay Wilentz separately address the dangers of essentialism. Though she reminds us that "the willingness to embrace a commonality might blind us to the uniqueness which distinguishes the separate peoples of the desired whole," Busia's work demonstrates that there are "common themes in the literature of black women in the diaspora," and she shows that a "rebellious process of self-definition and redefinition" are repeatedly evidenced in these texts (2,3). Gay Wilentz's work stresses the ways in which diaspora studies remains "dialectic," not "essentialist" (1992b 386).[8]

What I think the term diaspora captures, why I want to retain the term and the specificities it entails, are the memories of enforced migration, displacement, and racial slavery or colonial dominance which emerge in the cultural expressions of diasporic peoples.[9] This history could also be called the Fact of Slavery. In Du Bois's chapter, "The Concept of Race," in *Dusk of Dawn*, he writes, "as I face Africa I ask myself: what is it between us that constitutes a tie which I can feel better than I can explain?" By way of an answer Du Bois concludes, "one thing is sure and that is the fact that since the fifteenth century these ancestors of mine and their other descendants have had a common history; have suffered a common disaster and have one long memory.[. . .]The physical bond is least and the badge of color relatively unimportant save as a badge; *the real essence of this kinship is its social heritage of slavery; the discrimination and insult*" (117 emphasis added). In this passage in *Dusk of Dawn*, Du Bois revises Booker T. Washington's 1909 framing of diaspora. In *The Story of the Negro*, Washington writes:

There is, however, a tie which few white men can understand, which binds the American Negro to the African Negro; which unites the black man of Brazil and the black man of Liberia; which is constantly drawing into closer relations all the scattered African peoples whether they are in the old world or the new. There is not only the tie of race, which is strong in any case, but there is the badge of colour, which is specially [*sic*] important in the case of the black man. It is this common badge of colour, for instance, which is responsible for the fact that whatever contributes in any degree to the progress of the American Negro, contributes to the progress of the African Negro, and to the Negro in South America and the West Indies. (33–34)

Du Bois revises Washington in suggesting that the "badge of colour" itself is less important than the experiential history (i.e., the "social heritage") that it may signify.[10] Black international writing traces this kinship of experience, rather than a kinship based on blood or genealogy, and diasporic authors use their writing to resist, explore, and revise "the social heritage of slavery" as it is lived in contemporary discrimination. Against the "social death" of slavery and the social negations of contemporary racisms, black writers embrace authorship as a means of reinstating perhaps not one, but multiple resistant selves. In *Turning South Again: Re-Thinking Modernism/Re-Reading Booker T.*, Houston Baker explains the power of authorship: "What I shall call memorial and performative writing is our rite of black revisionary survival par excellence. In the most profound ways, writing, and especially revisionary writing, is our key to sanity, our prophylaxis against civil and social death" (5). Du Bois too holds out this hope in the "crooked marks" of his pen, the writing that was so central to his life, in the final words of *Souls*: "may infinite reason turn the tangle [of racism] straight, and these crooked marks on a fragile leaf be not indeed The End" (217).

Writing Home: More Than "Crooked Marks on a Fragile Leaf"

What does it mean to study the work of writers who have migrated from their "home?" Indeed, most people in the world have made such migrations, whether far or near. African diasporic writing shows us that the processes by which black people (and especially black writers) living in the West define their identities are in every way influenced by their relationship to what they call "home." The reasons why many black writers have left their "homes" have everything to do with the material experiences, as well as cultural memories of, slavery, colonialism, and contemporary racism—Du Bois's "tears and blood." Thus, their identities as diasporic peoples comprise an important element of their later status as migrants. Many migrant or exiled writers do not seek to enact a collective return to a particular home or country of origin. Rather, their very status as migrants in many ways represents a rejection of that national identity. What does it mean to say that someone is displaced from their home? One might ask today, "Who is not?" Contemporary critical discourse in the fields of cultural studies, literary studies, anthropology, and geography has pointed to "the instability of 'home' as a referent" (Bammer vii). Angelika Bammer continues, stating that "this instability is manifesting itself on a staggering—some believe, unprecedented—scale both globally and locally. On all levels and in all places, it seems, 'home' in the traditional sense (whether taken to mean 'family,' or 'community,' or 'homeland'/'nation') is either disintegrating or being radically redefined" (viii).

Heeding Bammer, perhaps we should revise the concept "home," rather than jettison it altogether. By acknowledging the persistence of a desire for home, perhaps especially among diasporic peoples, we can trace its redefinitions and identify the ways that this persistent desire influences the cultural production of black writers living in the West. Rosemary George's important examination of contemporary postcolonial and colonial literatures, in *The Politics of Home* (1996), claims that "The search for the location in which the self is 'at home' is one of the primary projects of twentieth-century fiction in English . . . [this literature] is not so concerned with drawing allegories of nation as with the search for viable homes for viable selves" (3, 5). My argument here is similar and also explains the ways in which diasporic writers use literature to critique the place they might call home. Furthermore, I want to ask in what sense we might think of the diaspora itself as a home, thereby uniting the two terms which are typically viewed as mutually exclusive.

Most commonly, one's diasporic location is juxtaposed to the concept of a perhaps imagined original homeland from which one is now displaced. However, by *uniting* the terms we may suggest that in the absence of any recoverable singular homeland of origin, the diaspora itself, a plurilocal (also imagined) community of peoples politically self-identified within its scope represents a home. This home is not bounded, singular, retrograde, or exclusionary. The vast range of black international writing questions notions of a singular community, implying as it does a "collective consciousness." Barnor Hesse defines the diasporic imaginary as "itself vitally emergent in the conditions set by the 'inability of collective consciousness to absorb' the enormity of the traumas associated with slavery and also the ultimate impossibility of a collective consciousness" (169). The notion of diaspora can represent a multiple, plurilocal, constructed location of home, thus avoiding ideas of fixity, boundedness, and nostalgic exclusivity traditionally implied by the word home.[11]

Studying black international writing can show us the ways in which black writers construct a home in diaspora via their literary production. Looking further at the constructed nature of home, Bammer presents the provocative idea that perhaps home is best understood as an "amalgam, a pastiche, a performance" (ix). She continues, referring to home as "an enacted space within which we try on and play out roles and relationships of both belonging and foreignness" (ix). Precisely what is this "enacted space" in which one's relationship to home or not-home is constructed, negotiated, and repeatedly revised? I suggest that one important realm is discourse, and specifically literary production. Judith Butler's work on the discursivity of gender can be informative here. In *Gender Trouble* Butler asserts, "genders can be neither true nor false, but are only produced as the truth effects of a discourse of primary and stable identity." In fact, the gendered body can be seen as performative since "it has no ontological status apart from the various acts which constitute its reality" (136). We may see this as similar to the nature of diasporic identification, in that there need not be an ontological Africanness to which a diasporic identification refers. And yet, conversely, the desire for home also is claimed in the language of literary narrative as a direct result of racial exclusions enacted "at home." We can understand the power of performative utterances and racist exclusion when we consider racist speech and police brutality. A feeling of statelessness, of the lack of state protection, has been described over and over by black writers living in the West. Chester Himes, James Baldwin, W.E.B. Du Bois, and others have all indicated the state-sanctioning of racism as the reason for their migrations and exiles away from their "home" country.[12] It has been the reason why these writers continually ask in what sense America can be a home to people of color. Writing diaspora, then, is part of the construction of an alternate community, part of the "search for viable homes for viable selves" (George 5), in opposition to this experience of statelessness. Barnor Hesse reminds us that "*The affirmation of Black community is its politicization,* even in a day-to-day sense. Categoric distinctions between public and private, personal and political, local and national, are blurred in the activities of diasporic identification" (177 emphasis added). This is the politically performative power of writing diaspora; and yet diaspora is not always written in the same way. As readers we must attend to the different accents and valences with which diasporic writers invest their writings of home(s).

The identification with a particular place as home is something which can be claimed in discourse, but which may have little or no ontological status. An obvious argument here is that certainly there is an empirically verifiable recourse to geography: home is where you were born. But this phrase has very little meaning for many diasporic peoples. Consider Toni Morrison's literary example in *Beloved* of a child born, literally on the run, to an escaping female slave somewhere in, or near, Ohio. Or the case of black writer, Caryl Phillips, who was born in St. Kitts, but emigrated to London with his family before he was one year old. Of course, there are many more examples of ways in which a geographic answer attempting to unite space and place, to fix this with a notion of time: one's entry into the world becomes an insufficient answer or an incomplete explanation of either what is home or what is one's geographic (or national) identity.

Prose narrative is one important site in which black writers enact their relationship to various notions of "home." By necessity then, a study of diaspora literature must move beyond traditional national boundaries secured by a geopolitical ordering of world events and spaces. Instead, by paying attention to both movement and settlement we can deconstruct the linguistic binaries in such term pairs as colony and metropole, dominant culture and subordinated culture, homeland and adopted land. It is in the ever-shifting interstices of these terms that diasporic identities are constituted, and these in-between spaces inform the cultural production of diasporic peoples. The texts of diasporic writers give us new ways to conceive of community and resistance to oppression and domination.

While geographic or generational displacement from a putative homeland can be seen as a common condition uniting many diasporic writers, we must also focus on the moments of movement (lived or invented) that inform a writer's work. That is, rather than posit a reified homeland from which each writer has been "displaced," perhaps we can instead study the ways that transatlantic shuttling between European, African, and "New World" locations informs their literary production. Barnor Hesse states that "journeys become movements in time, space and memory in *reconstituting archaeologies of places of attachment or bewilderment*, which are reinhabited in order to comprehend contemporary settings" (179 emphasis added). This is a key description of the way in which Chester Himes's detective novels, for example, revisit a Harlem constituted perhaps solely in his nostalgic imaginings—a place he was attached to, in a sense filled with bewilderment, having never lived there, yet desiring to journey there in memory, creating a community of African-American resistance to police invasion. Himes's literary attachment to Harlem can be understood by way of Stuart Hall's notion of a "homeland" as a symbolic imaginary, an "infinitely renewable source of desire, memory, myth, search, discovery," which therefore "fuels the engines of nostalgia and fetishization" ("Cultural Identity" 236). Indeed, for a writer like Chester Himes the very notion of "home" itself is problematized. Himes has said that he experienced "a sort of pure homesickness" in writing his detective novels, a homesickness that was also an intense "pleasure." From a position of expatriation—hurt by U.S. racial injustices and yet longing for the familiar streets of home—he invents a hyperbolic Harlem landscape he can control. But the "facts" of Himes's life make the ground of familiarity slip away: Himes never lived in Harlem. Through a fictive Harlem marked by named landmarks, streets, and neighborhoods, Himes transports himself to a mental space he desires to call "home." His detective novels bear witness to the power of nostalgia as symbolic imaginary. And yet it is important to delineate the political elements of this nostalgia. In other words, rather than condemn Himes's nostalgia as a facile, potentially regressive state of consciousness, we can look for the ways Himes's re-creations of what was paradoxically both home and not-home enable him to stage a political critique of that very location.

To take another example, Clare Savage, the protagonist of both *Abeng* (1984) and *No Telephone to Heaven* (1987) is, like author Michelle Cliff, a light-skinned Jamaican who has lived in Jamaica, the United States, and London. Clare struggles with her nostalgic longing for her Jamaican birthplace, what Cliff has called, "this landscape of her identity" ("Crossroads" 266). And yet Cliff's texts also refuse to construct Jamaica as idyllic or pure, instead presenting a critique of the island's class politics and homophobia.[13]

I am interested in the ways that diasporic writers negotiate their relationships to the various places they call home, in order to see how they use writing to perform a sense of home-ness in the diaspora. How does such a trajectory strain against the overdetermined discourses of nation, race, and family, by which the modern self is so often defined? The goal of this questioning is not to illuminate an imaginary construct, a fixed finality of selfhood which an author may achieve in and through narrative, since few performances end so simply. Rather we can study the discursive strategies they adopt, the literary performances they enact, and see the ways in which their texts represent a space of negotiation with multiple places called "home."

Literary performances that speak in the registers of nostalgia are complicated when they encounter notions of accountability, however socially constructed and discriminatory those notions may be. Judith Butler cautions, "if one always risks meaning something other than what one thinks one utters, then one is, as it were, vulnerable in a specifically linguistic sense to a social life of language that exceeds the purview of the subject who speaks" ("Sovereign Performatives" 365). Butler's warning can help us see the shaky ground between the utterance of diaspora identity in narrative, the politics of culture, and the material reception of "racially-marked" utterances. Black writers are often held unjustly accountable by a community of readers who assume they write a national narrative or represent a national discourse in the sense of speaking for all black people, all African-Americans, etc. For some French readers, for example, Chester Himes becomes a representative of all Black America, and the Harlem of his novels is consequently imagined as sociologically "true." Himes is held accountable both by European readers who consider him a native informant on American blackness, and by those critics who see his creation of a lurid Harlem as pandering to French tastes for exoticism.[14] And yet Himes clearly invests his nostalgic imaginings with the power of political critique.[15]

A perhaps nostalgic desire for "wholeness," or a definition of identity which is bounded and exclusive, is not only at times an internal desire on the part of the diasporic subject, but in many ways it is also externally imposed by the larger social system which may act against the acceptance of a mobile and/or multiple identity. In Michelle Cliff's second novel, *No Telephone to Heaven*, Harry/Harriet, a gay male friend of Clare Savage's who cross-dresses, warns Clare, "'Cyaan [can't] live split. Not in this world'" (131). According to Harry/Harriet, the Jamaican milieu demands that one choose among definitional categories. Clearly, however, the choice is often made for one, by others, dependent upon legal definitions and rulings such as *Plessy v. Ferguson* and the counting of "drops of blood." To what extent and in what contexts can Michelle Cliff choose to define herself as black, Jamaican, or lesbian? Audre Lorde illuminates this dilemma when she writes, "As a black lesbian feminist comfortable with the many different ingredients of my identity, and a woman committed to racial and sexual freedom from oppression, I find I am constantly being encouraged to pluck out some one aspect of myself and present this as the meaningful whole, eclipsing or denying the other parts of myself. But this is a destructive and fragmenting way to live" (1990 285). Many diasporic texts explore the social/political dilemma posed by Lorde and Harry/Harriet and address the ways that diasporic identifications might exist in tension with discourses of "wholeness." Richard Wright throughout his life described himself as "of the west," yet also not of it. His papers at Yale University Library contain a manuscript where he writes out 85 statements all beginning, "I am an American, but . . ." An analysis located in the space of Wright's comma can show us the ways that writers claim a transnational identity which becomes neither a seamless wholeness nor a debilitating schizophrenia, but perhaps something closer to the fruitfully multiple stagings of identity affirmed by Lorde.

The concept of diaspora identity is not new and begins perhaps with such texts as Olaudah Equiano's 1789 narrative, in which he charts his movements from his kidnapping from Africa to his claiming of an Afro-British identity, describing his many "homes" along this journey. To formulate a method of inquiry about diasporic texts demands that we develop reading strategies that will allow us to hear the doubleness in many diasporic texts, the critique and the construction. Vè Vè Clark introduces a key critical term as she explains that to acquire "diaspora literacy" readers must possess "a knowledge of historical, social, cultural, and political development generated by lived and textual experience" (42). It is this attention to historical detail, to geographical specificity, which will help us to avoid (mis)using diaspora as an overfull metaphor.

Though we may read the ways diasporic writers use fiction to perform their varied and multiple claims to home, I think many texts also importantly perform a "rhetoric of refusal," to quote Doris Sommer (411). That is, there are spaces in these texts which disrupt whatever impulses a reader may have to read these books "about" home as national narratives. Michelle Cliff's most recent novel, *Free Enterprise*, begins with an epigraph from Miles Davis: "I always listen for what I can leave out." This performative refusal to divulge all, to present the "perfect oppositional other," is a strategy diasporic narratives employ to remain oppositional, and it is a strategy which implicates the reader as well. That is, we must learn to listen for what the author has left out, yet paradoxically without assuming we can fill it in, master or know it. Sommer emphasizes the significant challenge posed by learning to read resistance as she points to the potentially coalitional political strategies of a reading which respects difference. This suggestion of a coalitional politics between writer and reader is a very hopeful and productive one, which presents an answer to the question, why literature? Does diasporic literature present us with a mode of engagement that must be attended, that demands our participation? Think of Toni Morrison's stunning conclusion to her novel, *Jazz*; the interpretive power she signals, between the reader and the book as the (talking) book, itself invites us: "Say make me, remake me. You are free to do it and I am free to let you because look, look. Look where your hands are. Now" (229). Doris Sommer's warnings also point to the oppositional interpretation, as well an oppositional pedagogy, which a study of diasporic literature enables. That is, we must learn (and teach) how to read the resistance in a text, how to recognize the spaces at least of what is left out. Perhaps diasporic texts point not only to a coalitional home in diaspora, but also to the potential of coalitional reading and teaching strategies.[16]

NOTES

1. This essay is a version of my Introduction to *At Home in Diaspora: Black International Writing*, forthcoming from University of Minnesota Press, 2005, and used by permission of the publisher.

2. Throughout this chapter I use this term cognizant of its shortcomings as a way to describe a group of writers whose very work aims to deconstruct notions of racial categories based on false science. I borrow from Stuart Hall's definition when he says that "The term black is referring to this long history of political and historical oppression; it's not referring to . . . genes; it's not referring to . . . biology" (Hall "Race: The Floating Signifier," Undated Video, Media Education Foundation).

3. In this volume, Asale Angel Ajani cautions against an easy use of the term "displacement," noting official United Nations High Commissioner for Refugees distinctions between the categories refugee and displaced person. My use of the term is indeed less official and hopefully retains a different specificity.

4. I am largely influenced here by Stuart Hall's "Cultural Identity and Diaspora." Hall writes, "Diaspora does not refer us to those scattered tribes whose identity can only be secured in relation to some sacred homeland to which they must at all costs return. . . . The diaspora experience as I intend it here is defined, not by essence or purity, but by the recognition of a necessary heterogeneity and

diversity" (235). Avtar Brah's conceptualization of *diaspora space* is also instructive: "'Diaspora space' (as distinct from the concept of diaspora) is 'inhabited' not only by diasporic subjects but equally by those who are constructed and represented as 'indigenous.' As such, the concept of *diaspora space* foregrounds the entanglements of genealogies of dispersion with those of 'staying put'" (16). Following Brah's lead, the discipline of literary studies itself can be reconceived as a *diaspora space*. This space then weakens the claims previously made by fiction, which had been constructed or read as national narratives.

5. Abena Busia's work on black women writers has been seminal in this field, as has the work of Gay Wilentz. Two other important books analyzing the concepts of diaspora, exile, and migration via a range of texts written by black women are Carole Boyce Davies, *Black Women, Writing and Identity*, and Myriam J. A. Chancy, *Searching for Safe Spaces*.

6. In *Dangerous Crossroads: Popular Music, Postmodernism and the Poetics of Place*, George Lipsitz shows how music can teach us about "place and displacement. Laments for lost places and narratives of exile and return often inform, inspire, and incite the production of popular music" (4). Lipsitz's analysis explains how these "new discursive spaces allow for recognition of new networks and affiliations; they become crucibles for complex identities in formation that respond to the imperatives of place at the same time that they transcend them" (6). Jayne O. Ifekwunigwe studies "the everyday words of working-class and middle-class 'mixed-race' people in England" in *Scattered Belongings: Cultural Paradoxes of "Race," Nation and Gender*, and makes oral testimonies central to showing how "'mixed-race' de/territorialized declarations delimit and transgress bi-racialized discourses and point the way toward a profound re-alignment of thinking about belonging" (xiii).

7. Several critics have pointed to a similar danger in using the term "postcolonial" to refer to localities and experiences which are characterized by importantly diverse power dynamics. The warning here is against erasing such differences or simply subsuming them under an academically convenient rubric. Sarah Suleri writes, "The concept of the postcolonial itself is too frequently robbed of historical specificity in order to function as a preapproved allegory for any mode of discursive contestation" (758). See also McClintock.

8. In addition to this article, see also Wilentz's book, *Binding Cultures: Black Women Writers in Africa and the Diaspora*.

9. When I use the term diaspora (or diasporic) henceforth, though I drop the qualifier African, I am specifically referring to African diasporic peoples, and I do not mean to imply a similarity of conditions for members of other diasporas, such as the Jewish or Greek diasporas.

10. For several important analyses of Du Bois's complicated and shifting arguments about race, especially in this section of *Dusk of Dawn*, see Appiah, Posnock, and Hall, "Race, the Floating Signifier."

11. Rosemary George's work reminds us that "Home is a way of establishing difference. Homes and home-countries are exclusive" (2).

12. Though there are far too many examples to mention, I here provide two passages which discuss ideas of belonging and the sense of exclusion caused by racist practices. In the second section of his autobiography, *Black Boy (American Hunger)*, Wright writes, "Negroes are told in a language they cannot possibly misunderstand that their native land is not their own" (355). Decades later, Patricia Hill Collins writes of her own childhood, "I now see that I was searching for a location where I 'belonged,' a safe intellectual and political space that I could call 'home.' But how could I presume to find a home in a system that at best, was predicated upon my alleged inferiority and, at worst, was dedicated to my removal? More important, why would I even want to?" (4).

13. See Walters 1998 for a discussion of the politics of nostalgia in *No Telephone to Heaven*.

14. See Tyler Stovall's chapter in this volume and elsewhere for further discussion of French interactions with black culture.

15. I develop this argument about the political critique in Himes's detective fiction in Walters 1994.

16. I am using the word coalition in the way described by Bernice Johnson Reagon in her influential essay, "Coalition Politics: Turning the Century," when she reminds us that a coalition is not an exclusionary home with a nipple and a bottle for comfort (359).

WORKS CITED

Appiah, Anthony. "The Uncompleted Argument: Du Bois and the Illusion of Race." *"Race," Writing and Difference*. Ed. Henry Louis Gates, Jr. Chicago: U Chicago P, 1985. 21–37.

Baker, Houston A. *Turning South Again: Re-Thinking Modernism/Re-Reading Booker T.* Durham: Duke UP, 2001.

Bammer, Angelika. "Editorial." *New Formations* 17 (Summer 1992), *The Question of 'Home.'* vii–xi.

Bhabha, Homi. (1994a) "Frontlines/Borderposts." *Displacements: Cultural Identities in Question*. Ed. Angelika Bammer. Bloomington: Indiana UP. 269–272.

———. (1994b) *The Location of Culture*. London: Routledge.

Brah, Avtar. *Cartographies of Diaspora: Contesting Identities*. London: Routledge, 1996.

Busia, Abena P. A. "Words Whispered over Voids: A Context for Black Women's Rebellious Voices in the Novel of the African Diaspora." *Black Feminist Criticism and Critical Theory. (Studies in Black American Literature, Vol. II)*. Eds. Joe

Weixlmann and Houston A. Baker, Jr. Greenwood, FL: Penkevill Publishing Co., 1988. 1–41.

Butler, Judith. *Gender Trouble: Feminism and the Subversion of Identity*. New York: Routledge, 1990.

———. "Sovereign Performatives in the Contemporary Scene of Utterance." *Critical Inquiry* 23 (Winter 1997): 350–377.

Chancy, Myriam J. A. *Searching for Safe Spaces: Afro-Caribbean Women Writers in Exile*. Philadelphia: Temple UP, 1997.

Clark, Vè Vè A. "Developing Diaspora Literacy and *Marasa* Consciousness." *Comparative American Identities: Race, Sex, and Nationality in the Modern Text*. Ed. and Intro. Hortense J. Spillers. New York: Routledge, 1991. 40–61.

Cliff, Michelle. *Abeng*. New York: Dutton, 1984.

———. "Clare Savage as a Crossroads Character." *Caribbean Women Writers: Essays from the First International Conference*. Ed. and Intro. Selwyn R. Cudjoe. Wellesley: Calaloux, 1990. 263–268.

———. *Free Enterprise*. New York: Dutton, 1993.

———. *No Telephone to Heaven*. New York: Vintage, 1987.

Collins, Patricia Hill. *Fighting Words: Black Women and the Search for Justice*. Minneapolis: U Minnesota P, 1998.

Davies, Carole Boyce. *Black Women, Writing and Identity: Migrations of the Subject*. London: Routledge, 1994.

Du Bois, W.E.B. *Dusk of Dawn: An Essay Toward an Autobiography of a Race Concept*. 1940. Rpt. New York: Shocken Books, 1968.

———. *The Souls of Black Folk*. 1903. Rpt. Intro. Donald B. Gibson. New York: Penguin, 1989.

Equiano, Olaudah. *The Interesting Narrative of the Life of Olaudah Equiano or Gustavus Vassa, the African*. *The Classic Slave Narratives*. Ed. and Intro. Henry Louis Gates, Jr. New York: NAL/Penguin, 1987.

Fanon, Frantz. *Black Skin, White Masks*. 1952. Trans. Charles Lam Markmann. New York: Grove, 1967.

George, Rosemary Marangoly. *The Politics of Home: Postcolonial Relocations and Twentieth-Century Fiction*. Cambridge: Cambridge UP, 1996.

Gilroy, Paul. *The Black Atlantic: Modernity and Double Consciousness*. Cambridge, MA: Harvard UP, 1993.

Hall, Stuart. "Cultural Identity and Diaspora." *Identity: Community, Culture, Difference*. Ed. Jonathan Rutherford. London: Lawrence and Wishart, 1990. 222–237.

———. "Race, the Floating Signifier." Video. Media Education Foundation, Kinetic Video, U.S.A., 1996.

Hesse, Barnor. "Black to the Front and Black Again: Racialization Through Contested Times and Spaces." *Place and the Politics of Identity*. Eds. Michael Keith and Steve Pile. London: Routledge, 1993. 162–182.

Himes, Chester. *My Life of Absurdity: The Later Years.* 1976. Rpt. New York: Paragon, 1990.

Ifekwunigwe, Jayne O. *Scattered Belongings: Cultural Paradoxes of "Race," Nation and Gender.* London: Routledge, 1999.

Iser, Wolfgang. "Why Literature Matters." *Why Literature Matters: Theories and Functions of Literature.* Eds. Rudiger Ahrens and Laurenz Volkmann. Heidelberg: Universitatsverlag C. Winter, 1996. 13–22.

Lipsitz, George. *Dangerous Crossroads: Popular Music, Postmodernism and the Poetics of Place.* London: Verso, 1994.

Lorde, Audre. "Age, Race, Class, and Sex: Women Redefining Difference." *Out There: Marginalization and Contemporary Cultures.* Eds. Russell Ferguson, Martha Gever, Trinh T. Minh-ha, Cornel West. New York: New Museum of Contemporary Art, 1990. 281–287.

———. *Zami: A New Spelling of My Name.* Freedom, CA: Crossing P, 1982.

Lott, Tommy. "Black Cultural Politics: An Interview with Paul Gilroy." *Found Object* 4 (Fall 1994): 46–81.

Lowe, Lisa and David Lloyd. "Introduction." *The Politics of Culture in the Shadow of Capital.* Durham: Duke UP, 1997. 1–32.

McClintock, Anne. "The Angel of Progress: Pitfalls of the Term 'Post-Colonialism.'" *Social Text* 10, 2 & 3 (1992): 84–98.

Morrison, Toni. *Beloved.* New York: Plume, 1987.

———. *Jazz.* New York: Alfred A. Knopf, 1992.

Posnock, Ross. *Color and Culture: Black Writers and the Making of the Modern Intellectual.* Cambridge: Harvard UP, 1998.

Reagon, Bernice Johnson. "Coalition Politics: Turning the Century." *Home Girls: A Black Feminist Anthology.* Ed. Barbara Smith. New York: Kitchen Table: Women of Color P, 1983. 356–368.

Richard Wright Papers. Yale Collection of American Literature, Beinecke Rare Book and Manuscript Library.

Sommer, Doris. "Resisting the Heat: Menchu, Morrison, and Incompetent Readers." *Cultures of United States Imperialism.* Eds. Amy Kaplan and Donald E. Pease. Durham: Duke UP, 1993. 407–432.

Suleri, Sarah. "Woman Skin Deep: Feminism and the Postcolonial Condition." *Critical Inquiry* 18 (Summer 1992): 756–769.

Walters, Wendy W. "Limited Options: Strategic Maneuverings in Himes's Harlem." *African American Review* 28, 4 (Winter 1994): 615–631.

———. "Michelle Cliff's *No Telephone to Heaven*: Diasporic Displacement and the Feminization of the Landscape." *Borders, Exiles and Diasporas.* Eds. Elazar Barkan and Marie-Denise Shelton. Stanford: Stanford UP. 1998. 217–233.

———. *At Home in Diaspora: Black International Writing.* Minneapolis: U of Minnesota P, forthcoming 2005.

Washington, Booker T. *The Story of the Negro: The Rise of the Race from Slavery.* Vol. I. New York: Negro Universities P, 1909.

Wilentz, Gay. (1992a) *Binding Cultures: Black Women Writers in Africa and the Diaspora.* Bloomington: Indiana UP.

———. (1992b) "Toward a Diaspora Literature: Black Women Writers from Africa, the Caribbean, and the United States." *College English* 54, 4 (April 1992): 385–419.

Wright, Richard. *Black Boy (American Hunger): A Record of Childhood and Youth.* 1944. Rpt. Intro. Jerry Ward, Jr. New York: Harper Perennial Restored Edition, 1993.

13

Displacing Diaspora
Trafficking, African Women, and Transnational Practices

Asale Angel-Ajani

> They say that behind mountains are more mountains.
> Now I know that this is true. I also know that there are
> timeless waters, endless seas, and lots of people in the
> world who's names don't matter to anyone but them-
> selves. —Edwidge Danticat, *Krik? Krak!*

In 1995, the Lawyers Committee for Human Rights reported that the situation for emigrant and refugee populations from the African continent was
the most severe in the world and the conditions were not improving. Currently, there are over 30 million Africans uprooted from their homes by
ethnic strife, economic upheaval, political persecution, or environmental
degradation. In this chapter, I discuss how, when thinking about the contemporary Africa Diaspora, we must recognize the realities of these conditions, these diasporic conditions, in the lives of subsaharan African
women who traverse borders.

To explore what I have called "diasporic conditions" (Angel-Ajani
2002), I draw on my research with imprisoned African women in Rome,
Italy as the framework. I look to the forms of movement that mark
their lives, for example, drug trafficking and being trafficked into Europe
for prostitution. The example of these imprisoned women's lives illustrates the importance of an analysis of transnational movements that
documents the racism, sexism, poverty, and violence that set in motion
their migrations. Exploring these forms of travel not only signals the

crises of these contemporary times, but also brings forth the challenges these kinds of travel pose to theories of diaspora and transnationalism. I will explore the parameters of diaspora and transnational studies from the disciplinary vantage point of anthropology. Today we can hardly discuss the concept of diaspora without fully acknowledging the contributions of transnational studies. Perhaps because of this, diaspora and transnational processes often occupy the same theoretical space. But obviously these two areas of studies are different. For example, however contested, the issue of identity is at the core of diaspora studies; while on the other hand, transnational studies, because of its link with the disciplines, has more conventionally preoccupied itself with the larger structural processes of cultural change, political economy, and the nation-state.

Mapping Diasporic Difference

While this chapter considers African travels to Italy, I am not writing about the African diaspora in Italy per se. As I detail below, I am not concerned with the roots/routes discussion that so many diaspora theorists have taken up qua Gilroy (1993) and Clifford (1997). While I draw on the term diaspora to frame my discussion I do so with certain caution. I evoke diaspora in a way that reveals the intersubjectivity of the construction of diaspora and loosely use the concept as a way of creating and acknowledging the gaps within and between theory and lived experience. Not unlike several other scholars, I write of diaspora as a fluid concept, one that is less fixed than currently imagined.

As Paul Gilroy (2000) discussed in his book *Against Race*, diaspora, in its crudest form, is a way to discuss the etymological roots of the term *scattering* (also see Helmreich 1993; Brown 1998). This scattering attends to the notion that communities (for example, African Americans) have been ripped from their original homeland. For others, diaspora is about a time-space continuum where location, culture, and memory take center stage and seek to explicate how and where diasporic communities live (Gilroy 1991, 1993; Clarke 1997; Brown 1998). For still others, the African diaspora is about Pan-Africanism, linking politically and culturally the struggles of people of African descent around the globe (Drake 1982; Lemelle and Kelley 1994). There are many variations on the diaspora theme, but the common ground of these literatures is the significance they place on notions of identity and community. But in all these literatures community is sewn together by race and notions of blackness.[1]

It is obvious that the significance of race has long shaped the interpretation of Africa and Africans (Mudimbe 1988). My own exploration on the significance of race and gender is grounded in criminological debates during the late nineteenth and early twentieth centuries. In this chapter I set out to understand the conditions of possibility or as I have called, "diasporic conditions," in an attempt to understand what renders African women immigrants as dangerous and possibly criminal others in Italy. While I suggest that "diasporic conditions" is a way of examining the conditions of possibility, it also refers to epistemology. The phrase, "diasporic conditions," signifies the need to think through the diaspora concept along the lines of shared (but not similar) experience, rather than through the telos of traditional notions of cultural survivals and continuity. The call to explore diasporic conditions has a necessary political tone, one that I hope compels us to look at the social and political conditions for Black people around the world.

Earlier theories of diaspora lend credence to my examination of diasporic conditions in Italy. St. Clair Drake's unabashed commitment to social justice in the context of writing about Pan-Africanism and diaspora has provided a framework for thinking about how theoretical explorations can also be politically engaged. For Drake, diaspora studies "must contribute toward maintaining and reinforcing black consciousness and must be oriented toward the goal of fostering understanding, solidarity, and cooperation throughout the black world" (1982: 453). Drake may be too prescriptive in his framing of diaspora studies, but I am nevertheless deeply influenced by his call for political commitment. Like many of the theorists of the mid-1960s to the mid-1980s, Drake's formulation of diaspora studies grows out of a critique of societies that are structured by racial dominance (Hall 1996).

In addition to recognizing the history of racial oppression (which is sorely lacking in contemporary studies on transnationalism), diaspora theory has had a preoccupation with notions of home for better or for worse. But "home" and homeland (Africa) do not figure into my research sites of longing or loss. For many women detained in Rebibbia prison in Italy, home was not thought of as the nation or continent they left behind. Sometimes, home was a memory space where their children lived—children—they had been forced to leave behind, in Italy or Africa. In fact, women's configurations of home were very different from those imagined in diaspora literature. As ex-convicts, former prostitutes, and overall "bad and dangerous" women, many did not want to go "home," conjuring the famous phrase from the African American poet and performer Wayne Corbit, who once said, "I cannot go home as who I am."

For my purposes, Avtar Brah's notion of a "homing desire" rather than a desire for a homeland is more useful. For Brah, diaspora provides a critique of fixed origins and ought not be "theorised as transhistorical codifications of eternal migrations." She observes, "the concept of diaspora should be seen to refer to historically contingent 'genealogies,' in the Foucauldian sense of the word. That is to say that the term should be seen as conceptual mapping which defies the search for absolutes, or genuine and authentic manifestations of a stable, pre-given, unchanging identity" (1996: 196). Importantly, Brah views power relations as central to her framing of diaspora, focusing on the intersections of gender, race, sexuality, and class in her analysis. Brah asks the ever-important question often ignored in diaspora studies: Who travels and how and under what circumstances? "What socio-economic, political, and cultural conditions mark the trajectories of these journeys? What regimes of power inscribed the formation of a specific diaspora" (1996: 182). Brah directs our attention to the necessity of analyzing diasporic groups by inquiring, what makes diasporic groups similar or different from one another (1996: 182).

Similarly, feminist critics Inderpal Grewal and Caren Kaplan have firmly claimed that "All diasporas are not alike; we must learn how to demarcate them, how to understand specific agendas and politics" (1994: 16). Although I agree with Kaplan and Grewal's call for demarcations between diasporic groups (for example, between the African and the South Asian diasporas), I would suggest that we also reconfigure the boundaries *within* individual diasporic groups.[2] For example, to be African American or Afro-Cuban in diaspora is much different than being an African (say from Nigeria or Ghana, for example) in diaspora.[3] In short, I am calling for an understanding of the differences that exist between and among African diasporic groups. It is crucial that differences get acknowledged within the African diaspora, where U.S. perspectives, particularly about race and notions of blackness, rule supreme (da Silva 1998). Indeed, national origin may mean much more than we care to admit.

Transnationalism

In diasporic literature, the nation is often constructed as monolithic and is seldom seen as a multilayered entity (Gupta 1995). In my research with African women who traverse state borders, the nation-state is necessarily a complicated and often contradictory space. I have found that the nation and its borders are internalized within prisons and not just at the frontier. For example, as Barbara Harlow writes, "prisons, deportations, immigration control, and forced exile indicate a nexus of bureaucratic power and its deployment in the service of the state [that is] central to the contemporary historical experience of much of the world's population" (1994: 150).

Herein lies the difference between diaspora and transnational studies. In a move away from area studies, transnationalism positions the nation and a critique of the fixedness of national boundaries at its center. Several scholars of transnationalism have argued that movements by populations across national boundaries disrupt and challenge the notion of the nation (Appadurai 1996; Glick Schiller, Basch, and Blanc-Szanton 1992; Yanagisako and Delaney 1995).[4] Anthropologist Michael Kearney, for instance, writes that "Transnationalism calls attention to the cultural and political projects of nation-states as they vie for hegemony in relations with other nation-states, with their citizens and 'aliens.' This cultural-political dimension of transnationalism is signaled by its resonance with nationalism as a cultural and political project" (1995: 548). Glick Schiller, et al. also define transnationalism through the lens of the nation.[5] They define transnationalism as "the process by which immigrants build social fields that link together their country of origin and their country of settlement" (1992: 1).

Yet, one of the most troubling aspects of the recent work on transnationalism and travel are the ways these concepts have become for many scholars "linked to a more postmodern moment of destabilized nations-states" or seen as operating beyond the boundary of the nation (Kaplan 1996; Appadurai 1996). Dorinne Kondo has noted that rendering the nation as deterritorialized is "too-celebratory" (1997: 176). Going a step further, Kamala Visweswaran has argued that these "uncritically theorized notions . . . trivializ[e] the political particularities of the phenomenon" (cited in Kondo 1997: 176). In short, it appears that, as Nina Glick Schiller has recently written, "In the first flurry of interest in transnational processes, scholars made a simplistic equation between the growth of transnational processes and the demise of the nation-state" (Glick Schiller 1997: 158).

Given the foregoing, it is unsurprising, then, that those who celebrate the supposed unbounded borders of the nation-state fail to acknowledge the significance of some of the major institutions that make up the nation-state—the border patrol, the police, prisons, and other centers of custody or detention that are increasing in power and expanding in jurisdiction.⁶ Unfortunately, there is little discussion by these scholars of such sites as key representational forces of the power of the nation-state. In addition, these penal or otherwise punitive institutions are seldom seen as among those locations that serve to reify the idea of citizenship and proper national belonging.

I view the current literatures on transnationalism as studies on the "plurality of presence," that celebrate the presence of Third World others who are now living in the First World (Miyoshi 1993: 750). This celebration, however, does not speak to the political context of travel between the Third and First Worlds. In fact, the literature on transnationalism, the Third World at home, and what Rosaldo calls the implosion of the Third World into the First (Rosaldo 1988), remark upon a kind of impossibility, with reference to the nation-state and the ability of people to cross its borders. Kearney, for instance, argues that this vision has reconfigured urban anthropology. He speaks with excitement of the Caribbeanization of New York City or Los Angeles as the capital of Latin America (1995: 554). Transnationalism, for Kearney, provides a new set of questions where immigration studies left off. He declares: "Former concern with assimilation in migration studies has given way in contemporary work to the examination of the persistence and creation of difference among, for example, Senegalese in Italy, Algerians in France, Moroccans and other nationalities in Spain, Turks in Germany, Asians and Mexicans in California, Indians in the United States, and West Indians and Sikhs in England" (1995: 554). What is striking about Kearney's list is how the First World is the point of arrival in all these studies. This speaks volumes about what types of travel and migration we value. Indeed, had Kearney listed lateral moves—from Colombia to Venezuela, for instance, or from Malawi to South Africa, or Burma to Thailand (all examples of contemporary sociopolitical displacement)—there might not be such cause for celebration. These lateral migration moves from so-called developing nations to developing nations—are the most common forms of movement for a majority of the world's population. As Avtar Brah (1996) reminds us, just as arrivals are important, so too are departures.

I have mentioned earlier that there is an inability within studies that focus on transnational processes to acknowledge the history of racial oppression. However, among the important aspects of transnationalism, the few notable studies that place an emphasis on gender and in particular women's experiences set the literature on transnationalism apart from African diaspora studies. As many of us have lamented, African diaspora studies fail women miserably, or at least much of the published works do.

Despite this, there is the possibility within diaspora studies to move away from the politically sanitized discourse that surrounds transnational studies. Since much of our work in African diaspora studies focuses on racial formation, racism, and white supremacy, we can bring a varied political, if not radical political, perspective to the study of transnational processes and globalization. We can and we should, but we should also take into account the everyday practical realities of people's lives. It is here that African diaspora scholars have much to learn from the transnational and globalization theorists who take great care in exploring both the contemporary moment and its historical underpinnings.

Displaced African Women and Transnational Discourses

Human rights, particularly what constitute women's human rights, are endlessly debated (Bunch and Reilly 1994; Cook 1994; Peters and Wolper 1995). Yet while there may be fissures among scholars and activists about the meaning of women's human rights and women's human rights violations, there seems to exist a general consensus that violations of women's rights are prevalent but gravely underreported.[7] It is estimated that women and children represent 75 to 80 percent of all refugees and displaced persons (Wali 1995). The situation confronting immigrant, refugee, and displaced women is extreme, resulting in what Sima Wali (1995) calls a human tragedy. Refugee Women in Development, Inc. (ReWID) reported that refugee and displaced women face extreme violence including, but not limited to, trafficking, rape, forced prostitution, and forced childbearing, abduction, physical and psychological torture, and murder. In a 1993 testimony to the Global Tribunal on Violation of Women's Human Rights in Vienna, Asha Samad from Somalia spoke of the experiences of refugee women, "[t]hose in refugee camps are almost all women and children.

Those suffering harassment, not only in Somalia, but when they are escaping the country into some neighbouring countries, are the women." She continues:

> Sometimes, the police of those countries, and other men from [the women's] own country and from those countries [in which the women have sought refuge], often also take advantage of their impoverishment. When they are trying to get food for their children, or for other people who have survived with them, when they're trying to get legalized status in the neighbouring countries or in developed countries, too, quite often men have to pay with bribes, and women have to pay with sex. (cited in Bunch and Reilly 1994: 44–45)

Within the international community, human rights scholars and activists recognize a difference between displaced persons and refugees. Displacement, which millions of Africans face, is largely viewed as internal displacement. According to the United Nations High Commissioner for Refugees (UNHCR), the term internal displacement is used to "denote those persons who, as a result of persecution, armed conflict or violence, have been forced to abandon their homes and leave their usual place of residence, and who remain within the borders of their own country" (UNHCR 1997: 1). The UNHCR identifies internal displacement as among the most pressing of humanitarian concerns. The distinction between refugees—those who cross borders seeking asylum—and internally displaced populations are "conceptually vapid," for, as the UNHCR notes, those who are internally displaced are at the threshold of becoming refugees. It is obvious that one's ability to leave the country is dependent on a number of variables. "With the exception of those who live very close to an international border (and those who have access to vehicles) people who have been forced out of their homes may have to walk for many days, or move in a number of stages, before they are able to seek asylum in another state" (UNHCR 1997: 5).

Despite the UNHCR's official distinctions between refugees and the displaced, many academics have used the term *displacement* to speak of immigration (Ong and Nonini 1997), diaspora (Lavie and Swedenburg 1996), and exile (Kaplan 1996). I do not want to debate the significance and nuances between *refugees* and *displaced persons*, nor the differences between the UNHCR's definition of the internally displaced and academic, particularly postmodern, notions of displacement. What I do want to signal are the myriad ways in which the postmodern conceptualization of displacement can in some cases obscure the realities faced by displaced populations, by failing to acknowledge how or why populations are displaced. Indeed, the disciplinary emergence of discursive notions of displacement within anthropology is problematic. Specifically, we need to ask what types of questions and areas of investigation this kind of discourse conceals.[8] As scholar Angelika Bammer writes, "the problem with this [postmodern] notion of displacement is that differences . . . disappear." She suggests that notions of displacement that elide differences are "appropriated for the purposes of elaborating a new, postmodernistically hip version of the universal subject" (1994: xxii–xxiii). In light of this critique, Caren Kaplan argues for "a more historically accurate and geographically specific representation of displacement" (1996: 102). But, for Kaplan, producing more accurate representations of displacement and of its processes is not about presenting the real displaced people but rather the "appropriations of their experiences by cultural theorists." According to Kaplan, this distinction is not "exactly the point" (102). But I wonder: If the point is not a concern with producing texts that move beyond the postmodern free play of difference to discuss the realities of displacement, what *is* the point?[9] I pose this question in the spirit of criticism as a gesture of respect. I am not attempting to present a moral argument, nor am I arguing against postmodernism or for vulgar empiricism. Instead, I argue for a more nuanced understanding of how displacement figures into the forms of transnational movements.

Trafficking in Women and Transnational Practices

Just as the term *displacement* has become more discursive, *transnationalism*—that is, a movement or migration that involves two or more nations—can be seen as another disciplinary emergence that has become, as Kearney (1995) notes, a prominent focus within anthropology.[10] In fact, I suggest that, as the literature on transnationalism or diaspora has grown, the term has become an emerging orthodoxy, used as both a frame of reference and an analytic category (Grewal and Kaplan 1994).

In an important attempt to bring women and feminism to the fore of these debates, Grewal and Kaplan have sought to "broaden and deepen the analysis of gender" within the studies of transnationalism and transnational projects (1994: 1). They advocate for transnational feminist practices that acknowledge the conditions of globalization which affect women's lives, writing:[11]

> If feminist political practices do not acknowledge transnational cultural flows, feminist movements will fail to understand the material conditions that structure women's lives in diverse locations. If feminist movements cannot understand the dynamics of these material conditions, they will be unable to construct an effective opposition to current economic and cultural hegemonies that are taking new global forms. Without an analysis of transnational *scattered hegemonies* that reveal themselves in gender relations, feminist movements will remain isolated and prone to producing the universalizing gestures of dominant Western cultures [italics mine]. (Grewal and Kaplan 1994: 17)

Grewal and Kaplan's call for understanding the material realities confronting women is significant. The following narrative of an imprisoned woman named Charlotte highlights the importance of understanding the lived experience of women's migration.

Inside Rebibbia Prison: Charlotte

"I am twenty-two years old." Charlotte added quickly after telling me her name. She sat in front of me at a small desk, her hair and make-up impeccable. She smiled sweetly as she watched me write down her name in my notepad.

"I used to work in Nigeria sewing clothes. I wanted to be a fashion designer. I lived near Lagos, but now I live here." She shrugged her shoulders and looked around the large room. It was a noisy room right off the main hallway, and from the moment Charlotte and I began speaking, two or three times Italian inmates walked by the open door, paused, and pointed to us and yelled to the guard, "What's going on here?" Or "What's this?" Charlotte would pay them no mind, but I would become distracted and angry. I was incensed that these women would shout their questions over our heads as if we were not in the room. I was even more angered by the reaction of the guard, who would only shrug his shoulders and send the women on their way.

Charlotte watched me struggle to keep my patience each time. "You get used to it," she said sympathetically.

Before being arrested, Charlotte had been living in Italy working as a prostitute.[12] She was one of the few women that I interviewed who spoke openly about being a victim of trafficking.

"When I was working [in Nigeria], a friend told me that she had a friend, a woman, who arranged visas to Europe for girls who wanted to study. I didn't pay her any attention, but she talked about it too much! She was going to go to Italy. I went to my parents one day and we chatted about the matter. I am their first daughter and they wanted me to study. We met the woman, as my friend told me. She told my parents what it would cost and where I would study. This was very big news for them, you know! The woman said that I would have to work, that I would work in [a house] with an Italian family, as I would have to pay her back. It was very expensive to come to Europe you know. Oh! My parents were very happy for me, and yes, we gave her some money for my journey. When I arrived, it was a different matter, very different." Charlotte laughed nervously.

"When I knew what was going on, you know, what could I do? I knew what they wanted me for in just a few hours after I arrived here and I was trapped. How could I escape, with no money, no car, no airplane ticket?" She paused. "I didn't even speak the language! Oh! It was impossible! This went on for some time. Sometimes I forget how long I was with them, sometimes I remember up to the very last minute. After awhile, working for them, you know, I met an Italian man and he rented an apartment for me and he squared my debts with the [Nigerian] woman to let me go.

"I still write my family, I have since I have been here [in Rebibbia for eight months]. At first I told them that my life is fine here, I was working and studying. I did not like to lie to them. I wrote one day and I told them everything, I told them the truth. At that time I was here, I was arrested. I have not received a letter, not even a common letter from them. They must not be getting my letters, so this is why I have started to give my letters to the sister."

Trafficking is a fast-growing problem in Europe and Italy. The Nairobi Forward-Looking Strategies for the Advancement of Women argues that "[f]orced prostitution is a form of slavery imposed on women by procurers. It is . . . the result of economic degradation that alienates women's labour through processes of rapid urbanization and migration resulting from underemployment and unemployment" (Bunch and Reilly 1994: 49). Suffering under these conditions, many women from Africa, Latin America, Asia, and Eastern Europe, like Charlotte, fall prey to criminal organizations that span borders.

The International Organization for Migration (IOM) reports that the trafficking in women from Nigeria into Italy is extremely well organized. In 1996, their study found that many of the Nigerian women are between the ages of fourteen to twenty-four. Girls from fourteen to eighteen make up the majority of the trafficked population. These women come mostly from areas outside of Lagos or Benin City. As in Charlotte's case, a Nigerian woman, often generically called Madam or Mama, acts as a contact person or recruiter. Sometimes, this woman will come with the girls to Italy, as was the case with Charlotte, or she may stay in Nigeria. IOM found that there are three levels of the "organization of the exploitation" (1996: 19) which, as discussed below, illustrate the difficulties that face Nigerian women if they try to escape.

The first level is located in Nigeria itself, with the older woman, the Mama, heading up the organization. According to IOM, "This organization is composed of members who prepare and organize the migration of the women and girls, and coerce them into prostitution by threatening their parents and relatives, and by offering payments to parents for their daughters" (1996: 19–20). The profits earned by the women are then collected, and a portion of the money is given to their parents. A second level of operation is one in which the Nigerian woman goes to Italy with the women and acts as "a mediator figure between the group of the women and girls and the usually male 'protectors'" (1996: 20). At this level, profits are collected by the Nigerian "Mama" and a nominal sum of money is given to the girls and the men involved in the operation. The rest of the profits go to Nigeria. The third level uses messengers or people who transfer or deliver money from Italy to Nigeria. IOM notes that at this level, money that is sent is "just . . . part for the girls' parents and the biggest part for the Mama (and other members of the organization) is directly rerouted into the criminal financial trafficking network: drugs, laundering of money" (1996: 20).

As the IOM research indicates, the trafficking in women often includes other forms of illegal conduct that extend the horrors of trafficking. One woman told me that she was first trafficked to Italy, where she worked for over a year as a prostitute, only to be used by the same criminal organization as a drug courier. Drug couriers are people, overwhelmingly women, who carry drugs on or in their bodies across national borders. This woman was forced to perform this task twice while working as a prostitute before she was arrested during the third attempt to bring drugs into Italy. When she was arrested, she confessed everything to the police and told them that she was trafficked to Italy. Although she feared reprisals from the men for whom she worked, she informed the police of their operations. The police, however, did not believe her and did not investigate the case.

The trafficking of women is a transnational practice. However, this practice, and the practice of using poor women as drug couriers or "mules" across international borders, is ignored in many scholarly discussions of transnational movements. Transnationalism is more than simply movement or migration. It seems to be a way of being in the world or a signifier of a kind of contemporary identity. The women that I work with are transnational agents because they have transcended the boundaries of the nation-state. It is the particular vulnerability of women that they are forced, out of the sheer necessity for survival, to take risks that may eventually get them arrested and sometimes killed.[13] These are the examples of Grewal and Kaplan's scattered hegemonies.[14]

It is important, indeed crucial, that we do more than just consider gender or gender politics in our analysis of travel, migration, or transnationalism. As anthropologist Paulla Ebron argues, "theorists who ignore the specificity through which gender is figured and reconfigured overlook a critical transnational aspect of the social construction of gender categories" (1997: 225). We must look to the lived experiences of women and men, listen to them, and incorporate their accounts into our theoretical and political explorations. As it stands, much of the current work on transnationalism, while important, only reflects, as Masao Miyoshi notes, a "presumably politically engaged intellectual [exercise]," adding that "if practice follows discourse, discourse must follow practice" (1993: 750).

NOTES

1. In my own research, I am less concerned with how African immigrants, either free or incarcerated in Italy, see themselves as black or construct notions of blackness than I am in understanding how the power of race and structural racism operates within their setting (Angel-Ajani 2000).

2. For example, diaspora as a signifier of multiple locations becomes a trope of postmodern fragmented, exiled displacements. If indeed, as Grewal and Kaplan suggest, postmodernism is a critique of "modernity and its related institutions" (Grewal and Kaplan 1994: 21), then I would not be so uncomfortable with linking diaspora to or as postmodernity. To my mind, to talk about a diasporic community—with all of its historical particularities—within a postmodern framework—

generally tends to move away from the political and material realities that could provide us with a richer political understanding of the phenomena of displacement, travel, and diaspora.

3. I acknowledge the contradiction implied by my own convenient placement of the label African on a diverse group of women whose culture, history, and personal circumstances shape their particularities of movement in the world.

4. Foregrounding how the concept of the nation functions within transnational configurations, Michael Kearney writes, "The 'nation' in transnationalism usually refers to the territorial, social, and cultural aspects of the nations concerned" (1995: 548).

5. Not all scholars of transnationalism situate the nation as Glick Schiller, Basch, and Szanton Blanc. I draw on them, however, precisely because within anthropology they have been the most prolific writers on the subject. For scholars who have alternative perspectives on transnationalism and the nation, see Kondo 1997; Hall 1996; Ebron 1997; Flynn 1997.

6. The incarceration rates in the United States alone are astounding—almost two million people. Women and immigrants are the fastest growing populations in U.S. and Italian prisons. See, for example, Basch, Glick Schiller, and Szanton Blanc 1994; Appadurai 1996; Lavie and Swedenburg 1996.

7. Women's human rights violations include, for example, denial of reproductive rights, rape during times of war, domestic violence, the trafficking of women, and economic and educational discrimination among them.

8. My thanks to Joseph Clarke for pointing me in the direction of the "disciplinary emergence" of displacement.

9. I am well aware that I may appear to fall prey to the fallacy of a prescriptive and descriptive argument. I am not attempting to create a corrective discourse.

10. For an expanded definition of the term *transnationalism*, see Basch, Glick Schiller, and Szanton Blanc (1994) or Kearney (1995).

11. Oyèrónké Oyewùmi (1997) poses a challenge to Western feminists, who include Grewal and Kaplan and myself, when she argues that in Òyó-Yorùbá society, as well as other cultures and societies, there was no gender category *woman*. She powerfully challenges us to remember that "the concept 'woman' as it is used and as it is invoked in the scholarship is derived from Western experience and history, a history rooted in philosophical discourses about the distinctions among body, mind, and soul and in ideas about biological determinism and the links between the body and the 'social'" (1997: xii). I raise this point precisely to demonstrate how scholarship could push our transnational understandings further, yet I am wary that I may dismantle the arguments of my own work. I am supportive of Oyewùmi's claims, but acknowledge, as she herself does, that Western domination has meant that transculturally the category woman exists, and indeed, they/we are discriminated against in multiple and varied ways because they/we belong to this category.

12. Prostitution is not a crime in Italy, although it has become increasingly criminalized. In 1958, the "Merlin Law" decriminalized private prostitution by an individual, but made it illegal to encourage, lead, or traffic women into prostitution (IOM 1996). For example, Charlotte was not arrested and serving time for prostitution but for other charges.

13. I want to be cautious of stepping into a victim/victimizer framework. I see many of the women who I worked with in Rebibbia as survivors, not woeful victims. It is important to remember that these women are oppressed and, like many oppressed and marginalized women, they employ oppositional consciousness and *la facultad*. However, I heed the words of Ebron when she writes of feminist scholarship on trafficking, "our scholarly tools have not been very helpful. We only think of agency as erasing 'oppression'; where there is a clear power imbalance, we reasonably want to show cohesion and vulnerability, not self-fashioning" (Ebron 1997: 242).

14. Consider the plight facing women working as couriers, who are frequently found dead or die shortly upon arrival because the contents of the "packages" that they have swallowed, for example, have been eaten away by the hydrochloric acid in the stomach.

REFERENCES CITED

Angel-Ajani, Asale
2000. "Italy's Racial Cauldron: Immigration, Criminalization and the Cultural Politics of Race." *Cultural Dynamics* 12(3):231–252.
2002. "Diasporic Conditions: Mapping the Discourses of Race and Criminality in Italy." *Transforming Anthropology: Journal of the Association of Black Anthropologists* 11 (1). Arlington, VA: American Anthropological Association.

Appadurai, Arjun
1991. "The Global Ethnoscapes: Notes and Queries for a Transnational Anthropology." *Recapturing Anthropology*, edited by Richard Fox, pp. 191–210. Santa Fe: School of American Research Press.
1996. *Modernity at Large: Cultural Dimensions of Globalization*. Minneapolis: University of Minnesota Press.

Bammer, Angelika, ed.
1994. *Displacements: Cultural Identities in Question*. Bloomington: Indiana University Press.

Basch, Linda, Nina Glick Schiller, and Cristina Szanton Blanc
1994. *Nations Unbound: Transnational Projects and the Deterritorialized Nation-States*. New York: Gordon and Breach.

Bohlen, Celestine
1997. "Exotic Imports Have Captured Italy's Sex Market." *New York Times*, July 9: A4.

Brah, Avtar

1996. *Cartographies of Diaspora: Contesting Identities*. New York: Routledge.

Brown, Jacqueline Nassy

1998. "Black Liverpool, Black America, and the Gendering of Diasporic Space." *Cultural Anthropology* 13(3):291–323.

Bunch, Charlotte, and Niamh Reilly

1994. *Demanding Accountability: The Global Campaign and Vienna Tribunal for Women's Human Rights*. New Brunswick, NJ: Center for Women's Global Leadership, Rutgers University.

Clarke, Kamari

1997. "Genealogies of Reclaimed Nobility: The Geotemporality of Yorùbá Belonging." Ph.D. dissertation, University of California, Santa Cruz.

Clifford, James

1997. *Routes: Travel and Translation in the Late Twentieth Century*. Cambridge: Harvard University Press.

Cook, Rebecca, ed.

1994. *Human Rights of Women: National and International Perspectives*. Philadelphia: University of Pennsylvania Press.

da Silva, Denise Ferreira

1998. "The Facts of Blackness: Brazil Is Not (Quite) the United States . . . and Racial Politics in Brazil?" *Social Identities* 4(2):201–234.

Drake, St. Clair

1982. "Diaspora Studies and Pan-Africanism." *The Global Dimensions of the African Diaspora*, edited by Joseph E. Harris, pp. 451–514. Washington, D.C.: Howard University Press.

Ebron Paulla

1997. "Traffic in Men." *Cultural Encounters: Gender at the Intersections of the Local and Global in Africa*, edited by Maria Grosz-Ngate and Omari Kokole, pp. 223–244. New York: Routledge.

Flynn, Donna

1997. "Trading Traitors: Cultural Negotiations of Female Mobility in a West African Borderland." *Identities* 4(2):245–280.

Foucault, Michel

1988. "The Dangerous Individual." *Politics, Philosophy, Culture: Interviews and Other Writings, 1977–1984*, edited by Lawrence Kritzman, pp. 123–151. New York: Routledge.

1997. "The Punitive Society." *Michel Foucault: Ethics, Subjectivity, and Truth, the Essential Works of Foucault 1954–1984*, vol. 1, edited by Paul Rabinow, pp. 22–37. New York: New Press.

Gilroy, Paul

1991 [1987]. *Ain't No Black in the Union Jack: The Cultural Politics of Race and Nation*. Chicago: University of Chicago Press.

1993. *Black Atlantic: Modernity and Double Consciousness.* Cambridge: Harvard University Press.

2000. *Against Race.* Cambridge: Harvard University Press.

Glick Schiller, Nina

1997. "The Situation of Transnational Studies." *Identities* 4(2):155–166.

Glick Schiller, Nina, Linda Basch, and Cristina Blanc-Szanton, eds.

1992. *Towards a Transnational Perspective on Migration: Race, Class, Ethnicity and Nationalism Reconsidered.* New York: New York Academy of Science.

Grewal, Inderpal, and Caren Kaplan, eds.

1994. *Scattered Hegemonies: Postmodernity and Transnational Feminist Practices.* Minneapolis: University of Minnesota Press.

Gupta, Akhil

1995. "Blurred Boundaries: The Discourse of Corruption, the Culture of Politics, and the Imagined State." *American Ethnologist.*

Hall, Stuart

1982. "The Local and the Global: Globalization and Ethnicity." *Dangerous Liaisons: Gender, Nation, and Postcolonial Perspectives,* edited by Ann McClintock, Aamir Mufti, and Ella Shohat, pp. 173–187. Minneapolis: University of Minnesota Press.

1996. "Race Articulation and Societies Structured in Dominance." *Black British Cultural Studies: A Reader,* edited by Houston A. Baker, Jr., Manthia Diawara, and Ruth H. Lindeborg, pp. 16–60. Chicago: University of Chicago Press.

Harlow, Barbara

1994. "Sites of Struggle: Immigration, Deportation, Prison, and Exile." *Criticism in the Borderlands: Studies in Chicano Literature, Culture, and Ideology,* edited by Héctor Calderón and José Saldívar, pp. 149–163. Durham, N.C.: Duke University Press.

Helmreich, Stephen

1993. "Kinship, Nation, and Paul Gilroy's Concept of Diaspora." *Diaspora* 2(2):243–249.

International Organization for Migration (IOM)

1996. *Trafficking in Women to Italy for Sexual Exploitation.* Washington, D.C.: IOM.

Kanneh, Kenneth

1998. *African Identities: Race, Nation and Culture in Ethnography, Pan-Africanism and Black Literatures.* New York: Routledge.

Kaplan, Caren

1996. *Questions of Travel: Postmodern Discourses of Displacement.* Durham, N.C.: Duke University Press.

Kearney, Michael

1995. "The Local and the Global: The Anthropology of Globalization and Transnationalism." *Annual Review of Anthropology* 24:547–565.

Kondo, Dorinne

1997. *About Face: Performing Race in Fashion and Theater*. New York: Routledge.

Lavie, Smadar, and Ted Swedenburg, eds.

1996. *Displacement, Diaspora and Geographies of Identity*. Durham, N.C.: Duke University Press.

Lawyers Committee for Human Rights

1995. *African Exodus: Refugee Crisis, Human Rights and the OAU Convention*. New York: Lawyers Committee for Human Rights.

Lemelle, Sidney, and Robin D. G. Kelley, eds.

1994. *Imagining Home: Class, Culture and Nationalism in the African Diaspora*. New York: Verso.

Miyoshi, Masao

1993. "A Borderless World? From Colonialism to Transnationalism and the Decline of the Nation-State." *Critical Inquiry* 19:726–751.

Mudimbe, V. Y.

1988. *The Invention of Africa: Gnosis, Philosophy, and the Order of Knowledge*. Bloomington: Indiana University Press.

Ong, Aihwa, and Donald Nonini, eds.

1997. *Ungrounded Empires: The Cultural Politics of Modern Chinese Transnationalism*. New York: Routledge.

Oyewùmí, Oyèrónké

1997. *The Invention of Women: Making an African Sense of Western Gender Discourses*. Minneapolis: University of Minnesota.

Peters, Julie, and Andrea Wolper, eds.

1995. *Women's Rights, Human Rights: International Feminists Perspectives*. New York: Routledge.

Rosaldo, Renato

1988. "Ideology, Place, and People Without Culture." *Cultural Anthropology* 3(1):77–87.

Sassen, Saskia

1982. "Recomposition and Peripheralization at the Core." *Contemporary Marxism* 5 (Summer):88–100.

Scott, David

2001. *Refashioning Futures: Criticism After Postcoloniality*. Princeton, N.J.: Princeton University Press.

United Nations High Commissioner of Refugees (UNHCR)

1997. "Statelessness and Citizenship." *The State of the World's Refugees: A Humanitarian Agenda*. Electronic document, consulted 5/4/2001 http://www.unhcr.ch/refworld/pub/state/97/ch6.htm

Wali, Sima

1995. "Human Rights for Refugee and Displaced Women." *Women's Rights, Human*

Rights: International Feminists Perspectives, edited by Julie Peters and Andrea Wolper, pp. 335–344. New York: Routledge.

Yanagisako, Sylvia, and Carol Delaney, eds.

1995. *Naturalizing Power: Essays in Feminist Cultural Analysis*. New York: Routledge.

About the Contributors

ASALE ANGEL-AJANI is an assistant professor in the Gallatin School at New York University. She is the coeditor of *Engaged Observer: Advocacy, Activism and Anthropology* with Victoria Sanford.

JERMAINE O. ARCHER received a Ph.D. in history from the University of California, Riverside. His interests include black abolitionists, slave narratives, and Atlantic world slavery.

CHOUKI EL HAMEL teaches in the History Department at Arizona State University. He is the author of *La vie intellectuelle Islamique dans le Sahel Ouest Africain* and is currently working on a new book entitled *Ethnicity, "Race/Color" and Gender in Moroccan Slavery*.

MICHAEL A. GOMEZ is Professor of History and Middle Eastern and Islamic Studies at New York University. He is the author of *Black Crescent: The Experience and Legacy of African Muslims in the Americas; Reversing Sail: A History of the African Diaspora; Exchanging Our Country Marks: The Transformation of African Identities in the Colonial and Antebellum South;* and *Pragmatism in the Age of Jihad: The Precolonial State of Bundu.* He is also director of the Association for the Study of the Worldwide African Diaspora.

FREDERICK KNIGHT is Assistant Professor of History at Colorado State University. His research interests include the history of slave labor in the Anglo-American colonies, and he is currently working on a book manuscript titled, *Gifts of Labor: The Contribution of African Workers to Agricultural Development in the Anglo-American World, 1650–1850.*

FRAN MARKOWITZ is Associate Professor of Anthropology in the Department of Behavioral Sciences, Ben-Gurion University, Beersheva, Israel. Her research and writings focus on community, identities, and diasporas, particularly the Jewish and Black diasporas and their overlaps.

ERIK S. MCDUFFIE is an assistant professor in the African American Studies and Research Program and in the Gender and Women's Studies

Program at the University of Illinois, Urbana-Champaign. He is currently working on a book entitled *"Toward a Brighter Dawn": Black Women and American Communism, 1930–1956*, and on other projects related to black women and the Old Left, black internationalism, feminism, and radicalism in the African Diaspora.

DIANE BATTS MORROW is an Associate Professor of History and African American Studies at the University of Georgia. She is the author of *Persons of Color and Religious at the Same Time: The Oblate Sisters of Providence, 1828–1860*, which received the Letitia Woods Brown Memorial Book Prize from the Association of Black Women Historians in 2002 and the Distinguished Book Award from the Conference on the History of Women Religious in 2004.

ELIZABETH PIGOU-DENNIS teaches at the Caribbean School of Architecture, University of Technology, Jamaica, where she is currently the Acting Head of the School. She has presented at conferences around the world and is author of several articles.

João José Reis is Professor of History at the Universidade Federal da Bahia, Brazil. He is the author of *Slave Rebellion in Brazil: The 1835 Muslim Uprising in Bahia* and *Death Is a Festival: Funeral Rites and Rebellion in Nineteenth-Century Brazil*.

TYLER STOVALL is a Professor of History at the University of California, Berkeley, where he specializes in the study of modern France. He has written several books and articles on labor, race, and post-colonialism, including *The Rise of the Paris Red Belt* and *Paris Noir: African Americans in the City of Light*. He is currently working on a study of Caribbean migration to France.

JAMES H. SWEET is an Assistant Professor of History at the University of Wisconsin. Sweet is the author of *Recreating Africa: Culture, Kinship, and Religion in the African-Portuguese World, 1441–1770*.

ROSE C. THEVENIN is an Assistant Professor of History at Florida Memorial University and cochair of the South Florida Consortium of Colleges and Universities. She is the Parliamentarian of the Association of Black Women Historians (ABWH) and has won numerous awards and fellowships, including Scholar of the Year at Florida Memorial University in 2004.

WENDY W. WALTERS is an Assistant Professor of Literature at Emerson College in Boston. Her first book, *At Home in Diaspora: Black International Writing*, is forthcoming. In 2001–2002, she was a nonresident fellow at the W.E.B. Du Bois Institute at Harvard University.

Index